The NetWare 4.0 Wor'

ATOTAL   Allows you to see a total of all the
you have turned on the accounting function fo.

AUDITCON   Allows an auditor, who works independently of network
supervisors and other users, to verify the security of your network.

CAPTURE   Allows you to redirect print jobs so that you can print to a network
printer from within network-unaware applications. You can also redirect screen
displays to a network printer, redirect data to a network file, set up a print job to
use a specific form, and specify the number of copies you want to print.

COLORPAL   Allows you to set the screen colors for NetWare menu utilities
and menus you create for users (using the NMENU utility).

CX   Allows you to see your context (where you are in the NDS tree). Also allows you to change your context and view other objects in the tree.

DOSGEN   Allows you to set up workstations so they can boot from a server
instead of from a boot disk or local drive.

FILER   Allows you to manage the NetWare file system.

FLAG   Allows you to view or modify a file or directory's attributes.

LOGIN   Allows you to log in to a NetWare server or an NDS tree. You can use
LOGIN options to determine a login script to run or to specify that you do not
want to run a login script.

LOGOUT   Allows you to log out of the network, or to log out of a specific
server while remaining logged in to all other connections.

MAP   Allows you to view, create, or change network and search drive mappings.

NCOPY   Allows you to copy files and directories from one location on the network to another and to specify how they are copied.

NDIR   Provides a powerful search function to help you find and sort information about files and directories in your file system.

Continued on inside back cover

NOVELL'S® GUIDE TO
NetWare® 4.0
NETWORKS

CHERYL C. CURRID

With STEPHEN SAXON

NOVELL
PRESS™

Novell Press, San Jose

Publisher: Peter Jerram
Editor-in-Chief: Dr. R. S. Langer
Series Editor: David Kolodney
Acquisitions Editor: Dianne King
Program Manager: Rosalie Kearsley
Developmental Editor: David Kolodney
Editor: Richard Mills
Technical Editors: Mark Hall and Nelson Cicchitto
Novell Technical Advisor: Kelley J. P. Lindberg
Book Designer: Helen Bruno
Production Artist: Charlotte Carter
Technical Art and Screen Graphics: Cuong Le
Desktop Publishing Specialist: Thomas Goudie
Proofreader/Production Assistant: David Silva
Indexer: Ted Laux
Cover Designer: Archer Design
Novell Press Logo Design: Jennifer Gill
Cover Photographer: Marilyn Bridges

Screen reproductions produced with Collage Plus.
Collage Plus is a trademark of Inner Media Inc.

Part VI, "Dictionary of Key Concepts," was adapted from the *NetWare Concepts* manual with permission from Novell, Inc.

SYBEX is a registered trademark of SYBEX Inc.

Novell Press and the Novell Press logo are trademarks of Novell, Inc.

TRADEMARKS: SYBEX and Novell have attempted throughout this book to distinguish proprietary trademarks from descriptive terms by following the capitalization style used by the manufacturer.

Every effort has been made to supply complete and accurate information. However, neither SYBEX nor Novell assumes any responsibility for its use, or for any infringement of the intellectual property rights of third parties which would result from such use.

Library of Congress Card Number: 92-83943

ISBN: 0-7821-1274-9

Manufactured in the United States of America

10 9 8 7 6 5 4 3 2 1

To Ray, Tray, and Justin.
—C.C.

To Diane, Rachel, and David.
I love you,
and I promise,
no deadlines next time.
—S.S.

Acknowledgments

Cheryl Currid would like to thank:

Tony Croes for his late-night help on the editing and willingness to jump in at any moment. We especially appreciate the efforts of our literary agent, Bill Gladstone, for working with us during the early conception of the book. And thanks again to the Currid & Company team, especially Dianne Davison, Diane Bolin, Josh Penrod, Kent Drummond, and Linda Musthaler.

Stephen Saxon would like to thank:

Chuck Conlin, my assistant; Ed Tittel, for his work on the early part of the book; Compaq Computers, for a really cool 486/33L, which worked flawlessly throughout this project; Nelson Cicchitto, Jennifer Wahlquist, and the gang of the 4.0 beta forum of NetWire; LaMont Leavitt, Sandy Stevens, and JD Marymee, for technical support and clarifications; Rose Kearsley (Novell Press), for Novell products and for encouragement along the way; Richard Mills (SYBEX), for some fine copy-editing and for the other stuff too; Marshall T. Rose, for writing *The Little Black Book;* Allan Saxon, for the late-night e-mail and for teaching me the CD command; God; and everyone who's taught me things along the way, especially the students.

Novell Press would like to express its gratitude to:

The expert review team in the Novell Technical Publications Department in Provo, Utah.

The team members are listed here (those who deserve substantial credit for particular chapters they "adopted" are noted): Meike Peters (Chapter 7), Kelley Lindberg (Chapters 8, 13, 14, and 15), Marj Hermansen (Chapter 9), Nicholas Wells (Chapter 11), Lin Sorenson (Part V), Rich Hillyard (Part VI), Craig Oler, Loren Russon, and Grace Whitaker.

The leader of the team, Kelley J. P. Lindberg, merits special recognition for organizing this effort with great competence, composure, and efficiency.

Thanks also to Lynn Christensen for volunteering his modem and Evelyn Sealander, Documentation Services Manager, for giving the team the go-ahead to work on this project.

CONTENTS AT A *Glance*

TABLE OF Contents

PART IV *Network Maintenance and Tuning* *391*

17 · Disaster Planning and Recovery 393

*I*ntroduction

Novell's Guide to NetWare 4.0 Networks is an easy-to-follow guide to installing and operating a microcomputer network using Novell NetWare version 4.0. Unlike the system documentation, which focuses on functions, this book demonstrates the process of actually setting up a network from start to finish and of tuning or adjusting an existing network for improved performance and access. In addition, the important topics of maintenance and troubleshooting are addressed along with advanced techniques and utilities. The context of the discussion is the installation and start-up of a new NetWare 4.0 network or an upgrade from an earlier version of NetWare to version 4.0.

Who This Book Is For

You will find this book to be valuable whether you are a microcomputer manager embarking on an installation of NetWare 4.0 or you are simply a network user wanting a better understanding of NetWare fundamentals and functionality. If you don't know much about networks and networking terminology, be sure to read the first three chapters of the book, which will give you all the background you need. If you have experience with NetWare already, you might want to just skim the first three chapters and go right to Chapter 4, which contains an overview of NetWare 4.0 and information on how to plan for installation.

How This Book Is Organized

The book is organized into six parts:

Part I (Chapters 1 to 4) covers networking basics, explaining what a network is, the types of networks, and the essential components of a network. There is also an overview of the different versions of NetWare and some hints on how to plan for your installation of NetWare 4.0.

Part II (Chapters 5 to 11) begins with an overview of the whole installation process and goes on to show you how to prepare your hardware, how to install NetWare 4.0 on a new server, how to install NetWare Directory Services (with a complete discussion of NDS concepts), and how to upgrade an existing version of NetWare. Later chapters show how to configure printing options and security.

Part III (Chapters 12 to 16) covers the creation of the user environment, including setting up individual DOS and Windows workstations, adding users and groups, writing login scripts and batch files, and creating user menus.

Part IV (Chapters 17 and 18) covers network maintenance, disaster planning, and recovery techniques. It also covers troubleshooting and monitoring your network's performance.

Part V contains descriptions of the graphical workstation utilities, text-based workstation utilities, and file server utilities, along with examples of their use.

Part VI defines all the key NetWare terms as well as general networking terms.

What's New in NetWare 4.0?

NetWare 4.0 is a whole new operating system. Everything from the workstation drivers to the memory allocation on the file server has been redesigned. Many of the concepts that were associated with NetWare 3.11 (and even more so with NetWare 2.2 and 2.15) do not apply to NetWare 4.0.

NETWARE DIRECTORY SERVICES

The most significant change in version 4.0 is that there is no longer any bindery for each file server. The authentication, security, and object organization information that used to be found in the bindery files is now administered by NetWare Directory Services (NDS). (NDS is based on the CCITT X.500 and OSI directory services specifications. It is not exactly X.500-compliant, but the differences are mostly due to the increased security needs of a NetWare environment, and data networks in general.)

To better understand NDS, you can think of logging in to a NetWare 4.0 *network* instead of to a NetWare *file server.* Security, access rights, object management, user administration, and just about everything else are now administered from a network point of view instead of from a file-server point of view.

DATA STORAGE

Many improvements and enhancements have been made to the already advanced NetWare file system. NetWare 4.0 supports *High Capacity Storage Systems* for online (direct access) or near-line (archived, but available) file storage.

You can think of *data migration* and its facility of near-line disk storage as analogous to the public library system. You can check out a book from your local branch, or if it is not in the stacks at your branch, you can request the book from another branch in the system. It takes a little longer, but it greatly enlarges the virtual storage possibilities.

Block suballocation allows the file system to store files in whatever block size you configure for a particular volume, but if the file is larger than an even division into file-system blocks, the remainder is stored in 512K miniblocks. This feature can greatly increase the efficiency of your file storage.

Data compression allows you to optimize the file system even more by compressing little-used files as a background operation of the file server. The settings are very detailed, allowing you impressive control over how and when compression will take place.

CLIENT SUPPORT

NetWare 4.0 ships with support for DOS, Windows, and OS/2 clients (workstations). No longer is the Windows workstation limited to a small set of "applets." Now the Windows environment has a complete set of user and administrative utilities. In many ways, managing a network is easier with the Windows utilities than with the standard DOS menu utilities.

INTERNATIONAL SUPPORT

NetWare 4.0 has incorporated international languages into the core of the operating system. Now you can see NetWare messages and utilities in English, French, German, Spanish, or Italian. Actually, NetWare no longer generates messages, but instead makes calls to its language modules. In that way, the same operating system can be switched from one language to another by simply issuing a console command, instead of reinstalling the whole operating system.

AUDITING

With NetWare 4.0, an independent auditor can keep track of operations and transactions on the network without needing sufficient rights to control those transactions. In this way, the management and auditing tasks can be isolated from one other and independently executed.

ONLINE DOCUMENTATION

A new help utility, Novell ElectroText, provides Windows and OS/2 users with a full-bodied online documentation source, including all the NetWare 4.0 manuals (except the *Quick Access Guide*).

CD-ROM SUPPORT

NetWare 4.0 comes on CD-ROM, which makes the installation procedure much easier. The same CD-ROM contains both the NetWare software and the electronic manuals.

SERVER MEMORY ALLOCATION

Memory allocation in the NetWare 4.0 operating system has been redesigned to avoid memory shortages, as sometimes occurred with previous versions. Instead of having multiple memory allocation pools, NetWare 4.0 has a single allocation area from which all operating-system functions and file-caching needs are serviced.

PROTECTED-MODE SERVER

You can now run questionable or test versions of NetWare Loadable Modules (NLMs) in a protected mode (with some performance degradation). If a module fails or tries to violate operating-system integrity, the module is shut down, but the file server remains fully functional and safe from ill effects.

PART I

Networks and Networking

CHAPTER 1

What Is a Network?

Fast Track

7   *Networks can be either of the following types:*

 ▸ Hierarchical networks, as are often found in mainframe or minicomputer installations

 ▸ Peer networks, as are many local area networks (LANs)

11   *The benefits of a LAN from a hardware-cost standpoint include*
the ability to share peripherals, such as expensive printers, high-capacity disk drives, specialty devices, and communications·devices, and to share common information, such as databases, project data, or directories.

11   *The benefits of a LAN from the user's standpoint include*
the capability to link people and groups together, resulting in improved communications.

The benefits of a LAN from a maintenance standpoint include   11
the capability to share centralized data-processing maintenance services,
such as backup services and software installation services.

To set up a network,   12

  1 · Select the hardware, cabling, and cabling layout (topology).

  2 · Install the hardware and network operating system.

  3 · Configure the server and load application software.

  4 · Create the user environment.

  5 · Set up procedures for ongoing network administration.

Over the past ten years, personal computer networks, called local area networks, or LANs, have arrived in the mainstream. Today, many companies use local area networks for crucial parts of their businesses.

Since 1985, American Airlines has used LAN technology to link its ticket agents, gate agents, and affiliated travel agencies over the Sabre Travel Information Network to its online reservation system. The LAN plays a critical role in requesting and presenting information for airline tickets and reservations, and for seat assignments and cancellations; it even permits American's flight crews to obtain electronic mail at any airport connected to the network. American's far-flung information empire includes over 150 airports around the world, and over 8000 affiliated travel agencies, each of which uses at least one LAN and some of which use many interconnected LANs.

The Chicago-based insurance claims processing company, HealthCare Compare, also uses LANs to run its business. At its headquarters operation, it has segmented its networks into two halves, each of which plays a vital role in processing claims. As one half of the network is used by keyboard entry staff, claims adjusters, and administrative staff to process the day's claims, the second half is churning out the thousands of checks and related paperwork needed to document and pay the preceding day's claims. This split design allows Health-Care Compare to double its productivity by doubling its LAN resources, so that each half can perform a specific task in parallel. In all, its LAN services over 800 regular users, supports a multi-gigabyte claims database, and allows the company to handle claims for health insurance organizations like Blue Cross/Blue Shield and the Kemper Insurance health-care subsidiaries.

Why did these organizations choose local-area-network technology in lieu of other data processing approaches? This chapter looks at some of the reasons why increasing numbers of organizations are building LANs. This chapter also outlines the simple steps that allow you to easily connect your computers and information resources to a network operating system such as Novell NetWare.

Types of Networks

In the not-so-distant past, when computers were large and expensive, organizations could not give employees entire computers for their personal use. Instead, the central processing unit (CPU) had to be shared. Thus, networks emerged as a way of sharing a precious and expensive resource.

The first networks were hierarchical. In this scheme, shown in Figure 1.1, the center of computing activity, where the CPU is located, is the host hardware unit. This host is usually a mainframe or minicomputer. Users access this host through satellite terminals, often called dumb terminals because they cannot perform any processing themselves. The basic purpose of dumb terminals is to provide an interface between the host and its users.

Hierarchical networks provide centralized computing, but they are limited in important ways. The users of the central processor are limited to the applications available on the host computer. The user's ability to perform custom analysis is therefore limited, because changes to host programs are invariably costly and time consuming, and because the host program must meet all the needs of every user on the network.

With the advent of highly integrated silicon-based circuitry and the corresponding drop in prices of computer processors, computing capability, in the form of personal computers, or PCs, has come to the individual desktop. Personal computers allow individual users to customize programs, to select unique combinations of off-the-shelf software, and to perform personalized data analysis to meet their particular needs. However, standalone, unconnected computers (Figure 1.2) do not offer direct access to an organization's data, nor can information and programs on one machine be easily shared with another.

Local area networks provide a solution to the limitations of both standalone and centralized processing environments. As Figure 1.3 shows, LANs can function as peer networks, where all devices on the network can communicate with one other. Instead of dumb terminals, LANs use independent computers—that is, microcomputers with their own central processing units that can communicate among themselves or with other minicomputers or mainframes. Because they are capable of independent operation, they can also function as terminals

► · ◄

FIGURE 1.1

A hierarchical network

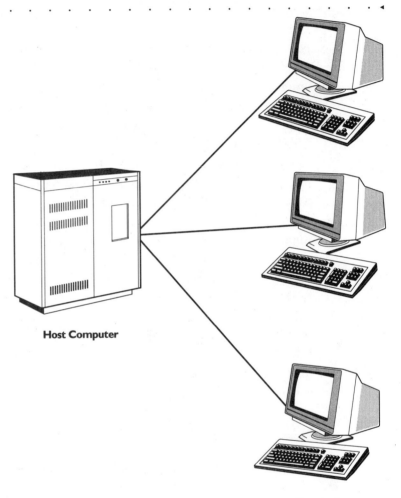

Host Computer

Terminals

attached to a host—in that role they are often referred to as smart terminals. LANs provide a bridge not only between people and information but also among individual users and among different types of computers.

FIGURE 1.2

Unconnected personal
computers

FIGURE 1.3

Smart terminals connected
to form a network

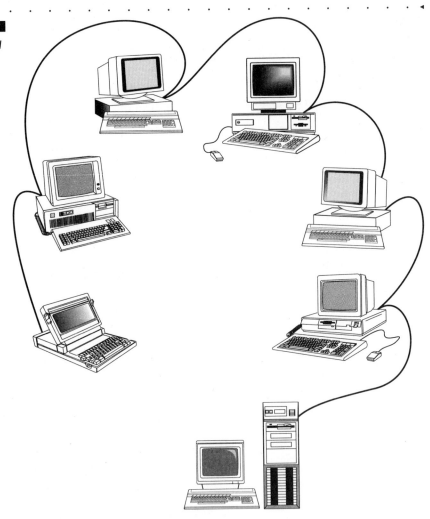

Benefits of Using a LAN

Often, the installation of a local area network is initially justified as a means of sharing peripheral devices. For example, a single large hard drive or disk array can be made available to an entire workgroup. Expensive output devices, such as laser printers and plotters, can be shared, as can other specialty devices, such as PC fax boards, CD-ROM players, high-speed modems, and color printers.

But as a network grows and becomes integrated into an organization, device sharing pales by comparison with other, more substantial advantages of networking. Local area networks link people as well as computers, resulting in a network of human beings as well as machines. LANs provide an effective tool for communicating through the use of electronic mail (e-mail) and other workgroup software. Messages can be sent instantaneously throughout the network, work plans can be updated as changes occur, and meetings can be scheduled without placing half a dozen phone calls. The same highway that moves data among machines also functions well to move information among the people who use those machines.

In fact, networking can reshape the way a company conducts certain business activities. The use of workgroup software reduces the need for face-to-face meetings and other time-consuming methods of information distribution. At the same time, networking allows increased interaction among workers from their workstations. Networking can also enhance the effectiveness of communication, because people tend to put more thought into written communications than into informal conversation.

Because LANs provide direct access to workgroup information from each desktop, productivity is also enhanced. Everyone on the network has access to data and, by using the tools available from the network, can manipulate it and share the results with others. It's also more efficient to put on the network any process that depends on input from many members of the organization. LANs reduce, or in some cases can even eliminate, the need for one person to finish working on a file before someone else can use it.

An important side benefit of local area networks is that software and data are much easier to maintain and protect than in a standalone environment. You can back up critical data daily, hourly, or even in real time if necessary. When software needs to be upgraded, you can do the job from a single workstation rather than having to sit down at every personal computer that runs the program. Even though users are distributed throughout an enterprise, a LAN supplies a powerful focus to bring them together. It provides ways to manage their shared requirements centrally, no matter how far-flung an organization might be.

Building a Local Area Network

Building a local area network is not difficult, but it does require thoughtful planning. Networks are inherently modular, so once the right base is established, additional functions can be added later as needed.

There are five basic steps to building a network:

1 · Select the cabling layout and hardware.

2 · Install the hardware and network operating system.

3 · Configure the system and load the applications.

4 · Create the user environment.

5 · Set up ongoing LAN administration.

The first step in building a network is to design the physical layout. Working with a network installer, you must decide which offices will be cabled for the network and where key components (computers, printers, cabling components, etc.) will be located. You must select the types of computers to use, the type of cabling to install, and the network scheme to use.

Your next step is to install the equipment and link the computers together with network interface cards and cables. At this point, you can load the operating system onto the hard drive of the computer you select as the server. You can configure the operating system to recognize the file server's components (such as network interface cards, communications adapters, and so on). You can now set up the subdirectory structure and organize the hard drive in preparation for loading the application software and other data. For multiple-server networks, you will also want to set up a Directory Services environment, to help end-users find their way around the network and its services.

Next, you create the user environment—the look and feel of the system—through the screens that appear when a user logs in and the menus that help guide him or her through the options available from the network. You also need to establish security schemes to protect the integrity of the data stored on the network, which can also be managed through Directory Services where appropriate.

Finally, since LANs require ongoing administration, you need to set up procedures to support the network. Since administration consumes the bulk of the time that a system manager will spend with a network during its useful life, this is not just an afterthought to installation—it's usually the principal duty. Future chapters discuss these steps in detail.

CHAPTER 2

Network Components and How They Work

Fast Track

A file server is

19

the core of the LAN. It is the microcomputer that runs the network operating system and controls the activities on the local network segments to which it is attached.

A network workstation is

19

a personal computer that has a network interface card installed and can physically access the server through network cables or cableless media. In addition, the network workstation must run a special program, called a network shell, requestor, or redirector, to communicate with the file server.

The network topology is

21

the route data travels along the network. It represents the shape of the network cabling system. Three popular topologies are bus, star, and ring.

Network routers   25

are a combination of hardware and software that connects networks that use similar communication protocols. They can be either internal or stand-alone. Standalone routers are usually faster and more expensive than internal routers. Novell's Multi-Protocol Router could be considered a stand-alone router, though it actually runs on top of a run-time NetWare OS and is therefore an internal router.

Gateways can be microcomputers that   31

are configured with hardware and software that enable communications with other systems, such as mainframes and minicomputers. A gateway's primary function is to convert from one protocol to another.

Novell NetWare allows you to shape your LAN (local area network) architecture to meet the specific needs of your organization. This flexibility applies not only to the applications you run on the network but also to the hardware and functions you use, and to the way your users perceive the network and the services it provides.

A LAN can consist of a single server supporting a small number of workstations or of multiple file servers, application servers, directory servers, and communications servers connected to hundreds of workstations. Some networks are designed to render relatively simple services, such as sharing an application and its related files, while also providing access to a single printer. Other networks support communications to mainframes and minicomputers, shared modems and fax servers, a variety of output devices (such as plotters and laser printers), and high-capacity storage devices (such as CD-ROM or magneto-optical disk drives). Still other networks may link hundreds of servers together across multiple locations, and rely on the existence of a shared set of Directory Services to let administrators and end-users find their way around a complex collection of servers and services. NetWare 4.0 provides the flexibility to support all of these configurations and includes support for hundreds of NetWare-specific applications from third-party developers.

This chapter discusses some of the major options to consider as you plan your own network's architecture. We'll begin by exploring the basics: a file server and the workstations that may use it. Then we'll look at how these computers communicate with one another through the personal computer and network operating systems. Next we'll briefly examine the physical layout of the network—its *topology*—a topic we'll explore in more detail in Chapter 3. Then we'll investigate some of the alternatives available for sharing peripheral devices and for communicating with other systems and other networks. Finally, we'll review some specific purposes appropriate for NetWare servers, all the way from the basics to platforms for specific applications.

Servers and Workstations

For most network environments, and for NetWare in particular, the server is the core of the LAN. This computer is typically a high-speed microcomputer with large amounts of random access memory (RAM) and lots of hard-disk space. It runs the operating system and manages the flow of data through the network. Individual workstations and any shared peripheral devices, such as printers, are all connected in some way to the server. In many ways, the server is the focus of the LAN for the workstations it services; it can act as a hub for the exchange of information on the LAN and as the gatekeeper for access to resources beyond the LAN.

Each network workstation is an ordinary personal computer running its own operating system or environment (such as DOS, OS/2, Windows, UNIX, or the Macintosh operating system). Unlike a standalone personal computer, however, a network workstation contains a network interface card and is physically attached to the file server via network cabling. In addition, a workstation runs a special program, called a network shell or a network requestor, that permits it to communicate with the file server, other workstations, and other network devices. This special software allows workstations to use files and programs on the file server as easily as those on its own local disks.

Figure 2.1 illustrates a simple local area network. This LAN consists of three workstations with a printer and plotter connected to the file server. All of the network files (both programs and data) can be stored on the hard disk in the file server, as opposed to on the workstation hard disk or on floppy disks. As the regulator of the network, the server manages access to network files, printer use, and other network activities.

For example, when the user of a workstation wants to run an application, such as the network version of WordPerfect, the program files are read from the file-server disk and sent across the wire to be loaded into RAM on the workstation. The application then runs just as if it had been loaded from a disk drive in the workstation computer. Since the application files for this version of WordPerfect are designated for sharing, they can be also be used by another workstation at the

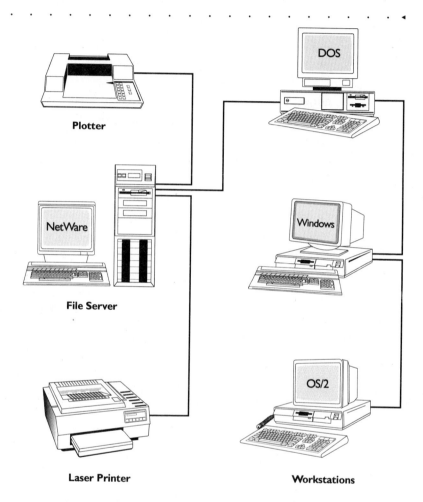

FIGURE 2.1

A simple local area network

Plotter

DOS

NetWare

File Server

Windows

OS/2

Laser Printer

Workstations

same time. Thus, both users can load the application from the same location on the server. However, if a network user is updating data in a file that is flagged with something called the nonshareable attribute, the file cannot be modified by another user until the first user is finished with it. (The options to make files shareable or nonshareable are discussed more fully later in this book.)

Workstation Operating Systems

Each workstation computer runs under its own operating system or environment (DOS, OS/2, Windows, UNIX, or the Macintosh OS). To make each workstation a part of the network, a network operating system extension is added to the computer's operating environment. This extension, commonly called a network shell, a redirector, or a requestor, preserves most of the underlying operating system's commands and functions, allowing the workstation to retain a familiar look and feel.

The network extension is what makes accessing network resources possible. That way the user relates to the network as an extension of the environment that is familiar. The user doesn't have to learn NetWare in order to use the network resources. If the user is familiar with DOS, NetWare looks like DOS; if the user is familiar with OS/2, NetWare looks like OS/2; and so on.

Topology

Network *topology* refers to the physical data path that traffic takes across the network. There are three basic types of topologies: bus, star, and ring.

In a bus, or linear, network (see Figure 2.2), each node (servers, workstations, etc.) is connected to a common cable called a *bus* or a *trunk*. In a star network (see Figure 2.3), each node is connected to a common hub device, but not directly to each other. In a ring network (see Figure 2.4), the cabling runs from workstation to workstation (and to the file server) without any endpoint.

Because topology selection is so important, and because cable selection is a large contributor to total LAN expense, you should seek the advice of a network consultant or installer to determine the best topology and cabling for your particular needs. For multisite organizations, this choice may even vary from site to site, especially if it is possible to take advantage of unused telephone cable at some sites.

FIGURE 2.2

Bus (or linear) topology

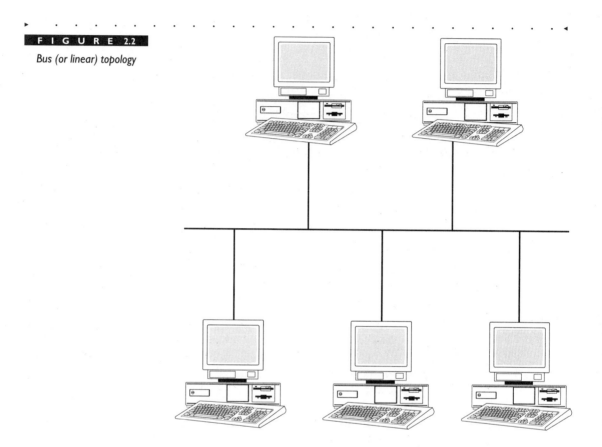

While IBM Token Ring uses a logical ring topology, its physical layout is that of a star, with the MSAU (multistation access unit) functioning as the star's hub. 10BaseT (commonly thought of as Ethernet over unshielded twisted pair—UTP—wire) can be seen as a logical bus, as is thin or thick Ethernet. However, like Token Ring, its physical layout is that of a star, the wiring concentrator serving as the hub.

FIGURE 2.3

Star topology

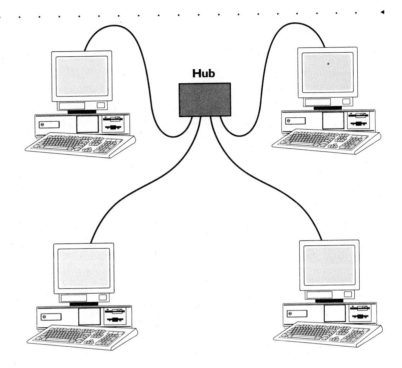

Star and modified star topologies tend to be easier to maintain and trouble-shoot than bus or ring topologies. Along with the common availability of UTP telephone cable in modern buildings, this is one reason why 10BaseT and UTP Token Ring have become so popular in recent years.

Shared Resources

Linking an organization's personal computers lets users share peripheral devices, common data, and other resources. Often, the efficiency of sharing

F I G U R E 2.4
Ring topology

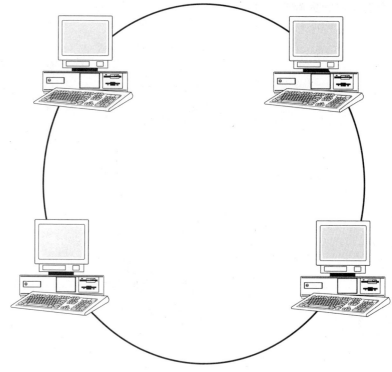

resources allows an organization to use more expensive, higher-quality output devices than might be attached to a standalone personal computer. For example, laser printers, color printers, plotters, film recorders, and specialized computer-aided design (CAD) output devices can be shared efficiently and economically on a LAN, because it is impractical to buy one of each of these devices for each user in an organization.

Some resources can be shared through a specially designed program called a NetWare Loadable Module (NLM). These applications can be linked to the operating system to expand the capabilities of the network server. The program code of an NLM is written to run on top of the NetWare operating system, to enhance its functionality without interfering with the network's regular operation, or to provide specialized services on a dedicated application server.

Companies like Oracle and Sybase offer NetWare-specific implementations of their database management systems—DBMSs—which very often run standalone on a server. Some typical NLMs offer services such as asynchronous or synchronous communications (such as the NetWare SAA gateway and the NetWare Asynchronous Communications Server—NACS), database services, archive/backup services, virus control, and more. The recent tendency of application developers seems to be to move all sorts of different network applications to the NLM architecture to provide better management of these services.

Communications with Other Systems

An entire LAN can be connected to other LANs or to external host computers, such as mainframes or minicomputers. Connection is accomplished through the use of routers, bridges, and gateways. Such products are available from Novell and third-party companies to support the kinds of connections that you need to access other computing resources within your organization.

ROUTERS

A *router* is a combination of hardware and software that connects networks that use similar communication formats, or protocols. With NetWare, routers can connect networks with different topologies, such as ARCnet, Ethernet, and IBM Token Ring networks, as well as with other network types. The NetWare operating system provides built-in support for the LAN protocols associated with each type of workstation that NetWare supports—namely, IPX/SPX for DOS, Windows, and OS/2; AppleTalk for Macintosh computers; and TCP/IP for UNIX workstations.

Routing services can be made a part of a NetWare server that provides other services (such as file and print sharing), or they can be dedicated to their routing functions. Both integrated and standalone routers function the same way, but performance differences can be considerable: Standalone routers—particularly dedicated hardware devices like those provided by companies such as cisco, Vitalink, Wellfleet, and others—almost always offer better routing performance; however, they are more costly to deploy and manage.

Internal routers reside within a NetWare server and consist simply of one or more network interface cards (NICs), along with additional NICs and protocol NLMs to provide routing services among them. Communications between multiple network segments (each serviced by a separate NIC in the file server) is managed by the NetWare operating system. Using internal routing, NetWare can interlink as many local area networks as there are distinct network interface cards in the server. The practical limit, based on cabling and common machine constraints, is six to eight distinct network segments. This simple and effective approach to creating an expanded network is illustrated by Figure 2.5.

In previous versions of NetWare, there was a utility called ROUTEGEN.EXE that could be used to generate an external router (ROUTER.EXE). This external router required a dedicated computer upon which to run, but that computer could be as simple as an IBM XT or compatible with 640K of RAM. The most significant limitation of ROUTER.EXE is that it can only route traffic using the IPX/SPX protocol. It does not support TCP/IP, AppleTalk, or any other protocols. Since NetWare 4.0 is so deeply involved with wide area networking and cross-platform internetworks, ROUTEGEN.EXE does not ship with the operating system.

The principal external routing solution from Novell is called the Novell Multi-Protocol Router (MPR). In fact, it is not a "generated" product at all in the sense that ROUTER.EXE is generated. It is rather a single-user, or run-time, NetWare operating system, combined with a number of NLMs that combine to support routing for various networking protocols. If you want to think of it as an internal router, you're actually correct, in a way. Although the MPR runs on top of a NetWare OS (either 3.x or 4.0), it doesn't support file services. If you accept the loose definition of an internal router—a file server with more than one NIC—the MPR isn't exactly an internal router. If, however, you think of an internal router as a NetWare server with more than one NIC, the definition fits.

FIGURE 2.5

*Connecting two LANs with
an internal router*

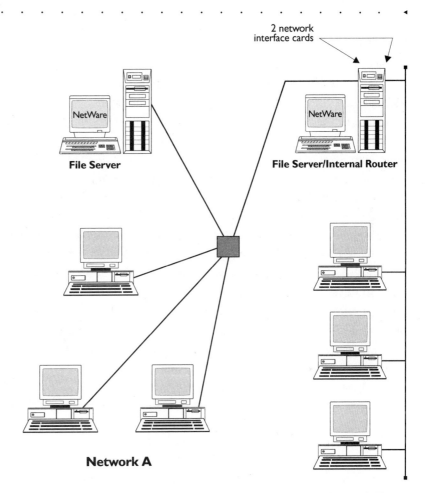

Network A

Network B

Here we get into a discussion that mandates a shift in attitude or perception. In the past, NetWare and the NetWare file server were, for all intents and purposes, the same thing. When Novell introduced NetWare 3.0 and the NLM architecture, that changed in theory, but it was still true enough in practice. Only after NetWare 3.11 and the release of a number of NLM-based applications (such as NACS, the NetWare SAA gateway, MPR, etc.) did the user community begin to see that one could take advantage of the NLM architecture in and of itself. They began to design networks with run-time NetWare servers that were dedicated to supporting the NLM applications, completely separate from NetWare file services. We call these NCP (NetWare Core Protocol) servers, since the operating system itself is NCP, but there are no file services present. We tend to call a NetWare file server an NCP server with file services (but only when we're being really nit-picky).

Getting back to routing, the NetWare Multi-Protocol Router can be loaded on a full-blown NetWare file services server, which makes it an internal router, or it can be loaded on run-time NetWare, which makes it an external router. If you think of the difference between the two as simply the presence or absence of file services, you'll have an easier time with the concept of the product. Since the MPR is in all other respects a NetWare 3.x or 4.x file server, it has the same requirements as a file server: 386 or better Intel-compatible CPU, 4MB of RAM or more (preferably 8MB or more for reasonable performance, depending on disk storage size), at least 25MB of disk space in addition to a DOS partition, etc.

When would you choose the MPR instead of allowing your server to act as an internal router? Some reasons are practical and others have to do with overcoming physical limitations. A short list of common reasons follows:

- ▸ The file server has no remaining expansion bus slots for additional NICs.

- ▸ The file server is already laden with activity, and performance is crucial.

- ▸ The file server is not conveniently located for interconnection of the dispersed networks.

- ▸ The applications in use are critical to the business, and all noncritical functions have to be off-loaded from the file server for fault tolerance. (Fault tolerance is the ability to avoid system failure due to problems with a single component or subsystem, whether hardware or software.)

▸ The routing functions are critical to the business and must be isolated from any possible causes of performance reduction, conflict, disruption, or failure.

▸ One of the links is a heavy-duty, high-traffic network segment that acts as a highway among multiple network segments. This type of segment is usually called a *backbone*. A backbone typically carries heavy traffic that might take up too much of a multipurpose server's processing capacity. Using a standalone router guarantees that the router will do its job properly and that local servers will not get bogged down by routing traffic on and off the backbone.

▸ A special-purpose link must be integrated. Sometimes, cable segments require 32-bit interfaces to be worthwhile—for instance, to get best use out of a 100 megabit-per-second technology like the Fiber Distributed Data Interface (FDDI). If the server doesn't offer a 32-bit bus like Extended Industry Standard Architecture (EISA) or IBM's Micro Channel Architecture (MCA), adding a new workstation that supports one of these permits the connection to be used to its best advantage. This can also be true for a variety of other WAN communications interfaces, including both asynchronous and synchronous connections of different kinds.

Figure 2.6 shows a multiprotocol internetwork using a Novell Multi-Protocol Router. The MPR in the illustration routes IPX/SPX (NetWare's native protocol), TCP/IP (the native protocol of UNIX systems), and AppleTalk (the native protocol of Apple Macintosh networks). Each of the separate networks can access each of the others by using the routing function of the MPR.

Of course, Novell isn't the only vendor producing routers that support multiple protocols. Wellfleet, cisco, Vitalink, and others provide dedicated devices that support many protocols. These products tend to offer higher performance at a higher cost than the Novell MPR. One advantage of the Novell MPR is that, being based on the familiar architecture of the NetWare operating system and using hardware that is as easily available as a personal computer, many system administrators feel less intimidated by the MPR than other dedicated devices. (The MPR is not yet available for NetWare 4.0, but Novell plans to release the product in the next year.)

▶ · ◀

FIGURE 2.6

Routing various protocols
with Novell's Multi-Protocol
Router

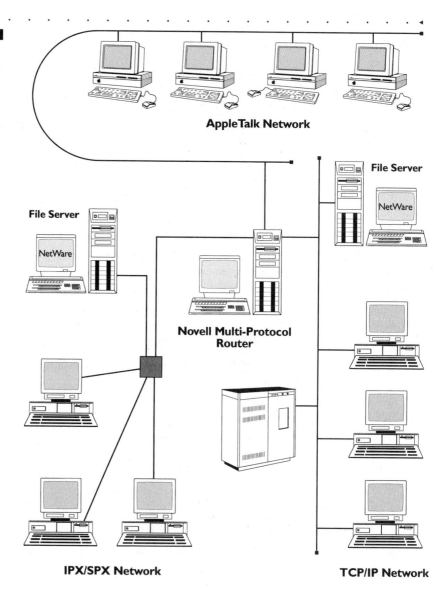

AppleTalk Network

File Server

File Server

Novell Multi-Protocol
Router

IPX/SPX Network

TCP/IP Network

Remote links can be configured when the distance between networks makes it impractical (or impossible) to physically connect them with standard network cables. In this case, telephone lines or public data networks (PDNs) are used to provide an intermediate transmission medium. You can connect networks that are located far apart from one another by configuring a router on each network with modems, as shown in Figure 2.7.

GATEWAYS

Communication gateways and special-purpose communications servers connect dissimilar systems. They can connect networks to mainframes and minicomputers. Similar to routers, such gateways or servers can be either local or remote, depending on whether or not the physical distance between the server and the other end of the link dictates an intermediate transmission medium.

Gateways have become a popular, cost-effective means of giving everyone on a network access to a mainframe computer. Instead of installing an interface card and cable for mainframe hookup in each personal computer, you can install one gateway computer. This computer gives everyone on the network access to the mainframe computer.

Gateways can be used in many ways. Although a detailed discussion of each way is beyond the scope of this chapter, we can look at how a local area network can be connected to a mainframe computer with a NetWare for SAA gateway. A coaxial cable connects a special interface board in the gateway to the mainframe directly, or the gateway can be connected to the host via synchronous phone lines. This architecture, illustrated in Figure 2.8, allows any workstation on the local area network to emulate a mainframe terminal as well as transfer files to and from the host computer.

As mentioned before, the NetWare for SAA gateway is a set of NLMs running on a NetWare operating system. In addition to offering 32-bit speed and enhanced services, NetWare for SAA can accommodate as many as 508 host sessions on a single NetWare server. It can run as a standalone, dedicated communications server or with other NetWare services.

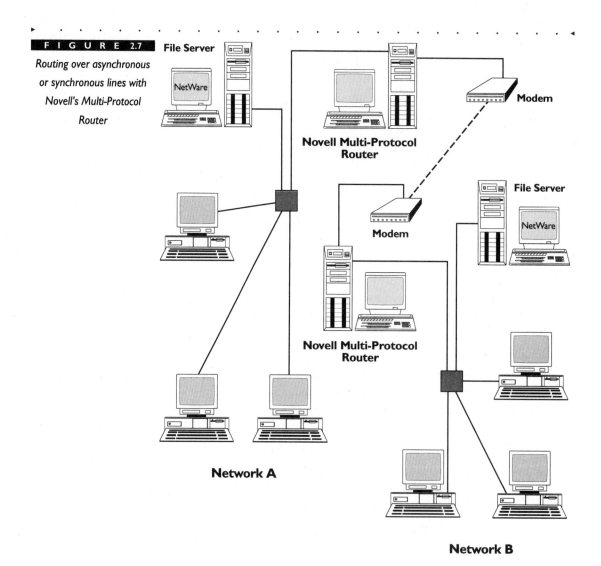

File Server

Novell Multi-Protocol
Router

Modem

Modem

File Server

Novell Multi-Protocol
Router

Network A

Network B

Figure 2.9 illustrates an example in which the NetWare for SAA NLMs share
a server with the file, print, and application services used by workstations on the

LAN depicted. Notice that the connection between the host and the LAN occurs through the server and does not require a separate dedicated workstation to manage the host link.

F I G U R E 2.8

Connecting a LAN to IBM hosts with the Novell SAA gateway

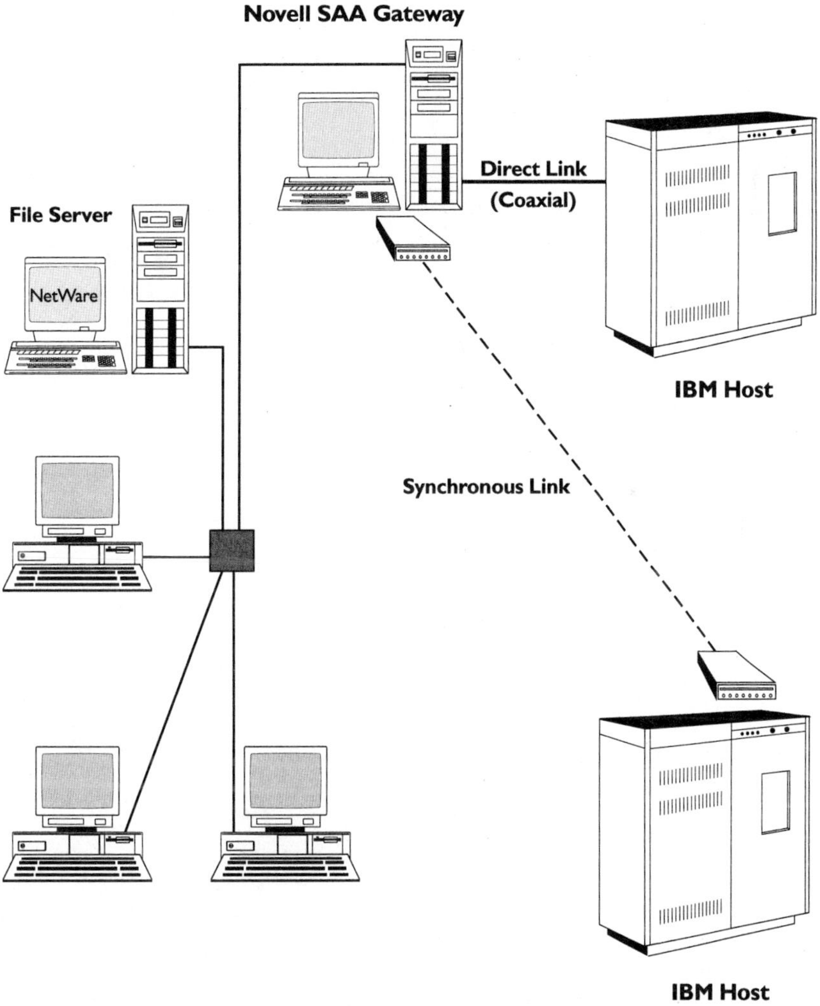

Novell SAA Gateway

File Server

NetWare

Direct Link (Coaxial)

IBM Host

Synchronous Link

IBM Host

F I G U R E 2.9

*Using the SAA gateway to
support other NLM-based
services*

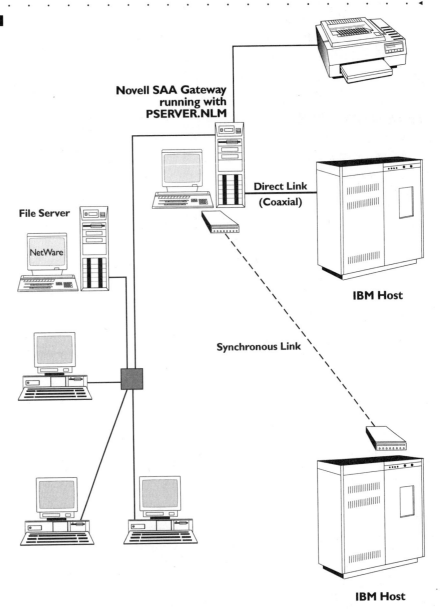

CHAPTER 3

Network Options

Fast Track

39   **_To pass data on a network,_**
three basic schemes can be used:

- ▸ Contention
- ▸ Token passing
- ▸ Polling

41   **_Communicating data over the network involves seven components:_**

- ▸ Source computer
- ▸ Sending protocol engine
- ▸ Transmitter
- ▸ Physical cabling
- ▸ Receiver
- ▸ Receiving protocol engine
- ▸ Destination computer

42   **_Ethernet networks use_**
the contention data-passing scheme. Depending on the requirements and brands used, Ethernet networks can be wired in either bus or star topologies. They can use coaxial, unshielded twisted-pair, shielded twisted-pair, or fiber-optic cables.

44   **_Token Ring networks use_**
the token-passing data-passing scheme. Token Ring networks are wired physically like a star, but they behave like a ring. They can run on unshielded twisted-pair, shielded twisted-pair, or fiber-optic cables.

One of the great strengths of Novell NetWare is its ability to run on a variety of network media and networking topologies. This gives the network manager much flexibility in deciding which network architecture to install. Because NetWare runs on all the major topologies, it's a matter of selecting the wiring and the topology that best fits your environment, rather than being restricted to a limited set of options.

This chapter reviews the key elements of popular networks. Its purpose is not to provide an exhaustive technical discussion, but it does offer an overview of network data-passing schemes, network systems, and cabling options (for more details, consult the references listed in the "Resources" section at the end of the chapter).

Terminology

First a word about terminology. In the LAN marketplace today, ARCnet (developed originally by Datapoint), Ethernet (developed by Digital Equipment Corp., Intel, and Xerox), and IBM's Token Ring dominate. The Institute of Electrical and Electronics Engineers (IEEE) has taken these technologies, modified their original specifications, and published them as IEEE standards. However, the IEEE specifications are not identical to the ARCnet, Ethernet, or IBM Token Ring standards.

Ethernet is closely related to the IEEE 802.3 specifications, ARCnet less closely to the IEEE 802.4 specifications, and IBM Token Ring remains very close to the IEEE 802.5 specifications. In general, the IEEE specifications are broader and more general than their original counterparts. For clarity in this chapter and the rest of this book, we will refer to both IEEE 802.3 and Ethernet generically as "Ethernet" and to both IEEE 802.5 and IBM Token Ring as "Token Ring." Since 10BaseT (sometimes referred to as unshielded twisted-pair Ethernet) is a subset of the IEEE 802.3 specification, it is also understood to be included in the term Ethernet.

Since ARCnet and the 802.4 specification are significantly different, and since the 802.4 standard has not become an industry standard as have 802.3 and 802.5, we will not refer to 802.4 much, if at all. Instead of being controlled by an IEEE standard, ARCnet is guided by the ARCnet Trade Association (ATA). More recently, the American National Standards Institute (ANSI) has more or less adopted the ARCnet specifications and hence has codified what had previously been a de facto industry standard.

Network Data-Passing Schemes

One of three basic schemes is used to send data along a network:

- Contention
- Token passing
- Polling

Contention

Networks that use contention schemes (Ethernet, AppleTalk) listen to the line before trying to send, and wait for the line to go quiet before sending out messages. If two computers happen to send messages at the same time, these messages will inevitably collide and be garbled. When this occurs, collision-sensing electronics take note of the event, and the lost messages are resent. Ethernet and AppleTalk systems use contention.

Token Passing

Networks that use token-passing schemes send data in a more orderly way. A *token* is a specific electronic signal that indicates a node has permission to transmit or receive. A limited number of tokens (usually one) circulate around the network—that is, messages follow a specific order of circulation, and the last recipient in the order passes the message back to the first recipient in the order. Messages to be transmitted are held at the local workstation until a free token arrives, which can pick up pending messages and deliver them to their destinations. Once properly delivered, the messages are stripped off the token, freeing it up for other messages. Both ARCnet and IBM Token Ring systems use token passing, as does the high-speed FDDI.

Polling

Polling is used only in hierarchical networks and therefore is not popular in LANs. It was used with the now obsolete S-Net system and is inappropriate for most modern LAN needs.

Performance Considerations

There is an ongoing debate about which scheme—contention or token passing—is more efficient. However, networks that use older token-passing schemes, like ARCnet and 4 megabit-per-second Token Ring, are usually slower but can be more predictable than those that use contention. Faster token-passing schemes can offer better performance than contention schemes, but they do so at an increased cost, which gets higher as the performance increases.

As more users join a network, systems that use token-passing schemes degrade more slowly than those that rely on contention. This advantage is because in a token-passing scheme, an increase in the number of users results in only a moderate slowdown of the token circulation time, whereas in a contention scheme, the presence of more users inevitably means more collisions.

The Token Ring scheme has the advantage of guaranteeing delivery of the token at some time (it is a *deterministic* architecture) as it circulates around the network. In extreme cases, the contention scheme can degrade to the point where the network becomes completely unavailable because collisions occur continuously. This is why contention schemes cannot support traffic levels that saturate the physical medium, but Token Ring schemes will continue to perform properly, although more slowly, at high traffic levels.

Network performance depends on many factors, one of which is the total amount of network traffic, which is not necessarily related to the number of active workstations. In a contention scheme, collisions occur when multiple workstations attempt to send data simultaneously. Thus, if most processing within a network occurs right on the workstation (for example, if workstations are used for local word processing), network performance may continue to be very good, even if the network has a large number of users.

With a token-passing scheme, performance is directly affected by the number of active workstations, not the total network traffic. Each additional user adds another address that the token must visit, whether or not the workstation needs to send data. However, in situations where traffic may be high, Token Ring will function more reliably than a contention scheme like Ethernet.

Network Communications

The process of communicating data across a network is managed by seven components: the source computer, the sending protocol engine, the transmitter, the physical cabling, the receiver, the receiving protocol engine, and the destination computer.

The source computer can be a workstation, a server, a gateway, or any computer or device on the network.

The protocol engine for both sender and receiver consists of the chip set and software driver for the network interface card. The protocol engine is responsible for the logic of network communication. At a very simple level, its job is to translate bits into appropriate signals when sending data, and signals into bits when receiving data.

The transmitter sends the resulting electronic signals produced by the protocol engine through the physical topology, while the receiver recognizes a network signal and captures it for translation by the protocol engine.

The data transmission cycle begins with the source computer submitting raw data to the protocol engine. The protocol engine arranges the data into a *message packet* that contains the appropriate request for services, information about how to process the request (including the destination address, if necessary), and the raw data to be transferred.

The packet is then forwarded to the transmitter for conversion into a set of network signals, called a *frame*. The frame flows through the network cable until it is delivered to the receiver, where the signal is decoded into data.

At this point, the protocol engine takes over. The protocol engine checks for errors and sends an acknowledgment of frame receipt to the source if required. It can also reassemble multiple frames into their original packet formats, and passes these packets on to the destination computer.

During the process of sending and receiving data over the network, the protocol engine controls network communications according to its built-in access scheme. Depending on the type of network system—the electrical topology—packets are either transmitted randomly via a contention scheme or systematically via a token-passing scheme. The NetWare operating system works in conjunction with the network system to manage the flow of data.

As previously mentioned, the three most important systems for local area networks are Ethernet, IBM Token Ring, and ARCnet. The standardization of these schemes helps maintain consistency among the sundry software and hardware manufacturers that use them. By following the established standards, vendors can closely monitor the compatibility of their implementations to ensure that components from different vendors work together.

Table 3.1 summarizes the most popular network and data-passing technologies.

ETHERNET NETWORKS

Ethernet uses a contention scheme to control data transmissions on the network. Ethernet networks can be wired in either bus or star topologies using coaxial (RG-6 for "thicknet," RG-58 for "thin-net," and RG-59 for Broadband Ethernet), twisted-pair (shielded or unshielded), or fiber-optic cables. (Cabling options are discussed later in this chapter.)

	ETHERNET (10 MB/S)	FAST ETHERNET (100 MB/S)	TOKEN RING (4 OR 16 MB/S)	FDDI (100 MB/S)	ARCNET (2.5 MB/S)	ARCNET PLUS (20 MB/S)	TCNS (100 MB/S)	APPLE-TALK (0.24 MB/S)
Coax	✓	?			✓	✓	✓	
Unshielded Twisted-Pair	✓	?			✓	✓	?	✓
Shielded Twisted-Pair	✓	?	✓		✓	✓	?	✓
Fiber-Optic	✓	?		✓	✓		✓	
Contention	✓	✓						✓
Token Passing			✓	✓	✓	✓	✓	

T A B L E 3.1   A Comparison of the Most Popular Network and Data-Passing Technologies

The key advantages of Ethernet are cost, availability, and convenience. Ethernet is currently the most widely used networking technology, according to industry sources like the Forrester Group and IDG, with somewhere between 60 percent and 70 percent of the installed base. A large Ethernet marketplace helps to lower the cost of the technology and ensures a large number of vendors to compete for consumer dollars. In turn, widespread competition provides a tremendous variety of components for Ethernet, including routers, hubs, network interface cards, repeaters, and bridges.

Finally, Ethernet's support for multiple wiring schemes—including fiber-optic cable, multiple types of coaxial cable, and both shielded and unshielded twisted-pair cable—makes it easy to mix and match cabling in an installation, and to make use of unused telephone wiring when available. All of these factors have contributed to Ethernet's current popularity, and it doesn't show any signs of abating.

With transmissions occurring at 10 megabits per second (Mbps or Mb/s), Ethernet was once one of the faster LAN technologies. However, its speed can also lead to problems. At such transmission rates, even a small amount of electromagnetic interference can degrade network performance. This fact accounts for the need to route twisted-pair and thin coaxial cable away from fluorescent light fixtures, transformers, and other sources of electromagnetic interference (EMI) and radio-frequency interference (RFI).

TOKEN RING NETWORKS

As indicated by its name, IBM Token Ring networks use a token-passing scheme for data transmissions. A Token Ring network is wired physically like a star, but the network behaves like a logical ring (see Figures 2.3 and 2.4). In other words, data flows from workstation to workstation in sequence (as in a ring network), but continually passes through a central point (as in a star network). Token Ring networks can run on unshielded twisted-pair, shielded twisted-pair, or fiber-optic cables. (Cabling options are discussed later in this chapter.)

Token Ring networks are available in two versions, supporting transmission speeds of 4 Mbps or 16 Mbps. Proteon developed a 10-Mbps variety of Token Ring, but it has fallen from favor. Although an individual network must run at either one speed or another, networks operating at different speeds can be bridged or routed together.

Token Ring networks are reliable, dependable under heavy loads, and fairly easy to install. However, when compared to the total costs of ARCnet and Ethernet networks, Token Ring networks are more expensive. Also, fewer vendors offer Token Ring equipment than Ethernet or ARCnet equipment. Together, all these factors conspire to keep the costs of Token Ring higher than the other two technologies.

Token Ring is a technology created and backed by IBM, and it is the topology of choice for environments where IBM mainframe connectivity is a consideration. Even so, now that IBM is pursuing the broader UNIX market, where Ethernet reigns supreme, IBM itself is beginning to offer Ethernet options.

ARCNET NETWORKS

ARCnet uses a token-passing scheme and can operate as either a bus or a star. A star usually provides better performance because this topology yields fewer collisions, and it is also a much more flexible type of wiring scheme. ARCnet is compatible with coaxial (RG-62), twisted-pair, and fiber-optic cables. (Cabling options are discussed later in this chapter.)

ARCnet systems are relatively slow. Transmissions occur at only 2.5 Mbps, which is significantly slower than in the types of systems discussed earlier. However, in at least one respect, slowness is an advantage. Because its speed does not challenge the capabilities of any of the cables, ARCnet is not especially sensitive to electromagnetic interference. Therefore, it is the best candidate for running on existing unshielded twisted-pair cables or existing RG-62 coaxial cables (used by IBM 3270 terminals), when they may be susceptible to electrical interference.

Despite its slow line-speed, ARCnet remains a popular choice. Its slow speed is somewhat offset by its efficient method of passing signals. ARCnet is relatively inexpensive and flexible, and it is easy to install, expand, and reconfigure. A 20-Mbps version of ARCnet, called ARCnet Plus, has been developed by Datapoint and is becoming more widely available, but it appears that this technology is unlikely to capture significant market share because of the cost of hardware and the significant competition offered by 100-Mbps technologies such as FDDI and TCNS.

APPLETALK

Developed by Apple Computers, Inc., AppleTalk is a protocol that gains market share with each Macintosh computer sold. The reason is that every Macintosh computer ships with AppleTalk network capabilities built in at the factory. Though it is used mostly for small workgroup environments, AppleTalk is gaining popularity as a viable linking technology where Macintosh computers need to communicate with other Macs or non-Macintosh computers or both.

OTHER TYPES OF NETWORKS

While the three types of networks discussed above—Ethernet, Token Ring, and ARCnet—certainly make up the bulk of local area networks in place today, there are numerous other types in use today, most of which are supported by NetWare.

Other technologies that are gaining popularity include Fiber Distributed Data Interface (FDDI), Thomas Conrad Network System (TCNS), and Datapoint's ARCnet Plus. A new Ethernet specification currently referred to as Fast Ethernet is also getting off the ground. The popularity of these technologies will increase as system designers need more and more bandwidth for their network traffic. With ARCnet Plus clocking in at 20 Mbps and FDDI, TCNS, and Fast Ethernet all offering 100 Mbps, these provide a new standard for high-speed local-area data communication.

NetWare drivers for IBM's PC-LAN, a 1-Mbps technology in wide use in primary and secondary educational institutions, are readily available, as are drivers for more esoteric technologies like Corvus OmniNet and Allen-Bradley 1- and 2-Mbps broadband.

In general, it's worth checking to see if a network already in place can support NetWare, before deciding to replace it with something else. A quick inquiry on the Novell forums supported on the CompuServe Information Service (collectively called NetWire), on Novell's NetWare Express forums on GE BusinessTalk, or with your NetWare reseller should help you to determine if you can use your "Pot-Luck-Net" with NetWare. While there are too many niche networking technologies out there for us to cover them all here, it's well worth checking anyway.

Cabling Options

Four types of network cables are commonly used today:

- ▶ Coaxial (or coax)
- ▶ Unshielded twisted-pair
- ▶ Shielded twisted-pair
- ▶ Fiber-optic

The first three conduct an electrical signal through metal wiring (typically copper). Fiber-optic cables convey light through special glass or plastic formulations.

Cabling is a more serious consideration than is often perceived. The cable you select for your network affects your future expansion options. Most networks allow several cabling options. You should, however, understand the consequences of using a particular cable type for a network.

For example, if a Token Ring network uses unshielded twisted-pair (type 3) cable, only 96 devices can be connected to a single ring. By contrast, if you use shielded twisted-pair (type 1 or type 2), 255 devices can be connected to a ring. Shielded cables also permit longer *lobe* lengths—the distance a wire can run from hub to workstation—allowing your cable plant (total cabling installation) to cover more ground, which can sometimes lower overall installation costs in far-flung offices or plants.

Although the cable in your building can always be replaced later, doing so is usually disruptive, cumbersome, and expensive. Thus, you should consider growth and expansion plans as well as present needs when choosing the kind of cable and topology to use. Also, you should be aware that telephone cabling is a form of unshielded twisted-pair and that telephone cabling systems, especially those with unused pairs, can sometimes be used for network data transmission. You should always consult a reputable cable installer to investigate your options; using an existing cabling plant will definitely be cheaper than installing new cable and should be investigated wherever feasible.

COAXIAL CABLE

Coaxial cable is a popular cable in buildings with IBM 3270 terminals. Coaxial cable consists of two conductors surrounded by two insulating layers. The first layer of insulation encloses a central copper conductor wire. The second layer is a conductor braided around the insulation of the first, and is clad with additional insulation and sometimes foil or metallic shielding as well.

Buildings that have ducts for air conditioning and heating can use either coaxial cable, which is covered with PVC (polyvinyl chloride), or a higher grade of cable—called plenum cable—that is covered with teflon. PVC cable is significantly cheaper than plenum cable.

If a building does not have duct work, the air system usually uses the space between a false ceiling and the next floor—the plenum space—for air circulation. When this is the case, strict codes are usually enforced pertaining to the materials that can be installed in the plenum space. If PVC cable is used and there is a fire, poisonous fumes from the burning PVC can enter the office through the air openings, and people can breathe them and suffer serious injury. That is why only teflon-clad cable can be used in the plenum space of a nonducted office.

Several types of coaxial cable are compatible with LAN topologies. If the building in which you are installing the network has mainframe terminals, a whole lot of IBM 3270 cable might run through the ceilings already, and you may want to consider using it.

Some types of coaxial cable are thicker than others. Thicker cables offer greater data capacity, can be run longer distances, and are less sensitive to electrical interference. RG-58 (50-ohm) cable is used for thin Ethernet, RG-62 (93-ohm) is used for ARCnet, and occasionally RG-59 (75-ohm) is used for IBM PC-LAN or 10Broad36 Ethernet.

Again, it's always wise to consult a reputable cabling contractor with network installation experience to decide which types of cable to use and where they should be laid.

UNSHIELDED TWISTED-PAIR CABLE

Because most buildings have an abundance of telephones, they also typically have an abundance of unshielded twisted-pair cable (it is commonly used as telephone wire). Telephone-grade twisted-pair cable is composed of two wires twisted together at six turns per inch to provide shielding from electrical interference plus consistent impedance, or electrical resistance. Another name commonly used for this wire is IBM type 3. Because existing buildings usually contain plenty of this wire, there is often a great temptation to save expense and time by using it.

However, using telephone wire, especially when it is already in place, can lead to several major problems. First, unshielded twisted-pair cable is sensitive to electromagnetic interference, such as the electrical noise created by fluorescent lights and passing elevators. The ring signal on phone lines running alongside the network cable can also cause interference. In addition, poor-quality twisted-pair cables may have a varying number of twists per inch, which can distort the expected electrical resistance. Though this cable is usually quite adequate for most telephone communications, network data transmission demands much smaller tolerances.

Also important to note is that telephone wires are not always run in straight lines. Cable that appears to run a relatively short distance between two offices might actually run through half the building. A misjudgment could cause you to exceed the maximum cable length specifications.

In short, unshielded twisted-pair cable is inexpensive, easy to install, and may work for your network. But be careful: The money that you save may be more than offset by additional costs later if the network doesn't function properly because of cable problems. The best way to decide if using such cable is worthwhile is to hire an experienced wiring or cable installation contractor to come out and test the signal quality and actual cable lengths of the wiring in your building. True, this will add to the cost of your network, but it is the only sure way to avoid encountering cable-quality problems later on.

SHIELDED TWISTED-PAIR CABLE

Shielded twisted-pair cables are similar to unshielded twisted-pair cables except that they use heavier-gauge conductors—thicker wire— and are protected from interference by a sheath of insulation and foil shielding. The most common type of shielded twisted-pair cable used in local area networks is IBM's type-1 cable. The standard developed for type-1 cable calls for a shielded cable with two twisted pairs of solid wire. For new buildings, type-2 cable might be a better option because type 2 includes two pairs of data wires as well as four unshielded pairs of solid wire for voice telephone transmissions. Type-2 cable thus permits the use of a single multistranded cable for both voice and network data communications.

The shielding and close attention to the number of twists per inch make shielded twisted-pair cable more reliable than its unshielded cousin. However, with this reliability comes additional cost. For new buildings or replacement installations, modular wiring like type 2 that combines voice and data wires into a single cable bundle makes wiring (or rewiring) much easier and helps to control overall costs. It also permits the use of modular wall plates, where connectors for phone and network connections can be provided and easily accessed when needed.

One thing that you want to avoid if at all possible is having too little cable available for your future needs. For that reason, you should consider installing twice as much cable as you immediately need. Doubling the amount of cable can be highly cost-efficient. Even if you don't foresee your network having much immediate growth, you can count on significant expansion over time. Remember that it is not the cable itself but the labor that is usually the most expensive part of the cable installation. Installing ample cable to begin with can save you in the long run (no pun intended). Also, since it's cheaper to install cable only once, combining telephone and network cabling can definitely save money.

FIBER-OPTIC CABLE

Fiber-optic cable transmits data in the form of light pulses through glass or plastic cables. Most major network systems support fiber-optic cabling, including ARCnet, Ethernet, Token Ring, TCNS, and FDDI.

Fiber-optic cable has significant advantages over all the metallic cable options. Fiber-optic cable is more reliable because it is not susceptible to packet loss through electromagnetic or radio-frequency interference. This feature makes fiber-optic cable appropriate for highly secure or electromagnetically noisy environments. Since the light pulses that carry the data are restricted to within the cabling itself, it is virtually impossible to surreptitiously tap into the medium without getting down into the actual core of the cable. In electromagnetically noisy environments like those around large cranes and massive mechanical equipment, fiber-optic cable is often used to bypass the interference of the engines and generators when transmitting data from one logic unit to another.

Fiber-optic cable is also very thin and flexible, making it easier to move than the heavier copper cables. Because signal losses while traversing the medium are less than those for metallic conductors, fiber-optic cable also supports much longer cable runs than do any of the wire-based alternatives.

Unfortunately, even though the price of fiber-optic cabling is declining, it is usually still more expensive than copper. Installing fiber-optic cables also can be more difficult than installing copper cables because the ends must be precisely polished and aligned in order to make a dependable connection. However, where long runs or links between buildings are required, fiber-optic cabling is often the only viable alternative.

While it is likely that you or someone on your staff is competent at cable installation for any of the wire-based types, we strongly recommend that you allow only qualified professionals to install fiber-optic cables. Not only does the technology demand close tolerances for tapping and termination, it also requires sophisticated, expensive test equipment using laser interferometry in order to test the quality of the fiber-optic lines installed.

Since small errors can lead to large problems, insist that your cable installer provide customer references and be sure to check them. You do not want to pay the added costs of training a fiber-optic cable installer. Unless your company is in the business of installing such cables, this job should be left to the professionals!

Resources

For information on networking topologies and technologies, we recommend the following:

▸ William Stallings, *Local Networks,* 3d. ed., Macmillan Publishing Company, New York, 1990.

This is one of the best general introductory books on LANs around. In addition to covering basic topologies and technologies, it also provides valuable information about networking protocols, wide-area-network links, and internetworking techniques and equipment.

▸ Andrew S. Tanenbaum, *Computer Networks,* 2d ed., Prentice-Hall, Englewood Cliffs, N.J., 1988.

This book covers much of the same ground as Stallings', but in more detail and with a better set of additional references. We'd still recommend Stallings as the first place to look, but no serious LAN library should be without this book.

▸ Frank Derfler, *PC Magazine Guide to Connectivity,* Ziff-Davis Press, New York, 1991.

Derfler's book covers a wide range of LAN topics, from cabling and topologies to networked applications, network operating systems, and electronic mail. It is an excellent reference to available products and technologies and, unlike the other books, looks at competing products rather than the academic models that spawned them.

For information on cabling and signaling issues, we recommend an encyclopedic resource that points to a galaxy of other references in this area (and many others):

▸ Paul J. Fortier, ed., *The Handbook of LAN Technology,* 2d ed., McGraw-Hill, New York, 1992.

Fortier's book covers most conceivable LAN topics from an engineering perspective. It's a clear case of overkill for those who may be merely curious; for the seriously inclined—or those with detailed questions to answer—the book can be a godsend.

CHAPTER 4

NetWare Overview and Planning for Installation

Fast Track

59   **If you have a very small network,**
you should choose NetWare Lite. However, the functions and growth opportunities of such a network are limited.

62   **If you have a medium-size network,**
you should choose NetWare 2.2 or NetWare 3.11, depending on the type of services and workstations involved. Version 2.2 is appropriate for homogeneous, NetWare-only environments.

64   **If you have a medium- to large-size network,**
you should choose NetWare 3.11. It is better suited to environments with different client (workstation) operating systems, or where multiprotocol connectivity is a must. It is also necessary if third-party NetWare Loadable Module (NLM) products will be incorporated.

65   **If you have a large to very large network,**
you should choose NetWare 4.0, especially if multiple servers and multiple sites are involved, or if large numbers of users must be accommodated. NetWare 4.0 is the most advanced version of the NetWare operating system and contains a number of features not available in other versions.

67   **The servers should be located**
in an area that is well ventilated, is well secured, and has stable and sufficient electricity. For small workgroups, servers can be close to their users along with other essential peripherals, like printers. For large workgroups, remote printers make it possible to place printers where needed while still controlling server access and location.

Cable placement options include   68

routing all cables back to a central wiring closet. This approach may be
somewhat more expensive, but it helps reduce maintenance and troubleshooting problems. Also, every cable should be labeled as it is installed,
and cable runs should be documented on site plans or engineering drawings for easy identification.

The location of network printers   69

should be carefully planned so that people who use them a lot can get to
them easily. NetWare includes a remote print server utility that facilitates
sharing local printers over the network.

Planning for NetWare 4.0 Directory Services   70

before installing NetWare is essential to providing the most workable installation. This can be time-consuming and may involve organizational
politics, but it is critical to a successful installation.

Migrating from older versions of NetWare to 4.0   71

is best managed by a combination of advanced planning, controlled
trials, and phased implementation. Though migration tools help to automate this task, understanding the migration process and testing the plan
before it goes on line are the keys to success.

The previous chapters provided an overview of networks in general and device, topology, and cabling options. This chapter discusses how to distinguish among NetWare versions and factors you should consider in setting up a NetWare 4.0 installation.

What Is NetWare?

NetWare is an operating system for networks, much like DOS is an operating system for standalone personal computers. The primary difference between NetWare and an operating system like DOS is that NetWare is designed to manage the programs and data among several computers instead of just one.

A NetWare LAN usually uses a Token Ring, Ethernet, or ARCnet *access scheme* and can have a bus, star, or ring topology. The network access scheme provides the electronic highway for transporting data; NetWare provides the mechanisms for controlling system resources and their use along that highway.

As you'll see when you configure the NetWare operating system, one of NetWare's strengths is that it can accommodate a variety of network configurations.

Choosing a NetWare Version

Although this book specifically covers Novell's current flagship operating system, NetWare 4.0, we have included this section to help you distinguish NetWare 4.0 from other members of the NetWare product family. Because the network operating system controls all resources and servers, determines individual service capabilities, and provides these services to each of the workstations and users connected to the network, your choice of an operating system is critical to the effectiveness of the network.

Novell NetWare is available in several different forms. The one that's right for you depends on the size and complexity of your network. In general, the version you select will be determined by the kinds of services you expect from your network and the total number of servers and workstations to be connected on your network. In some cases, however, you may also want to consider such factors as the number and kinds of links to other, non-NetWare environments you expect to use and whether or not your network will ultimately be part of a wide area network (WAN).

When selecting a NetWare version, remember that networks grow, and often they grow quickly. For this reason, you should estimate the total number of workstations that might eventually be connected to the network, and then prepare as if you were going to connect all of them. Because networks are so flexible and easy to add on to, you should also plan for the level of complexity to increase as your network grows.

Generally, network users find they expand their software applications well beyond traditional spreadsheets and word processing programs. Because users often store critical company data on the network, security is another important factor in selecting the operating system. For large, multisite installations, remote management and network-based software distribution may also be important factors to consider. In general, with larger numbers of users per server, larger overall networks, and/or greater numbers of non-NetWare resources that must be accommodated, you will find that a higher version number of NetWare will probably be appropriate.

Table 4.1 summarizes available NetWare products and their uses. The primary criteria in your selection will be the number of users and the overall complexity of the network as determined by the need for such features as inter-LAN bridging, sophisticated backup procedures, the total number of servers and individual networks, and the need for global directory services.

CHOOSING NETWARE LITE FOR PEER-TO-PEER SERVICES

If all you need is simple file and print sharing, and there will never be more than 25 users on your network, NetWare Lite may be the right product for you. NetWare Lite is a peer-to-peer networking solution that offers simple file and print sharing among up to 25 simultaneous network users, where access to network disk resources and printers acts like an extension of the same kinds of resources available through DOS on your local workstation. Though the theoretical limit of NetWare Lite is 25 simultaneous users, a more realistic and functional

TABLE 4.1

A Comparison of NetWare

Versions

NETWARE VERSION	NUMBER OF WORKSTATIONS (Theoretical Limits Are in Parentheses)	KEY FEATURES
NetWare Lite	2–5 (25)	Simple file/print sharing
		Simple security structure
		No dedicated file server (peer-to-peer)
NetWare 2.2	5–50 (100)	Usually dedicated file server, though can be nondedicated
		Full-featured file and print services
		Full-featured and extremely configurable security structure
		Full-disk-channel fault tolerance allows protection from disk or disk controller failures (SFT level II)
		Supports Macintosh file system
		Can support Macintosh clients with NetWare for Macintosh (additional product)
NetWare 3.11	10–200 (250)	All the advances of 2.2, plus the following:
		Must be dedicated file server
		Advanced file services, supporting DOS, Macintosh, HPFS (OS/2), FTAM, and NFS (UNIX) file systems

	NETWARE VERSION	NUMBER OF WORKSTATIONS (Theoretical Limits Are in Parentheses)	KEY FEATURES
T A B L E 4.1 *A Comparison of NetWare Versions (continued)*			NetWare Loadable Module (NLM) architecture allows third-party products and services (database, communications, virus protection, system management, etc.) to be integrated into the operating system Multiprotocol support Supports Macintosh, UNIX, and OS/2 clients (additional products)
	NetWare 4.0	100+	*All of the advances of 3.11, plus the following:* NetWare Directory Services supplies an architecture for large network interconnection and relationship planning On-disk file compression makes better use of disk storage space High Capacity Storage Systems (HCSS) Data Migration GUI utilities

limit is around 5 to 10 users. Above that range, network design and operation really dictate a more powerful operating system.

NetWare Lite offers basic networking services, but it will also operate with other NetWare versions. Since a NetWare Lite workstation can act as a client and as a server, provided the right software modules are installed and loaded, it can be a simpler system to run.

If your users just need to share each other's files and an occasional printer, Net-Ware Lite might be a great solution. This product works well as long as your needs are simple and the network is small, but it is unsuited for larger groups of users or for mixed environments involving more than DOS workstations (for example, where data sharing needs to embrace Macintoshes, OS/2 machines, or UNIX workstations, in addition to DOS).

If you'd like more information on NetWare Lite, see the "Resources" section at the end of this chapter.

CHOOSING NETWARE 2.2 FOR A SMALL NETWORK

For networks that require more full-featured capabilities, Novell's entry-level operating system—NetWare 2.2—may be a good choice. This version of Net-Ware is Novell's most basic file-server-based operating system. It can be configured to run in nondedicated mode, so the computer configured as the file server can also function as a workstation, but unlike NetWare Lite a machine must be configured to operate as the file server for the network.

NetWare 2.2 will run on an Intel 80286, -386, or -486 processor, but since performance increases with the power of the CPU, we recommend that you buy a 386 or 486 machine. Not only will such a machine run NetWare 2.2 more effectively, it leaves the door open to migrate to more advanced versions of NetWare without having to upgrade your hardware.

When you are shopping for a file server, we advise that you buy as much power as you can reasonably afford. The difference between the purchase price of a Novell-approved and -tested file server based on a 486 CPU and a 386 CPU is minimal. The couple of hundred dollars extra that you might spend will be a good long-term investment. There is little or no reason to run any operating system (except possibly NetWare Lite) on anything less than a 386-based computer. Even though NetWare 2.2 will run on a 286, it is a waste of employee resources to do so since the operating system will run much more efficiently on a more advanced computer.

With the advancing complexity of operating systems and applications, a 286 will be obsolete in a normal office environment very soon. Sure, you can run

WordPerfect 5.1 with DOS 3.3 on a 286 and get a lot of work done. However, the nature of the industry is that active support for older products is withdrawn after a certain amount of time.

NetWare 2.2 file services are optimized for sharing data and program files using a central file server. The file server is the central point of reference for a 2.2 network. It is at the file server that all security, file, and print services are based. Because it is the most basic standard NetWare version, NetWare 2.2 does have some important limitations. NetWare 2.2 does not offer all the rich features offered by other, higher-numbered versions. It supports only DOS, Macintosh, and OS/2 clients, and cannot handle sophisticated Macintosh print services. It cannot support TCP/IP or OSI protocols directly, nor can it operate as a Multi-Protocol Router. All of these features limit NetWare 2.2's ability to function effectively in a heterogeneous, multiprotocol computing environment.

As already mentioned, NetWare 2.2 can be configured with a file server that doubles as a workstation. In this mode of operation, it is called a *nondedicated* file server. Any nondedicated file server is limited to 640K of RAM in its DOS sessions and may not be able to run all DOS software (especially where extended or expanded memory support is required).

NetWare 2.2 is available in versions for 5, 10, 20, 50, and 100 users. It is suitable for smaller, moderately sophisticated environments where external computing resources and protocols don't need to be accessed. It functions well as a workgroup solution, for linking together groups of individuals who work together regularly, and for building homogeneous NetWare-only internetworks. It is not optimal for networks that are likely to grow beyond 10 to 20 servers, networks that need to span multiple sites, or networks that need to interact with UNIX workstations or minicomputers, or that need to connect to DEC or IBM mainframes.

Novell has publicly announced that, though it will continue to support NetWare 2.2, there will be no further changes to the core operating system. That means that 2.2 will not be revised or rereleased, according to Novell's current plans, although enhancements may be made to drivers, utilities, etc. Development teams and a whole lot of programming talent are currently devoted to 3.*x* and 4.*x*. Such is no longer the case for 2.*x*. Accordingly, if NetWare 2.2 fits your needs as it is, it may be an appropriate solution for you. If you find it lacks certain services that you need, consider 3.*x* or 4.0.

CHOOSING NETWARE 3.X FOR A MEDIUM- TO LARGE-SIZE NETWORK

For networks of 30 to 250 or more workstations, or those with a potential for complex applications or heterogeneous connectivity requirements, you should choose NetWare 3.11. This product is a more powerful version of NetWare. Net-Ware 3.11 requires a file server that uses an 80386 or 80486 processor. However, as with all versions of NetWare, DOS workstations can be based on a variety of CPUs, including 8088 (IBM XT–compatible), 80286 (IBM AT–compatible), 80386, and 80486.

NetWare 3.11 has a number of advanced features not available in NetWare 2.2. Among them are

- ▶ Enhanced security

- ▶ Ability to support a greater number of users per server

- ▶ Enhanced file system

- ▶ Ability to support larger files (e.g., database and graphics files)

- ▶ Optional file attribute (Purge) to immediately purge erased files

- ▶ Dynamic operating-system configuration

- ▶ Improved manageability

- ▶ Add-on options for enhanced UNIX and Macintosh support

- ▶ Ability to add individual services, called NetWare Loadable Modules (NLMs), to the operating system

For larger, more complex networks, the extra functions in NetWare 3.11 make it possible to fully integrate the needs of network users, where NetWare 2.2 would be insufficient. This product provides more powerful functions and a more capable operating platform, which is required for supporting mission-critical applications—the functions that are at the core of a company's operations.

NetWare 3.11's limitations are related to the size of the user community to be supported, to the complexity of the computing environment in which it is situated, and to the desire for end-users to interact more simply and effectively with the network. NetWare 3.11 is available in versions for 5, 10, 20, 50, 100, and 250 users, offering a wide range of options for the size of the user community to be supported by an individual file server. NetWare 3.11 lends itself to deployment in large, multisegment internetworks, but you can quickly see that its use becomes increasingly complex as the number of servers and resources increases.

In a way, NetWare 3.11's most significant weakness is directly related to one of its most significant strengths. There are a vast number of utilities available for system configuration, navigation, maintenance, monitoring, security, and so on. This variety allows a system administrator to choose the method that he or she can relate to best (menu utilities versus command-line utilities). On the downside, there are a whole lot of menus and commands to become familiar with. While basic network functionality can be attained with the working knowledge of a few utilities (SysCon, PConsole/Capture, NDIR, etc.), real mastery of NetWare 3.11 requires no small amount of advanced training and experience.

CHOOSING NETWARE 4.0 FOR A LARGE OR COMPLEX NETWORK

NetWare 4.0 is Novell's latest implementation of NetWare. It offers all the capabilities found in 3.11, plus significant functionality not present in the 3.11 version. While these benefits are most obvious in a large, complex networking environment, they can confer considerable benefits on end-users and administrators alike, even for single-server, smaller networks.

NetWare 4.0's significant new features are as follows:

▸ NetWare Directory Services

▸ On-disk file compression

▸ Improved network management features (Windows-based management utilities)

From the standpoint of pure convenience, NetWare 4.0 offers significant improvements over NetWare 3.11. Background authentication means that users need only enter their login name and password once, and thereafter can access any 4.0-based network resources to which they are entitled without having to go through a login sequence again. Of course, this isn't just a convenience; it is part of an improved login security mechanism, which makes a NetWare 4.0 network more protected against unauthorized access.

NetWare 4.0 also offers a new, consolidated set of end-user and administrative utilities that greatly simplifies interaction with NetWare and also provides the option of using GUI-based tools to Windows 3.1 and OS/2 2.0 users and administrators. DOS command-line and menu utilities are still supplied, but you will probably find that the GUI (graphical user interface) tools are much better suited to effective system management and understanding.

The most significant new feature is NetWare Directory Services (NDS), in which, at last, the file server is no longer the focal point of the network. Users can log in to the network itself rather than a particular server. This seemingly simple shift confers tremendous advantages on users and administrators. These gains are explained later in this chapter and are covered in detail in Chapter 8.

Some of NetWare 4.0's other features will appeal to different audiences: For those who wish to operate NetWare in a language other than English, NetWare 4.0 supports French, German, Italian, and Japanese directly. Language development tools are available from Novell for third-party developers to produce and distribute other language modules on their own. This language support is integral to the NetWare utilities, so you can switch languages as needed and receive messages and utility prompts in any of the supported languages.

NetWare 4.0 also allows support for EDP (electronic data processing) audit, built-in disk compression, and jukebox (near-line storage) or removable (offline storage) media support.

Start-up Considerations

If NetWare 4.0 is the version you've elected to install, you must make a number of start-up decisions. Some have to do with your physical situation: You must determine where to put the file server, the cables, and any network printers. Some have to with environment planning: particularly, the design and deployment of a Directory Services environment, including choosing names and naming conventions for users, servers, services, and other network objects and resources managed within the NetWare 4.0 environment.

Working with Directory Services also includes figuring out where to put the Directory database and (optionally) how to partition it into multiple databases, and addressing creation and placement of Directory database replicas. If gradual or progressive migration from earlier versions of NetWare is a consideration, this too will benefit from advanced planning and scheduling, particularly in organizations where large numbers of NetWare servers have to be upgraded.

DETERMINING WHERE TO PUT THE SERVER

For NetWare 4.0, the location of the file server can be important, especially if it is the repository of Directory Services or another mission-critical service. In general, we recommend that you put your server into secure areas where there is little chance that they can be accessed by unauthorized personnel. A locked room or at least a separate, unshared space is most appropriate for your server.

Whether your server resides in a dedicated computer room, telephone closet, or other secure space, make sure its space is well ventilated. Most NetWare servers run continuously, 24 hours a day, and should be in an area that does not get too hot or too cold.

You should also be sure to check the available electricity. A typical server is likely to have extra disk drives and possibly tape drives or printers attached to it, and these will require more power than an ordinary personal computer. If you will be using a laser printer, which typically requires a circuit rated at at least 30 amps, it is especially critical to have a qualified electrician check the power supply to ensure that there is adequate and consistent current.

If it is possible, keep the laser printer and the file server on separate electrical circuits. Doing so will prevent the sometimes drastic power drains generated by typical laser printers from affecting the server adversely.

We strongly recommend renting or obtaining a power monitor to check the quality of power on a server's circuit for no less than a week. Often, such monitoring can indicate the need for power-conditioning equipment where a casual spot check might not.

For smaller networks or workgroups or to obtain maximum performance, you could put the file server near the users. This location is for the users' convenience, particularly if a printer is attached directly to the server. If the server needs to be located far from its users, you can connect remote printers to a DOS workstation if the remote printer utility (NPRINTER) is loaded on that machine.

Use of NetWare 4.0 permits a great deal of flexibility. It is possible to locate a server close to the users or several floors away. As with other versions of NetWare, advanced printer services are available that allow special queuing of printers. These services also allow local printers to be configured as network printers. For this reason, it's not really critical to have the server located close to the users. All things considered, a server should be located in the very best place, with climate and physical security in mind.

DETERMINING WHERE TO PUT CABLES

The network topology you select will most likely determine the cable type the network uses. You will, however, likely have some options regarding cable placement in wire closets or hubs.

Where possible, you should route all cables back to a common area, usually in a wiring closet. Your office or building likely has a central closet or demarcation point for telephone wire. This area usually makes an excellent place for LAN cables too. Although this method can be more expensive than stringing cables in a long, bus fashion, it is much easier to maintain later on. Finding a cable problem is much easier when all wires come to a common area.

You also should start a cable-numbering scheme even before your network is installed. To facilitate debugging, you should label every cable and connection point on the network. This can be done easily while the network is being installed. Once the network is in place, however, determining what cable goes to what location can be difficult and frustrating. It's also wise to plot cable runs on a set of site plans or architectural drawings. Should you ever need to change the cabling, having a clear diagram will make it easier to find and replace the cable.

Remember that installing cables for a LAN can be disruptive for everyone in the office. Therefore, be sure to do it right the first time, and try to do installation during off-hours if there are already people in the office. The best time to install cables is before walls and ceiling are completed, during construction, but in the real world this is not often possible.

DETERMINING WHERE TO PUT NETWORK PRINTERS

Make sure you adequately plan printer locations for your network. If you put your printers in inconvenient spots, your users will get very upset. Unlike most other peripherals, printers are used regularly by almost every user of the network.

As a general rule, place the best printers as close as possible to their most frequent users. In practice, this means keeping them close to clerical and administrative personnel, who typically produce the greatest volume of printed material in an organization. Many printers are put in copier rooms or document production centers, where they fit right into the paper management business so prevalent in many companies. This type of placement may require the use of extra-long cables, dedicated print servers, or connection options that allow the printer to attach directly to the network cabling system. These additional costs will quickly be offset by the additional productivity and access they provide.

As with versions 3.11 and 2.2, NetWare 4.0 has special printer service functions that allow you to configure local printers as remote printers. This procedure requires running a special program on the workstations that share the printers. Because this software runs as a terminate-and-stay-resident (TSR) utility, it decreases the available memory on the workstations that share the printers. Problems may surface if the amount of memory available is no longer sufficient to load a particular application.

It is wise to map out a target workstation's memory, interrupts, and ports before trying to add remote printer software. This precaution will help to identify, and sometimes even to cure, potential problems or conflicts. It's also wise to educate users who host a remote printer that their machine should never be turned off when other users expect the printer to be available. Remind them that their machine is also a network resource and that other people depend on access to "their printer."

PLANNING FOR NETWARE DIRECTORY SERVICES

NetWare Directory Services (NDS) acts an information hub for all network access for NetWare 4.0. End users and applications alike can use NDS to find the resources they need, such as printers, print queues, users, servers, and volumes, regardless of where those resources are located on the network.

In previous versions of NetWare, you logged in to a file server so that you could user the files, print queues, users, or other resources that were located on that server's network. To access a file or print queue on a different file server, you had to attach to that server separately.

With NDS, you no longer have to log in to each file server that has resources you'd like to access. Instead, you log in once to the network, and that single login gives you access to every resource on the entire network, regardless of the servers involved. How you can use those resources is then controlled by NetWare security features, such as trustee rights and file and directory attributes. NDS allows you to remove the physical barriers to network resources without compromising security.

NDS consists of a database of information about every object on the network. Objects are the resources and entities that use the network: servers, print queues, printers, print servers, users, groups, volumes, and so on. This Directory database (also called the Directory Information Base) is, generally speaking, duplicated on every file server in the network, so that all the file servers contain the same information.

What all of this means to users is that when they want to send print jobs to a printer, they can simply select that printer from the list of network resources. They no longer have to worry about which file server the printer is connected to or whether they have valid user accounts on that server. Likewise, when users want to access files, all they need to know is the volume that contains the file; they do not need to know which file server contains the volume.

Since resources are now available to the entire network instead of being restricted to a given file server's network, planning your network setup is crucial. There are three critical steps to planning for NetWare Directory Services:

► Plan the organizational structure of network resources: You will need to group network objects into a logical hierarchical structure so that users can easily find what they are looking for. This hierarchy is called the Directory tree. You also need to decide how to name objects, whether network administration will be centralized or distributed, and how bindery-based NetWare servers will fit into the NetWare 4.0 network.

► Plan for partitions and replicas of the Directory database: Partitions divide the overall Directory database into more manageable segments. Replicas of those partitions are then placed on various servers so that if one server goes down, the Directory database can continue to operate and remain available.

► Plan for time synchronization: Because all the file servers on a NetWare 4.0 network work together to maintain the Directory database, you must ensure that they are all keeping time accurately and consistently with one other. To do this, you specify some servers to be reference or primary time servers (which set the time) and others to be secondary time servers (which get their time from the reference and primary servers).

These NDS issues are described more thoroughly in Chapter 8.

PLANNING FOR MIGRATION TO NETWARE 4.0

Migration (or upgrading) is only an issue if you are converting from NetWare 2.2 or 3.11 to NetWare 4.0. In these cases, the activities described in the following sections should always be planned for.

Plan How to Migrate the Bindery

In previous versions of NetWare, information about the objects that use the network was stored in a database called the *bindery*. Each file server had its own bindery. In NetWare 4.0, these individual binderies are replaced by one Directory database, which contains information about all objects on the entire network.

When you upgrade a file server from a previous version of NetWare to Net-Ware 4.0, the migration utility you use transfers the information from the file server's individual bindery into the overall Directory database. If you upgrade two or more servers to 4.0, NetWare migrates all of their binderies into a single Directory database. This can cause problems if you have the same names for objects on different file servers, such as two different users named Lynn. While this may not have been a problem when neither Lynn needed access to the other's file server, it will be a conflict when the two binderies are migrated into a single Directory database.

Make sure you plan the migration of your servers so that existing objects do not conflict with one another when they are combined in the Directory database. You may want to change object names on your NetWare 3.11 or 2.*x* network so that they are all unique before you begin migrating to NetWare 4.0. Chapter 8 explains more about installing NetWare Directory Services on your server.

Make Sure NetWare 4.0 Supports All Your Production Needs

In many ways, NetWare is more than just a network operating system. It is also a platform for add-on services, both from Novell and from third-party developers. While the initial release of NetWare 4.0 is guaranteed to provide basic NetWare services, add-on protocols and services for Macintosh, UNIX, or IBM host environments may not be ready at the time that NetWare 4.0 actually ships. Don't start migrating until you're sure that the services you require can migrate with you.

Alternatively, you may want to plan for a phased migration that moves key application servers to NetWare 4.0 only when those key services can move as well. This problem is typical of most complex software systems and is likely to affect third-party products more than Novell products, simply because third parties typically do not have the benefits of as much advance information about or exposure to new NetWare releases.

Adequately Test the Migration Utilities in a Limited Setting Before Converting Your Production Environment

Before attempting to switch your production servers from an earlier version to NetWare 4.0, take the time to install a test server with the older version and perform a test run of the migration tools. This will prepare you to deal with the real thing based on experience rather than a set of manuals or books, and will help to identify potential problems along the way. No book (not even this one!) can take into account every nuance and wrinkle that your network may incorporate. The more your test server resembles your actual production servers, the more dependable your results will be (installing a standalone server from a production backup is a great place to start this exercise).

For Each Server to Be Migrated, Create Three Complete Backups of the Earlier Environment

The second full backup is a form of insurance and will let you at least go back to your old environment should the first one fail for some reason. In general, major changes are best anticipated by creating two backups, and migrating from 2.2 or 3.11 to 4.0 certainly qualifies as a major change. We have experienced a double failure of backup systems at least once. This is why we recommend three backups. If you only realize that something is destroying your tapes in the middle of the second restore (it's happened!), you still have a third fresh backup to rely on.

It's been said that a backup is only as good as it restores. We follow this view and therefore suggest that you attempt and confirm a full restore (to a neutral machine) before placing your trust in any backup. You don't want to be like the graduate student (it has happened to more than one person) who came into our computer center in tears, explaining that his dissertation was on "this" floppy disk and he couldn't read it all of a sudden. "Where's your backup copy?" was the response, to which the student replied, "It's on this disk also!"

Train Local Administrators Before the Migration Takes Place

It's better by far to delay migration and have your network administrators up to speed with newly upgraded servers than it is to upgrade willy-nilly and live with the ensuing chaos. Advanced training for support staff and administrators is the ounce of prevention that can avoid the pounds (or tons) of cure that you'll need to administer after the fact.

Train End-Users As Soon As Practical

Because end-users significantly outnumber administrators, training all of them before a migration is not always possible, even if you decide that it is a good idea. At the very least, let them know a change is coming, and try to prepare them for it. The availability of extensive online help and documentation in NetWare 4.0 can offset lack of direct training in the short term, but at the very least, a short class or document on how to use help and access the system's online documentation is crucial.

Run Mission-Critical Applications in Parallel

If an application is the lifeblood of your business, planning the cutover from an old environment to a new one can be served properly only by bringing up the new version alongside the old and letting the new version demonstrate its workability before abandoning the tried and true implementation. This will require extra time and hardware (renting or leasing is a great option here), but it can completely pay for itself if it helps to avoid downtime. If the application is truly mission-critical, no one should balk at the time and expense. The alternative is to put your whole operation at risk unnecessarily.

This combination of planning ahead of time, dry runs, phased migration, and parallel operation should help to smooth out the transition and to avoid unnecessary loss of network services during the process. It's almost axiomatic that the only time a network gets noticed is when things go wrong, so your basic goal should be to traverse the migration path without attracting too much attention.

Resources

For additional NetWare product information, consult *The Novell Buyer's Guide*. This semiannual publication, available from Novell in both paper and electronic form, documents all current components of the Novell product line. This document brings technical and marketing information together in a reasonably useful form, and can be obtained by requesting a copy from your Novell reseller or by calling 1-800-NET-WARE and requesting a copy (single copies only).

For more specific information on NetWare Lite, you can read *The Official Novell NetWare Lite Handbook* by Ed Liebing, published by SYBEX/Novell Press, 1992.

Most of the PC- and LAN-focused publications review new Novell products as they ship and can be excellent sources of information. We've become leery of competitive benchmarks over the last two years, simply because benchmarking has always been and remains an imperfect method of evaluation. That sounds like sour grapes, but in fact, NetWare consistently shows well in these reviews. It's just that no benchmark can adequately take into account the needs and various parameters of your particular environment.

All things considered, we've seen very good coverage of NetWare and other LAN-related products and software from the following magazines:

- *LAN Technology,* published monthly. M&T Publishing, 411 Borel Avenue, Suite 100, San Mateo, CA 94403-3522.
  Phone: (415) 358-9500.

- *LAN Times,* published (roughly) semimonthly. McGraw-Hill, 1900 O'Farrell Street, Suite 200, San Mateo, CA 94403.
  Phone: (415) 513-6800.

- *NetWare Solutions,* published monthly. Data Base Publications, Inc., 9390 Research Boulevard, Suite II-300, Austin, TX 78759.
  Phone: (512) 343-9066.

- *Network Computing,* published monthly. CMP Publications, 600 Community Drive, Manhasset, NY 11030.
  Phone: (516) 562-5701.

▸ *Network Management,* published monthly. PennWell Publishing Company, 1421 South Sheridan, Tulsa, OK 74112. Phone: (918) 831-9424.

▸ *Network World,* published weekly (except around Christmas). IDG Publications, 161 Worcester Road, Framingham, MA 01701. Phone: (508) 875-6400.

▸ *PC Magazine,* published biweekly, except for July and August. Ziff-Davis Publications, One Park Avenue, New York, NY 10016. Phone: (212) 503-5255.

Believe it or not, this is just the tip of a large iceberg. If these publications don't appeal to you, there are a lot more publications that review microcomputer and LAN technology. Over time, we've found these to be well worth reading.

PART II

Installing and Configuring Your NetWare Network

An Installation Overview

You can follow many paths when you install a NetWare 4.0 network. However, no matter how you proceed, preparing—and using—a checklist can save you a lot of time and headaches later.

This chapter outlines a step-by-step process that can help ensure success as you put the parts in place and begin to "turn on the lights" for your NetWare network. This outline illustrates the sequence of events and activities. Later chapters describe each step in detail.

Preparing for the Installation

As discussed in Part I, even before the equipment arrives, you should have a plan for the LAN installation. Your file server will have greater stability and longevity if it operates in a dust-free, static-free, temperature-controlled environment. Although a file server does not require the strict climate control of a mainframe or minicomputer, it nevertheless will not function well if you lock it in a hot broom closet, for instance. In addition, to reduce any problems associated with electrical noise, you should make sure that a dedicated and grounded uninterruptible power supply (UPS) is available for the file server.

You will also need to begin running the workstation cables. Here the best approach is to obtain assistance from a professional cable contractor. Unless you are installing a very small local area network, running cables through ceilings and walls can be messy and frustrating. In addition, special tools are required to properly terminate the cable ends and attach the connectors. Installing cable is not a good job for an amateur to tackle.

If any of the cable is fiber-optic, don't attempt to install it yourself. The proper tools and terminators for fiber-optic cable are quite pricey, so unless you do a lot of fiber-optic work, it doesn't make much sense to invest in them. Additionally, the tolerances for fiber-optic cable are minuscule. Although a competent copper-cable installer might be able to get away with an imprecise crimp here and there without affecting the functionality of the installation, any variance from perfection in a fiber-optic environment will result in serious problems. We don't mean to overstate the case, but fiber is not a specialty to dabble in.

An Installation Checklist

Here is a checklist to follow in installing your NetWare network. Later sections in this chapter elaborate on these steps, and later chapters discuss them in detail.

1 · Prepare the hardware.

- Take an inventory of the servers and workstations for your network. Record manufacturer information for all components on the server, and the make and model of the CPU and network interface card for each workstation.

- Ensure that NetWare supports the server and its various components. Do the same for the workstations.

- Take an inventory of the network services you'll need (or are already using, if you're upgrading).

- Run setup routines as necessary.

- Record peripheral device characteristics and settings as necessary for printers, modems, synchronous links, host links, etc.

2 · Configure and install NetWare.

- Install network interface cards and any other hardware devices.

- Partition and format the boot hard-disk for DOS.

- Load the operating system.

- Load disk drivers.

- Partition the hard disks for NetWare.

- Create volumes.

- Copy NetWare files.

- Load LAN drivers.

- Install and configure NetWare Directory Services.

- Apply current patches and fixes.

3 · Install and configure add-on NetWare Services. For each service identified in your inventory (printing, asynchronous or synchronous communication, etc.):

  ‣ Configure and install hardware devices.

  ‣ Install and configure software.

4 · Define printer options.

5 · Add security features.

  ‣ Add login and password security.

  ‣ Add directory (and file) trustee rights security.

  ‣ Add file (and directory) attributes security.

  ‣ Add object security.

6 · Install and configure network workstations.

7 · Establish the on-disk directory structure and load applications.

  ‣ Set up the basic on-disk directory structure, taking into account security, convenience, and logic.

  ‣ Make sure selected applications are designed for, or at least compatible with, network use.

  ‣ Test applications and services.

8 · Set up login scripts, users, and groups.

  ‣ Write system login scripts.

  ‣ Write profile and individual-user login scripts.

  ‣ Set up users and groups (directory utilities).

9 · Create menus (if appropriate).

➤ Use a text editor to create source scripts.

➤ Use the NetWare MENUMAKE utility to compile the source scripts.

➤ Use the NetWare NMENU utility to execute the compiled menu scripts.

➤ Test the menu-based environment.

10 · Plan network administration.

Preparing the Hardware

The first step in installing NetWare is to prepare your hardware. You can read about hardware preparation in detail in Chapter 6.

INVENTORY THE SERVER AND WORKSTATIONS

Before installing the LAN hardware, you need to ensure that the server and workstations are supported by NetWare 4.0 and that they are adequate to do their jobs. You can check with your Platinum or Gold authorized Novell reseller to confirm that a particular computer model or component has been approved and tested by Novell for NetWare compatibility. You can also call Novell at 1-800-NET-WARE to obtain the NetWare buyers guide, which contains a list of all tested and approved hardware and software.

We strongly discourage using a nonapproved computer for a file server. Would you want to take regular business trips on an airplane that doesn't meet FAA regulations? We'll discuss Novell's testing program later in this chapter.

You should begin the task of installing NetWare on servers and workstations by performing an exhaustive inventory of the server and its components, because many, if not most, of these components' settings will come into play during an installation. Likewise, you must also perform a workstation inventory, gathering information about each machine, its operating system and version, and the network interface card it will use, to make sure that the machines are compatible with NetWare client software and to determine what kind of networking software is needed to support your network interface cards.

Your primary motivation for doing these inventories is to gather information about what kinds of driver software you'll need to make your installation work. Most components in a server—the disk controller and disk drives, the tape controller and tape drive, the network interface cards, etc.—require their own drivers. Documenting what you've got will also help you to determine what you'll need to perform a successful installation.

More than one NetWare installation has stalled midway because of missing software (we know, from hard, cruel experience); getting your requirements straight is a key to collecting the ingredients needed to complete an installation. Having all necessary ingredients on hand before starting an installation will save you time and energy and eliminate frustration. If you are working as a consultant or in a service organization, it looks very bad to the customer for you to get stuck without the proper components or drivers.

The same is true for workstations: Knowing what version of client software and network interface card is needed lets you gather them in advance. That way, they're there when you actually need them.

There's another benefit to your preinstallation inventory: It's a whole lot easier to maintain and troubleshoot a network when you know what you've got around. It's easy to include information about where each computer or peripheral is located. You may want to do that part on a copy of the floor plan or on an architectural drawing. This comes in handy for more than just network issues and makes a good addition to any well-run system management regime. If possible, make the documentation changeable—that is, make the notations in pencil if it's on a floor plan. There are a lot of reasonably priced (even shareware) programs to let you draw and annotate floor plans. Of course, if you happen to be lucky enough to be working for an architectural firm, pass the actual documentation off to the CAD department.

For the purposes of installation, the most important information for you to know is what unique configurations you have to support. An inventory will also add how many of each variety or configuration you have.

ESTABLISH SUPPORTED COMPONENTS

Novell operates an aggressive testing and certification program for hardware, called the Independent Manufacturers' Support Program (IMSP). For a fee, it accepts hardware from vendors and subjects it to a number of rigorous compatibility and interoperability tests, to make sure it works with NetWare and that it works well with other common system components. Novell Labs publishes IMSP bulletins for each test it performs, and the best way to determine if a particular computer or component is NetWare-certified is to peruse the listing of certification tests published in the IMSP bulletins.

Note that server certification is also keyed to the version or versions of NetWare that the server is tested against. Also note that server certification is different from—as well as much more rigorous than—workstation certification. IMSP bulletins can be obtained from a number of sources, including the NetWire libraries on the CompuServe Information Service (!GO NOVLIB), NetWare Express on GE BusinessTalk, direct from the IMSP group in Provo, or from your local Novell sales office or Novell-authorized reseller.

Your Platinum or Gold authorized Novell reseller should have direct access to the bulletins on their copy of the Network Support Encyclopedia (NSE) or by downloading current test results from NetWire. Of course, if you have a current copy of the NSE (professional edition) or care to download the appropriate files from NetWire, you can have direct access to the current information yourself.

In fact, we recommend strongly that you consult the IMSP bulletins before purchasing servers and workstations, just to make sure that the hardware you own is in fact supported by NetWare. This will sometimes mean choosing more expensive hardware than you otherwise might, but it will pay for itself in the reduction or elimination of the potential headaches that come from trying to make NetWare work on off-brand equipment.

INVENTORY NETWORK SERVICES

The next step is to build the list of network services you'll want from your server. This includes, for example, the number and kinds of print queues to be created, the types of printers to be supported, and the types of connections they will use (direct attachment to server, remote printer TSRs, etc.). The information to be gathered should include the settings you'll need in order to configure this equipment during installation (for example, for serial printers, this means baud rate, parity, number of stop bits, and COM port).

At this stage, it's also time to establish what kinds of protocols and services you'll need to support the various workstations that will be attached to your NetWare network. Table 5.1 summarizes the basic protocols and services for each type of workstation supported by NetWare, and mentions built-in and add-on Novell products that will be needed to provide these services.

RUN SETUP ROUTINES AS NEEDED

If the computer workstations to be installed on the network are new, you should run the setup routines shipped with them. NetWare 4.0 lets you boot with DR DOS 6.0's FDISK.COM and FORMAT.COM as part of the installation procedure.

RECORD DEVICE REQUIREMENTS AND CHARACTERISTICS FOR ADD-ON SERVER DEVICES

The other side of the services coin is to look beyond the local network and to decide what kinds of remote resources and external computing environments you need to access. For remote access, evaluate possible wide-area connections, evaluate what kinds of connections you'll need, and compile a best-guess estimate of how much usage you expect from those links.

For access to external computing environments—perhaps an IBM mainframe or a UNIX server—you'll need to figure out what kinds of services will be needed, and what types of applications and protocols will have to be supported in order to provide them. This information should also be captured in some kind of inventory. Building it will require that you talk to the intended users of the network to see what they want, and to management at your organization to find out what you can live with (and without).

CLIENT	CLIENT OS OR OPERATING ENVIRONMENT	CLIENT COMMUNICATIONS PROTOCOL	CLIENT SHELL OR SOFTWARE REQUIRED	SERVER SUPPORT MODULE REQUIRED
IBM Compatible	DOS	IPX/SPX	ODI drivers, VLM drivers	No additional modules
IBM Compatible	Windows	IPX/SPX	ODI drivers, VLM drivers, Windows Client Kit	No additional modules
IBM Compatible	OS/2	IPX/SPX	NetWare OS/2 requester	No additional modules
IBM Compatible	DOS (connecting to a UNIX host)	TCP/IP	ODI drivers, VLM drivers, LAN WorkPlace for DOS*	No additional modules
IBM Compatible	Windows (connecting to a UNIX host)	TCP/IP	ODI drivers, VLM drivers, LAN WorkPlace for DOS*	NetWare for NFS*

* denotes additional product available from Novell

T A B L E 5.1   Common Protocols and Services for Supported NetWare Clients

CLIENT	CLIENT OS OR OPERATING ENVIRONMENT	CLIENT COMMUNICATIONS PROTOCOL	CLIENT SHELL OR SOFTWARE REQUIRED	SERVER SUPPORT MODULE REQUIRED
Macintosh	System 6 or 7	AppleTalk	AppleShare client software included with Macintosh OS; drivers for non-LocalTalk interface should be included with network interface cards	NetWare for Macintosh*
Workstation	UNIX	TCP/IP	NetWare for NFS*	NetWare for NFS*
NeXT	NeXTstep	TCP/IP	NeXT Client Kit*	

* denotes additional product available from Novell

T A B L E 5.1   *Common Protocols and Services for Supported NetWare Clients (continued)*

It is now that you should define characteristics of any and all additional peripherals to be attached to your server. Typically, this includes devices like CD-ROM readers, tape drives (for backup and restore), asynchronous modems, and other add-ons that enhance a server's capabilities. For each device, you should identify it by type, manufacturer, and model (including all the settings for the controller or interface card, if it uses one), the kinds of protocols and physical connections it requires, and so on. Many of these devices can also be checked against the IMSP bulletins for compatibility, and the bulletins may even help you figure out which drivers you need to use for installation.

If all the activities described in this section sound as if you're designing a complete network environment, you've got the right idea. Knowing what needs to be done, which hardware and software components are needed, and where installation activities must occur, is the biggest part of getting ready for an installation. If you do your homework correctly at this stage, everything else will go much more smoothly later.

Configuring and Installing NetWare

Installing and configuring NetWare 4.0 requires three basic steps:

1 · Configure the hard-disk subsystem and network interfaces.

2 · Run the DOS front end to create and format a DOS partition and to load the operating-system kernel (SERVER.EXE).

3 · Install and configure the operating system by using INSTALL.NLM.

The installation and configuration of NetWare on a new server is covered in detail in Chapter 7.

CONFIGURE THE HARD-DISK SUBSYSTEM
AND NETWORK INTERFACES

When you start up a server for the first time, first configure the elements that will become the contents of the STARTUP.NCF and AUTOEXEC.NCF files to enable the server to recognize its basic hardware components (such as disk drivers or network interface cards). These components include the storage media installed on the server, the types of connections and communications the server is supposed to support, and the file system the server is supposed to handle. Net-Ware 4.0 creates the two configuration files during the running of the installation program and adds commands you specified during the installation. The remaining details of these two .NCF files get supplied during the ensuing installation process, as a consequence of defining your environment through the INSTALL program.

STARTUP.NCF can be as simple as a single line that loads the appropriate driver so that the operating system can communicate with the hard-disk controller. Optionally, it can include variations from the basic default settings for the file system (including alternate name spaces), the communications environment (including minimum packet receive buffers), and memory allocation (including cache buffer size). STARTUP.NCF is saved on the DOS (boot) partition so that NetWare can read it before it mounts any NetWare volumes. That makes sense when you figure that NetWare can't mount a volume without first loading the disk driver.

AUTOEXEC.NCF is usually more complex than STARTUP.NCF. In a NetWare 4.0 AUTOEXEC.NCF, there are some settings that you might not have used in your 3.11 environment. Set Timezone, Set Daylight Savings Time Status, Set Daylight Savings Time Offset, and Set Default Time Server Type all pertain to the time context in which NetWare Directory Services operates. As in 3.11, AUTOEXEC.NCF then continues with the server's name and internal IPX address information, to uniquely identify it to itself and the rest of the networks that may be connected to the internetwork.

NetWare 4.0 uses add-on programs, called NetWare Loadable Modules, to extend the basic functionality of the NetWare operating-system kernel. The configuration information supplied for network interface cards and disk drives provides the basic information needed to use these fundamental subsystems on the server. Without them, network communication and file-system access could not operate.

For this process to be successful for the disk drives, you'll need to have the disk-driver software for your drive controller available and also know the interrupts, port addresses, and, for Micro Channel (PS/2) and EISA file servers, the slot numbers where the drive's controllers are installed.

For this process to be successful for the network interface cards, you'll need to have their driver software, know what protocols each card must handle, and be aware of similar hardware interrupt channel, memory, port address, and slot information as for the disk controllers.

Each of the modules (drivers) mentioned above can also be loaded manually from the file server console and incorporated later into the NCF files. Once you have a functioning network interface and an accessible disk subsystem, you're ready to install the other NetWare services and devices that will ultimately make up your server configuration.

RUN THE DOS FRONT END

The new DOS front end automates the process of creating and formatting a DOS partition that will contain your boot files. If you already have a DOS partition on your hard drive, you can choose to retain it, provided it is big enough. The minimum recommended size is 5MB. The front end (called NWNSTLL.EXE but invoked by the INSTALL.BAT batch file) then copies the boot file to the newly created partition. You can also choose to have this program create an AUTOEXEC.BAT file for this server. This file contains the command to execute SERVER.EXE (the operating-system kernel) every time you reboot the server. Next, the front end "invokes," or loads, the NetWare kernel, SERVER.EXE.

In computer science lingo, the *kernel* of an operating system is that part of the operating system that is always resident and that controls and orchestrates all the other activities and programs that make up a multitasking, multithreaded execution environment. Since NetWare 4.0 can do more than one thing at a time— that's what multitasking means—and can let individual programs run in the form of multiple sets of operations at the same time—that's what multithreaded means—the first order of business in the installation process is to load the kernel software and let it take over the server hardware.

If you want to compare the NetWare kernel to a DOS environment, think of COMMAND.COM. When you boot to DOS, COMMAND.COM is loaded into the computer's memory and interprets various commands. Some of those commands are internal—that is, they are part of the executable code of COMMAND.COM itself. Other commands are external and require separate executable sets of code.

In DOS the internal commands include DIR, VER, CD, CLS, MD, RD, and COPY. External commands are those you see in your DOS directory, such as CHKDSK, FORMAT, SYS, MEM, and XCOPY. DOS external commands can have the extensions .COM, .EXE, or .BAT. Actually, .BAT (or batch) files must depend upon COMMAND.COM to interpret their code, so they are kind of a cross between internal and external commands.

With NetWare, the kernel is the file SERVER.EXE. Internal commands are called console commands in the NetWare environment and include LOAD, BIND, CLS, CONFIG, DISPLAY SERVERS, and TRACK ON. External routines, programs, and drivers are NetWare Loadable Modules (NLMs) and have the extensions .DSK (disk drivers), .LAN (LAN drivers), .NAM (name-space modules), or .NLM (all other NLMs).

Technically, SERVER.EXE is a DOS program that lets an Intel 80386 or higher-numbered processor boot the NetWare operating system. Upon loading, SERVER.EXE looks for two NetWare configuration files, STARTUP.NCF and AUTOEXEC.NCF. These files play the same role in starting NetWare that CONFIG.SYS and AUTOEXEC.BAT play in starting DOS—the first one specifies device and environment settings, and the second provides information about software and settings to be executed as a part of the start-up process.

Once SERVER.EXE starts up, it takes the CPU away from DOS (you cannot run DOS programs on the file server itself while NetWare is running), and it begins running the kernel of the NetWare operating system on the server.

RUN THE INSTALL NLM

All the activities required to install NetWare (or to alter an existing installation) can be managed by a single menu-driven NetWare module called INSTALL.NLM. This module is loaded automatically by the DOS front end. Even though it executes some extremely sophisticated operations, its user interface is relatively easy to understand and operate. The real trick is to understand what you're doing.

At a simplistic level, configuring the operating system entails selecting the operating-system options to be included in the network and defining the server hardware to be installed. Based on these selections, a customized operating environment is built from the pieces that you specify while using the INSTALL NLM.

You can use INSTALL to perform a number of important setup and configuration tasks. You can do the following:

- ▶ Configure and load disk drivers.

- ▶ Create NetWare disk partitions.

- ▶ Add enhanced server disk capabilities, including disk mirroring or disk duplexing (both optional).

- ▶ Create, configure, and mount NetWare volumes and build a usable file system.

- ▶ Copy the NetWare 4.0 operating system and user utilities (SYSTEM and PUBLIC files).

- ▶ Configure and load LAN drivers.

- ▶ Install NetWare Directory Services.

- ▶ Create and edit the STARTUP.NCF and AUTOEXEC.NCF files.

Installing and Configuring NetWare Directory Services

If you have constructed a design for your overall NDS environment before you install your first NetWare 4.0 server, installing and configuring NDS is a whole lot easier, but it can still be time-consuming. If you haven't done your homework ahead of time, you'll have to allow at least one additional day (and that's an optimistic estimate) to read and understand the directory documentation and the environment it describes, and to build your basic Directory Services database. In fact, the broad concepts involved in NetWare Directory Services are a significant change of context for most people, and you should give them a good deal of thought before you commit to your planned structure.

We recommend that you take the time to investigate and understand the Directory Services environment before trying to build one. Planning for Directory Services, especially in large, complex environments, takes time and effort, and can even require political maneuvering to design. Be sure to leave adequate time for the planning phase, even if it must immediately precede your first NetWare 4.0 deployment.

To begin with, you'll determine where Directory servers will reside and how the Directory database must be partitioned and replicated. With this information in hand, you can begin with a first Directory server installation, to begin to grow the Directory environment that you need. Although defining the Directory is an interesting process, it's just the beginning of using this environment.

You can find more information on installing NDS in Chapter 8.

Applying Current Patches and Fixes

Because NetWare is a complex and dynamic software environment, changes and enhancements to NetWare 4.0 will be made all the time. This is generally a good thing, because it is a way for Novell engineers to fix bugs and address problems that inevitably show up no matter how exhaustive the testing process is. Patches may add new functionality to NetWare, or simply make the program behave as required by its specifications.

By the time NetWare 4.0 shows up on your doorstep, chances are a collection of patches and fixes has already been defined. Since the box you purchased has been sitting on a shelf somewhere, there's no effective way to add this software into the box itself; rather, it's your responsibility to find out if patches and fixes have been defined and if so, to get them and then apply them to your server. This is the only sure way to make certain you've taken advantage of the best implementation that NetWare 4.0 has to offer.

As with the drivers and IMSP bulletins mentioned earlier, you can get patches and fixes from a number of different sources. You can get them on line from CompuServe in the NetWire forums in the New Novell Downloads library (!GO NOVLIB), or you can find them on GE BusinessTalk in the NetWare Express area. You can also check with the reseller who sold you your copy of Net-Ware or with a local Novell sales office. In most cases, your reseller will simply have downloaded the patches in the first place, so your best bet is usually to download them yourself.

Whatever your source, make sure you check to see if any patches or fixes are available before beginning to install NetWare. If you have these materials at hand during the installation, you can apply them as the last step in the process. That way, you can successfully avoid learning why they were needed in the first place.

Even if you are installing NetWare after version 4.0 has been on the market for a while, the software in the box will probably be the same as when it was first released. Occasionally there will be a minor revision of the operating system (NetWare 2.15 went as high as rev. C). However, don't count on patches being incorporated into the product as it ships. Making modifications without raising the revision number is a practice commonly called "slipstreaming," and Novell has fairly consistently avoided it in previous product releases.

Installing and Configuring Add-on NetWare Services

Because we can't know exactly which collection of services you'll be installing on your server in addition to basic NetWare functionality, and because there are so many services available, it's beyond the scope of this book to go into much detail about what's involved in installing them. Some of the Novell extended services can be installed with INSTALL.NLM, while others come with their own documented procedures or installation utilities.

We recommend that you read any product's installation documentation in advance so that you can be more familiar with the process and the specific steps of the installation. You can contact or contract with your reseller for additional information and help, or even consult one of the online information resources or a local user group for answers from people with prior experience with the products you're going to be using.

Once you've installed these services, you should test them thoroughly to make sure they work properly before bringing them on line in your production environment. In most cases, a service that doesn't work dependably is even worse than no service at all.

Configuring and Testing Network Printers

The next step is to configure network printer services and the printers themselves. Many tools are available to help you define printers and establish the way print jobs are handled by the various output devices attached to the file server, to remote workstations, or directly to the network cable. Although your ability to perform rigorous testing might be limited at this point if some application software has not yet been installed, you can make sure that the printers are at least operating by printing a text file from the workstation prompt. You can fine-tune later, as you add more applications and services. (You can find more information on configuring printing in Chapter 10.)

Adding Security Features

NetWare allows five types of security:

- ▸ Login and password security
- ▸ Directory (and file) trustee rights
- ▸ File (and directory) attributes
- ▸ Network audit security
- ▸ NDS object and property trustee rights

After studying these options and matching them to your particular needs, you should implement the types of security appropriate for your local area network.

The first level of security is login security. To access the LAN, a user must enter a valid user name. To add an additional layer of security, entry of a password can (and should) be required. NetWare also allows you to customize the degree of security associated with login and password security. For example, you can restrict the number of concurrent connections, limit access to specific workstations or times of day, and force users to select new, unique passwords after a specified period of time.

Once the user has gained initial access to the network, the primary security mechanism is trustee rights security. Trustee rights regulate a specific user's ability to use a particular directory or service. NetWare can limit users' rights to read files, to write to files, to open files, to access named services, and so on. Trustee rights must be explicitly granted to an individual or a group by a system or directory administrator.

The final level of file-system security is file and directory attributes security. This type of security determines whether particular files or directories can be altered. For example, you can flag an individual file as read-only, which means that no user, regardless of any other right the user has, can write to, rename, or delete the file. You can set similar attributes for directories and subdirectories.

Network audit security provides a powerful option for recording system activity in a NetWare environment. Network audit security depends on the definition of a special class of user, called an *auditor,* who is granted exclusive use of space on a network drive. This drive space will be occupied by such file system and NetWare Directory modifications as the auditor decides to log, where the data is stored in encrypted form visible only to the auditor.

This function was provided primarily to satisfy government requirements for an EDP (electronic data processing) audit, used mainly in the banking and securities trading industries, where accountability for file transactions and system definitions is required. Although the auditor can track all file-system activity, all logins and logouts, and any modifications to the NetWare Directory, in practice, logging should be restricted to auditing access to sensitive files and to system and directory administrator actions. Otherwise, the amount of file space needed to log activity might actually exceed the size of the file system being audited!

Just as there are trustee rights for files and directories, there are also trustee rights for objects and their properties. These object and property trustee rights control how objects work with one other. For example, network administrators may be assigned rights to create, change, or delete other objects, while end-users may be assigned rights to merely view other objects. You can use object and property rights in a variety of ways to make your NetWare Directory security as flexible as you need.

Novell offers comprehensive security features. It is important to plan your security strategy properly so that you can protect essential and sensitive files and can manage access to network services, while at the same time ensuring that users are not unnecessarily constrained. Where accountability is an issue, audit functions might also come into play.

You can read more about security in Chapter 11.

Setting Up Network Workstations

Before end-user workstations can access the network, you must configure workstation software for DOS and OS/2 workstations to make this possible, and check the viability of AppleShare and/or Network Filing System (NFS) installations for Macintosh and UNIX clients if applicable. In many cases, it helps to create a simple batch or script file to allow easy network access for your users. In general, the easier you make using the network, the more use your users will make of it.

Since networking is not built into DOS, you will have to install network drivers and protocol software for those workstations. The collection of drivers and protocol support used to be referred to as the NetWare shell. Now the DOS workstation components are referred to collectively as the Name requester. Novell's Open Datalink Interface (ODI) drivers allow users to connect to the network without actually generating the unique executable files used in previous versions of NetWare (IPX.COM).

The ODI drivers do not require custom generation, but there are three separate pieces involved, and a configuration file called NET.CFG must be defined as well. The typical ODI driver components include the following:

- ► LSL.COM, a driver that supplies the basic NIC (network interface card) interface for your computer's CPU. LSL stands for Link Support Layer.

- ► <MLID_DRIVER>.COM, where the driver portion is the name or abbreviation for the NIC in use. It supplies the hardware-specific driver for the NIC. MLID stands for Multiple Layer Interface Driver.

- ► IPXODI.COM, which supplies the ODI version of the native NetWare transport protocols (IPX/SPX).

The previous implementation of the NetWare shell included NETX.COM. This file provided redirection services for DOS workstations on a NetWare network. With NetWare 4.0 this component has been replaced with Virtual Loadable Modules (VLMs). Just as IPX.COM was broken into pieces in order to make the ODI drivers more easily configurable, NETX.COM has been broken into VLMs to make the requester more configurable and more functional.

You will load the VLMs by running VLM.EXE. When VLM.EXE executes, it checks the current directory for files with the VLM extension and loads them into the workstation's memory. If you want to disable an individual VLM, simply rename it to another extension.

You can attach and log in to a NetWare 4.0 server running IPX.COM and NETX.COM, but doing so prevents you from taking advantage of the features of NDS and limits you to the bindery emulation mode of NetWare 4.0.

The requester executables can be executed with other DOS batch-file commands in the AUTOEXEC.BAT file to create a custom user interface for your network that executes the network requester and prompts the user for a login ID and password.

NET.CFG defines the hardware configuration for the workstation NIC and specifies protocols to load for use on the workstation. Additionally, it specifies parameters for the workstation's network environment that may be necessary to utilize particular network services. NET.CFG *must* be located in the directory from which you run the ODI drivers and VLM.EXE. If it is not, the configuration parameters will not be incorporated. This means that if you have your drivers and NET.CFG in a directory C:\NET, but you execute the driver files from C:\, NET.CFG will not take effect, even if C:\NET is on your DOS path. This is a frequent mistake, so don't get caught!

Some access schemes, particularly Token Ring, may require additional drivers for routing services, remote boot capability, etc., but the list above covers the basics. The files required may appear overly complex, but the NetWare Workstation for DOS installation utility (there are also related utilities for Windows and OS/2 workstations) makes their choice much easier than it may seem.

If memory management is a concern, one advantage of the ODI drivers is that it breaks up the requester into enough small pieces that most, if not all, of them can typically be shoehorned into high memory by using a third-party memory manager or even the capabilities built into DOS 5.0. Doing so, you can conserve more of the 640K area where DOS applications must run.

Once you've installed your DOS drivers, you can test your network by logging in from a workstation. The installation process for an OS/2 workstation is similar to that for a DOS workstation, except that it uses a collection of driver and protocol software called a NetWare Requester for OS/2.

Typically, Macintosh and UNIX workstations make use of built-in AppleTalk and TCP/IP networking software. You have to purchase separate products to actually let these workstations function on a NetWare network (NetWare for Macintosh and NetWare for NFS).

You can read more about setting up network workstations in Chapter 12.

Establishing the Directory Structure and Loading Applications

With your network up and running, your end-users will be able to access the server for file services and Directory Services, plus any additional NetWare-based services you might have installed. Once you install printing services, they will become available as well. However, this does not exhaust the full set of services that NetWare can provide.

Because the file services on the server are inherently shared, the server makes an ideal location to install end-user applications. This doesn't mean that the server actually runs those applications; it means that the server can act as a repository for DOS, OS/2, Macintosh, and UNIX application and data files, which get downloaded to the end-user workstation as they are used.

Installing applications in one place—on the server—instead of in many places—on the individual workstations—makes them easier to install, easier to meter (to make sure the number of users doesn't exceed the number of valid licenses for the software), and lets them be managed at a single location rather than on each individual workstation. In fact, this is probably the most common use of NetWare technology today and will continue to be for the foreseeable future.

Consequently, once you've got the NetWare server configured and ready to use, it's time to start making decisions about the directory structure and where workstation applications will be loaded on the server's hard disk. Special considerations affect where programs and user files are stored. Because security is usually an issue, you may want to isolate user files by user name (give each user a "home" directory). In addition, you may want to facilitate the backup process by grouping together data files that are frequently updated.

When you prepare to load applications on your file server, make sure that the programs you load are intended (and licensed) for a local area network. Running single-user programs on a LAN can cause problems, and these programs may perform inconsistently. In addition, such use is almost always in violation of the program's license agreement.

You can read more about the basics of the NetWare directory structure in Chapter 13.

Setting Up Users, Groups, and Login Scripts

The next step in preparing the local area network for use is to create user accounts so that users can access the network. Then you can also create groups and other types of objects, such as profiles, aliases, and so on. Then you write login scripts.

Login scripts are a set of instructions that direct DOS and OS/2 workstations to perform various functions. Login scripts are frequently used to produce a greeting message, such as that shown in Figure 5.1, and to assign drive letters to specific subdirectories. NetWare allows you to create three types of login scripts: system login scripts, which apply to everyone who accesses the network; profile login scripts, which apply to all member of a particular profile; and user login scripts, which are specific to a particular user. Additionally, there is a default login script that supplies the minimal system settings necessary for network operation if no user login script is present.

Creating groups allows you to grant access rights to several users at once instead of assigning them individually. You create and modify groups by using the NETADMIN utility or the NetWare Administrator graphical utility.

You can read more about creating users and groups in Chapter 14. You can read more about login scripts and batch files in Chapter 15.

FIGURE 5.1

A sample greeting message

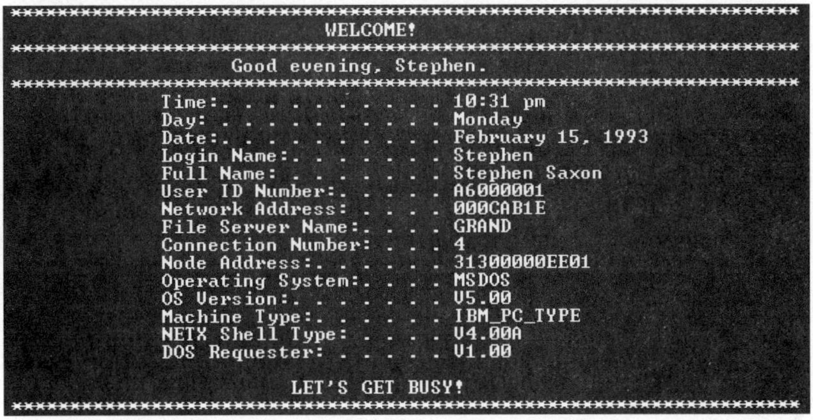

```
************************************************************
                         WELCOME!
************************************************************
                  Good evening, Stephen.
************************************************************
          Time:.  .  .  .  .  .  .  .  .  10:31 pm
          Day:.  .  .  .  .  .  .  .  .  Monday
          Date:.  .  .  .  .  .  .  .  .  February 15, 1993
          Login Name:.  .  .  .  .  .  Stephen
          Full Name:  .  .  .  .  .  .  Stephen Saxon
          User ID Number:.  .  .  .  A6000001
          Network Address:.  .  .  .  000CAB1E
          File Server Name:.  .  .  .  GRAND
          Connection Number:  .  .  .  4
          Node Address:  .  .  .  .  .  31300000EE01
          Operating System:.  .  .  .  MSDOS
          OS Version:.  .  .  .  .  .  V5.00
          Machine Type:.  .  .  .  .  IBM_PC_TYPE
          NETX Shell Type:  .  .  .  .  V4.00A
          DOS Requester:  .  .  .  .  .  V1.00

                    LET'S GET BUSY!
************************************************************
```

Creating Menus

If you plan to insulate your users from the internals of the network, the final step in the installation process is to create a menu system for them. The menu utilities, included with NetWare, let you create easy-to-use custom menus for your local area network for DOS workstations. An example of a menu created with the NMENU utility is shown in Figure 5.2.

The NetWare 4.0 menu utilities (MENUMAKE and NMENU) were developed by Saber. The Saber menu system is powerful, is popular, and has been well received by the industry. One of the significant advantages that this system has over the old Novell menu system is that it requires less workstation memory.

You can read more about creating menus in Chapter 16.

Administering the LAN

All local area networks require at least some degree of ongoing maintenance. You must back up files and the NetWare Directory regularly. Also, over time,

FIGURE 5.2

A sample menu created
with the NMENU utility

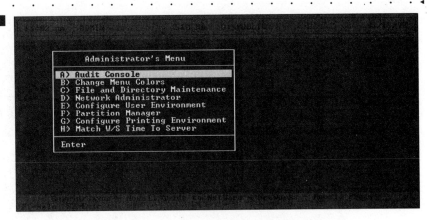

additional users will need to be added, software will need to be upgraded, new programs will need to be added, and security requirements will change.

A part-time system administrator can manage many of these activities. If possible, the network administrator should also be involved in the installation process, to be better able to understand its structure. In any case, you should publish a set of standards and practices and distribute it to each of the network's administrators. The document should clearly outline each person's responsibilities and the steps necessary for each administrative task.

It's also wise to construct a maintenance schedule, particularly for activities whose benefits come primarily from regular repetition, like backup. Designing a schedule for backup and automating backup as much as possible are the best ways to ensure that this onerous task actually gets done. Be sure to schedule full system backups often enough to avoid time-consuming application of numerous incremental backups to get to the freshest state (once a week is a good place to start, though full backups every day are preferable).

Make sure that the tape rotation allows you to have the most recent tape on site, but keep the next most recent tape somewhere safe off-site in case of catastrophic failure (earthquakes and hurricanes come to mind). Also, be sure to schedule test restorations quarterly or semiannually. The backup and restore procedure is another case where knowing how the environment works can save expensive loss of time and data because of midcrisis learning. It may be time-consuming, but it's better to practice when the payroll isn't at stake than when it is.

Also, be sure to investigate the add-on Network Management products available for NetWare 4.0. NetWare ships with an excellent remote management utility (RCONSOLE, for managing a server from a network workstation), but the add-on products, particularly the Network Management System (NMS) and its Management Agent components, provide a much richer set of network management tools than those supplied as a part of the basic NetWare operating system. These tools can be invaluable for larger, more complex networks, or for environments where servers and administrators are placed inconveniently far apart. They make it possible to manage an entire internetwork from a single Windows or OS/2 workstation, thereby saving lots of travel time. More and more outstanding network management tools (many compatible with NMS) are available from third parties as well.

Chapters 17 and 18 cover maintaining, troubleshooting, and monitoring your network in more detail.

Preparing
Your Hardware

Fast Track

112   ***Site preparation should include***
protecting your servers from static electricity and power-related problems (noise, interference, sags and surges, and outages). Server requirements include equipping the file server with sufficient RAM and disk space. For best results use a fast 486 or better, with at least 12MB of RAM (see the formula for RAM calculation for the most applicable number). A fast SCSI controller and SCSI-based hard drives are also recommended for best server performance and dependability.

120   ***Workstation requirements vary, depending on the operating system used:***

- For DOS PCs, any IBM-compatible computer (PC/XT, PC/AT, 80386, or 80486) should work, given a minimum of 512K RAM.

- For Microsoft Windows or OS/2, the practical minimum is an 80386, with a minimum of 4MB RAM for Windows and 8MB RAM for OS/2 (for both environments, more CPU power, more memory, and more disk space are highly recommended).

- For Macintoshes, any system capable of running AppleShare services (Macintosh OS release 6.05 or better) will work. Apple System 7 is recommended, because of its superior networking support, but older (1MB) Macintoshes will have to stick with System 6.05.

123   ***Minimum preparation for network computers requires***
a working machine. This includes setting up and configuring the hardware, installing the operating system, and testing to ensure that systems are running properly as standalone computers before installing networking software.

Configuring network printers 123

is most important for serially attached devices, but before installing networked printing software it's important to know what type of connection a given printer will use and where the printer is to be located before installing networked print software.

Document your cable layout 126

with a map, a spreadsheet, or a database capable of producing up-to-date reports about cable locations, lengths, and other layout information. Be sure to keep this layout current as new devices are added and as your layout changes. Post a layout chart in the wiring center, and tag each cable with its corresponding destination for easy identification and troubleshooting.

Attach network printers appropriately: 127

- ▶ For networked printers, attach the printer to the network cable.

- ▶ For server-attached printers or for printers attached to dedicated print servers or remote workstations, run a serial or parallel cable from the server or remote workstation to the printer as needed.

The first step in building a local area network is to prepare the hardware for use. To begin with, you'll want to select the sites where the NetWare server and the workstations will be located, to make sure they are suitable. Next, you will need to check and prepare the computers, disk and tape drives, printers, and any other equipment that you plan to use, to make sure they meet NetWare's requirements and to properly configure them for your systems. Last, you must attach all the computers to your network cabling, attach and configure your printers, and then test your new network to make sure it works.

If this is your first LAN installation, don't try to go it alone. Because installing hardware can be difficult and complex, get as much assistance as you need from a reputable network specialist or service company. You should feel confident that the company that sold you your systems and software can also provide expert installation assistance; if not, it's wise to consider hiring a contractor to oversee the installation process.

This chapter assumes that you possess hardware skills or have obtained qualified assistance to set up and install hardware, and provides an overview of the various steps in the installation process. There are simply too many different kinds of systems and peripherals on the market today for us to do a thorough job of guiding you through all of the ins and outs of installing each one. Also, equipment changes much more rapidly than software. Our goal is to get you through a successful installation and configuration of NetWare, so we have to assume that the hardware end of things is working in order to proceed.

Preparing the Server Location

The environment surrounding your NetWare server is vital to the stability and reliability of this key computing resource. The server needs to be protected against static electricity, temperature extremes, and the full range of electrical insults it is likely to encounter in daily use—namely, electrical noise, power sags and surges, and power outages. It's also a good idea to consider placing servers in locked rooms or closets, to protect against theft or unauthorized access.

PROTECTING AGAINST STATIC ELECTRICITY AND TEMPERATURE EXTREMES

Because static electricity can destroy the kinds of sensitive electronic components that computers are made of, it's essential to protect any and all computer hardware against static discharges. This includes taking proper precautions when handling electronic components, as well as for computers situated in a workaday environment. Such precautions are crucial for your NetWare server, since it is the linchpin upon which your entire network depends.

We recommend that you take steps to control static in your environment. One way is to treat your carpets regularly with antistatic chemicals. That might sound very intimidating on the face of it. In fact, the chemicals themselves are not too expensive and are not particularly dangerous to anyone's health.

You can also dilute fabric softener with distilled water and apply that to your carpets. Though we haven't tried this (we usually purchase commercially available static dissipation formulas), we know of some who have done so successfully. Alternatively, you can use electrically conductive covers for carpets or linoleum flooring. There is even conductive floor wax for treating linoleum.

Once the floors (and chairs) are made safe, make sure to place the file server on a work surface that is grounded. To do so, attach a heavy-gauge copper cable to a metal work surface with a sheet-metal screw, and then attach the other end of the cable to a water pipe or to the ground line of a properly grounded electrical outlet.

Excessive temperatures, both hot and cold, are also bad for your computer equipment, and for your server or servers in particular. Because computers themselves produce heat, sometimes in surprisingly high amounts, overheating is more often a problem than excessively low temperatures. The key to successful operation is maintaining the temperature range between 65 and 85 degrees Fahrenheit (18 to 30 degrees Celsius), and making sure that air can circulate freely inside and around the computer. Keeping a computer's case off to facilitate air cooling is not a good idea. The power supply's fan depends on the case to function effectively. Without the case, the air doesn't really circulate through the computer and you get stagnant, hot air around components instead of good circulation.

In fact, because air circulation inside the server's enclosure is so important, we recommend buying a full-size tower case whenever possible. Tower cases typically offer more room inside. They not only accommodate more interface cards and disk drives, they can also provide vital room for the system and its components to "breathe." In areas where dust or other airborne particles may be a problem, some type of air filtration may also be necessary.

ELECTRICAL PROTECTION

Electrical disturbances come in many forms, and each must be dealt with properly to avoid potential mishaps to your server. Electrical noise is caused by interference in the line that delivers power to your server or by inconsistencies in the delivery system itself. The best way to protect against the influence of other devices in your server's power is to install a dedicated power line exclusively for its use. Otherwise, you will have to protect against sags and surges that other devices can create when they're powered up or down. (If you're not sure what we mean, think about how the lights in your home go dim when the refrigerator or other heavy-duty appliances kick on.)

The power source should also be a standard three-wire grounded A/C outlet, preferably an "orange plug" type of installation, where a ground to true earth is created and tested. Power quality is more important for this type of outlet than for normal home or office use. If a dedicated line is not an option, you should consider purchasing some kind of transformer-based power-conditioning equipment, which can isolate your server from power fluctuations on the line and even provide backup power in the event of a power outage.

You might have read the last paragraph and thought, "Oh, that's not a problem for my office; our file server only shares its circuit with the laser printer." Well, let's examine the kinds of devices you may have in your office that could cause power inconsistencies. That laser printer is a big one. In warming up periodically throughout the workday, typical laser printers can draw large amounts of power, subjecting any other device on the same circuit to a significant sag in voltage. Consequently, we recommend against putting the server and laser printer on the same circuit, or even the same UPS (uninterruptible power supply).

Other power-hungry devices that may be in your office include refrigerators, microwave ovens, copy machines, drink machines, coffee makers, and so on. Remember that these need not be in the same room to be on the same circuit. To truly determine the electrical design in your office, you must consult your office's electrical design documentation. If no such documents are available, you may want to hire a competent electrician to determine the condition and design of your electrical circuits.

You should always use a UPS for any server in regular use. Most UPS's include power-conditioning capabilities, as well as a finite amount of battery-supplied operation time following a severe power sag or an outright power outage. The NetWare operating system on your server will accommodate special monitoring and alarm software to notify you in the event of a power outage, and some implementations can even track power fluctuations over time.

You may also want to install UPS's for workstations that run critical applications, to protect them from loss of data during a power failure. In addition, all of your computing equipment should be fitted with surge protectors to prevent damage in the event of a severe power spike (such spikes are most commonly caused by lightning). It's generally not a good idea, however, to use a surge protector and a UPS for a single machine, since most of these devices include heavy-duty surge and spike protection. Be sure to check with your UPS manufacturer to see if an additional surge protector is needed before installing the two devices in tandem.

Preparing Your Computers to Run NetWare

Once you have decided where to place your server and workstations, and you have taken care of environmental and electrical considerations, the next step is to check each computer that will be used on the network to make sure each one meets NetWare's requirements.

CHECKING COMPUTER REQUIREMENTS

Although NetWare supports most PCs that can run DOS on the market today, many older machines may not meet the minimum hardware and memory requirements. For both file servers and workstations, you should confirm with your NetWare dealer that the brand you choose has been tested and certified by Novell, or you can check the IMSP bulletins (or the NetWare buyers guide) referenced in the preceding chapter to see if your machines are certified.

Server Memory Requirements

The amount of RAM needed for a server depends on a number of factors and must be calculated from your intended configuration. For NetWare 4.0, as with NetWare 3.*x*, the more RAM the better; any RAM not consumed by specific system needs will automatically be used as a disk cache, thereby enhancing overall system performance.

While the formula below may indicate lower minimum requirements, it's not uncommon to see NetWare servers with 32MB of RAM or more. A good rule of thumb is to fill your server's motherboard with as much RAM as it can accommodate, simply because it's easier to buy and install everything at once, and typically, because it's often easier to budget the money all at once.

Novell uses the following to calculate the minimum RAM for servers running NetWare 4.0:

▶ NetWare 4.0 kernel: 2.5MB RAM.

▶ For each NetWare volume, up to a total of one gigabyte or less, add the results of the formula shown below. For disk storage over about a gigabyte in a single file server, this formula is not really dependable. When in doubt, err on the side of adding more RAM, not less.

Minimum RAM = 0.023 * volumesize/blocksize

▶ For each volume with support for an additional name space (to accommodate Macintosh, OS/2, or UNIX NFS files), the formula is

Minimum RAM = 0.032 * volumesize/blocksize

▶ Each additional NetWare Loadable Module (NLM) that you intend to use on your system will typically have its own memory requirements that can be determined from the product's documentation. Since you're trying to put together a system and may not have all the software in hand just yet, a general rule of thumb is to allocate 2MB to 6MB of RAM per additional NLM service (for example, 2MB for NetWare for Macintosh, 6MB for NACS, and 6MB for Novell's SAA gateway).

▶ The actual memory requirements for NetWare Directory Services will depend on the number of entries in the Directory database at any time, but here again, we recommend an additional 2MB or more to accommodate NDS data on your server.

▶ Round up (to the next even megabyte) the total of all the preceding memory needs or to the next highest number of RAM components that your system can handle easily. For example, if the formula produced the number 14.4MB, it would be wise to install 16MB because that number is one of the common memory configurations supported on most Intel-based 386 or 486 computers and is the nearest "round number" higher than the calculated figure.

To give this formula some meaning, let's apply it to a typical server configuration: a 486 machine with 1.2GB of disk space. The NetWare partition consists of three volumes: SYS, MAC, and OS2-NFS. The 500MB SYS volume supports only DOS name spaces and uses 4K blocks (that's NetWare's default), the 200MB MAC volume supports the Macintosh name space and uses 8K blocks, and the 500MB OS2-NFS volume supports OS/2 and NFS name spaces and uses 64K blocks. We would evaluate the formula as shown in Table 6.1.

The total for our sample configuration comes to 10.43MB. Applying the rule of thumb that says to round up to the next highest "easy" memory configuration, we'd want to round up to either 12MB or 16MB of RAM, depending on the RAM format to be used in the server. Following the "more is better" philosophy, 16

TABLE 6.1

*Calculating Memory
Requirements for a
Sample Server*

VOLUME	SIZE (in MB)	NAME-SPACE MULTIPLIER	BLOCK SIZE (in K)	TOTAL RAM (in MB)
SYS	500	* 0.023	÷ 4	= 2.88
MAC	200	* 0.032	÷ 8	= 0.8
OS2-NFS	500	* 0.032	÷ 64	= 0.25
NetWare OS				= 2.5
NDS				= 2.0
NetWare for Macintosh				= 2.0
NetWare for NFS				= 2.0
GRAND TOTAL				10.43

would be a better choice than 12, because it leaves room to grow by adding more users or more NLMs to the initially configured environment. More important, the higher number leaves more space for disk caching, supporting heavier network use more efficiently. If you are planning on supporting a larger number of users or heavy application services, like a relational database, the greater the amount of RAM on the server, the better your system will perform.

Other Server Requirements and Recommendations

The server itself must be an 80386, 80486, or better computer to support NetWare 4.0. As with memory, more CPU horsepower is better than less. Even though NetWare 4.0 will run adequately on an older 386/20 or 386/25 machine, we'd recommend buying the most powerful processor that you can afford for your system. This will have a higher price tag (though the differential seems smaller every day), but will offer a definite performance boost that may be over-kill at first, but will definitely come in handy as the load on the server increases over time.

For your server's disk subsystem, NetWare will support most of the common disk controllers and most disk drives, including IDE, ESDI, and SCSI. Of these three technologies, ESDI (Enhanced Small Device Interface) is the oldest and possibly least desirable. It is based on the ST-506 interface, as are MFM (modified frequency modulation), RLL (run-length limited) and to a lesser degree IDE (Integrated Device Electronics). Some feel that ESDI is not as fault tolerant as SCSI (small computer system interface) and does not offer the same level of performance. On the positive side, the ESDI specification supports high-capacity drives comparable to SCSI devices and is a stable technology, supported by many of the better drive manufacturers. That stability makes compatibility between different manufacturers a bit easier than one finds with SCSI devices.

IDE is newer, but cannot support as many drives as SCSI can, nor does it offer the kind of performance that SCSI can.

We recommend using fast SCSI drives, with a 32-bit controller and a minimum of 300MB of disk space. Most commercial users purchasing new systems typically start with 1.2GB of disk space, often as a pair of 600MB drives or a single 1.2GB drive unit. Larger installations may require up to 20GB of disk space or more on individual NetWare servers. For these kinds of situations, SCSI is the only workable technology available today.

Your network should include a tape backup unit, preferably using a high-capacity helical scan format like 4mm DAT (digital audio tape) or some type of 8mm technology. The larger your collection of on-disk data, the better such choices will accommodate your needs, and the more worthwhile some consideration of a jukebox type of backup unit becomes. These units automatically support collections of up to ten or more cartridges, raising the backup capacity ceiling to as high as 250GB or more for the highest-density DAT and 8mm tapes.

We don't consider backup devices to be optional; they are critical to any serious network environment. If you aren't convinced of the need, consider how much of your computer-based work your business can do without. If your computer system has no live information (contact lists, databases, documents, vital applications, etc.), and you can survive without the use of the computers, then the possibility exists that you could do without a backup device. If, however, you are like most businesses and store at least some of your business's critical information solely on computers, you cannot afford to be without a backup system and a workable disaster plan. Of course, the more critical the information you deal with, the more often you should back it up.

For more important data, you should also consider disk mirroring or disk duplexing for your NetWare server, which creates two working copies of your disk subsystem and can automatically bypass one drive, controller, or set of drives in favor of another in the event of a subsystem failure. Disk mirroring pairs redundant drives on a single controller and can function despite individual drive failures. Disk duplexing pairs controllers and drives to overcome a potential controller failure as well as individual drive failures.

Workstation Requirements

This section details requirements for the individual workstations in your network.

DOS PCs   For DOS-based PC workstations, you can select from a broad range of computers. Any of the following computers can be used as workstations, as long as they have a minimum of 512K of RAM:

- ▸ IBM or Compaq 80386- or 80486-based computers

- ▸ IBM Personal System/2 (any model)

- ▸ Compaq Deskpro (any model)

- ▸ IBM PC/AT, PC/XT, or PC (or compatibles)

Even though 512K is the minimum memory requirement, you should consider adding memory to any machine that has less than 640K. The NetWare redirector environment typically consumes between 35K and 60K, and DOS itself consumes between 17K and 70K, depending on the version, high memory access, and other factors. The upshot is that most commercial DOS applications require at least 400K of RAM, and unless you have at least 640K available, you'll be hard-pressed to run DOS, attach to the network, and run any such applications. For maximum performance, expandability, and useful product life, we recommend using workstations based on either the 386 or 486 processor. Older machines should be phased out; either upgrade them to at least an 80386SX or replace them with an 80386DX or 80486 machine.

Windows PCs   Windows puts so much more demand on a PC that some of the models that will work with NetWare running DOS will not work with Windows. Essentially, the list of machines supported for Windows and NetWare is a subset of the list above:

- IBM or Compaq 80386- or 80486-based computers
- IBM Personal System/2 (models 25 and 30 not recommended)
- Compaq Deskpro (any model)
- IBM PC/AT (or compatibles)

Of these models, even though Microsoft will tell you that any of them will work if equipped with 2MB of RAM, we recommend that an 80386 with 4MB of RAM be the minimum platform for using Windows in a networked environment. Because PCs are currently so affordable, even for 386s and 486s, we'd recommend buying a faster machine (25MHz 80386 or better), with a Super VGA color monitor, a mouse, a minimum of 80MB of hard-disk space, and at least 4MB RAM. You're far better off exceeding these recommendations than just meeting them. Even though it's not a specific requirement per se, we'd recommend equipping a Windows machine with a 3.5" high-density floppy drive if it doesn't already have one, simply because 3.5" disks are the most common format in use for Windows software.

Windows and DOS workstations can be configured without hard disks (though you should do so only if your environment's security requirements absolutely demand it). However, if you run Windows on a computer without a hard disk, plan on a minimum of 8MB to 16MB of RAM. You must also configure Windows to refrain from using virtual memory to avoid the abnormally heavy network traffic: Add the line **Paging=off** to the [386Enh] section of your SYSTEM.INI file.

OS/2 PCs   For PCs running OS/2 version 2.0, adding NetWare to the recommended configuration does not normally change the initial requirements for OS/2 itself:

- ▶ 80386SX or higher Intel-based PC

- ▶ 4MB RAM minimum

- ▶ 3.5" floppy drive

- ▶ A mouse

- ▶ 20–35MB of free hard-disk space (15–30MB for the operating system; 5MB for NetWare-specific files)

Here again, it's better to overshoot these minimum requirements, especially for RAM and hard-disk space. Both Windows and OS/2 consume lots of hard-disk space, and the need for more disk storage, whether on the file server or on the local drive, will soon make itself felt in either of these environments.

Macintoshes   Any machine that can run Apple's AppleShare networking software can communicate with a NetWare server. Practically speaking, this dictates a Macintosh Classic or better, and a version of the Apple operating system number 6.05 or higher. (System 7 is preferable to System 6 because of its improved networking capabilities, but you can't use it on 1MB Macintoshes.)

CHAPTER 6
. . . . .
PREPARING
YOUR HARDWARE

PREPARING NETWORK COMPUTERS

If any of the computers on the network, including the server, have not yet been configured using the manufacturer's supplied setup software or system installation disks, you should now complete that first step. In order for a machine to run on a network, it must be able to boot up standalone or to boot itself from a server—the key is to make sure the equipment works by itself before trying to use it on the network.

DOS workstations are often delivered with DOS installed and every other standard device already configured correctly. If the machine boots to DOS (or if you don't know exactly what you're doing) don't bother going into the setup facility. You could do more damage than good.

Preparing Network Printers

NetWare 4.0 can support up to 256 printers per print server NLM. Printers can be directly attached to the server, remotely to other workstations, or even to another server running PSERVER.NLM (or PSERVER.VAP for 2.x servers). NetWare services print requests by placing them into holding tanks, called *queues*, where print image files reside until they get shipped to a printer. After they are printed, NetWare deletes them from the queue.

Larger, higher-volume printers are commonly attached directly to the print server or, better yet, directly to the network cable through a built-in network interface card. By attaching to the network cable, you can avoid the bottleneck of the personal-computer printer ports. Both serial and parallel ports are significantly slower than network access technologies such as ARCnet, Token Ring, and Ethernet.

On networks with already heavy traffic, you can even install a dedicated network segment for the printers themselves. You should install an extra network interface card in the file server and run its cable only to the network printers. The advantage of this configuration is that no data passed across the network to the printers affects the traffic that is not printing-related. You can put lightly used devices where they're convenient, possibly at user workstations.

The configuration information for printers varies, according to whether a printer is serial or parallel, or is a device connecting directly to the network cable. If any of the printers are indeed serial devices, you will need to document the data transfer protocols. You'll use this information in the next chapter when you configure the NetWare 4.0 operating system. Neither parallel printers nor printers attached to the network cable need similar communications parameters to communicate with a NetWare server.

Serial printers are most commonly configured using the following parameters and values:

- ► Baud rate: 9600

- ► Word length: 8 bits

- ► Stop bits: 1 bit

- ► Parity: None

- ► XON/XOFF: No

These are the default settings used by NetWare 4.0 during serial printer configuration. Therefore, using these settings greatly simplifies the installation procedure. If you use these communications parameters, however, make sure they do not reduce the printer's performance. Check the printer's documentation to determine the communications parameters that provide the best performance, rather than blindly following the defaults.

Representatives of Hewlett-Packard have been known to recommend that XON/XOFF flow control be switched on both in the NetWare configuration and at the printer. The reasoning is that the NetWare print utilities can sometimes make demands on serial communication cables that would not be made in a normal DOS environment. Using XON/XOFF can overcome some cable problems that would otherwise arise because of these additional demands.

Cabling the Computers

The major culprit whenever local area networking problems arise is most commonly the cabling. One cable-testing manufacturer claims that up to 80 percent of all network failures are cabling-related. While we take that figure with a grain of salt, we also tend to think it's not too far off the mark. Be they simple connectivity issues—unplugged interfaces, opens, shorts in the cable, accidental cable breakage—or more subtle problems, the cabling is the first place to look when things go wrong and is unfortunately the cause of many problems that are difficult to diagnose. The best thing to do right for a network is to make sure that the cabling is correctly installed in the first place, by a reputable cable installer. After installation, be sure to test the cabling plant before you even bring up the network.

OBEY NETWORK LIMITATIONS

For each type of topology and each kind of wiring, specific rules govern network limitations such as the maximum number of workstations per cable segment, the maximum allowable cable length, and the kinds of connections and terminations needed to make the cable plant work correctly. Even if you employ an experienced cable contractor, it's essential for you to understand these limitations and to make sure that your network does not exceed them. These rules are covered in detail in the topology supplement that accompanies NetWare. You would be well-advised to dig up the details on the set that applies to you, and to go over your network design before installation to make sure that no violations are present. It may be helpful for you to go use a scale map of your network when the installation is complete to make doubly sure that no violations have crept in by mistake.

ADD COMPONENTS ONE AT A TIME

The best approach to establishing a network is to start small and to expand from there in limited increments after testing what's already in use. Start your installation with just two machines: the server and a single workstation. Make sure that these machines are working properly and that they are communicating with each other correctly. Then expand the network one machine at a time. This incremental approach will let you diagnose more readily any problems that might occur during the initial installation and will make it clear exactly when problems began to appear. If possible, it's also wise to test first on one cable segment and then to move on to others only after the first one has proved to be functioning properly. As always during installation and testing, the idea is to keep the number of variables or configuration changes to an absolute minimum.

DOCUMENT THE CABLE LAYOUT

The last step of the installation process should be to draw a detailed network map. This map need not be precisely to scale, but it is important to document individual cable lengths and the location and type of connectors and terminators in use. This is especially true if your network is configured as a trunk (a backbone cable that services multiple individual branches or cable segments) or as a star, where cables branch out from a central location or wiring closet.

Because cables run through walls and ceilings, after they are installed, it's an excellent idea to perform a low-voltage test to make sure that you can identify cables at both ends. You can perform this type of test with a volt-ohmmeter, with a time domain reflectometer (TDR), or (for Token Ring environments) with a Token Ring scanner such as are included in Microtest's line of cable-scanning equipment. While Microtest offers the best-known line, other manufacturers offer comparable equipment.

If your network is relatively large, set up a spreadsheet or database to generate a cabling chart, and then be sure to keep this chart up-to-date. Post the cabling chart in the wiring closet or your wiring center, so it can be easily referenced while troubleshooting any problems. In addition, it's wise to tag cables on both ends with their corresponding office locations. (All cables coming through a conduit look alike, so some form of tagging is essential to proper identification.)

Installing the Network Printers

Following the instructions outlined by the printer manufacturers, attach the network printers to the server, to the network, or to the remote print server or workstation, as you determine to be appropriate. Be sure to document the printer ports you use for each printer (e.g., LPT1 or COM1 for the first parallel and serial ports, respectively). For a network printer, this will require defining and recording a unique network address for that device, so it can be accessed on demand. You will need this information when you configure the software for the NetWare 4.0 operating system.

CHAPTER 7

Installing NetWare 4.0 on a New Server

Fast Track

You can install NetWare 4.0   *136*
by using the NWNSTLL.EXE utility on the NetWare 4.0 INSTALL disk,
or you can create a 5MB DOS partition, format the hard disk, and use IN-
STALL.NLM.

To start the NetWare operating system,   *145*
run SERVER.EXE. The operating system must be running to prepare the
server for NetWare installation.

After NetWare is running,   *147*
use INSTALL.NLM to load disk drivers and LAN drivers, to create a Net-
Ware partition, to create and mount volumes, to load the system and
public files and install NetWare Directory Services.

In this chapter we'll walk through the basic installation procedure for Net-Ware 4.0. We will use a relatively simple example LAN to illustrate the process of installing NetWare on a network designed to support a small business or professional organization, but we will also explore the issues you're likely to en-counter for larger, multiserver networks as well.

To begin with, you must configure the NetWare operating system for the server on which it resides. You'll start by running a program that gives NetWare the ability to launch itself from DOS. Then you'll add support modules for your network connections and disk subsystems. After that, you can start configuring your server environment in earnest.

If you're going to be upgrading an existing NetWare server to version 4.0, we recommend that you skim this chapter and proceed to Chapter 9, which deals with migrating data and bindery information from an earlier version of NetWare. Even though your approach will be different from the one outlined in this chapter, it's a worthwhile read because it will show you a lot about what's different in NetWare 4.0 when compared with earlier versions.

Configuring the Operating System

Configuring NetWare 4.0 begins with the following steps necessary to turn a PC into a functioning NetWare server. The DOS front end (NWNSTLL.EXE) ac-complishes the first six steps. Then INSTALL.NLM takes over to complete the in-stallation process.

1 · Install a DOS partition on the first hard drive.

2 · Format the DOS partition.

3 · Copy server boot files to the DOS disk partition, and run SERVER.EXE.

4 · Supply a unique server name.

5 · Supply a unique internal network number.

6 · Load INSTALL.NLM.

7 · Load disk drivers.

8 · Create NetWare partitions.

9 · Create and mount NetWare volumes.

10 · Copy NetWare SYSTEM and PUBLIC files.

11 · Load LAN drivers.

12 · Load other modules and services, as needed.

13 · Create and edit the STARTUP.NCF and AUTOEXEC.NCF files.

14 · Provide Time Synchronization Information.

15 · Install NetWare Directory Services (covered in detail in Chapter 8).

We'll tackle each of these steps one at a time in its own section. The goal of this exercise is to get the basic NetWare operating system up and running. After we've covered the basics, we'll go on to point out some additional, optional activities that may make sense for your installation and show you where they fit into the overall procedure. We will postpone detailed discussion of NetWare Directory Services (step 15) until Chapter 8, which is devoted entirely to that topic. We do, however, strongly suggest that you read Chapter 8 before you actually begin a NetWare 4.0 installation, irrespective of your degree of familiarity with earlier versions of NetWare.

Preinstallation Checklist

Before you can install NetWare 4.0, here's the hardware you'll need:

► An 80386 or 80486 PC.

► A minimum of 8MB of RAM (for information on how to calculate RAM requirements for NetWare 4.0, consult the preceding chapter). Remember that more RAM is *always* better.

▶ A hard drive with adequate storage space for your user community. (The absolute minimum is 50MB for the NetWare SYS volume plus the size of your DOS partition. If you plan to install online documentation from CD-ROM, count on an additional 25MB.)

▶ A CD-ROM reader if you are installing from CD-ROM.

▶ At least one network interface card (two or more if you plan on configuring your server as an IPX router, or if you plan to integrate Novell's Multi-Protocol Router NLMs).

▶ Network cabling appropriate to the network interface cards.

▶ While an uninterruptible power supply (UPS) is not actually required to run NetWare, it is required to run NetWare responsibly.

▶ Though a backup device is not absolutely required, it is strongly recommended. Backup devices may be configured and operated as workstation devices or as peripheral devices of the file server. We don't hold strong views on which is preferable; both have strengths and weaknesses. The backup utility provided with NetWare 4.0, SBACKUP, requires a backup device to be attached to the file server.

Before you actually begin to install NetWare, you should have installed the hardware, and it should all be functioning properly under DOS. This step will help you resolve any potential interrupt or memory conflicts that can crop up when installing multiple interfaces. For dealing with such conflicts, we recommend a diagnostics tool like Microsoft Diagnostics (MSD.EXE), which ships with Windows 3.1, or a configuration management package like Check-It, QA Plus, or System Sleuth.

It's also an excellent idea to document all the configuration settings for the server and the interfaces, so that you'll have this information handy when you start installing NetWare. We often print these out and affix the settings to the file server's power supply or inside the case (though you should make sure that the paper itself won't bother any of the computer's functions in any way).

If you're installing from floppy disks, you'll need the following software:

- ▸ The NetWare disk labeled INSTALL.

- ▸ All the disks labeled *LANGUAGE_NAME-n,* for installing the user interface in the language of your choice (where *LANGUAGE_NAME* represents ENGLISH, DEUTSCH, FRANCAIS, ESPANOL, etc.). The *-n* indicates that the disks are numbered in series beginning with 1.

- ▸ The NetWare disks themselves.

- ▸ The License disk.

- ▸ The Registration disk.

Then insert the disk labeled INSTALL in drive A.

If you're installing from CD-ROM, you'll need

- ▸ The NetWare 4.0 CD-ROM

- ▸ The License disk

- ▸ The Registration disk

In an installation from CD-ROM, you also need to install the CD-ROM and its drivers according to manufacturer's instructions, then insert the NetWare 4.0 CD-ROM into the reader and turn on the CD-ROM reader. Next, reboot the computer, change to the CD-ROM's drive letter, and go to your language's subdirectory on the CD-ROM.

If you're installing from a network drive, you need to copy the following NetWare 4.0 disks to a drive on an existing server: INSTALL, ENGLISH_n, and NETWARE_n. Then install DOS workstation software on the computer that will be your server, and create a DOS partition of at least 5MB. Next, map a drive to the NetWare server that contains the NetWare 4.0 files and change to that drive.

With all these preparations, you'll be ready to start the installation.

Preinstallation Considerations

If you're recycling an existing PC or disk drive and you want to keep any of its contents, you'll need to back it up. If you decide to repartition and format the server's drives, you will lose all data that's currently on those drives. If you're upgrading from a previous version of NetWare, the details are covered in Chapter 9, but upgrading makes it even more imperative to back up all your NetWare volumes before proceeding.

As we've mentioned before, we recommend that you do three complete backups before proceeding to migrate from one version of NetWare to the next. The first backup is to ensure that you have a working copy of your environment before you start changing things. The second backup is to save your behind if for some reason the first backup is corrupted or unusable. The third backup is a form of "paranoia insurance," designed to make sure you have a working copy, even if the first two backups are damaged somehow. We have been in at least one situation where the third backup was the only thing between us and data loss.

Setting Up and Formatting a DOS Partition

The SERVER.EXE program that starts NetWare is actually a DOS program that instructs the computer to switch over from DOS to the NetWare operating system. While it's a common misconception that NetWare is a DOS application, NetWare actually takes over the file server CPU and completely supplants DOS to control the server on its own.

If you want to try an experiment that will illustrate this concept, you can get the same effect with NetWare 2.x by executing the operating-system file (NET$OS.EXE) after booting the file server to DOS. If you currently run 2.2 in its nondedicated mode, you are already doing this every time you boot the server.

SERVER.EXE will run from a floppy disk, so it's not strictly necessary to install DOS on your server before setting up NetWare. Working with earlier versions of NetWare (3.11 in particular), we've learned that a modest-size DOS partition (20 to 30 megabytes) lets your server function as a DOS machine when NetWare is not running and makes the rest of the installation much easier. Even though the DOS partition is mostly a convenience, it's one that has proven to be worthwhile, so we recommend it strongly. It's also the default method for NetWare installation, so it's what most support organizations and engineers expect to find.

This is particularly true if you intend to load up your server with add-on NLMs and services. It is usually a whole lot easier to copy the distribution files for extra services to the DOS partition and then install them from there once the server is running. In addition, with some services (like NACS and the SAA gateway), you may need to reinstall or at least reconfigure them once they are installed. One reinstallation or reconfiguration from floppy disks is one too many! We feel that the investment of 20 to 30 megabytes for a DOS partition is well worth the benefits gained in the long run.

Here are some more reasons to have a DOS partition on the file server:

▸ SERVER.EXE is a very large file, and loading almost a megabyte from floppy disk is a whole lot slower than loading it from a hard drive, so the file server boots faster from a hard disk than from floppy.

▸ Because floppies wear out with repeated use, the risk of boot media failure is far greater for a floppy than for a hard drive.

▸ The DOS partition makes an excellent home for troubleshooting and repair NLMs (like the INSTALL program itself, and a disk repair utility called VREPAIR), and also for the server boot files (like the disk and other device drivers you may need for your server). Because hard drives are faster than floppies, and because you won't have to swap floppies to load the files and tools you'll need, the DOS partition boot method offers better performance, helps to guarantee that you'll have all the things you'll need in one place when you do need them, and is a lot more convenient all the way around.

Some administrators decide to boot the file server from floppy despite the advantages we've mentioned. The most common reason, though not very persuasive in our opinion, is that they consider it a waste of file-server hard-disk space to have a DOS partition. True, the NetWare partition will be a little smaller because of the DOS allocation, but as we've already stated, we feel that the investment is justified. Then again, when you compare a 20MB DOS partition with a 1.2GB disk drive, you're talking drops in a bucket.

Another reason—and in some cases this one actually makes a good deal of sense—is security. If the file server boots from floppy disk and then the floppy disk is removed, the file server is secured from unauthorized restarts. This adds a bit of control, especially if the devices in the file server don't use the loadable modules that come directly from Novell. If the boot disk contains a unique disk driver (let's say, OUR_DISK.DSK), and it's been secured somewhere, a potential intruder cannot reboot the server and have his or her way with the system unnoticed. If the server is rebooted, you will surely know about it, because NetWare won't load without a copy of OUR_DISK.DSK.

Of course, this kind of arrangement has obvious and serious difficulties. For example, if the power goes down (and the UPS is exhausted), someone will have to restart NetWare manually to bring the file server back online.

STARTING THE INSTALLATION

NetWare 4.0's INSTALL utility is capable of partitioning and formatting your server's drives and of installing DR DOS 6.0 in your DOS partition. If you've already set up the hard drives and installed this or another version of DOS, you can elect to repartition your drives and install DR DOS, or you can skip ahead in INSTALL to bypass those initial steps.

NetWare 4.0 greatly simplifies the formatting and partitioning phases with DOS:

1 · Follow the instructions under "Preinstallation Checklist."

2 · Type INSTALL.

3 · From the Select An Installation Option menu, select *Install new NetWare 4.0.*

Depending on whether you've already installed DOS and set up a bootable DOS partition, you'll have a number of different options that you can follow:

1 · You're not required to have a DOS partition on your hard disk. We don't recommend this approach unless your site absolutely requires it.

2 · If you've already defined a DOS partition that is 5MB or larger and you want to preserve it, you may. If you want to get rid of the partition, proceed as with item 2 above, and go to the next section. If your DOS partition is smaller than 5MB, you have to redefine it (there's not enough room on it to accommodate all the necessary NetWare files), so proceed as with item 2, and go to the next section. Remember that repartitioning a drive destroys *all* data on that drive. Don't say we didn't warn you!

3 · If no DOS partition has been defined for the drive, proceed with "Setting Up a DOS Partition" below.

SETTING UP A DOS PARTITION

If you'd rather run a DOS version other than DR DOS 6.0—for example, IBM's PC-DOS or Microsoft's MS-DOS, or some other OEM version that may have shipped with your server—rather than Novell's DR DOS, we recommend that you use the DOS FDISK and FORMAT utilities that come with the version of DOS that you do want to use before running INSTALL and setting up your DOS partition the way you want it. Then, when you do run INSTALL, you can skip right to "Naming Your Server" and bypass the partitioning and formatting options that INSTALL will ask you about. Just make sure to define a DOS partition that's 5MB or greater in size, and everything should be OK.

If your hard disk is unpartitioned when you select the new installation option, the following message appears on the server's screen:

> The NetWare installation utility requires a
> DOS partition on your hard drive in order
> to install the NetWare operating system.

> If you do not want to create a DOS partition
>   on your hard disk, you should exit and
>   perform the installation manually.
> If you want to create a DOS partition with another utility,
>   you should exit, create the partition, and restart the installation.
> If you continue, you will be guided through
>   the process of creating a DOS partition on
>   your hard disk.

To use INSTALL to create a DOS partition, follow these steps:

1 · Press ↵ to grant permission for INSTALL to set up a DOS partition.

2 · The default partition size is 5MB. We recommend a larger partition, usually 10 to 20 megabytes or more, depending on the extra services you plan to install. Press ↵ again to continue. INSTALL will define the partition for you.

Once you've defined a DOS partition, it must be properly formatted in order for you to deposit the files that you'll need it to accommodate. This is the next important step in the installation process if you are starting from scratch. It is covered later in the section "Formatting Your DOS Partition."

HANDLING AN EXISTING DOS PARTITION

If you start INSTALL and it detects that the hard drive already has been partitioned, it responds by listing all the existing disk partitions on drive C, with the active DOS partition marked with an asterisk. If your active partition is smaller than 5MB, you'll need to destroy it and define a new one. If your active partition is larger than 5MB, you can elect to retain the current partitions and proceed to name your server, skipping the activities covered in the next section ("Formatting Your DOS Partition"). If you elect to destroy your active partition and define a new one, you'll be prompted for the size of the new partition to be defined, as described above.

To define a new partition and do away with your old ones, you must perform the following actions:

1 · Enter the size of the new DOS partition as a whole number (it must be 5MB or greater), and hit ↵. The following prompt will appear on your server's screen:

Add this partition and destroy the data on
    your hard disk?

2 · Select Yes to define a new DOS partition. You can elect to abort the process by selecting No and then exiting the INSTALL program, but if you select Yes, INSTALL will inform you that a new partition has been created.

FORMATTING YOUR DOS PARTITION

After defining a new DOS partition, it's necessary to format that partition so it can be used. If you're using the NetWare INSTALL utility from floppy disks and elect to reboot the machine after defining the partition, it will automatically jump to the format menus after rebooting. If you've already defined a DOS partition and will be keeping it intact, you should skip to "Naming Your Server."

Formatting an existing partition destroys all the data stored on that partition, so be sure you've backed up anything that you might need before proceeding with the format (in most cases, you'll be starting with a blank hard disk, so there won't be anything to save). If you elect to continue, INSTALL loads DR DOS 6.0's FORMAT.COM and proceeds to format your hard disk. Just to be on the safe side, this message appears on the screen when FORMAT.COM runs:

Warning   All existing data on nonremovable
disk C: will be destroyed! -- Continue (Y/N)?

Since formatting the disk is just what you want to do, type **Y** and press ↵ to continue.

After the disk is formatted (formatting will take a few minutes—longer for large DOS partitions), FORMAT.COM will produce information about your drive, showing the total amount of formatted space available in the DOS partition, and the total amount left over after the partition has been formatted and the basic files for the DR DOS 6.0 operating system have been installed.

If you plan on using this DOS partition, either regularly or occasionally, you should plan on loading the rest of the DR DOS operating-system files and utilities, and whatever DOS applications you might wish to use, at the next available opportunity (i.e., the next time you down the server it will reboot in DOS, and that makes a perfect opportunity to continue setting up and configuring your DOS partition).

If you're interested in learning more about disk formatting and partitioning, consult the entries "disk format" and "disk partition" in Part VI.

Naming Your Server

Every server in the NetWare environment must have a name, to let it be identified and distinguished from other servers. If you're using Directory Services exclusively, names must only be unique within individual NetWare Directory Services (NDS) container objects, rather than across an entire internetwork. Since most larger internetworks will contain a mix of NetWare 4.0 and older versions for some time to come, we recommend using names that are unique across the entire internetwork, to avoid possible compatibility problems when older and newer versions must communicate with each other.

NetWare server names can include alphanumeric characters (A–Z, 0–9), hyphens, and/or underscores (_), but cannot include spaces. They must be between 2 and 47 characters in length. If you really want to use spaces, try using underscores instead.

It's a good idea to keep server names short, because server names get used in lots of NetWare-specific commands, but they should also be descriptive of location and function. Typing a few extra characters for a name will help users and administrators locate individual servers. For example, 4EDB_SRVR could indicate fourth floor, east wing, database server. A server name like Gollum or Frodo, which says a lot about the vintage of your network administrators but not much about what the server actually does or where it is, probably isn't as clear. Also, publishing a server listing for your administrators and users is a good idea.

It may be useful to give servers in a specific area names that are organized yet not location-specific. One scheme is alphabetical names. You could use alphabetical lists of colors for one division (Azure, Blue, Crimson, etc.), composers for another division (Albinoni, Bellini, Chopin, Debussy, Ellington, etc.), and minerals for a third division (Amethyst, Beryl, Crystal, Diamond, Emerald, etc.), or you can come up with your own naming scheme. The most important thing is that the names be consistent in some way and that they be manageable in the long run. FS1, FS2, FS3 is fine for a small network, but it just doesn't cut it with a large internetwork.

While you're running INSTALL, select the *Name the server* option. A dialog box will pop up for the server name, which you type in at the keyboard. At this point, pressing the F1 key for help provides detailed instructions on naming rules. If you are using Novell's server worksheet, be sure to record the name on the worksheet as well. If not, record the server name and its other address information in a notebook or some other place where the data will be easy to retrieve at any time. If you keep it only on your computer and the computers go down, you won't be able to get the data.

Assigning an Internal IPX Network Number for Your Server

NetWare is built from the ground up as a network operating system. Its users are consumers of services provided by NetWare servers. Interestingly, the same model is used for internal communications among multiple processes running on an individual NetWare server. The purpose of the internal IPX network number is to provide a mechanism for internal communications that works the same as for external communications. For example, two NLMs might need to communicate with each other (let's say CLIB.NLM and STREAMS.NLM). They actually use the internal IPX network for their communication back and forth.

For this reason, the internal IPX network number has to be unique—that is, it has to be different from any IPX addresses assigned to any physical cable segments out there on your network, and also from any other server's internal IPX network number. NetWare will generate a random number for you that is guaranteed to be unique as a part of the installation process at this point, or you can override this number with one of your own if you choose.

It's important to understand the distinction between the server's internal address and any external addresses. Just remember that each network interface card on a server has an associated network address and that each server's internal IPX network number must be different from all other defined IPX addresses. For server-to-server links, the network cards attached to the same cable segment must have the same (external) network address, since they're attached to the same network cable.

Though the analogy's a bit of a stretch, think of it like this: Each house on a street must share the same street name; that's the network address. Each house on the street has a different house number; that's the node address or media access control (MAC) address. Now imagine a house that's so big that it requires a whole internal street of its own just to facilitate transport from one end of the house to another. Maybe a factory or a campus would be a better analogy than a house. It still has a street address for the outside world, but it has an internal street address as well.

Now further imagine that this campus uses the U.S. Mail service to facilitate its communications, both internal and external; that's what NetWare is, a communication service that serves needs both internal and external to the OS itself. OK, now imagine what would happen if there were two separate campuses next to each other that had identical internal street names. The mail service would not be able to correctly deliver the packets that used that redundant street address because there would be two from which to choose. That's why the internal IPX address must be absolutely unique across the internetwork.

One of our enterprise clients decided that the internal IPX number was a good field to use for support purposes. They place the phone number of the primary help line in the internal IPX address field (5551234), and if they have more than one server for one phone number, they add a letter to the end (5551234a, 5551234b, etc.). That way there can be up to 26 servers for each help line, and the help-line number is always close in an emergency.

Aside from that, we can't think of any compelling reasons why you might want to assign your own internal IPX network number, unless you've designed an explicit numbering scheme in advance. In most cases, it's perfectly safe and valid to let NetWare generate the number for you. If you do use a numbering scheme for the internal IPX network number of your server, make sure to record it somewhere, either on the Novell worksheet or in your configuration notebook.

Copying Server Boot Files to the DOS Partition and Running SERVER.EXE

From NetWare's perspective, the whole reason for the DOS partition is to provide a home for the NetWare boot and configuration files that let NetWare boot and take over the server. At this point, INSTALL will ask if you want to accept the default DOS directory for the NetWare 4.0 files (a directory named C:\SERVER.40), or if you want to supply a substitute. We can't think of any reasons why you'd need to use a different name, unless SERVER.40 is already taken. To accept the defaults, you need only press ↵ at the "accept default" prompt.

If you do want to define an alternative directory name, press the F4 key at the prompt and enter a directory name. When asked if you want to create C:*directory_name,* select Yes and press ↵. The name you've entered will be created if it doesn't yet exist, and INSTALL will begin to copy and expand the NetWare boot files. Whether you elect to use the default directory or define a directory of your own, INSTALL will copy all the necessary files to your target directory for you. If you are installing from floppy disks, the installation program will prompt you for the necessary disks.

The last step is to answer a prompt from INSTALL that inquires, "Do you want AUTOEXEC.BAT to load SERVER.EXE?" If you answer Yes, a line invoking SERVER.EXE is appended to your AUTOEXEC.BAT file. Even though it's convenient, we don't recommend doing so until the installation is complete and flawless. Only when everything is complete and stable should you generally add the following lines to the AUTOEXEC.BAT of the file server. If you want to boot without intervention, omit the first five lines.

```
@echo off
cls
echo Press <Ctrl>-C to abort NetWare.
echo To boot as a NetWare server, strike any key. . .
pause > nul
cd \SERVER.40
SERVER
```

The ECHO statements write the following message to the screen:

```
Press <Ctrl>-C to abort NetWare.
To boot as a NetWare server, strike any key. . .
```

By redirecting the output of PAUSE to NUL, the normal message "Strike a key when ready…" is not displayed. If you hit any character key or ↵, AUTOEXEC.BAT will continue and load SERVER.EXE. If you hit the Ctrl-C combination instead, the DOS batch file interpreter will ask you: "Terminate batch file (Y/N)?" Strike the Y key to abort AUTOEXEC.BAT if you want to stay in DOS instead of booting the NetWare server.

Of course, if your server has special remote reset hardware, or you want it always to boot into NetWare, have INSTALL invoke SERVER.EXE for you, and your machine will always boot into NetWare. This is a good idea when your server is in a remote, inaccessible location, or when you want to keep tight control over access to the DOS partition.

Once you've completed this process, the installation program automatically loads SERVER.EXE, along with a NetWare program called INSTALL.NLM, which you will use to complete the rest of the NetWare installation. After this point, you're really running NetWare (not DOS), and the NetWare Loadable Module, INSTALL NLM, will allow you to complete the file server installation.

Running INSTALL.NLM

The INSTALL NetWare Loadable Module (NLM) is a NetWare program that will control the server installation process from here on. It's also a tool that you will use from time to time for maintenance purposes, since it is the primary tool for changing system configurations. As the hardware and peripherals on your server change with time, you can use INSTALL.NLM to help manage that process.

For this initial installation, the INSTALL NLM loads automatically. For future use, it will be necessary to go to the server console and type **LOAD INSTALL** at the server's colon (:) prompt. From this point you will use INSTALL.NLM to handle the following activities:

1 · Load disk drivers, to let NetWare access the hard disks attached to your server.

2 · Create NetWare partitions, to let NetWare know how much of your hard disk it can use.

3 · Create and mount NetWare volumes, to organize NetWare file space into logical file groupings and to set up the basis for the NetWare file system.

4 · Copy the NetWare SYSTEM and PUBLIC files, which are the core of the NetWare environment.

5 · Load LAN drivers, to let the server use the network interface cards (NICs) to communicate over the network.

6 · Install NetWare Directory Services, to set up your NetWare processing environment. (This will be mentioned only briefly in this chapter but is covered in detail in Chapter 8. As we mentioned before, please read Chapter 8 *before* you install any NetWare 4.0 servers.)

7 · Edit the STARTUP.NCF and AUTOEXEC.NCF files.

After you've completed these steps, you'll have a server that's live, with a usable file system, ready to interact with clients on the network.

One of the most common causes of NetWare installation problems is having an outdated version of a driver (usually a NetWare Loadable Module). A driver is a very special piece of software that sits between a specific device and an operating system—in this case, NetWare—and is what makes it possible for the operating system to use the device being driven to do its job, be that to read and write files or to enable networked communications.

Both disk-drive subsystems and network interface cards require that specific NetWare drivers be supplied during the installation process. Before starting an installation, you should always do the following:

1 · Make a list of all of the disk controllers and drives and network interfaces to be installed, making note of the manufacturer, capacity, model number, etc. Find out which ones need drivers and which ones already have drivers on the NetWare distribution disks. (For a list of supported devices, consult the NetWare 4.0 documentation.) Building a spreadsheet or a handwritten table is a good way to represent and track this information. Using the DOS DIR command, record the driver's exact file name, creation date, and size.

2 · Check with your reseller or on a public forum, such as CompuServe's NetWire or GE BusinessTalk's NetWare Express, to make sure that you have the most current driver for each item that needs one. Often, driver files must be checked by comparing the size and date of the file you have against the one available online or from your dealer. Unless the one you have is newer than the one online, which seldom happens, it is a good idea to get the latest and greatest from whatever source you use. Also, many of the equipment manufacturers for disk or tape drives, disk controllers, network interface cards, etc., either have bulletin boards or their own forums on CompuServe (as a last resort, you can call their technical support numbers for help).

3 · Make up a listing that represents the proposed configuration for your server. Ask your dealer, your local NetWare user's group, people online, or anyone else knowledgeable if they can spot potential gotchas

before you start installing. Getting stuck midway through an installation waiting for software can be costly and time-consuming; don't get caught short. Asking for help ahead of time will also help you identify potential sources of support if you do hit a snag midstream.

4 · Once you've identified the drivers you need, you'll have to obtain them, either from your dealer or from an online source. Make sure you collect all the ones you need and have a complete set before starting the installation.

There's no question about it: Going through the numbers is work, plain and simple. Overlook these precautionary measures at your own risk!

LOADING DISK DRIVERS

A disk driver acts as the software interface between NetWare and the hard disk's controller. The controller is an interface card that lets your computer's CPU access data from or write data to one or more hard disks that work with the specific controller in use. Usually, you load one disk driver for each disk controller in operation in your server, even if a controller is managing multiple drives (as is the case when you have disk mirroring installed).

Most NetWare 4.0 disk drivers include an individual description file that appears as you highlight the driver in the INSTALL NLM. You should refer to these descriptions, or to Table 7.1, to figure out which driver or drivers you'll need to install.

For each disk driver you need to install, there are four basic steps:

1 · Select the driver you want to load.

2 · Accept or change the default parameter settings.

3 · When a message indicating a successful load appears, press ↵ to continue.

4 · Select a new menu item.

TABLE 7.1

NetWare 4.0 Default Disk
Drivers

DRIVER	DISK CONTROLLER
IDE.DSK	Integrated Device Electronics (IDE) interface; also called ATA-compatible interface. The IDE interface may be on the motherboard or installed as an expansion card. Up to four interface adapters are supported by the driver, though not all of them can be configured as a second, third, or fourth adapter. The driver must be loaded once for each adapter (including on-board).
ISADISK.DSK	ST-506 Standard disk controllers. These include MFM, RLL, some ESDI, and some IDE controllers. The driver can be loaded twice to support two controllers.
PS2ESDI.DSK	Specifically designed for use with IBM PS/2 ESDI disk controllers.
PS2SCSI.DSK	Specifically designed for use with IBM PS/2 SCSI disk controllers.

Selecting the Driver You Want to Load

If you can find your driver on the list of available drivers in the selection menu, you're in luck. That indicates that it is one of the drivers already present, probably because it shipped with NetWare's distribution disks. After selecting the driver, a description message may appear on the screen. Press ↵ to proceed. If a message tells you that the driver has to be loaded manually, follow the prompts to install it from the file server console.

If the driver isn't listed, you'll have to load it from a third-party disk. Press the Insert key. INSTALL will prompt you to insert the necessary disk and then let you select the required driver to be loaded. The distribution disk labeled NETWARE-2 contains the drivers listed in Table 7.2.

	DRIVER	DISK CONTROLLER
TABLE 7.2 *Third-Party and Additional Disk Drivers Provided on the NETWARE-2 Disk*	ADTAPE.DSK	TAPE DAI
	ASPITRAN.DSK	UltraStor NetWare 4.0 ASPI Administration driver
	BT40.DSK	BusLogic BT40 (ISA, EISA, MCA) NetWare 4.0 SCSI driver
	DCB.DSK	ADIC SCSI DCB, disk driver v4.0 (ISA)
	DCB3200.DSK	ADIC BusMaster SCSI DCB, ASPI driver v4.0 (EISA, MCA, ISA)
	DTC80AS4.DSK	DTC3280 ASPI Manager for NetWare 4.0
	DTC80HD4.DSK	DTC3280 disk driver
	DTC90AS4.DSK	DTC3290 ASPI Manager for NetWare 4.0
	DTC90HD4.DSK	DTC3292 disk driver
	DTC92AS4.DSK	DTC3292 ASPI Manager for NetWare 4.0
	DTC92HD4.DSK	DTC3292 disk driver
	IDE.DSK	Novell IDE (ATA-compatible) driver
	ISADISK.DSK	Novell ISADISK (AT-compatible) driver
	U124_40X.DSK	UltraStor U124 disk array controller
	U14_40X.DSK	UltraStor U14F SCSI host adapter
	U22_40X.DSK	UltraStor 22X EISA ESDI controllers
	U24_40X.DSK	UltraStor U24F SCSI host adapter

Accepting or Changing the Default Parameter Settings

If your controller can accommodate the default settings, press F10 to initiate driver installation; otherwise, use the up and down arrow keys to scroll through the parameter list and select the proper values, then press F10 to continue.

Continuing with the Installation

A message will indicate that the driver was able to load properly. It means you can press ↲ to proceed to install another disk driver or move on to defining your server's file system. This should be a routine step. However, if an error message appears, make sure you've documented all the interrupts and memory locations that are already taken on your server; interrupt conflicts are the most common causes of driver installation failures.

Loading Additional Drivers

If you have multiple disk controllers of the same type, you can proceed to select the "Load *driver* again" menu item. Proceed as before, but make sure you select a different set of parameters for the duplicate controller. You can also elect to install a different driver to match another type of controller. In that case, select "Load another driver" and proceed with steps 1 through 4 (as outlined above) for each driver.

When you've loaded all appropriate disk drivers, select *Continue with installation* and move on to the next phase of the installation process: creating and organizing your NetWare file system.

Here's an important tip: If you use a specialized disk coprocessing system, it will have its own special drivers. For example, if you use the Novell disk coprocessor board (DCB), you must run DISKSET to configure it. DISKSET puts identification information about external hard disks into the programmable read-only memory (PROM) of the DCB. If you use a DCB, run DISKSET after the NetWare installation is completed. The Novell DCB is a discontinued product, but there are DCBs available from other manufacturers.

CREATING NETWARE DISK PARTITIONS

Every server disk drive must have a NetWare partition defined in order to function as part of the NetWare file system. Only one NetWare 4.0 disk partition can be defined per disk. Thus, after you have a DOS partition on the server's internal hard disk, you can use the rest of the disk space as a NetWare disk partition.

You might want to set up a machine with multiple operating systems (e.g., DOS, NetWare, and UNIX; or DOS, NetWare, and OS/2) . In such cases you must allocate multiple non-DOS partitions and designate one of them as the NetWare partition. This is not common for servers put into production use, but it is sometimes used in test labs and other environments where a single machine must be able to fill multiple roles. For this kind of setup, it's best to use the DOS FDISK and FORMAT utilities outside of NetWare and to establish the NetWare partition during normal NetWare installation.

For those who may be hazy on the concept, Figure 7.1 illustrates the difference between a partition and a volume. The partitions determine the operating system that controls an area of the disk. Volumes are subsets of the partitions. With Net-Ware (since version 3.*x*), you can have volumes that span multiple physical

The difference between a
partition and a volume

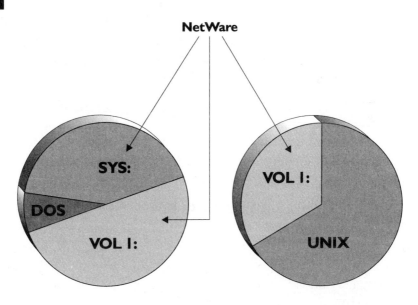

Partitions: DOS, NetWare, UNIX
NetWare Volumes: SYS:, VOL1:

disks, as VOL1: does in the illustration. You can see that there is only one Net-Ware partition per physical disk, but that there may be more than one volume per NetWare partition (SYS: and the first segment of VOL1: on the first drive) or a single volume (or volume fragment, as with the second segment of VOL1: on the second drive), depending on your preference and design needs.

INSTALL NLM offers two approaches to creating disk partitions: letting IN-STALL grab whatever's available on a given drive and converting it to NetWare use or manually specifying partitions. In most cases automatic creation is preferable, simply because it requires no additional effort or planning.

Three reasons to manually create a partition are listed below:

▸ If you're going to be mirroring or duplexing disk partitions (because this requires two partitions to be identical to each other). Mirroring re-quires at least two physical disks.

▸ If you want to change the size of the Hot Fix redirection area. The percentage allocated to the Hot Fix redirection area on every NetWare partition depends on the size of the disk. When NetWare's read-after-write verification is unable to verify that data has been recorded cor-rectly, the block is marked bad (to prevent its use in the future), and the data is written to the Hot Fix area.

▸ If you want to delete existing disk partitions from within INSTALL, you must use manual setup. We recommend doing this in DOS with FDISK before starting INSTALL, but it's nice to know the capability is there if you forget.

Creating NetWare Partitions Automatically

This option automatically consumes all unallocated disk space for a NetWare partition. On the primary drive (drive 0), this means that all disk space outside the DOS partition (if it is already defined) gets allocated as a NetWare partition. On a secondary drive (drive 1 or greater), it means that the entire drive is allo-cated to NetWare.

To use the automatic partition option, select Automatically from the Create NetWare Disk Partitions menu. If your server has more than one drive installed, the Available Disk Drives menu will pop up. Cycle through this menu as many times as you have disk drives to define a NetWare partition for each one. When you have defined all the partitions, you can proceed to the section "Creating and Mounting NetWare Volumes."

Creating NetWare Partitions Manually

When you select the Manually option from the Create NetWare Disk Partitions menu, INSTALL presents the Disk Partitions and Mirroring Options menu. Select *Create, delete, and modify disk partitions.* For servers with multiple hard disks, you will be asked which disk to partition on the Available Disk Drives menu.

From this point forward, defining a partition is the same for each drive, including any and all mirrored or duplexed drive pairs. When you've selected a drive, choose *Create NetWare disk partition;* you should see the Disk Partition Information menu. Specify the size of the partition, in megabytes.

As we've mentioned, the Hot Fix redirection area is by default set to 2 percent of the total storage area. You can change this ratio, but we strongly recommend that it never be adjusted for a Hot Fix area of less than 2 percent. If you have a drive with a higher-than-usual number of surface defects, this might warrant setting a larger Hot Fix area, but it might be more appropriate to swap out the drive instead. Changing the number for one component automatically adjusts the value for the other, so if you increase the Hot Fix allocation, INSTALL automatically decreases the size of the data area by an equivalent amount. When the ratio is correct, press F10 to save the setting, and continue with the manual partition creation. INSTALL asks for confirmation by displaying the message "Create NetWare partition?" Select Yes and press ↵.

Repeat the preceding steps (from the Available Disk Drives menu through "Create NetWare partition?") for each drive on your server. Once you've defined partitions for all drives, return to the main installation menu by pressing Esc twice, then press F10 to continue with the next phase of setting up the file system.

In the next section, we'll cover the steps needed to mirror or duplex pairs of drives. Though this is an optional step, it must take place between partition creation and file-system setup. For this reason, we cover it now. If you are not interested in disk duplexing or mirroring, you should skip to the section "Creating and Mounting NetWare Volumes."

Installing Mirrored or Duplexed NetWare Partitions

Hot Fix redirection, as described above, allows NetWare to overcome bad media on a disk drive; if there is a bad block, it is remapped dynamically. Hot Fix redirection is called System Fault Tolerance level I (SFT I). However, if the drive itself fails, the operating system fails with it. This is why disk mirroring and disk-channel duplexing were designed into NetWare. Termed SFT level II, mirroring and duplexing can overcome a drive failure and a disk controller failure, respectively.

With disk mirroring, a single disk controller directs two physical drives simultaneously, writing the same information on each. In effect, the second drive is a mirror image of the first, hence the name. When one drive fails, the other drive is already online and prevents the system from failing. No data is lost and the users don't even know that a failure has occurred.

While it is possible to mirror up to eight partitions together (that is, as eight physical copies of one single logical data collection), mirroring two partitions is most common. Higher degrees of duplication should only be considered for unusually critical systems. Otherwise, the cost is hard to justify.

With disk-channel duplexing, not only the disks themselves are duplicated but the controllers as well. If one of the controllers fails, the other is already online and takes over all operations. Again, the operating system and the users don't suffer any downtime.

If any single hard disk fails and cannot be accessed by the server, the drives can be unmirrored and the affected volume can be salvaged from the still-functioning drive. NetWare ensures that data access to the still-functioning drive continues unabated in the event of a single drive failure (or a single controller failure, for duplexed drives).

Mirrored and duplexed disk partitions must be the same size, so NetWare will automatically adjust the size to that of the smaller of the pair if they were not originally created to be the same size. Disk-channel duplexing offers a higher level of confidence, at a slightly increased hardware cost. Additionally, duplexing offers an incremental increase in performance over both mirrored and nonmirrored systems because NetWare looks to whichever drive/controller happens to be closer to the location of data needed to service a read request. Similarly, systems with disk mirroring are slightly less efficient than nonmirrored systems. If it is feasible for your system, we feel that disk-channel duplexing is definitely the configuration to opt for. The cost of an additional controller is usually far outweighed by the increased security from device failure, and to a lesser extent by the incremental performance boost.

The INSTALL processes for mirroring and duplexing are the same. When all the drives have been partitioned for NetWare, you can choose *Mirror and unmirror disk partition sets* from the INSTALL menu. This option calls up a Disk Partition Mirroring Status list, which displays the current status for each partition.

Using the information from the status list, select one of the disk partitions that you wish to mirror or duplex. The partition you select first will be the primary partition of the mirrored set that you build. To add one or more secondary disk partitions, press Insert and then select the desired partition from the Available Disk Partitions list. Highlight the partition you want to add to the set, and press ↵. If the partition to be mirrored or duplexed is different in size from the primary partition, you will be warned and given the opportunity to change your mind before INSTALL automatically adjusts the partition size to the smaller of the two values.

To complete the mirroring operation, press Esc to return to the Disk Partition Mirroring Status list, which will now list the disk partitions that are mirrored to one another. At this point, you can elect to define additional members of a mirrored set, define different mirrored sets, or press F10 to go on to create and mount your NetWare volumes.

CREATING AND MOUNTING NETWARE VOLUMES

A *volume* is a fixed amount of hard-disk storage space that is treated as a named portion of the file system. It is the highest level in the NetWare directory structure, analogous to a drive letter in the DOS environment. Whereas DOS can break up a single hardware disk into multiple logical volumes—for instance, where you might partition a 300MB drive into five separate 60MB volumes—NetWare 4.0 allows you to create logical volumes that span multiple physical drives (as illustrated in Figure 7.1).

NetWare's abilities in setting up a file system are numerous, to say the least. Theoretically, it supports from 1 to 64 volumes per server, and a total of 32 terabytes (TB) of disk storage (that's 32 million megabytes!). Though it is clear that these are theoretical limits and not realistic ones, Novell has tested and demonstrated systems as large as 75 gigabytes (that's 75,000 megabytes). It's clear that disk-space needs are growing astronomically, but NetWare still offers plenty of headroom for hardware designers to fill.

Segmenting Volumes

No matter what their size, NetWare volumes can be divided in two ways. Logically, volumes are divided into directories by network administrators and those users who have appropriate rights to create directories. This represents the way the file system appears to its users—how files and directories are structured within a given volume.

Physically, volumes are composed of volume segments, where a single segment can be stored on one or more hard disks. This makes the relationship between a NetWare volume and a given hard disk interesting, since it means that a single drive can store multiple volumes or multiple parts of a single volume, a single volume in its entirety, or part of a volume that consumes segments on one or more other hard disks. A single hard disk can handle up to 8 volume segments, which may belong to one or more NetWare volumes. A volume can consist of up to 32 separate volume segments.

Volume segmentation can confer distinct performance advantages, because placing segments of the same volume on multiple disk drives confers the ability to read and write to each of those drives simultaneously, thereby improving overall disk input/output. In other words, segmenting a heavily used volume across multiple hard disks will actually make it respond more quickly than devoting only a single hard disk to that volume, no matter how fast that single drive might be. The NetWare term for a volume created from a collection of segments is *spanned* volume.

If you use this approach, Novell recommends that you protect the data on those drives by mirroring or duplexing them. The main reason is that spreading a volume across multiple segments on multiple hard disks increases the chances of failure. If a single drive in a multidrive volume fails, the entire volume becomes unavailable. Mirroring ensures that even if the primary mirrored partition fails, the mirrored volume stays up and running.

If any disk on a spanned volume fails, gets corrupted, or becomes unavailable, the offending segment must be repaired or replaced, and the entire volume must be restored from backup across all segments before it can be reaccessed through NetWare. This is why Novell recommends that all spanned volumes be mirrored or duplexed.

In addition, you can increase a volume's size simply by adding another hard disk to a NetWare server, defining a NetWare partition for that disk, and adding this new partition to the existing volume as a new volume segment. In many cases (e.g., where external disk subsystems are in use) volume sizes can be increased without having to take the NetWare server offline.

Naming Volumes

The first network volume must be named SYS. The SYS volume in all current versions of NetWare contains the following directories:

SYSTEM This directory contains files and directories for the NetWare operating system. Additionally, the programs that are commonly thought of as system administrator utilities are located in SYS:SYSTEM.

PUBLIC This directory contains files and directories for end-users, including a set of login utilities, as well as the full suite of NetWare user utilities. The various versions of DOS to be supported on the network are commonly kept in subdirectories of SYS:PUBLIC. Default access is limited so that NetWare utilities can be freely executed but not modified. These utilities are covered in depth later in this book and in the NetWare documentation as well.

LOGIN   This directory contains NetWare utilities such as LOGIN.EXE or NLIST.EXE and is commonly used to store operating- system boot images for diskless workstations (NET$DOS.SYS) or other programs that network supervisors decide should be made available to all users without restrictions; for example, a virus scan program, to make it a part of network login.

MAIL   This directory contains subdirectories for each user. These directories are keyed to each user ID number as assigned by NetWare and are created automatically by the operating system when a user is created. Way back in the deep dark history of NetWare, there was a mail utility that used these user mail directories, but that has long since been excised from the operating system. However, other functions were attached to the mail directories, so the directories were kept. These functions are primarily the storage of user login scripts (LOGIN and LOGIN.OS2) and the individual print-job configuration file (PRINTCON.DAT). Some electronic-mail applications make use of the NetWare mail directories as mailboxes, which brings them full circle to their original purpose.

DELETED.SAV   NetWare has the ability to recover recently deleted files using the SALVAGE utility (unless they have been purged). When the directory in which the file resided is removed, the deleted file is moved to the hidden directory SYS:DELETED.SAV. If an administrator then finds it necessary to undelete the file, it is restored from the DELETED.SAV directory.

With NetWare 4.0, some additional default directories are installed. They are primarily associated with the NetWare language services, which allow networks in non-English environments to operate NetWare with all menus, prompts, and error messages in the local language.

The SYS volume is mandatory, and INSTALL automatically constructs it in the free space available on the first storage device on your server (listed as device 0 by INSTALL). The minimum size for SYS is 50MB, but most installations use drives of 100MB or larger.

INSTALL creates default volume names for all other hard disks on your server for which NetWare partitions have been defined. These defaults take the form VOL*n*, where *n* is an incremented number, so the first volume after SYS is named VOL1, the second VOL2, and so on. However, you can modify these names during the INSTALL process.

INSTALL will prompt you with these default names, providing an instant opportunity to change them, as each individual disk device is discovered. Once it's stepped through the collection of available disk devices, INSTALL presents a summary list of all volumes. At this point, you can press ↵ to reconfigure volume parameters, such as file compression, block suballocation, and data migration (these concepts are covered later in this chapter), or you can accept the defaults and press F10 to continue with INSTALL to the next step, copying the NetWare files to the SYS volume. We recommend that you read the next few sections before deciding whether or not you can live with these defaults.

Adding Name Spaces

If your network supports workstation operating systems that require non-DOS name spaces (for example, Macintosh, UNIX's NFS, OS/2's HPFS, FTAM, or Windows NT's NTFS), be sure that you install name-space support when you create the volume. You can do it later, but over time it will cause the file system to slow down. Why is that? When you create a volume, you also create the File Allocation Table (FAT) for the volume. The primary difference between a volume that supports only DOS file names and one that supports extended name spaces is in the FAT.

When you add a name space to a new volume, every file on the volume has both file names as soon as it is copied to the volume or created. That helps the FAT avoid fragmentation and therefore allows the file system to operate more efficiently.

On the other hand, when you add a name space to an existing volume, the files that already exist on that volume must be "caught up" in the FAT. That tends to fragment the FAT somewhat, and over time it can affect the overall response of the volume. When the FAT has to catch up with a new name space, the FAT entries for the different names of a particular file are not necessarily adjacent to one other. Consequently, when a file is read from the disk, the FAT has to read from different areas of the disk and that's not efficient. That's why we recommend that if you have an existing volume, you back it up (three times), delete the volume, re-create the volume, and right away add the necessary name-space modules. Then when you restore from backup, the FAT will be optimized for the new name spaces.

Suggestions for File-System Setup

Here, we present a few rules of thumb for setting up a simple NetWare file system, based on experience with prior versions and common system-administration practices:

▸ It's best to use volume SYS for NetWare and possibly for program files that won't change much from day to day. Set up one or more additional volumes for data and applications that change a lot.

▸ For reliability, it's a good idea to mirror the SYS volume, since NetWare's system files are there. It's a whole lot easier to restore a non-SYS volume from backup than to reinstall NetWare. It's also a good idea to mirror any spanned volumes, SYS or otherwise.

▸ Mirror or duplex disks for volumes that contain mission-critical or important data (employee records, business records, payroll, etc.).

▸ If performance is paramount, span a single NetWare volume over multiple hard disks, with only one segment of that volume on any hard disk.

▸ If you decide to span a volume over two or more hard disks, use disk-channel duplexing for maximum speed and reliability.

▸ Create separate volumes for files (such as Macintosh or OS/2 HPFS files) that require longer name spaces. This will simplify maintenance, repairs, and disk space usage.

Modifying Volume Segment Sizes

If your file-server hard disks contain multiple volume segments, you'll need to change the default segment size created by INSTALL. To change the size of a volume, follow these steps:

1 · From the Manage NetWare Volumes screen, press F3 to request a change. This calls up the Volume Disk Segments list.

2 · Select the volume segment to be resized, and the Disk Segment Parameters list appears.

3 · Type the new volume size (in megabytes) into the *Disk segment size* field.

4 · Press Esc twice to return to the Manage NetWare Volumes screen.

Modifying Volume Names

You can rename your volumes to replace the default volume names with more informative ones. To rename a volume, follow these steps:

1 · From the Manage NetWare Volumes screen, highlight the volume to be changed and press ↵.

2 · Highlight the name field in the Volume Information list.

3 · Press ↵.

4 · Type in the new name and press ↵ (press F1 for help on volume-naming rules).

You can now proceed to modify other volume parameters, or press Esc to return to the Manage NetWare Volumes screen.

Modifying Volume Block Size

Blocks are the unit of storage for a volume. NetWare volumes default to different block sizes, depending on the volume's size. You can either accept the defaults or configure a volume's block size to 4K, 8K, 16K, 32K, or 64K. When a file is saved to a NetWare volume, it is saved in increments of the volume's block size. Consequently, on a volume with 4K blocks, a 24-byte batch file will not take 24 bytes on disk but 4096 bytes, because it will claim a single block.

If you have a volume that holds primarily large files, it can benefit from a larger block size. The reason is that when a large file is read from disk, it is read block-by-block. If it is saved over many blocks, the read is less efficient, but if the file is in a limited number of blocks, the read is faster. So if you have a bunch of 4MB database files, for example, you may be able to get better performance by configuring the volume to 64K blocks. Just remember that every little batch file or e-mail message will also take up 64K, regardless of its actual size.

That would be the end of the story if we were talking about NetWare 3.*x*, but NetWare 4.0 has improved the situation. Now you can configure the volume to support suballocation blocks to avoid the drawbacks of volumes with large blocks. Suballocation blocks allow NetWare to handle small files and remainders without wasting disk space. We'll discuss block suballocation a little later. Select the block size carefully, because you cannot change it once the volume is created.

If you want to set a block size other than the default size, follow these steps:

1 · In the Manage NetWare Volumes list, highlight the volume to be changed and press ↵.

2 · Use the arrow keys to move the cursor to the Volume Block Size field, and press ↵.

3 · Select a new block size from the list.

4 · Press Esc to return to the Manage NetWare Volumes list.

Setting File Compression

One of NetWare 4.0's most interesting new features is its ability to perform on-the-fly file compression at the file-system level. NetWare 4.0 file compression can increase a drive's capacity by 40 to 75 percent. The speed-space trade-off inherent in compression can influence your file system's design, because you may decide to create some volumes for data that needs to be accessed regularly and quickly and separate volumes for voluminous data sets, like graphics files, that would be appropriate for data compression.

Once you install file compression for a volume and files have been written to that volume, compression cannot be disabled for that volume. Once established, the only way to change its status is to back up the volume, delete its contents and its definition, re-create the volume with compression turned off, and restore the volume's contents.

If you plan to use data migration (which is explained later in this chapter), do not enable file compression.

NetWare 4.0 file compression is very configurable. As you can see by the parameters in Table 7.3, you have control over many options of the file compression, including the option to globally (at the file server level) turn compression off. You can set the parameters shown in Table 7.3 at the file server console either with the SET server utility or through the SERVMAN.NLM server menu utility.

To turn on file compression for a volume, follow these steps:

1 · From the Manage NetWare Volumes screen, highlight the volume whose compression setting you wish to change and press ↵. If you are modifying a volume sometime after the initial installation of NetWare, choose the Volume Options menu item in INSTALL.NLM, highlight the volume whose compression setting you wish to change, and press ↵.

2 · Use the arrow keys to move the cursor to the File Compression field and press ↵. This field is a simple toggle, so pressing ↵ will reverse the value of the field (from On to Off or from Off to On).

3 · Press Esc to return to the Manage NetWare Volumes screen.

For more information on the NetWare 4.0 file compression scheme, see the entry "file compression" in Part VI.

TABLE 7.3

*File Compression
Parameters*

PARAMETER	DEFAULT	LIMITS	MEANING
Compression Daily Check Start Hour	0	0–23	Start checking for compressible files at midnight.
Compression Daily Check Stop Hour	6	0–23	Stop compressing files at 6:00 a.m. If this parameter is the same as the start time, compression will begin at that time and continue as long as it takes to process all files meeting the compression criteria.
Minimum Compression Percentage Gain	2	0–50	The minimum percentage a file must be compressed to remain compressed.
Enable File Compression	On	On/Off	Allow file compression to occur on compression-enabled volumes. If disabled, no compression will take place. Immediate compress requests will be queued until compression is allowed.
Maximum Concurrent Compressions	2	1–8	The number of simultaneous compressions allowed by the system (simultaneous compressions can occur only if there are multiple volumes).
Convert Compressed to Uncompressed Option	1	0–2	What to do to the uncompressed version when the server uncompresses a file:

0 = always leave compressed version |

TABLE 7.3

*File Compression
Parameters
(continued)*

PARAMETER	DEFAULT	LIMITS	MEANING
			1 = if compressed file is read only once within the time frame defined by Days Untouched Before Compression, leave the file compressed (on second access, leave uncompressed) **2** = always change to the uncompressed version
Deleted Files Compression Option	1	0–2	How to compress deleted files: **0** = don't compress **1** = compress next day **2** = compress immediately
Days Untouched Before Compression	7	0-100,000	The number of days to wait after a file was last accessed before automatically compressing it.

Setting Block Suballocation

A little earlier we mentioned disk-block suballocation. In essence, this is another way for you to get the most disk storage space for your money. How does suballocation work? Imagine that you have a volume with 8K blocks. When you save a 16K file, it will take up two complete 8K blocks. Now consider saving a 28K file. Since 28 is not evenly divisible by 8, you would normally have some slack, or unused space, in the last 8K block. However, if you have suballocation on, the remainder of the file is saved in $1/2$K (512-byte) increments. These two examples are illustrated in Figure 7.2.

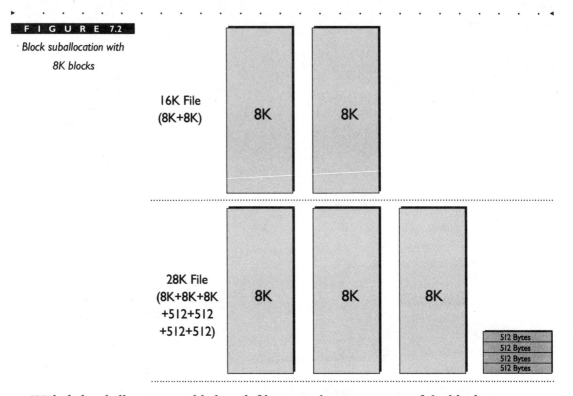

FIGURE 7.2

Block suballocation with
8K blocks

16K File
(8K+8K)

28K File
(8K+8K+8K
+512+512
+512+512)

8K

8K

8K

8K

8K

512 Bytes
512 Bytes
512 Bytes
512 Bytes

With disk suballocation enabled, each file is saved in increments of the block size, and the remainder is saved in increments of 512 bytes. You may not think that this makes a whole lot of difference to your network, but many applications generate small or temporary files that really eat up disk space. A common example is e-mail. Each message is usually stored separately as at least a single file. Sometimes each message is stored as two or more files—that is, one outgoing message and one incoming message. Also, database applications are often written to use many small information module files. The advantage is that if one file is corrupted, the loss is isolated. The disadvantage is that it uses up disk space. While disk suballocation does not eliminate the problem altogether, it mitigates it significantly.

If you plan to use data migration, do not enable block suballocation. To activate block suballocation, follow these steps:

1 · From the Manage NetWare Volumes screen, highlight the volume for which you want to activate suballocation. If you are modifying a volume sometime after the initial installation of NetWare, choose the Volume Options menu item in INSTALL.NLM, highlight the volume whose suballocation setting you wish to change, and press ↵.

2 · Use the arrow keys to move the cursor to the Block Suballocation field and press ↵. This field is a simple toggle, so pressing ↵ will reverse the value of the field (from On to Off or from Off to On).

3 · Press Esc to return to the Manage NetWare Volumes screen.

Enabling Data Migration

Data migration manages where and how NetWare stores your data. As data ages (sits for long periods of time without being accessed), it becomes a more and more likely candidate to get moved off a fast, expensive hard disk and onto a slower, cheaper optical or tape device. Data migration lets you actually move data to these slower devices but maintains a directory entry for the migrated file in the NetWare file system.

When a file that is not physically on a hard disk is requested, NetWare takes care of issuing the right operator requests, or of accessing a multitape or multi-platter device, to retrieve the file for you. This capability frees valuable hard-disk space for more frequently accessed data but still permits infrequently used files to be treated as if they're part of the overall file system. In exchange for a delay in accessing migrated files, you can expand your virtual space on a volume to as large as 256GB for high-capacity storage systems (HCSS's).

Data migration is turned on or off at the volume level in INSTALL, but it is also possible to mark individual files in a volume so that they are not migrated, even though the volume might have migration enabled. The directory attribute Don't

Migrate (Dm) and the file attribute Don't Migrate (Dm) override the Data Migration setting at the volume level. The file attribute Migrated (M) indicates that a file has been migrated already. The Migrated attribute cannot be set manually, but is set by NetWare when migration is performed.

To enable data migration, follow these steps:

1 · From the Manage NetWare Volumes screen, select the volume for which you want to enable data migration. If you are modifying a volume sometime after the initial installation of NetWare, choose the Volume Options menu item in INSTALL.NLM, highlight the volume whose suballocation setting you wish to change, and press ↵.

2 · Use the arrow keys to move the cursor to the Data Migration field and press ↵. This field is a simple toggle, so pressing ↵ will reverse the value of the field (from On to Off or from Off to On).

3 · Press Esc to return to the Manage NetWare Volumes screen.

Saving and Mounting Volumes

After going through all the steps to set volume parameters, you're finally ready to save the volume information and proceed with the rest of the INSTALL process. At the Manage NetWare Volumes screen, press F10 to accept the volume definitions and save all volume information. INSTALL will then proceed to mount all the volumes you've defined to make them accessible to network users. After the volumes are mounted, you are prompted to insert your NetWare license disk in drive A.

Only mounted volumes will be automatically sensed as volume objects when you install NetWare Directory Services. Therefore, don't dismount any of the volumes you've just defined so laboriously, lest they be left out of the NetWare Directory database definition that will occur a few more steps down in the INSTALL process.

Finally, you're ready to copy the NetWare files onto your server and start setting up the network!

COPYING THE NETWARE SYSTEM FILES

At this point, INSTALL automatically copies all NetWare system files and utilities to the SYS volume. These files include the NetWare utilities in the SYSTEM, PUBLIC, and LOGIN directories that were created by INSTALL when it defined the SYS volume earlier.

Most files on the distribution disks are compressed to reduce the total disk space required. INSTALL automatically decompresses the files during the "Copy System and Public Files" process.

To avoid installing some of the NetWare files that your system won't require, follow these steps:

1 · Look through the file groups in the File Groups list, and determine which ones should not be copied over.

Hint: If you don't plan ever to use Macintosh or OS/2 workstations, you won't need the Macintosh or OS/2 workstation files, nor will you need AppleShare File System support. Skipping these files will save about 8MB of disk space. You can do likewise for other file groups you may not need. Remember: You can always run INSTALL again at another time to add files from the distribution disks.

2 · To unmark a file group that you do not wish to copy, highlight the file group and press ↵. To unmark additional groups, use the cursor keys to highlight each group and press ↵ until all unnecessary groups are unmarked.

3 · After you've finished tailoring your selections, press F10 to start copying files.

4 · When prompted, "Are you finished selecting file groups?" choose Yes. If you change your mind at this point, you can select No and return to the menu from step 2, to deselect or reselect additional file groups. At this stage, the server copies the file groups that have remained marked for copying during the preceding steps. (If you are installing NetWare from floppy disk, insert the disks for which you are prompted in drive A and press ↵.)

Hint: To use a different drive or source for the data to be loaded, press F3. This will let you copy the files from across an existing network or from another floppy drive, if necessary.

5 · When a message appears indicating that the file copying is completed, press ↵ to proceed to the next step in the installation.

LOADING LAN DRIVERS

LAN drivers supply the same interface between NetWare and the file server's network interface cards that disk drivers provide between NetWare and the file server's hard-disk controllers. They make it possible for NetWare to communicate with these resources.

NetWare ships with drivers, right on the distribution disks, for most of the commonly available network interface cards. You can peruse the description files that come with each driver to determine exactly what it is you've got, or you can consult Table 7.4 to determine which driver to load.

If a driver for your specific network interface card does not appear on the list, don't despair. Many vendors build cards that emulate other cards—for instance, at least half a dozen vendors offer Ethernet cards that emulate the Novell/Eagle/Anthem NE2000. All of these cards work with the NE2000 driver that ships with NetWare, so you could have the proper driver in the list of default options and not even know it.

In any case, any network interface card that has been tested and approved for NetWare 4.0 file servers should ship with a disk containing the proper LAN driver. We advise you to check with the manufacturer to confirm that the driver is indeed certified for NetWare 4.0 and that it is the most current, bug-free driver available. If it is not, take the trouble to obtain the latest driver, either by downloading it from the company's electronic bulletin board or CompuServe forum or by having the company ship you a new driver disk. It's worth the effort to have a bug-free piece of software.

TABLE 7.4

*Novell File-Server LAN
Drivers That Ship with
NetWare 4.0*

LAN DRIVER	COMPATIBLE NETWORK INTERFACE CARDS	DRIVER CHARACTERISTICS
NE1000.LAN	Novell Ethernet NE1000	Supports up to four NICs
NE1500T.LAN	Ansel M1500 All-in-One-Networking; Novell Ethernet NE1500T	Supports only one 16-bit NIC
NE2_32.LAN	Novell Ethernet NE/2-32	Supports up to four 32-bit (MCA) NICs
NE2.LAN	Novell Ethernet NE/2	Supports up to four (MCA) NICs
NE2000.LAN	Novell Ethernet NE2000 or NE2000T	Supports up to four 16-bit NICs
NE2100.LAN	Ansel M2100 All-in-One-Networking; Novell Ethernet NE2100; Wearnes 2110T or Wearnes 2107C	Supports only one 16-bit NIC
NE3200.LAN	INTEL EtherExpress32; Novell Ethernet NE3200	Supports up to four 32-bit (EISA) NICs
NE32HUB.LAN	Novell Ethernet NE32HUB	Supports up to four 32-bit (EISA) BASE adapters with up to nine TPE adapters per BASE adapter
NTR2000.LAN	Novell Token Ring NTR2000	
TOKENDMA.LAN	IBM Token Ring 16/4 BusMaster	Configuration of the board should also include downloading the required microcode

	TABLE 7.4			

LAN DRIVER	COMPATIBLE NETWORK INTERFACE CARDS	DRIVER CHARACTERISTICS
TRXNET.LAN	Novell Turbo RX-Net, RX-Net II, and RX-Net/2 (ARCnet); Standard Microsystems Corp. NICs: PC170 = Novell RX-Net; PC130 = Novell RX-Net; PC120 = Novell RX-Net II; PS110 = Novell RX-Net/2	Micro Channel machines (RX-Net/2, PS110) should disable the Preempt option, if available, to prevent hanging the system bus

Novell File-Server LAN Drivers That Ship with NetWare 4.0 (continued)

The first step in the process of loading a LAN driver is to locate and highlight the driver you need in the Driver list and then press ↵ to select it. Much like the disk drivers, there are three situations you're likely to encounter:

▸ You find the driver you need, select it, and for most drivers a description file appears on the screen. In this case, you can proceed to edit the parameter values, as described in the next section.

▸ You find the driver you need and select it, but this produces a message that the driver must be loaded manually from the console prompt. In this case, follow the prompts to configure the driver, and INSTALL will pass the parameters as a console command.

▸ The driver you need is not listed, probably because Novell did not include your particular driver with the distribution disks. Since you'll need to read the driver from a disk (usually included with the network interface card), press Insert and follow the prompts to insert the manufacturer's disk and load the required driver.

Editing LAN Driver Parameters

The next step is to set the values for each network interface card (NIC). To accept the defaults, simply press F10 and continue to the next section, "Binding IPX to a LAN Driver." However, if you don't want to use the default parameters for the NIC, move the cursor to the fields that need to be changed and supply the correct values. This is where a specific configuration list or table (as we recommended you build in the previous chapter) will come in handy. It should supply all the information you will need to configure the LAN driver correctly.

If you are using Ethernet drivers, the next step is to add any additional Ethernet frame types to the LAN driver that you may need. To do this, select Frame Types from the driver parameter list (the default 802.2 frame type should already be marked). Highlight the frame types you want to add, and strike the ↵ key to add them. When finished, press Esc to exit the frame-type list, and press F10 to accept the frame types chosen.

NetWare will inform you if it detects a conflict in parameter settings, which can happen when the default values conflict with other settings. Here again, your configuration list (or the Novell networking worksheet) should help you to catch and resolve potential conflicts before you get to this point. If conflicts show up anyway, scroll down the parameter list and look at other supported values for the parameters that are in conflict. You may have to change hardware settings on the network interface card to use the supported values. Once you find a value that your hardware can accommodate, double-check the settings, and press F10 to accept that value as the parameter setting.

Keep in mind that whereas earlier versions of NetWare used a so-called raw 802.3 frame type for Ethernet, NetWare 4.0 Ethernet drivers default to using the Ethernet 802.2 frame type. If you are using earlier versions of NetWare with 4.0 in your network, chances are you'll need to load the frame type for 802.3 as well. Be warned, though, that some routers do not support the Ethernet 802.2 frame type—in particular, this includes the external router (formerly called an external bridge) supplied by Novell with NetWare 2.x versions. If these routers are necessary to maintaining your internetwork, you should replace the NetWare 4.0 default frame type (802.2) with the older-style frame type (802.3).

Binding IPX to a LAN Driver

INSTALL automatically binds the default NetWare protocol, IPX (Internet Packet Exchange), to any LAN drivers that you install. Since NetWare also supports additional protocols, you can proceed to bind other protocols to the LAN driver. This will be covered in the next section.

Once the LAN driver has been loaded successfully, you will be prompted for a network address. You must supply or verify the network address for the cable that you've just loaded the LAN driver for. The reason why you might be verifying an address, rather than supplying one, is because NetWare will sense if the cable segment to which the NIC is attached already has an address. If so, it will sense the address and bind IPX to that address. If it doesn't sense an address, IN-STALL will automatically generate a unique random address (much like it does for the internal IPX network number on the server) and ask you to approve it. In any case, you have the option of changing a generated address.

Repeat the process for binding IPX to the LAN driver for as many network interface cards as you have installed in your server. You can load the same driver again, assuming that you have two interface cards that match the card, or you can load other drivers. In either case, for each additional network interface card in the server, you should repeat the steps previously outlined for loading LAN drivers and setting driver parameters. Once you've completed loading and customizing the driver settings for all the interfaces, you can proceed to the installation of NetWare Directory Services.

Binding Other Protocols to a LAN Driver

If you need to bind other protocols supported by NetWare to a LAN driver, the installation details should be covered in the documentation for the various modules that support the protocols. For AppleTalk—a subset of SNA—and TCP/IP, the details are included in the NetWare documentation. For enhanced IPX and TCP/IP routing, and for OSI and full SNA routing, consult the documentation shipped with Novell's Multi-Protocol Router product. In any case, except for the names of the protocols to be bound to interfaces and the different formats for addresses associated with a given protocol, the process remains nearly identical to that for binding IPX to a LAN driver.

INSTALLING NETWARE DIRECTORY SERVICES

Since NetWare Directory Services is by no means a trivial matter, and since it represents a significant change from the way that most people, even extremely experienced NetWare engineers, are used to approaching NetWare and NetWare installation, we will cover the installation of NetWare Directory Services in depth in Chapter 8. We will also cover the editing of the STARTUP.NCF and AUTOEXEC.NCF files in that chapter.

LOADING OTHER MODULES

At this late point in the INSTALL process, a final menu appears, Other Installation Options. Selecting any item in the list of products will display context-sensitive help on that product. If you want to use any of these options, simply highlight it and proceed from there.

EXITING INSTALL

When you exit (or bypass) the Other Installation Options menu, you will have completed the INSTALL process. A lengthy message appears, stating that your initial installation is complete and pointing you to other sources of information for the rest of the necessary installation maneuvers. It concludes with the reminder that you can always run INSTALL again to make more changes to your server's environment, if need be.

To really be sure that the server is completely configured, you may want to reboot and watch the file server come up on its own. If volume SYS won't mount, we suggest looking at the STARTUP.NCF file for possible errors. If errors occur later on, check AUTOEXEC.NCF for mistakes in syntax or configuration parameters.

CHAPTER 8

NetWare Directory Services: Overview and Installation

Fast Track

182   NetWare Directory Services
must be installed on each file server to make it part of the Directory tree.
Before installing NetWare Directory Services on a server, you must carefully plan your Directory tree. When you are ready to install NDS, you
will use INSTALL.NLM.

182   Completely plan your organization's Directory tree
before you install NetWare Directory Services on the server. You must
decide on the overall structure of your company or organization and the
hierarchy of objects in the Directory tree. To plan your Directory tree,
you must understand the different types of objects, what name context
means, and how to plan for bindery emulation. You must also understand how the file system relates to the Directory tree.

192   Plan for Directory partitions and replicas,
which are the tools NetWare 4.0 uses to distribute, manage, and protect
the Directory database.

195   Plan for time synchronization
by deciding which servers will be Primary time servers (they provide
time to the network) and which servers will be Secondary time servers
(they get their time from the Primary time servers).

197   Begin installing NetWare Directory Services on a server
by using INSTALL.NLM.

Select a Directory tree name   **198**
to begin creating the tree itself. Each organization or company should
have only one tree.

Set up time synchronization   **198**
by using the Time Configuration Parameters screen. Specify the server's
time zone, daylight and standard time status, and variance from Coordinated Universal Time (UTC).

Specify the server's context   **200**
to create the Organization object and any Organizational Unit objects
that will contain this server. This will also create partitions for each new
container object.

Specify the administrator's password   **200**
for security reasons.

View and edit the STARTUP.NCF and AUTOEXEC.NCF files   **202**
to see the commands that were added to them automatically during installation and to add any necessary commands, such as those required to
load name spaces.

Use the Other Installation Options menu   **203**
to install additional products on the server and to complete a registration
disk, which you can mail to Novell to register your server.

Because NetWare Directory Services (NDS) is a scheme for arranging your entire organization's network into a unified structure, careful planning is critical. Imagine a network with thousands of objects, hundreds of servers, and dozens of network administrators in various departments. For the first time, all of these objects and servers will exist in one network database. With an overall plan for consistency and logical organization in place, this huge network can greatly streamline the jobs of all those network administrators. Without such a plan, the network will be more confusing and cumbersome than ever.

To plan for NetWare Directory Services, consider the following issues:

▸ What organizational structure of the Directory tree makes the most sense for your network resources?

▸ How do you want the Directory database to be partitioned, and where do you want to store replicas of those partitions?

▸ How should time be kept and synchronized among the servers on the network?

Each of these issues is discussed in the following sections.

Planning Your Organization's Directory Tree

To begin planning your Directory tree, look first at your organization's structure, functions, and needs. NetWare Directory Services is designed to reflect a hierarchical structure. Generally, this means that your Directory tree will be patterned according to some logical structure of your organization, whether or not that structure is formal.

For example, if your organization is formally divided into departments, you may decide to structure your Directory tree by departments as well. On the other hand, if people in several departments work together on long-term projects and need access to common resources, it may make more sense to divide your tree by project teams instead of departments.

When planning your Directory tree, also consider who will be running the network. With NetWare 4.0, you can centralize network administration so that a single person or small group of people controls the entire Directory database, or you can distribute administration so that many network administrators throughout the enterprise control their own portions of the Directory database.

If network administration will be distributed, it is crucial that everyone who will be administering the network be involved in planning for it. They must also be kept informed of all decisions and rules made about creating and naming objects, assigning security, and so on. Otherwise, there is no way to ensure the consistency that makes NetWare Directory Services so powerful. Designing by committee always has its downfalls, but in this case, designing in a vacuum could be even worse. Making massive, fundamental changes to a Directory tree once it has been established can be difficult.

Designing the Directory tree so that every network administrator is happy could become a political issue, but in most cases, a smooth outcome is in everyone's best interest. Therefore, try to concentrate on simplifying the hierarchy as much as possible. Then publish a description of all rules and guidelines for naming objects and defining information about those objects. Published guidelines will make it much easier for network administrators to create new users with correct electronic-mail names, consistent addresses and phone numbers, and so on.

At some point in the Directory-tree planning stage, someone may suggest that different portions of the organization could have separate Directory trees. Resist this temptation. There are several problems with having multiple trees:

▶ The point of NetWare Directory Services is to unify the organization's network resources. Having separate trees defeats this.

▶ It is difficult to get from one tree to another. If you are in one tree, the only way you can access another tree is to log in to a server on the second tree using bindery emulation. This makes it impossible to use the second tree in NetWare Directory Services mode, which eliminates many of the useful features of NetWare 4.0. Bindery emulation is explained later in this chapter.

▶ Although it is possible to merge two trees after they've been created, it is much easier and less problematic to set up a single tree in the beginning.

▶ If the reason people want two trees is because different people or groups want to "own" their own portions of the network, it is easy to set up a single tree so that administration is distributed to different people. A single person does not have to have control of the entire Directory. You can set it up so that several people each have ultimate control over their own portion of the tree.

NetWare Directory Services was designed in large part around the CCITT specification X.500. This specification is an attempt to standardize worldwide telecommunications. Although the X.500 specification is not yet complete, Novell attempted to comply with as much of the specification as possible, while at the same time simplifying some of the characteristics that are less directly related to computer networking.

If you need more information about X.500 directory services so that you can plan your NetWare 4.0 network, the most helpful resource on the topic is Marshall T. Rose's book *The Little Black Book (Mail Bonding with OSI Directory Services)*. Rose is an expert in the field, having participated in the design and implementation of the X.500 directory services specifications.

The following sections explain more about planning your Directory tree.

THE HIERARCHY OF OBJECTS

In its purest, most basic form, your organization can probably be broken down into a beautifully simple pattern. This simple pattern is what NetWare Directory Services uses to organize objects in the Directory tree:

▶ There is a top-level, all-encompassing entity to which everything else belongs. This entity may be a company, an organization, an association, a government agency, a school district, or the like. In NetWare Directory Services, this level is called an *Organization object*. Your Directory tree must have at least one Organization object.

▶ Within the top-level entity, there may be subgroups, each of which have their particular responsibilities. These subgroups may be divisions, departments, subsidiaries, workgroup units, schools, offices, project teams, and so on. In NDS, these subgroups are called *Organizational Unit objects*. Organizational Unit objects can contain other Organizational Unit objects as well. For example, the sales department of a company may contain sales teams called Inside Sales, Outside Sales, and Sales Support. If your organization is very small, you may not need any Organizational Unit objects. If your company is very large, you will probably have many Organizational Unit objects, and you may even have several levels of them.

▶ Finally, within any Organizational Unit, you find all the individual resources that make up the Organizational Unit: people, computers, printers, and similar single entities. Each of these entities has its own object in NetWare Directory Services. There are Server objects, User objects, Printer objects, Print Queue objects, Computer objects, and so on.

These three elements—Organization objects, Organizational Unit objects, and single-entity objects—are what you will use to set up the hierarchy of your network.

There is a fourth level of objects that you can use if you wish, but that level is less useful. The Country object is an optional object that is even higher than the Organization object. If your Organizations span countries, you can use the Country object to designate which country your Organizations are located in. However, it is better to divide a multinational organization into Organizational Units than into Countries. We recommend against using the Country object because it will make it more difficult for users to navigate the Directory tree. This will be explained more fully in the section on naming objects, later in this chapter. Country objects are not necessary for complying with X.500 directory services guidelines, so there really are few reasons to use the Country object.

The last type of object you need to know about is the Root object (sometimes spelled [root]). The Root object is the very first object in the Directory tree, and it cannot be deleted or modified. All other objects, including Organizations, are contained within the Root object.

Container Objects vs. Leaf Objects

All of the different types of objects fall into two categories of objects: container objects and leaf objects. Container objects can contain other objects. Country, Organization, and Organizational Unit objects are all container objects.

Single-entity objects are leaf objects, because they cannot contain any other objects, just as a leaf on a tree cannot contain other leaves or branches. For more information about container and leaf objects, see Chapter 14.

Considering Object Security in the Directory Tree

Another aspect of objects you may need to consider when planning your Directory tree is object security (trustee rights).

Just as there are NetWare trustee rights that control what users can do with directories and files, NetWare 4.0 includes an additional set of trustee rights that affect objects and their properties. These object rights and property rights control how objects can work with one other. For example, a User object might have rights to read the telephone-number property of another User object. The same user might also have the rights necessary to change the postal address property of another User object.

Like trustee rights in the file system, trustee rights for objects and properties can be inherited. If you have certain rights to a container object, you can inherit those rights and exercise them in the objects within that container. However, each object has an Inherited Rights Filter (IRF) that can be used to block other objects from inherited rights.

This concept of inherited object rights is one that may help you plan your Directory tree. Grouping users with similar security needs within the same container object may simplify some network administration tasks.

Files and Directories Are Not Objects

It is important to make a distinction between the Directory database and the file system. The Directory database contains information about all the resources on the network, including volumes. However, the Directory database does *not* include files and directories. The files and directories on a network are components of the file system instead.

In some ways, the distinction between the Directory database and the file system is quite clear. In others, the line is blurred, if not erased.

The two different sets of NetWare trustee rights are a good example. One set of trustee rights in NetWare 4.0 is the traditional set of NetWare rights that control what users can do with directories and files. Previous versions of NetWare have included these file-system trustee rights as an integral part of NetWare. In NetWare 4.0, file-system trustee rights still exist and operate just as they did in NetWare 3.11.

In addition to these trustee rights, NetWare 4.0 introduces an entirely different set of trustee rights that affect objects and their properties. Object and property rights are separate from file-system rights. They do not affect each other.

Another example of the separation between the file system and the Directory database is in Directory partitions. Replicas of the Directory database partitions are stored on several servers on the network so that there is no potential single point of failure. This means that if one server disk crashes, the database is not lost—replicas on other servers continue to provide the database information. However, the file system is not part of the Directory partition, so the files and directories stored on the crashed disk will *not* be available to the network. (This is a good reason for ensuring that you have established disk mirroring or disk duplexing on all of your critical servers.)

These examples illustrate how the file system and the Directory database are separate. However, to smooth the transition between the two systems, NetWare 4.0 has integrated the two systems so that you can easily work with both of them from within the same utilities. This is where the line blurs between the two.

For example, with the NetWare Administrator utility, which is a graphical-user-interface utility that runs under Windows or OS/2's Presentation Manager, you can browse through the Directory tree to see the objects on your network. As you open each container object, a list of the objects within that container appears. When you reach a leaf object, you cannot open it, because there are no objects within it.

However, when you open a Volume object, which is a leaf object, it does appear to open and list the files and directories within it. This is the point where NetWare seamlessly melds the Directory database with the file system.

Also, although object rights and file-system rights are separate, they again overlap at the Volume object. The ADMIN user is granted the Supervisor object right to the Volume object when the Volume object is created. That assignment automatically grants the ADMIN user the Supervisor file-system right to the files and directories within that volume.

PUTTING YOURSELF IN THE RIGHT CONTEXT

Finding your way around the Directory tree requires that you understand how objects are named and what their context is in the tree. The following sections explain these concepts.

What Is an Object's Complete Name?

Each object in the Directory tree has a name, such as Fred, Anne, Queue1, or Sales_Server. Each object also has a complete name. An object's complete name in NetWare Directory Services is actually more of an address that indicates the object's position in the tree. An object's complete name includes the name of each container object that precedes it, all the way to the Root object.

For example, to find Mary at her home, you have to know the country she lives in, the state or province, her city, her street, and finally her house number. In essence, you could say that this "address" actually defines Mary's complete name. It is a more complete definition than simply "Mary." Without all that information about Mary, you might never reach her.

Similarly, to find Mary on the network, you need to know the Organization object and any Organizational Unit objects that contain her. If Mary is located in an Organizational Unit object called Sales, which is in an Organizational Unit called Lab_Products, which is in an Organization called HighTech, Mary's complete name is Mary.Sales.Lab_Products.HighTech. Periods are used to separate the object names. They act as backslashes do in a DOS directory.

Depending on the tasks you wish to perform, you may need to specify an object's complete name when you work with it in the Directory tree.

Using Name Types

Another element of an object's name, called a *name type,* can complicate the picture slightly. In some cases, you may need to specify not only the complete name but also the type of object each portion of the complete name indicates. For example, Sales is an Organizational Unit object. To show what type of object Sales is, you use the abbreviation OU, and you would enter OU=Sales.

Each container object has its own abbreviation to indicate its name type:

C	Country
O	Organization
OU	Organizational Unit

Leaf objects all have the same name type: CN (for "Common Name"). Therefore, regardless of whether the leaf object is a NetWare Server object, a User object, a Printer object, an Alias object, or any other object, its name type is CN.

Therefore, if you have to indicate Mary's complete name *with* name types, you must use the following syntax:

CN=Mary.OU=Sales.OU=Lab_Products.O=HighTech

This is obviously a more cumbersome method of indicating an object's complete name, and it is another good reason for avoiding the use of the Country object. If you use the Country object, you will always have to use name types in object names. This is because with the Country object, there are four possible object types, and it is more difficult for the system to know which object type you are indicating.

The Name Context

Fortunately, it is not always necessary to use an object's complete name if you are in the same *name context* as the object you are referring to. An object's name context is its position in the Directory tree. If two objects are located in the same container object, they have the same context.

For example, suppose you are trying to tell someone else where Mary lives. If you are both already standing in the city where Mary lives, you can skip the country, state or province, and city in your explanation. All you need to specify is her street and house number, because all three of you are in the same context—the same city.

Similarly, in the Directory tree, Mary's context is Sales.Lab_Products.High-Tech. If a printer called FastPrinter is also in the Organizational Unit object Sales, Mary probably would not have to indicate the printer's complete name when she wants to access it, because the printer is in the same context as she is. Instead, Mary could just select the printer's *partial name:* FastPrinter. When Mary selects FastPrinter, NetWare will look in Mary's context (meaning within the Organizational Unit object Sales) for the printer.

Now suppose Mary wants to use a wide-carriage dot-matrix printer that is located in another Organizational Unit, called Accounting. The printer's complete name is WIDE_DOTM.Accounting.Lab_Products.HighTech. Mary could enter the printer's complete name, or she could enter only the part of the printer's name that is different from Mary's own context. Mary and the WIDE_DOTM printer are both located in the Lab_Products.HighTech context, so Mary would have to enter only the partial name WIDE_DOTM.Accounting in order for the system to find the printer.

Hints for Planning Contexts and Names

Because names and contexts can become confusing for users, you may want to consider the following hints:

▶ Seriously consider limiting the levels of container objects you have in your tree. Since it is difficult for users to remember long complete names with multiple layers of Organization Units, try to avoid having more than two or three levels of Organizational Units and keep the names as brief as possible. For instance, using the name *Lab* instead of *Lab_Products* would eliminate some typing on Mary's part.

▶ You can have up to 1000 objects in a container object.

▶ If users frequently need to access an object that is not in their context, use Alias objects to simplify your user's work. For example, you could create an Alias object for Accounting's WIDE_DOTM printer and put the Alias object in Mary's context. Then Mary could find the printer in her own context, and she wouldn't have to remember the longer "real" name of the printer. Chapter 14 explains more about creating leaf objects such as aliases.

▶ When naming objects, you can use spaces in the name, but spaces will appear as underscores in some utilities. In other utilities, you may have to enclose the name in quotations marks to avoid having the utilities treat the two-word name as two separate commands or objects. Therefore, you should avoid using spaces in names.

MIXED NETWORKS: UNDERSTANDING BINDERY EMULATION

In many cases, large enterprises may upgrade their NetWare networks to NetWare 4.0 over an extended period of time. Therefore, they may be running some servers with NetWare 3.11 or 2.*x*, and other servers with NetWare 4.0. However, they still need all of their servers to be able to function together on the same network, regardless of which versions they're running.

To address this potentially common situation, NetWare 4.0 has included a feature called *bindery emulation*. Bindery emulation is a way for bindery-based NetWare servers to become part of the NetWare 4.0 Directory tree and for NDS objects to appear like bindery objects to bindery-based servers.

The bindery is a "flat" database, meaning that there are no container objects and there is no hierarchy, unlike the Directory database. Therefore, for bindery-based servers, clients, applications, and utilities to function in the Directory tree, somehow the Directory database needs to be able to look like a flat database. That is what bindery emulation does.

By default, bindery emulation is installed automatically whenever a new NetWare server is added to the tree. The container object that contains the new server is established as the context for bindery emulation. This means that whenever a bindery-based client logs in to a server in that container object, the user at that client will see all the objects in that container as being bindery objects. Whenever

NetWare 4.0 clients log in to the network at that container object's context, those users will see all objects as being Directory Services objects. This way, both groups of users can function. The NetWare 4.0 users can use NetWare 4.0 utilities and work with the Directory tree normally, and NetWare 3.11 or 2.x users can use their bindery-based utilities and still accomplish their tasks.

When you install NetWare 4.0 on a server, the INSTALL utility will ask you for the context for bindery emulation. However, if you decide you do not need bindery emulation, you can turn it off after installation by using either the SET server utility or SERVMAN.NLM. You can also use SET (or SERVMAN) to change the bindery emulation context to a different container object.

Planning Directory Partitions and Replicas

The key to NetWare Directory Services is its single, unified database of network information. This Directory database makes it possible for an entire networked enterprise to function smoothly as a whole. However, it's also easy to see how a single, huge Directory database could become unwieldy and difficult to manage, especially if portions of the database are separated by WAN (wide area network) links.

There is also, of course, the issue of where to store the Directory database. If you store it on a single server and that server fails, it would be a catastrophe for the whole enterprise.

Clearly, it is critical to establish a way to divide the database into manageable pieces and then to ensure that those pieces survive even if one or more servers fail. The solution: partitions and replicas.

USING DIRECTORY PARTITIONS

Directory partitions are portions of the overall Directory database. Every time you create a new Organization or Organizational Unit object by using the INSTALL utility, a new Directory partition is created. The new partition includes the new container object, all objects in that container, and all the Directory information about those objects. Directory partitions do not include files or directories, because those are part of the file system, not the Directory database.

You can also create new Directory partitions after you've installed a server, by using the NetWare Administrator graphical utility or PARTMGR text utility.

The Root object is included in the Directory partition that is created for the first Organization or Organizational Unit object you install.

To make it easier for users to use the Directory tree, users do not see Directory partitions. To users, all of the Directory database appears as a whole.

USING REPLICAS TO PROTECT THE DIRECTORY DATABASE

Even with the Directory database divided into partitions, if a partition is stored on a single server and that server goes down, all the information in that partition will be unavailable. Users won't be able to log in and won't be authenticated to use network resources. To prevent this from happening, NetWare 4.0 makes copies of the Directory partitions, called *replicas*.

There are three types of replicas:

- ▸ Master

- ▸ Read/Write

- ▸ Read Only

You can store these different types of replicas on servers throughout the network so that there is no single point of failure for that partition. Make sure you have at least two replicas of every partition on your network. If you have only one partition and the server that contains it is damaged, you may not be able to recover the partition. By default, every server you install in a partition automatically gets a replica stored on it, so it's wise to install at least two servers in every container object. This will ensure that there are at least two replicas of that container's partition.

The Master replica is created and stored on the first server that is installed in a new container object. From the Master replica, you can change objects. In addition, the Master replica is the only one you can use to change the partition's relationship to the rest of the Directory database. You can also use the Master replica to create new partitions.

A Read/Write replica is the default type of replica that is stored on every other server you install within the same container object. A Read/Write replica lets you make changes to objects within the partition, but you cannot use a Read/Write replica to create new partitions or change the partition's relationship with the rest of the database. A Read/Write replica of a container object's partition is placed on the server that contains the *parent* container's Master replica. (Read/Write replicas are required on every server for bindery emulation. This is why these replicas are installed by default.)

Read Only replicas are not installed on servers by default, but you can create them and install them on additional servers. Read Only replicas only provide information about the partition. You cannot use them to change objects in the partition.

Replicas are useful for two reasons:

▸ They prevent the partition from being lost if one server goes down.

▸ They allow users in different partitions to have local access to each other's objects, which is especially useful across WAN links.

Servers can contain several replicas of different partitions. In general, 486-based servers can contain more replicas than 386-based servers because the 486-based servers' increased speed allows them to handle more updates to the various replicas.

If your enterprise covers a large geographical distance, you may want to consider placing replicas of your partition on a server in another area. This accomplishes two things: It allows users in that area to see your partition, and it protects the existence of your partition if a disaster, such as a fire, destroys your own servers and replicas. (Of course, this does not protect your files, so be sure to mirror your file server disks and keep up-to-date backups of your data in a secure location, as explained in Chapter 17.)

Storing a Read Only replica on servers that are across a WAN link can be helpful because it cuts down on the traffic that has to cross the link when users try to access the other partition's information. With a replica of a distant partition stored locally, users have immediate access to the objects they need. The only time that information needs to cross the link is when the replicas are being updated.

To change replicas after you've installed them, you can use either the NetWare Administrator utility or the PARTMGR utility.

Planning Time Synchronization

Because you can have more than one replica of a Directory partition from which changes can be made, it is very important that all the servers in your network are running on the same, synchronized time. Otherwise, changes made to the partitions from different places could get out of order, and an earlier change could overwrite a later one. *Time synchronization* is a method of specifying how servers keep time consistently with one other.

With time synchronization in NetWare 4.0, you can specify which servers actually set the time and which servers simply set themselves to the other servers' time.

There are two ways to set up your network's time synchronization scheme:

▶ If you have a small network, you can select the default configuration. In the default setup, the first server is designated as the only timekeeper and all other servers are set so they get their time from the first server.

▶ If you have a larger network, you can customize your time synchronization setup by specifying which servers set the time and how they synchronize with each other.

USING DEFAULT TIME SYNCHRONIZATION

When you install a server, the INSTALL utility will prompt you for the type of time server you want that server to be. If this is the first server you are installing in your network, the default type of time server offered by the INSTALL utility is called *Single Reference*. A Single Reference server is the only server on the network that sets time for the other servers. All other servers on the network will be installed as *Secondary* time servers, which means they get their time from the Single Reference server. Workstations can get the network time from either Single Reference or Secondary servers.

All Secondary servers must be able to contact the Single Reference server with as few links as possible, so that they can be synchronized without undue delays.

If you have a relatively small network, the default setup is a good choice.

CUSTOMIZING TIME SYNCHRONIZATION

If you have a large network, you may not want to have a single server that distributes time to the entire network. In this case, you can use three different types of time servers that work together to keep network time (workstations can synchronize with any of the following types of time servers):

> **Reference time server:** Similar to a Single Reference server, this server is the central point of time-keeping on the network. On a large network, this Reference server can be synchronized to an external time source, such as the server's own internal hardware clock or a radio clock. There are third-party NLMs available that allow you to set your server's time to a radio clock or other national time service. Ideally, there should be only one Reference server on a network. However, it is possible to have more than one, which might be desirable if the servers are far apart, such as on opposite sides of a WAN link. If you have more than one Reference server, they should each be connected to an external time source.

> **Primary time server:** Polls other Primary or Reference servers to establish an average time as the "correct" time and provides that time to Secondary servers. Place at least one Primary server in each geographic location so that Secondary servers don't have to cross WAN links to synchronize themselves. One Primary server can provide time for up to 150 Secondary servers.

Secondary time server: Gets its time from a Primary or Reference server. Secondary servers do not participate in establishing the network time. This means that no other time server will use a secondary time server as a synchronization source.

When you install a server, you can specify which type of time server you want it to be, or you can accept the default time-server types that the INSTALL utility offers you.

SAP VS. CUSTOM CONFIGURATION

By default, time synchronization uses a method called Service Advertising Protocol (SAP) to allow the different types of servers to find each other and share time information. Secondary servers use the SAP information that Primary and Reference servers send out to locate a time server to follow. In networks that are fairly stable (in which servers aren't constantly being added and removed), SAP is recommended. It generates a small amount of traffic on the network when servers are advertising themselves to each other, but it is generally not enough to be a problem.

In larger networks where servers are frequently added and removed or where the extra SAP traffic is undesirable, you can use several parameters in the SET server utility to turn off SAP and set up time synchronization in a custom configuration. You add these SET commands to the TIMESYNC.CFG file, located in SYS:SYSTEM. When you reboot the server, this file executes and specifies which time servers should be contacted by Secondary servers.

Custom configuration of your time servers gives you more control over time synchronization and requires more planning so that servers are synchronized efficiently.

Installing NetWare Directory Services on a Server

In Chapter 7, you used the NWNSTLL.EXE and INSTALL.NLM utilities to install the network operating system and load NetWare files onto the server. To allow the server to become a part of the overall NetWare Directory Services network, use the instructions in the following sections to continue running INSTALL.NLM and to add NetWare Directory Services to the server.

The procedures for installing NDS on a file server vary slightly, depending on whether this is the first server or an additional server that you are installing in the tree. The following sections assume that you are installing your first server and indicate where steps may be different if this is not the first server in the tree.

SELECTING A DIRECTORY TREE

You are probably already running INSTALL.NLM, in which case you have just finished binding IPX to your LAN drivers (as explained in Chapter 7), and you are now being prompted for a tree name. (If you are not already running the installation utility, type **LOAD INSTALL** from the colon prompt at the server, select Maintenance/Selective Installation, then select Directory Options to install Directory Services.)

When prompted for the Directory tree name, either type in the name of the tree you are creating (if this is the first server you're installing) or select the tree to which you want to add this server. If this is the first server and you are creating a new tree name, press the F1 key to see the rules you must follow to name your tree. If a tree already exists, but you want to create a new one anyway, press the Insert key and type in a name for the new tree.

SETTING UP TIME SYNCHRONIZATION

After you select a Directory tree, you set up the server for time synchronization. (Time synchronization is explained earlier in this chapter.) To specify this server's time information, follow these steps:

1 · Choose the time zone in which the server is located. If your time zone is listed on the screen, select the zone by pressing ↵. If your time zone is not listed, press the Insert key.

2 · Select the type of time server you want this server to be. The default for the first server in the tree is Single Reference. If you choose this

default, all subsequent servers will have to be Secondary time servers. To choose a different type of time server, move to the *Time server type* field and press ↵.

3 · Select the standard time zone for this server. Enter a three-letter abbreviation for the zone. Since not all time-zone abbreviations are standardized, you may have to enter your own abbreviation. Just ensure that other servers on your network use the same abbreviation if they are in the same time zone.

4 · In the Standard Time Offset from UTC field, enter the number of hours that separate your time zone from the Coordinated Universal Time (abbreviated as UTC; it is sometimes referred to as Greenwich mean time). You must also specify whether your time zone is ahead of or behind UTC. Press ↵ to toggle between Ahead and Behind. If your time zone is east of UTC, use Ahead. If your time zone is west of UTC, use Behind. For example, if you are installing this server in Paris, your server is one hour ahead of UTC, so specify *1 Ahead*. If you are installing this server in San Francisco, specify *8 Behind*.

5 · Indicate whether your time zone uses daylight savings time. Move to the field *Does your area have daylight savings time (DST)* and press ↵, then use the arrow keys to toggle between Yes and No.

6 · If your time zone uses daylight savings time, fill in the appropriate information in the remaining fields.

  ‣ Enter the three-letter abbreviation for Daylight Savings in that zone. (Again, not all abbreviations are standardized, so make sure every server uses the same abbreviations.)

  ‣ Enter the difference between standard time and daylight savings time. The default is one hour (1:00:00) ahead.

  ‣ Specify the starting and ending days for daylight savings time.

7 · When you are finished, press the F10 key and answer Yes to save the time configuration information.

SPECIFYING THE SERVER'S CONTEXT AND THE ADMINISTRATOR'S NAME

Next, indicate where in the Directory tree you want this server to be created, and then specify the Administrator user's name and password. The steps are different, depending on whether this is the first server or not. Read whichever of the following sections applies to you.

If This Is the First Server

If this is the first server in the tree, you must indicate the server context, which is where the server is located in the tree. This step also creates the Root object for the tree and creates a new partition for the container objects you specify.

In the *Company or Organization* field, enter the name of the top-level Organization object that will contain this server. Then, in the Level 1, Level 2, and Level 3 fields, you can fill in the names of any Organizational Unit objects that will contain this server. You can use letters, numbers, or the underscore character, but other characters are invalid. For example, to create a server in the Organizational Unit called Sales, which is in the Organizational Unit called Lab_Products, which is within the Organization called HighTech, enter the following information:

- **HighTech** in the *Company or Organization* field.

- **Lab_Products** in the *Level 1 (Sub)Organizational Unit* field.

- **Sales** in the *Level 2 (Sub)Organizational Unit* field.

- Leave the *Level 3 (Sub)Organizational Unit* field blank. If you want to enter more than three levels of Organizational Unit objects, specify them here, separated by periods.

- If you want to create a Country object, use the Server Context field. Press ↵ and type *.C=countrycode,* substituting the CCITT-approved country code for *countrycode.* Approved country codes are listed in Appendix C of the *NetWare 4.0 Installation and Upgrade* manual.

After you specify the server's context in the tree, you can enter a password for the administrator. Obviously, the password is important for network security; it is critical that you do not forget it. The administrator's name—ADMIN by default—is also displayed on the screen. ADMIN is created directly beneath the Organization object and has Supervisor rights to that Organization object, and therefore to the entire Directory tree. You can change user ADMIN's name and rights later, using the NetWare Administrator graphical utility or the NETADMIN text utility.

When you have finished entering the password, press the F10 key to save all the NetWare Directory Services information you have entered. A message indicates that the installation was successful and shows how many volumes were installed in the Directory tree. Now you can go to the section on editing the STARTUP.NCF and AUTOEXEC.NCF files, later in this chapter, to complete the installation.

If This Is Not the First Server

If this is *not* the first server in the tree, after you finish specifying the time synchronization information, you are asked to enter the administrator's complete name and password. By default, the administrator's name is ADMIN, but if you have changed it with the NetWare Administrator or NETADMIN utility, enter the new name instead. Remember to enter the administrator's complete name, such as ADMIN.HighTech.

Then select a context for the server. To install this server in an existing context, press ↵ at any organizational level to see the list of existing container objects. Then select a container object from the list. To install the server in a new context (which means you will be creating at least one new container object, and therefore at least one new partition as well), type in a new context, including name types, such as the following:

OU=Accounting.OU=Lab_Products.O=HighTech

When you have finished specifying the context, press the F10 key to save all the NetWare Directory Services information you have entered. A message indicates that the installation was successful and shows how many volumes were installed in the Directory tree. Now you can go to the next section to complete the installation.

EDITING THE STARTUP.NCF AND AUTOEXEC.NCF FILES

STARTUP.NCF and AUTOEXEC.NCF are the NetWare server configuration files that execute commands and load files that the server needs to run properly. The extension NCF stands for NetWare command file. These NCF files are similar to batch files; they are ASCII files, and the commands in them must follow legitimate server-utility syntax. You can execute them at the server console by typing their names, but more commonly they are run automatically when the file server is booted.

During the installation process, much of the information that you specified for your server is automatically added to these two NCF files. Therefore, there are options in INSTALL.NLM that allow you to view and edit these files.

You can also edit these files after the installation is complete by using a simple server-based text editor called EDIT.NLM. To use EDIT.NLM, type **LOAD EDIT**, then enter the path and name of the NCF file you want to edit (SYS:SYS-TEM\AUTOEXEC.NCF or C:\SERVER.40\STARTUP.NCF). When you have finished adding commands to the file, press the Escape key to confirm that you want to save the changes you've made and exit the utility.

To add SET commands to the NCF files, use SERVMAN.NLM. This NLM is a convenient menu utility that allows you to select SET parameters to include in these files instead of forcing you to type them. (SET commands tend to be long and are inconvenient to type, especially if you are prone to making typos.)

The following sections explain how to view and edit the NCF files from within INSTALL.NLM.

The STARTUP.NCF File

STARTUP.NCF is loosely analogous to the CONFIG.SYS file on a DOS computer. It executes immediately after SERVER.EXE and establishes configuration parameters that must be set before the operating system can become fully functional.

The most important of these functions is to allow access to the server's NetWare partition. Since STARTUP.NCF executes before the NetWare partition is accessible, it resides on the DOS boot partition and contains commands to load necessary disk drivers. Any modules (such as name-space modules) and commands (such as the "SET Minimum File Cache Buffers" and "SET Minimum

Packet Receive Buffers" commands) that affect the operating system's basic interface with its NetWare partitions must be executed in STARTUP.NCF.

The STARTUP.NCF file automatically appears on the screen. If necessary, add any commands to the STARTUP.NCF file. For example, you may want to load name-space modules for Macintosh or NFS support (make sure these commands are listed before the commands to mount the volumes that use these name spaces). You can also add certain SET commands to this file so that they are automatically executed when the server is booted.

Then save the file by pressing the F10 key. Changes to this file will only take effect when you reboot the server. See the NetWare documentation for more information about the STARTUP.NCF file.

The AUTOEXEC.NCF File

After you save your changes to the STARTUP.NCF file, the AUTOEXEC.NCF file appears on the screen. AUTOEXEC.NCF is similar to the AUTOEXEC.BAT file on a DOS computer and resides in the SYS:SYSTEM directory. It executes after STARTUP.NCF executes and after the SYS: volume is mounted. The INSTALL utility automatically creates the AUTOEXEC.NCF file and adds commands to complete the booting process for the server, including the information you specified earlier in the INSTALL utility, such as time-zone SET commands, the bindery context (set at the server's context), the server's name and IPX number, and commands to load LAN drivers.

To edit the AUTOEXEC.NCF file, add necessary commands. When you are finished, press the F10 key to save the file. Changes to this file will only take effect when you reboot the server. See the NetWare documentation for more information about the AUTOEXEC.NCF file.

FINISHING THE INSTALLATION

At the end of the installation process, the Other Installation Options menu appears. You can use this menu to install additional products on your server. You can also use it to copy the online documentation from the CD-ROM to the server. Selecting any item in the list of available products will display context-sensitive help on that product.

If you want to install any of these products, simply highlight that product and press ⏎ to begin installing it. If you want to install an unlisted product, press the Insert key and follow the instructions to insert that product's disks. When you are finished loading additional products, press the F10 key.

You can also select the Create a Registration Disk option from the Other Installation Options menu. This option lets you record your company name and address, your reseller's name and address, and your file server's configuration information. If you create this registration disk, you can send it to Novell to register your copy of NetWare. More important, perhaps, Novell will store the configuration information from the disk in a database. Then, if you have to call Novell Technical Support, they can pull up all your configuration data from the database, saving time for you and them.

When you exit (or bypass) the Other Installation Options menu, you will have completed the installation process. A lengthy message appears, stating that your initial installation is complete and pointing you to other sources of information for the rest of the necessary installation tasks.

To ensure that the server is completely configured, you may want to reboot the server and watch it come up. If volume SYS: won't mount, try looking at the STARTUP.NCF file for possible errors. If errors occur after SYS: mounts, check AUTOEXEC.NCF for mistakes in syntax or configuration parameters.

After the Installation

When the installation is finished, the basic elements of your Directory tree will be in place.

You will have a tree, an Organization object, and any Organizational Unit objects you specified.

You will also have a Root object and an ADMIN User object. The ADMIN User object is located in the Organization object's context and has the Supervisor right to the Root object. Because it has the Supervisor right to the Root object, ADMIN inherits the Supervisor right to all Volume objects in the Directory tree. The Root object gets the Browse right on all User objects in the tree and the Read right to the Member property of any Group object. It also gets the Read right to all

Volume objects' host server names and host resources (the physical volumes that the objects represent).

Directory partitions will be set up for each container object, with a Master replica on the first server installed in the object, and Read/Write replicas installed on every other server in the partition and on the server that contains the Master replica for the parent container object's partition. To change how the partitions and replicas are set up, you can use either the NetWare Administrator or PARTMGR utility.

A Server object and Volume objects, including SYS: and any other volumes you specified, will be located in the container object in which you installed the server. The SYS: Volume object will have the server name added to the beginning of it. For example, if the server's name is BARGAIN, the SYS: Volume object's name will be BARGAIN_SYS. The server name is only part of the Volume object's name; if you looked at the volume's name from the server console, it would still appear as SYS:. The server name is added to the beginning of the SYS: Volume object name because there could be several SYS: volumes in a given container object, and the server name makes them unique.

You will also have a User object named Supervisor, but this object only exists for compatibility with bindery-based utilities. Supervisor cannot be recognized by NetWare 4.0 utilities. User Supervisor takes ADMIN's password and is located in the same context as the server.

The [Public] trustee is created and is granted the Browse right to the Root object. This trustee allows all users who log in to the Directory tree to view objects in the tree.

All container objects are granted the Read and File Scan (RF) file-system trustee rights to the PUBLIC directory on every SYS: volume in that container. This means that all users who are later created in that container object will also inherit the Read and File Scan rights in each SYS:PUBLIC directory, which will give those users access to the NetWare utilities.

Upgrading to NetWare 4.0

Fast Track

Before you begin an In-Place upgrade from NetWare 2.x to 3.x,   *219*
make sure you have the following:

- ▸ A source file server

- ▸ A NetWare-compatible backup device

- ▸ All the drivers and auxiliary software that you'll need for your
  NetWare 4.0 installation

- ▸ The copy of the version of NetWare from which you are
  upgrading

Before you upgrade from NetWare 3.11 to 4.0,   *224*

  1 • Use the NetWare SALVAGE utility to restore deleted files.

  2 • Make sure you have a fully functional backup.

  3 • Log users out of the NetWare 3.11 server.

  4 • Specify the frame type for Ethernet LAN drivers.

There are several options for upgrading to NetWare version 4.0. If you are already running a version of NetWare that is at least version 2.10 or 3.10, you can use the NetWare Migration Utility, which ships with NetWare 4.0. If your current file server is running a version of NetWare before 2.10 or 3.10, either you must upgrade to a more recent version and then upgrade to version 4.0, or you must install your NetWare 4.0 server from scratch, including the users, groups, and security.

Assuming that your current version of NetWare is 2.10, 3.10, or higher, there are two basic methods of upgrading to NetWare 4.0. The first method is called the Across-the-Wire method, and it does what you might guess by the name: It transfers all applications, data, users, groups, security information, and so on from the source file server (version 2.x or 3.x) to a preinstalled NetWare 4.0 server.

The second method for upgrading to NetWare 4.0 is called the In-Place method. Again, the name provides a fairly accurate description of the process. This method expects you to use the original 2.x or 3.x file server as the file server for your NetWare 4.0 installation. There are some significant drawbacks to this method, and we'll get to these a little bit later. All in all, we recommend the Across-the-Wire method for all upgrades.

The Differences between Upgrading from NetWare 2.x and Upgrading from 3.x

The upgrade procedure for each method depends somewhat on the version that you are currently using and the version you plan to run on the upgraded file server. With an Across-the-Wire migration from NetWare 2.15, 2.2, or 3.x, you can go directly to NetWare 4.0.

If you use the In-Place upgrade from 2.15 or 2.2, you must first upgrade your file system to 3.11 and then add the operating system with the 3.11 to 4.0 upgrade. We'll get into more detail later.

The Argument for Installing from Scratch

As we already mentioned, if your current version of NetWare is not 2.10, 3.10, or higher, you may not have the option to upgrade at all. If that is the case, you should go back and review Chapter 7, which covers performing a new installation.

However, even if your current NetWare version is 2.10, 3.10, or higher, you may want to consider a new installation of NetWare 4.0 anyway. If you plan to significantly restructure your data or volume structures, your user- and/or group-naming conventions, your system's security structure, or any combination of these components of your system, a new installation might turn out to be less trouble in the long run.

Give it some thought. If the time and effort involved with planning, executing, and supporting an upgrade are not worthwhile, you may benefit from a new installation. If you would like to install your NetWare 4.0 server from scratch, see Chapter 7.

Probably the most persuasive reason to install NetWare 4.0 anew instead of upgrading is that it gives you the opportunity to reorganize your network. An important facet of NetWare Directory Services is the implementation of global naming services. In fact, this will complicate the jobs of many network administrators in the short run as they try to reconcile conflicting or redundant naming conventions in use on their networks. (For more information on NDS, see Chapter 8.)

While the user community is almost always better served by a smooth migration from one system to a newer one, you may find that the costs involved in planning a smooth transition are prohibitive and that a new installation makes a lot of sense.

Be that as it may, don't make the decision to install NetWare 4.0 from scratch lightly. It requires a great deal of planning and foresight. In the short run, it is much more difficult to handle a sudden shift of systems at the moment the new system comes on line than it is to manage a gradual migration. Use your own needs and capabilities as your guide. If you cannot manage the task of engineering a gradual shift of systems, bite the bullet and just change over en masse. If, on the other hand, you cannot afford to have any significant downtime, it may be well worth the cost to contract with a reputable integrator to codesign and manage the 4.0 migration for you.

How an Across-the-Wire Migration Works

When you perform an Across-the-Wire migration, the bindery information and network data (but not the operating-system files) are transferred from the old file server to an existing NetWare 4.0 server. A DOS workstation is necessary to translate the data format. This is the safest method, since even after the migration is complete, all of the original contents are still on the 2.x or 3.x server. If a software or hardware error occurs during the migration and data is corrupted during the transition, all the data should be safe because nothing has really changed on the old file server.

How an In-Place Upgrade Works

The process of upgrading 2.x and 3.x file servers differs when you use the In-Place upgrade. Actually, there is an additional step with the 2.x upgrade, since the second half is identical to an In-Place upgrade of a 3.x server.

IN-PLACE UPGRADE OF A 2.X SERVER

With an In-Place upgrade, the data from a 2.x server is backed up to a backup device; the file server configuration is erased and replaced by NetWare 4.0; and the backed-up data is restored to the new NetWare 4.0 server.

There is some risk of data loss with this method, because if there is a problem with the first step (the backup) that doesn't manifest itself right away, you could have no way to recover or to return to the original file server configuration. Since the new file server is using the hardware of the old server, your only source of recovery is your backup device.

IN-PLACE UPGRADE OF A 3.X SERVER

Since the basic architecture and disk format of NetWare 3.*x* and 4.*x* are quite similar, the disk drives don't have to be repartitioned. This means that the risk to your data is minimized when compared with an In-Place upgrade from 2.*x*.

Even so, it is still safer to perform an Across-the-Wire migration if you have any qualms at all about your ability to return to the original state of the network, should the upgrade fail for some reason. The risk can be caused by things that aren't completely within your control. For example, a power outage or hardware error could result in corruption and loss of data. We strongly recommend the Across-the-Wire method for our clients.

Performing an Across-the-Wire Migration

The following section explains the steps and some of the theory behind an Across-the-Wire migration (using the Migration Utility). First we will provide a list of numbered steps so you can keep track of them as you perform them in real life. After that we will expand upon the basic steps so that you can understand what you're doing a little better.

PREREQUISITES

Before you begin the upgrade, make sure you have the following:

- ▸ A source file server. This is the 2.*x* or 3.*x* server that you want to upgrade to NetWare 4.0.

- ▸ A destination file server. Usually, this is a new computer with large hard drives and/or disk controllers, a minimum of 16MB of RAM, and a fast CPU. Don't make the mistake of buying a computer that isn't approved and tested by Novell for NetWare 4.0 compatibility as a file server!

- ▸ A DOS workstation with a fast CPU and a 16- or 32-bit network interface card. The upgrade can be done with an 8-bit interface card, but the throughput of the NIC will be put to the test in the upgrade process more than virtually all other uses. All that will be going on are file transfers and manipulations from the source file server to the DOS workstation and on over to the destination file server.

Of course, all these computers have to be connected to the same LAN, preferably over a high-throughput network.

STEPS TO FOLLOW

The steps for an Across-the-Wire migration are as follows:

1 · Install NetWare 4.0 on your new file server (see Chapter 7).

2 · Run BINDFIX.EXE on the 2.x or 3.x file server.

3 · Perform a *full* backup of your 2.x or 3.x file server (three times, on three separate tapes!).

4 · Make a directory on the DOS workstation for the NetWare Migration Utility, and copy all the contents of the disk into it.

5 · Change to that directory and type **MIGRATE**.

6 · Select Standard Migration.

7 · Select Source LAN type (2.x or 3.x, IBM LAN Server 1.3, or PCLP).

8 · Select Destination LAN type (3.x or 4.x).

9 · Press the down arrow key to accept the default working directory, or press ↵ to specify another working directory.

10 · Select the source server you want to migrate from.

11 · Select Source Volume(s).

12 · Select Destination Server.

13 · Select Destination Volume and Directory.

14 · Press F10 when you are finished filling out the *Volumes' destination* field.

15 · Select the Passwords option (random or none).

16 · Press F10 to begin the migration process.

17 · Examine the report file MIG000.LOG.

18 · Fully test the functionality of the new file server.

EXPLANATION OF THE STEPS

The following sections give more detailed explanations of the steps for performing an Across-the-Wire upgrade.

Installing NetWare 4.0 on Your New File Server

The Across-the-Wire migration processes each file and bindery object to translate it into a NetWare 4.0 format. Since this is a migration of one server's files and data to another, you will need to configure and install the destination server as a first step.

Running BINDFIX.EXE on the 2.x or 3.x File Server

The bindery files of NetWare 2.x and 3.x are the database of security and network object information. Just as with any other kind of database, it must be optimized or reindexed from time to time. This process eliminates blank records and mislinked information.

Performing a Full Backup of the 2.x or 3.x File Server

We tend to go a little overboard on the backups. Well, after experiencing a loss of two backups once in your career, it kind of sticks with you. We always demand three full backups before any major reconfiguration or restructuring of data. This may seem like a waste of time and tape, but it can save your business. Given the alternatives, we feel that the cost is well justified when weighed against the possibility of data loss.

Making a Directory on the DOS Workstation for the Migration Utility and Copying All the Contents of the Disk to It

At this point, we've configured the destination (4.0) server and prepared the source (2.x or 3.x) server. Now it's time to prepare the workstation that is going to perform most of the work. All the file servers will have to do is read and/or write files. That's not very difficult for a file server; after all, that's what it's designed to do!

The workstation needs at least 5MB of free disk space and 480K of free conventional memory. It also requires NETX.COM 3.02 or later. For the sake of performance and a quicker migration process, we recommend a 486 workstation with a 16- or 32-bit network interface card and a fast hard drive (it should have an access time of under 18 milliseconds). If you can't get such a machine, the installation process will go slower but there shouldn't be any other problems.

Changing to the Working Directory and Typing MIGRATE

MIGRATE.EXE is the replacement for the 3.11 utility UPGRADE.EXE. The interface has been reworked, and the flow of it is a little more straightforward.

Selecting Standard Migration

Until you have gone through the utility a few times and are familiar with the process, choose the Standard Migration option. If you have multiple servers to upgrade, and you are confident of the server configuration parameters and are familiar with the Migration Utility, go ahead and try the Custom Migration option.

Selecting Source LAN Type (2.x or 3.x)

In fact, the NetWare Migration Utility supports source servers that are NetWare 2.x (2.10 or above), NetWare 3.x (3.10 or above), IBM LAN Server version 1.3, or IBM LAN Server PCLP 1.0. Most likely you will be upgrading from a NetWare file server, so we will restrict our discussion to that process.

Selecting Destination LAN Type (3.x or 4.x)

If you are upgrading from 2.x, you may want to go to 3.x or 4.0. The Migration Utility replaces UPGRADE.EXE in NetWare 3.11 and is therefore required to function as a 2.x to 3.11 upgrade utility as well as a path to 4.0.

Selecting the Source Server

If you are on an internetwork with many servers, this choice may require a bit more thought. Many, and possibly most, of those who run the Migration Utility, however, will have an easy time choosing the source and destination file servers. The source file server is the one you are upgrading from. The DOS workstation must be connected to the source file server via the LAN.

Selecting Source Volume(s)

If your source file server has more than a single volume, you may need to think about how and if you want to restructure your file storage areas. You can migrate multiple volumes to a single destination volume or leave the structure as it is currently.

Selecting the Destination Server

The destination server is the NetWare 4.0 file server. The DOS workstation must be connected to the destination file server via the LAN.

Selecting the Destination Volume and Directory

As we mentioned before, you have the ability to set the destination for each source volume. If you have many volumes that you want to combine during the upgrade, you may want to give them their own destination directories so that after the migration itself is complete, you can sort through the upgraded files as needed in order to organize the new file server volumes the way you want to.

Selecting the Password Option (Random or None)

The Migration Utility either generates random passwords for each user by default or assigns no passwords at all. In this case, you must institute password security at a later time, as you see fit. If you choose to assign random passwords, a list of users, print servers, and their passwords is created in the SYS:SYSTEM directory, in a text file called NEW.PWD. Since it is placed in the SYS:SYSTEM directory, only those with SUPERVISOR equivalence or specifically assigned rights can view it.

Beginning the Migration Process

Once you are satisfied with the migration parameters, you are ready to begin.

Examining the Report File MIG000.LOG

When a file is encountered on the destination file server that has the same name as one on the source file server, an error is generated on the DOS workstation and is also written to the Migration Utility report file, MIG000.LOG. You can choose to abort, continue, or ignore all further errors. Since this error will occur for every redundant file (and there are many), it is usually a good choice to ignore all errors. Since they are added to the report file in any case, you can go back and figure out if anything important was not migrated and act accordingly.

Fully Testing the Functionality of the New File Server

Once the migration is finished processing files, the real work begins. You should verify that every user can log in and function as he or she must, including—but not limited to—printing, executing all applications, and generating reports and special projects (especially those that occur infrequently). It is important to go through the uncommon processes, since by the time they are performed normally, the installation is usually long over and there is nobody around to fix the problem quickly.

Remember that if you encounter serious problems with the new server (incompatible applications, drivers, etc.), you still have the original file server in its original state.

Performing an In-Place Upgrade from 2.x to 3.x

The steps for an In-Place upgrade are different, or at least longer, if you are upgrading from a NetWare 2.x server. The reason is that you must first upgrade it to version 3.x and then perform the In-Place upgrade from 3.x to 4.0. As we mentioned above, you don't have to have a copy of 3.x hanging around to make this happen. The necessary 3.x components are included with the upgrade package.

The process of upgrading a NetWare server includes two parts: First the file system is upgraded and then the new operating system is installed.

The file-system upgrade has four phases:

1 • The 2.x file system is analyzed and inventoried.

2 • The 2.x disks are analyzed.

3 • The 2.x disks are modified.

4 • A 3.11 bindery is created to replace the 2.x bindery.

PREREQUISITES

To perform an In-Place upgrade from 2.x to 3.x, you must have a source file server, a NetWare-compatible backup device, and all the drivers and auxiliary software that you'll need for your NetWare 4.0 installation. Don't assume that a driver that works with NetWare 3.x will work with 4.0. Contact your vendor to make sure that you have the current Novell tested and approved drivers, patches, and fixes for use with NetWare 4.0.

As a precaution, you should also have a copy of the version of NetWare from which you are upgrading. That way, in the worst of all cases, you can reinstall the old version, restore your system from backups, and lose nothing but the time you've spent in the upgrade attempt. If you don't like that prospect, we advise you to reconsider the Across-the-Wire upgrade method.

STEPS TO PERFORM

The steps for performing an In-Place upgrade from NetWare 2.x are listed below. Once complete, continue with the steps for an In-Place upgrade from 3.11 to 4.0.

1 · Log in to the 2.x server as SUPERVISOR and run BINDFIX.

2 · Perform a full system backup (three times, really!).

3 · At the file server console, type **CONFIG** and write down the information that is displayed.

4 · Type **DOWN** and press ↵ at the system console.

5 · Turn off the computer.

6 · Load the NetWare 3.11 operating system by placing the In-Place Upgrade disk in drive A and typing **SERVER**.

7 · When the file server boots to 3.11 NetWare, type the server name.

8 · Assign an IPX internal network number.

9 · Load each disk driver by typing **LOAD A: disk_driver**.

10 · Load the network-interface-card driver by typing **LOAD A: LAN_driver**.

11 · Type **A:2XUPGRDE**.

12 · Press Y to continue after you have read the warning messages and verified that you have backed up your server.

13 · Enter the DOS partition size you would like (5MB–32MB), and press ↵.

14 · Follow the prompts through the four phases as indicated.

15 · Press Y to continue.

16 · Mount all volumes and monitor that they mount successfully by typing **MOUNT ALL**.

17 · Down the server and go to DOS.

18 • Format the drive-C partition with system files: Type **A:FORMAT C: /S /X**. (Use /X only with DR DOS.)

19 • Use COPY CON to create a new STARTUP.NCF file, including commands to load disk drivers and any necessary name-space modules (MAC, OS2, FTAM, NFS, etc.).

EXPLANATION OF THE STEPS

The following sections give more detailed explanations of the steps for performing an In-Place upgrade.

Logging In to the 2.x Server as SUPERVISOR and Running BINDFIX

The first step is to log in to the source (2.x) file server as SUPERVISOR and run BINDFIX.EXE. As we explained in the description of the Across-the-Wire upgrade process, BINDFIX corrects problems with the bindery database on the source server, eliminating any stray fields and unassigned or out-of-place values. Run BINDFIX before an upgrade so that any misalignments in the database can be resolved, rather than migrated to the new system. The NetWare 4.0-equivalent utility is DSREPAIR, which optimizes and reindexes the NetWare Directory Services Database.

Typing CONFIG

This is the easiest way to monitor the current configuration of your file server's hardware. Since the 2.x system is running, the software configuration must be correct. The console command CONFIG displays the current LAN and DISK configuration information. Write it down; you'll need it later.

Downing the Server and Turning Off the Computer

If everything goes right, this is the last time you'll see your 2.x file server running. Say good-bye and hope the procedures that follow go smoothly.

Inserting the Upgrade Disk and Booting NetWare 3.11 on the File Server

The NetWare 4.0 In-Place Upgrade disk is a bootable floppy, formatted with DR DOS version 6.0. It has the necessary components of DOS for partitioning, formatting, etc. Since this is a Novell product, distributed by Novell's desktop division, you don't need to worry about licensing when you use DR DOS for your file server's disk partition.

Entering the Server Name

The file server name can be up to 47 characters, but it cannot start with a control character (such as an asterisk, a slash, a backslash, a colon, or a semicolon), and it cannot contain any spaces. Make the name informative but not too limiting, because the location or function may change over time.

Entering the IPX Internal Network Number

This number can be up to eight characters in hexadecimal (base 16) format. Hexadecimal uses the characters 0–9 and A–F, so there are quite a few English words that function as valid hexadecimal numbers (such as CAB, DEAD, BEEF, BABE, DECAF, and FACE). This number must be unique throughout your internetwork. It cannot be the same as any other internal network number, nor can it duplicate a LAN (cable) address.

Loading the Disk Driver

If your disk controller is a standard AT controller (this includes most MFM, RLL, and ESDI drives), load A:ISADISK. If your controller is an IDE type, load A:IDE. If your controller came with a customized disk driver, load that driver. Remember that the driver must match the disk controller, not necessarily the disk drive itself. NetWare wants to talk to the controller, and the controller talks to the drive.

Loading the NIC Driver

If you are using a Novell NE3200 card, load NE3200.LAN; if you are using the NE2000 or a compatible card, load NE2000.LAN; and so on. This driver should be available from the manufacturer of your network interface card. If it doesn't ship with the NIC itself, contact the manufacturer and acquire the current driver.

Loading A:2XUPGRDE.NLM

This is the special In-Place Upgrade NLM. The first thing that you should see when you load it is a warning message. It is an unambiguous declaration of the severity of the next action to be taken. If you approve of the next step, you will not be able to recover your 2.*x* file server short of reinstalling it from scratch. Make absolutely sure that you have adequately backed up your system before continuing.

Entering the DOS Partition Size (5MB–32MB)

You should use a larger DOS partition of around 15MB or so. The total on a large, gigabyte-range server disk is usually not noticeable, but the extra space can come in handy on the DOS partition. If you plan to load extra services at some time in the future, such as the SAA gateway, NACS, or any other substantial NLM-based services, their installation and maintenance is often more efficient if you have some slack space on the server's DOS partition.

Scanning of the Disks

The analysis of the file server disks is a critical step in the conversion. It is the only way that the previously installed volume structure can be maintained.

Mounting All Volumes and Monitoring That They Mount Successfully

If the volume or volumes don't mount successfully at this point, you should pursue the reasons right away. The fault often lies with the disk driver or the disk driver configuration.

Downing the Server and Going to DOS

At the file server console, type **DOWN** and press ⏎. Then type **EXIT** and press ⏎ to return to the DOS prompt.

Formatting the Drive-C Partition

Type **A:FORMAT C: /S /X**. The /X parameter is necessary for DR DOS when you are formatting a fixed disk. It's OK to format the drive, since the NetWare partition has already been reserved by now. Don't forget that you must specify that the partition will be bootable, and install the system files (/S).

Using COPY CON to Create the STARTUP.NCF File

The STARTUP.NCF file includes commands to load disk drivers and any necessary name-space modules (such as MAC, OS2, FTAM, and NFS). This step will help you avoid typing the opening commands and load statements every time you boot the file server. Of course, with a little luck, you'll only be booting it once before you continue with the NetWare 4.0 portion of the upgrade.

Performing an In-Place Upgrade from 3.11 to 4.0

At this point, you have only a 3.11 file system. The new operating system and utilities have not been installed in the SYSTEM and PUBLIC directories on volume SYS yet.

PREREQUISITE TASKS

Before you begin the upgrade process to 4.0, complete these prerequisite tasks:

1 • Use the NetWare 3.11 SALVAGE utility to restore deleted files.

2 • Make sure you have a fully functional backup.

3 • Log users out of the NetWare 3.11 server.

4 · If you are upgrading a 3.11 server into an existing Directory tree, find out the following information from the network supervisor:

  ‣ Tree name

  ‣ Which context to place this server in

  ‣ Administrator's name (user ADMIN or another user with Supervisor object rights in this context)

  ‣ Administrator's password

5 · Specify the frame type for Ethernet LAN drivers.

COMPLETING THE UPGRADE

To complete the upgrade to NetWare 4.0, follow these steps:

1 · Insert the NetWare 4.0 INSTALL disk in drive A, and run IN-STALL.BAT (or NWNSTLL.EXE). Just as if you were installing on a brand-new machine, this is the way to begin a NetWare 4.0 upgrade.

2 · Select *Upgrade NetWare v3.1x to v4.0*. This menu selection is the difference between an upgrade and a new installation.

3 · Press ↵ to accept the source and destination paths. The default source path is A:\, and the default destination path is C:\SERVER.40. If you would like to change either or both of these, do so now.

4 · Type the path to the STARTUP.NCF file if you have created one. If you've just finished the 2.x to 3.1x upgrade, you may have already created a STARTUP.NCF file. If you are starting with a 3.1x server that is already fully configured, your STARTUP.NCF file will generally be in the directory that contains SERVER.EXE. Supply the correct path to STARTUP.NCF if you have one.

5 · Type the file server name and press ↵. The file server name can be up to 47 characters long, with no control characters.

6 · Choose your disk driver.

- ▸ Press ↵ to see a list of disk drivers.

- ▸ Insert the driver disk.

- ▸ Highlight the driver for your disk.

- ▸ Press ↵.

- ▸ Enter the base I/O (PORT) address and press ↵.

- ▸ Enter the hardware IRQ and press ↵.

- ▸ Press ↵ to accept "Allow BIOS redirection…."

- ▸ Press F10 to continue.

- ▸ Press ↵ to acknowledge "Driver…was successfully loaded."

- ▸ Press ↵ to continue.

7 · This is an optional step: At the Copy NetWare Files screen, deselect file groups by pressing ↵. If you are in doubt, load all groups of files. There isn't a particularly persuasive reason to avoid loading any of them, unless you are very conservative of space.

8 · Press F10 to continue.

9 · Insert disks as prompted.

INSTALL will prompt you to insert a number of disks. If you want to make this step go faster, you can copy all the files to a single directory on the DOS partition (this is another example of where that extra space can come in handy). That done, specify the directory as the source drive at the beginning of the installation. In fact, the difference in speed is quite significant. It's a good trick if you are going to reinstall from time to time in a laboratory or test-bed environment, for example.

10 · Press ↵ when all files have been copied.

11 · Load the first LAN driver.

    ‣ Press ↵ to see a list of LAN drivers.

    ‣ Enter parameters for LAN drivers. Note that NetWare 4.0 supports Ethernet 802.3 and 802.2 frame types. If you are running on a multiple-server LAN, you will probably want to use the 802.3 frame type to maintain compatibility with earlier versions of NetWare when running Ethernet.

    ‣ Press ↵.

12 · This is an optional step: Repeat the previous step to load other LAN drivers. NetWare 4.0, like NetWare 3.1x, has no upper limit on how many NICs it can support. However, the physical limitation of the computer is usually around six NICs or less.

13 · Highlight *Continue with Installation* and press ↵.

14 · Upgrade bindery and volumes.

15 · Continue with the installation of NetWare Directory Services as described in Chapter 8.

Configuring NetWare Printing

6 · Load (or run) PSERVER.

7 · Run (or load) NPRINTER.

8 · Run CAPTURE.

9 · Send a print job.

The easiest way to configure NetWare print services is   *248*
to use the Quick Setup option of PCONSOLE.

In this chapter we'll look at some of the similarities and differences between local and network printing, and then we'll go into a fairly detailed explanation of just how the NetWare print services work. After that, we'll analyze some of the print utilities themselves, and finally, we'll perform a step-by-step installation of basic print services on a NetWare 4.0 LAN and then test them out by logging in to the network and printing.

Local vs. Network Printing

To the user, printing on a NetWare LAN is very much like printing in a stand-alone environment. However, in the background there are some fundamental differences.

LOCAL PRINTING

When you print from a standalone personal computer, there is a printer connected directly to a port on the computer. No one shares the printer, so it is dedicated to the needs of the person using that computer. This arrangement is very expensive, especially in a business setting where many people need access to printers almost constantly.

NETWORK PRINTING

Printing on a NetWare network allows many people to share individual printers. These printers can be attached to print servers, which are computers that are set up to control the activities of up to 256 separate printers, or they can be attached to normal workstations that run a small program to advertise their attached printer as a shared device.

This arrangement is much more economical, since it allows a group of people to pool their purchasing power and share the enhanced capabilities of a more expensive printer, saving the money they would have had to spend on individual printers.

How Does NetWare 4.0 Printing Work?

NetWare 4.0's print services are similar in concept to those in 3.x, but there are also significant differences. If you are experienced with earlier versions of Net-Ware, you will probably catch on fairly easily, but don't take the changes lightly; they are not trivial.

THE WORKSTATION

The basic job of the workstation is to send a print job to a NetWare queue. The print job is the same information that would normally go directly to the local printer port. It's not the file itself, but the print image information, usually generated by a software application.

The Application

Some applications can print directly to a NetWare print queue. WordPerfect was an early example of a "NetWare-aware" application that could print to a queue instead of a local printer port.

More commonly, the application sends the job to the DOS device LPT# (LPT1 through LPT9). Note that there's a difference between the DOS device LPT1 and the physical LPT1 port. If an application writes information directly to the port's I/O address instead of to the DOS device, NetWare utilities cannot intercept the job and redirect it to the network print queue.

If you're unsure whether your application is printing to the DOS device, configure it to print to a file called LPT1, LPT2, or LPT3. Most applications will support three printer ports, though NetWare 4.0 supports up to nine local printer configurations.

The Redirector

When you run VLM.EXE, one of the modules that should load is PRINT.VLM. This software handles print job redirection. In previous versions of NetWare, this function was part of NETX.COM. Another program, CAPTURE.EXE, works with PRINT.VLM to assign parameters and information about just how the print redirection should be handled. For more information on CAPTURE.EXE, see the command-line utilities overview in Part V.

THE FILE SERVER

The print queue is actually a directory on the file server, and each print job is a file in that directory. When a workstation sends a print job to the queue, a file is opened in the queue directory and when the job is complete, the file is closed.

Some people are confused about just where the print job is stored while it waits for an available printer. If you think about the print job as a file, it starts to make sense that it is stored on the file server. After all, what is the main job of a file server? To serve files!

In previous versions of NetWare, the print queues were always directories under SYS:SYSTEM with a pseudo-random hexadecimal number for a name and the extension .QDR. Except for the location, this is unchanged with NetWare 4.0. Now you can choose the volume that you want to hold the print queues, and they will be created in a directory called QUEUES. QUEUES will be directly under the root of the volume you specify.

THE PRINT SERVER

Just as with NetWare 2.2 (optionally) and 3.11, NetWare 4.0 print services are separate from the operating system. You may load them or not, as your requirements dictate. In fact, you can load the print services on the file server or on a dedicated DOS computer (called a print server).

The NetWare print server manages all print services for its configured printers. Once a complete print job is in the queue, the print server notices it and moves it from the queue to an appropriate printer. The print server is a combination travel agent and traffic cop for all print jobs on the NetWare highway.

A single print server can manage up to 256 network printers, with a maximum of 5 attached directly to the print server. In previous versions of NetWare, this limit was 16 printers. You can see that a single print server will now accommodate the entire printing environment that may have previously required numerous print servers.

Loading PSERVER.NLM on the File Server

The NetWare print server is available as a NetWare Loadable Module (PSER-VER.NLM), which can run on any NetWare 4.0 operating system, including a 4.0 file server, Multi-Protocol Router, communications server, backup server, etc. As long as NetWare 4.0 is running, you can load PSERVER.NLM along with other services.

If you have a fairly unsophisticated network with few demands made on the file server, you might decide that combining the tasks of managing print services with the normal file services will not make a significant difference to the stability or performance of your network. If that is the case, you can add the NetWare print services to the NetWare server by loading PSERVER.NLM.

Under normal circumstances, the demands of managing print services is not a big deal and should not affect your file server to a great degree. Remember that loading *any* NetWare Loadable Module on a file server will use RAM on the server that would otherwise go to file caching. If you are using a 486-based computer, you probably won't notice a slowdown due to CPU stress.

In previous versions of NetWare, there was a version of the print server that ran on top of DOS instead of the NetWare OS. With the release of NetWare 4.0, PSERVER.EXE is no longer an option.

THE PRINTER

You can attach a printer to the network in any of three ways:

- ▸ To the print server directly

- ▸ To a DOS workstation on the network

- ▸ Through a built-in network interface card connected directly to the network cable itself

Wherever the printer attaches to the network, the network printer utility, NPRINTER, must be loaded or somehow emulated. In previous versions of NetWare, this utility was called RPRINTER.EXE and was not available as a separate NLM.

Attaching a Printer to a Print Server

When a print server is physically located in a convenient place, it can be a good idea to attach the network printers (up to five per server) directly to the print server. If PSERVER.NLM is the form you're using, the printers would be attached directly to the NetWare server. In this case, NPRINTER.NLM will automatically load if the print server is configured to have a printer attached directly.

Attaching a Printer to a Workstation

If the printer is attached to a DOS workstation, that computer can run NPRINTER.EXE, a small "terminate-and-stay-resident" (TSR), or memory-resident, software utility that advertises the availability of the printer across the network to a particular print server.

When NPRINTER.EXE is running on a workstation, that workstation should always redirect local print jobs through the NetWare print services, instead of printing directly to its local printer.

Attaching a Printer Directly to the Network Cable

If the printer is equipped with a network interface card, you may be able to attach it directly to the network cable, bypassing the slower transmission media of parallel and serial interfaces. When compared with serial transmission, parallel transmission is about four to six times faster. When compared with parallel transmission, direct connection to the cable can be ten to fifty times faster, depending on the transmission media, protocol, etc. Realize that this speed improvement is not assured, however, because at a certain point, the internal formatting device of the printer cannot keep up with the potential of the network connection, so it becomes the bottleneck instead. Still, direct connection is the best way to improve printer throughput for a heavily used network printer.

It should be noted here that devices such as Intel's NetPort and the Microtest LANPort are not the type of network connection we're talking about. While they are very useful devices, they attach to the network and then go through serial or parallel interfaces to connect to the printer. As you can well imagine, using one of these devices is simply replacing a PC with another device to translate between the network cable and the printer port.

For direct connection to the network, a printer requires an expansion card that is configured and installed internally to the printer. Since it is an internal device, a single unit cannot service more than one printer. As a rule of thumb, if you don't have to open the printer with a screwdriver to get the network interface card installed, it's probably not what we're talking about.

Each implementation of this type of device will come with a way to affect the services of NPRINTER. Consult the printer or network interface card documentation to learn how to configure the card for NetWare 4.0. Don't count on a device designed for NetWare 3.11 to work automatically with a 4.0 network. You will likely need to get an upgrade of the software and possibly replace some or all of the components of the interface device itself.

The Print Job

Up until this point in the process, the print information has been generated by the application, redirected by CAPTURE.EXE and PRINT.VLM, stored at the file server in the print queue, and managed from that time forward by the print server. Once the information reaches the printer, it should be interpreted exactly as if it were going directly to a local printer. In effect, all the network processes are no more than a brief "layover" for the job itself. At this point it arrives and is transformed by the printer into hard copy.

The NetWare Print Utilities

Some of the NetWare print utilities are of primary importance and others are optional. You may never use them all, but there are some that you will not be able to do without. We will cover these utilities in depth in Part V, but we'll examine them briefly here so that you can get a general idea of what's used for which purposes.

THE CRUCIAL UTILITIES

There are four crucial NetWare printing utilities:

- ► PCONSOLE
- ► CAPTURE
- ► PSERVER
- ► NPRINTER

PCONSOLE

PCONSOLE.EXE is the print console utility. Use PCONSOLE to create, configure, and monitor print queues, print servers, and shared network printers. It is found in SYS:PUBLIC, so it can be used by any normal user of the network. However, what users can accomplish within PCONSOLE is limited by the types of users and their rights to perform certain actions.

CAPTURE

CAPTURE.EXE is the print job redirector. As we mentioned earlier, it works in conjunction with PRINT.VLM (part of the DOS/Windows NetWare requester) to allow non-NetWare-aware applications to use the network's printing services. Such applications usually allow printing only to a DOS printer, not to a NetWare print queue. CAPTURE.EXE configures the printing portion of the NetWare requester that is already loaded in a workstation's memory (PRINT.VLM) to accept and redirect any data bound for the local printer ports to the NetWare print queues instead.

PSERVER

As we've mentioned, PSERVER is a NetWare Loadable Module (PSERVER.NLM). Once you have configured your print server with PCONSOLE, load PSERVER and specify that print server's name. The print server utility loads with the configuration specifications set up in PCONSOLE.

Remember that PSERVER only reads the configuration of the print server at the time it loads. If you reconfigure the print server later, the changes will not be enabled until you unload PSERVER and reload it. At that time, the configuration information is loaded anew.

Also remember that you should never type DOWN PSERVER at a NetWare console. DOWN is a console command that accepts no parameters, so if you type DOWN, the NetWare server will shut down and discontinue any and all services that may be running on the server. If you want to reload PSERVER.NLM, type **UNLOAD PSERVER** and try reloading it once you have returned to the console colon (:) prompt.

NPRINTER

Also mentioned above, NPRINTER is the utility that advertises a shareable printer across the network. When a shared printer is attached to a workstation, NPRINTER.EXE must run at that workstation. It loads into memory at the workstation and does its job in the background while other DOS activities run in the foreground. The reduction in the workstation's performance is very small (around 2 percent according to some independent tests).

If the printer is attached directly to a NetWare server running PSERVER.NLM, NPRINTER.NLM loads automatically when PSERVER is loaded to advertise the printer across the network.

OPTIONAL PRINT UTILITIES

The utilities listed below are described in Part V. They are useful in configuring a NetWare printing environment, but even without them, you can create a printing environment on a NetWare LAN by using the utilities described in the preceding section.

- PSETUP.EXE

- PUPGRADE.NLM

- PRINTCON.EXE

- PRINTDEF.EXE

- ▸ NETUSER.EXE

- ▸ NPRINT.EXE

- ▸ PSC.EXE

Installing Basic NetWare Print Services

You can use either PCONSOLE or the NetWare Administrator graphical utility to create NetWare print objects. We will focus on PCONSOLE because it will be the most familiar print utility if you have worked with previous versions of NetWare. The basic steps involved in configuring NetWare printing are as follows:

1 · Create a print queue.

2 · Create a print server.

3 · Create a printer.

4 · Assign the printer to the print server.

5 · Assign the print queue to the printer.

6 · Load (or run) PSERVER.

7 · Run NPRINTER, if necessary.

8 · Run CAPTURE (at the workstation).

9 · Send a print job (at the workstation).

CREATING A PRINT QUEUE

Log in as a user with sufficient rights to create leaf objects at your chosen context. If your network is brand-new, ADMIN should work. At a DOS prompt, type

PCONSOLE

You should see an opening screen similar to the one shown in Figure 10.1.

The opening screen of
PCONSOLE

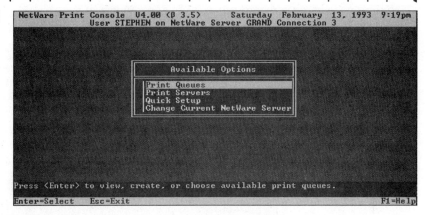

Make sure that Print Queues is highlighted, and press ↵. If your network is brand-new or has no print services installed yet, the list of print queues will be empty. As with most of the NetWare menu utilities, you can add to the list by pressing Insert. This should bring up a prompt similar to the one in Figure 10.2.

Type the name of your new print queue. It can be up to 57 characters long and cannot include any of the normal NetWare control characters (* : ;\ / | = + < > ? " [ ]). In Figure 10.2 a queue has been configured named *Q1*. Press ↵ to accept the queue name, then press Esc to return to the main menu.

Creating a print queue in
PCONSOLE

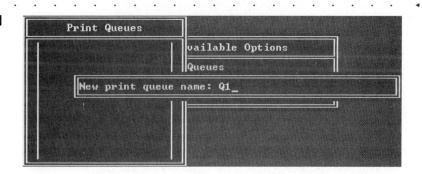

CREATING A PRINT SERVER

Highlight Print Servers and press ↵. As you can see in Figure 10.3, creating a print server is very similar to creating a print queue. Press Insert, enter a name for your print server (*PS1* in this example), press ↵, and then press ↵ again to select the new print server for configuration. You should see a menu similar to the one in Figure 10.4.

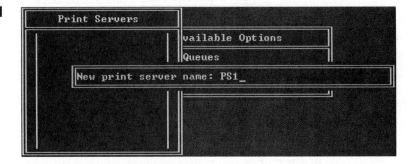

F I G U R E 10.3

Creating a print server with
PCONSOLE

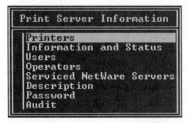

F I G U R E 10.4

The Print Server
Information menu in
PCONSOLE

CREATING A PRINTER

The first option on the Print Server Information menu is Printers. Make sure that Printers is highlighted and press ↵. Just as you did with the print queue and print server, press Insert to add a printer to what is probably a blank list. Type the name of the new printer (STEPHEN'S_HPLJ_IIIP in this example), and press ↵ to accept the name. Highlight the printer in the list and press ↵ once again to bring up a Printer Configuration screen similar to the one shown in Figure 10.5.

```
              Printer STEPHEN'S_HPLJ_IIIP Configuration
  Printer number:             0
  Printer status:             <Unavailable>
  Printer type:               Parallel
  Configuration:              <See form>
  Starting form:              0
  Buffer size in KB:          3
  Banner type:                Text
  Service mode for forms:     Minimize form changes within print queues
  Sampling frequency:         15
  Print queues assigned:      <See list>
  Notification:               <See list>
```

The *Printer number* field defines the relationship of this printer to the print server. Each NetWare 4.0 print server can manage up to 256 printers. Of course, if you have anywhere near that many printers on your network, we don't advise controlling all of them from one print server, but 256 is the theoretical maximum.

The *Printer status* field cannot be edited. It informs you about whether the printer is waiting, offline, out of paper, etc.

If you press ↵ while highlighting the *Printer type* field, you'll see a menu similar to the one shown in Figure 10.6. This is where you can define the printer's connection to the network. The most common options are Parallel (attached to a parallel, or LPT, port of a workstation or print server) and Serial (attached to a serial, or COM, port of a workstation or print server). You can also configure a network printer that attaches as a UNIX printer, a printer attached to an Apple-Talk network segment, an XNP (eXtended Network Printer) connection, an AIO (Asynchronous Input/Output) connection, or you can configure a printer as Remote Other/Unknown. You may need to choose Remote Other/Unknown for some printers that attach directly to the network cable.

Press ↵ while highlighting the Configuration field to go to the screen shown in Figure 10.7. This screen has some important details. First is the exact port to which the printer will be connected (LPT1, LPT2, or LPT3); the default is LPT1.

FIGURE 10.6

The Printer Type menu

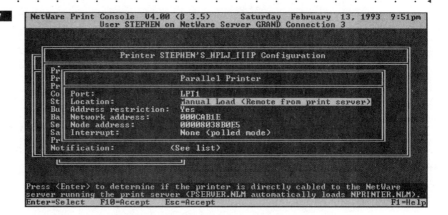

FIGURE 10.7

*Configuring a parallel
printer*

The second important field is Location. By default, this is defined as *Automatic Load (Local to print server),* which means that the printer is attached to one of the print server's ports directly. If this printer will be a remote printer (attached to a workstation running NPRINTER.EXE), you must change this field to *Manual Load (Remote from print server).*

In Figure 10.7 we have enabled the address restriction and defined a network and node address at which this printer will be connected. This might be useful if you have similar printers configured but want to avoid misdirected print jobs by explicitly defining where each printer is located.

The Interrupt field defaults to *None (polled mode),* which means that NetWare won't use the hardware interrupt request line (IRQ) normally associated with the particular port. Since standard parallel printers do not generate interrupts (they are purely output devices), polled mode is fine for them. Not using interrupts also avoids any possible conflict in a computer that may be configured with another device using what would normally be a parallel printer port's IRQ.

ASSIGNING THE PRINT QUEUE TO THE PRINTER

Toward the bottom of the Printer Configuration screen (Figure 10.5) is a field labeled *Print queues assigned.* Leaving this unconfigured is one of the most common mistakes in setting up a printing environment. This parameter defines what device can respond to jobs in any particular print queue. It is only at this critical point that the queue is connected to a printer.

Press ⏎ to see a list of the currently attached print queues, which will probably be blank. If you have created any print queues at this context, they will be displayed in this list. Highlight one of them and press ⏎. You should see a screen that requests a priority setting.

The default priority is 1, and the range is from 1 to 10. We recommend that you choose a priority other than 1 at this point. If every printer serves its queues at priority 5, the overall action will be identical to every printer serving its queue at priority 1. In fact, most network administrators don't utilize the print queue priority settings.

However, even if you don't plan on using the queue priorities anytime in the near future, configuring every queue at priority 5 will give you the possibility of configuring an URGENT or EMERGENCY queue sometime in the future. Actually, we've heard of at least one administrator who configured all the normal queues at priority 5, his own personal print queue at priority 3, and (after some pressuring) his manager's queue at priority 1 so that their waiting times would be minimized. We recommend that your configuration considerations be based on true performance needs instead of organizational status or techno-elitism.

LOADING (OR RUNNING) PSERVER

If you plan to print from a NetWare server, go to the server console and enter

> LOAD PSERVER *print_server_name*

substituting the name of the print server you configured in PCONSOLE for *print_server_name*.

You should see a main menu with two options on it: Printer Status and Print Server Information. Use Printer Status to see a list of the printers configured for that print server. Highlight one and press ↵ to see configuration information and status information, including Type, Current Status, Queues Serviced, Mounted Form, Printer Control, and more. Press ↵ at the Printer Control field to have direct control over the printer's functions, including Abort print job, Form feed, Mark top of form, Pause printer, Start printer, and Stop printer.

Return to the main menu (by pressing Esc), highlight Print Server Information, and press ↵. You will see a screen that displays the version of the print server software, the type of print server, the name of the print server, the number of printers, the number of queue service modes, and the current status of the print server. If you highlight Status and press ↵, you can choose to unload the print server, to unload the print server after the current print job is complete, or to leave its status as running.

RUNNING NPRINTER

If you are running PSERVER.NLM and the printer is configured to be attached to the print server, you don't have to load NPRINTER.NLM manually; it loads automatically.

If you have configured a printer that is attached to a workstation, you must go to that workstation after the print server is loaded and run NPRINTER.EXE. NPRINTER.EXE will not function correctly on a workstation running Windows in 386 enhanced mode.

The first NPRINTER screen shows a list of currently active print servers. Choose one and the next screen shows a list of that print server's available printers. Highlight the correct printer and press ↵ to load the NPRINTER driver into memory. From then on (until the workstation reboots), the printer will be available to users as a shared network printer.

RUNNING CAPTURE

Now go to any DOS workstation, and log in as a valid user. When your login is complete, change to the SYS:PUBLIC directory and type

CAPTURE /l=1 /nt /nb /ti=15 /Q = *print_queue*

where *print_queue* is the name of a queue (/Q) serviced by the printer you just enabled. The other parameters stand for Local Printer captured is LPT1 (/l=1), No Tab conversions (/nt), No Banner (/nb), and an inactivity Time Out of 15 seconds (/ti=15).

SENDING A PRINT JOB

The easiest way to send a test print job is to print from DOS, instead of from a program or an application. This makes certain that there are no configuration details in the software that might cause problems and make it seem that the print utilities were at fault.

An easy way to send a print job from DOS is to move to the SYS:PUBLIC directory and enter the following commands:

```
DIR *.EXE > LPT1
ECHO ^L > LPT1
```

The first line routes a listing of all files with the extension .EXE to the printer port (and if CAPTURE is working correctly, to the print queue). The second line sends a page-feed character to the same destination, so that the page will eject automatically when it is complete. To enter the page-feed character, press Ctrl-L.

An Easier Way to Skin This Cat: Quick Setup

We've focused on the PCONSOLE configuration method described in the previous section because it most closely resembles the method used in previous versions of NetWare. A new method added to PCONSOLE in version 4.0, however, makes the configuration process a good deal easier.

While logged in as ADMIN (or as any other user with sufficient rights to create a printing environment), go to SYS:PUBLIC and enter **PCONSOLE**. Instead of manually configuring a print queue, print server, and printers, choose Quick Setup. You should see a screen similar to the one shown in Figure 10.8.

If you have no print servers or print queues configured, Quick Setup will probably choose P1 as the printer name and Q1 as the print queue name. The print server will probably be PS-, followed by the name of your file server. You can change any of these names by highlighting the name fields, pressing ↵, and modifying the name you see displayed.

The banner type defaults to Text. If you have an Adobe PostScript–compatible printer, you can change the banner type to PostScript.

FIGURE 10.8

PCONSOLE's Print Services

Quick Setup screen

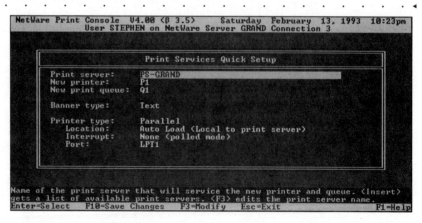

You can also change the default values from Auto Load (Local to print server) to Manual Load as we did in the previous example. Make sure that the Port configuration is correct before pressing F10 to save the configuration.

Wasn't that a whole lot easier than doing everything manually? Well, yes, but you don't have quite as much control over some of the configuration parameters, such as the queue service priority, the file servers to be serviced, and some other things. However, if your printing environment is fairly simple, this is a much better way to set up things.

From this point, the loading steps are identical to the previous example (load or run PSERVER, run NPRINTER, run CAPTURE, and print).

Security

Certain access rights can be granted to users or other objects so that they can access specific files or directories to complete assigned work. These rights include such things as Read, Write, and Erase. There are eight possible rights to a file or directory.

Rights to access files and directories on a NetWare 4.0 volume are controlled by trustee assignments to objects, such as users, that are part of the Directory tree.

Inheritance and security equivalence allow network administrators to make a few trustee assignments that affect a large number of users or access to a large part of the file system, if that is needed.

Access to the information stored in objects in the Directory tree is controlled by the same type of mechanisms used to access the file system. Trustee assignments are used to grant one object access to another object or its properties.

As in the file system, inheritance and security equivalence are used to avoid the need to make dozens of trustee assignments in an organization in order to complete even a simple task.

NetWare's powerful, granular security on objects includes the ability to control access to individual properties of an object.

In order to simplify the setup and operation of your network, NetWare will grant certain rights when it is first installed on your network. This will allow you to begin working without immediately entering trustee assignments yourself.

NetWare also creates certain trustee assignments when you create certain classes of objects or create a home directory for new users. Again, these things are done to allow you to work without first creating trustee assignments. When you have set up objects in your Directory tree and determined their access needs more fully, you can create or change trustee assignments.

Using the NetWare Utilities to Grant Rights   277

NetWare provides several utilities to grant rights and check access to files, directories, and objects. These include command-line utilities, menu utilities, and graphical (GUI) utilities.

The GUI NetWare Administrator utility is usually the easiest place to see and change trustee assignments, though you need a fast computer with a good color display and a lot of memory to appreciate using it. You can also perform all necessary security functions in the NetWare Administrator.

In contrast, if you prefer to use the character-based menu utilities, you must use NETADMIN to work with object rights, and FILER to work with file and directory rights.

The command-line utility packs all of the functionality of FILER into one command. It can be difficult to learn to use, but is the fastest way to make assignments or changes once you are familiar with it. You cannot change rights to objects from the command line; you can change only rights to files and directories.

NetWare 4.0's security system involves the assigning of various rights to users and administrators. Default settings allow operation of a simple network without an in-depth understanding of all of these new features. However, if you are operating a large network, or if you are particular about protecting the data on your network, you will want to take the time to learn all about the security options that NetWare 4.0 has to offer.

Although rights security is one of the most powerful features of NetWare 4.0, it can be a challenge to learn to use every option effectively. The options include file system rights, object and property rights, trustees and trustee assignments, inheritance, security equivalence, effective rights, and using rights to control access to the Directory tree.

You can use these security features to define roles in NetWare 4.0 to create positions with exactly the authority that you feel is needed to complete assigned tasks.

Another major benefit of 4.0 security features is the possibility to divide the administration of the network among several individuals, each with authority over only their area of the Directory tree.

Used correctly, the security system in NetWare 4.0 can provide you with a highly secure, very structured, and understandable networking environment.

Rights in the File System

Rights to the file system in 4.0 are basically identical to those that were used for NetWare 3.11, though a few differences will be mentioned later.

Basically, a user is given rights to any file or directory by a *trustee assignment* that is created by a network administrator. Any user who has rights to a file is a trustee of that file. A trustee assignment contains a list of rights that are granted to a certain user for the file where the trustee assignment is created.

Inheritance allows a trustee assignment that is granted at one point to apply to everything below that point in the file structure. Because of inheritance, network administrators do not have to create trustee assignments for every file that every user needs to use. Inheritance is the main reason that rights can be granted to directories. If a trustee assignment grants a user certain rights, that trustee (user) has those same rights to every file and subdirectory in the directory where the trustee assignment was granted.

A distinction must be made here between a trustee who has *explicit rights* to a file and a trustee who has *implicit rights* to a file. Explicit rights are granted to a file when a user has a trustee assignment on that file. Implicit rights are granted when a user does not have a trustee assignment to the file, but inherits rights from another trustee assignment.

For an example of how inheritance works, see Figure 11.1.

▶ . . . . ◀

How inheritance works, a simple example

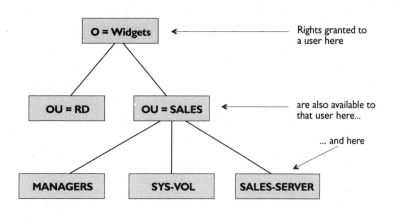

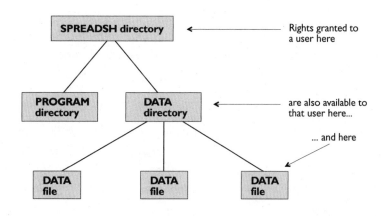

Suppose that you do not want anyone to inherit rights to a certain file. You can *block* all trustees from inheriting rights to a particular file by creating an *Inherited Rights Filter* for that file. An Inherited Rights Filter contains a list of rights, just as a trustee assignment does, but the rights listed in the filter are not granted to any user; rather, they are the rights that a trustee who already has them can keep for the file where the Inherited Rights Filter is created. If a right that the trustee was granted is not listed in the Inherited Rights Filter, that right is blocked by the Inherited Rights Filter and cannot be used by the user to which it was assigned.

Another key mechanism used to simplify the assignment of rights to files and directories is *security equivalence*. If a network administrator decides that one user should have all of the rights that another user has been granted, the network administrator can make the first user security-equivalent to the second user, and the first user will then have all of the rights that the second user was granted.

The rights that a user can actually use for a file or directory are called that user's *effective rights*. These are a combination of a user's trustee assignments, inheritance, and security-equivalent rights, as shown in Figure 11.2.

All of the trustee assignments for a file, as well as the Inherited Rights Filter, are stored in the Directory Entry Table for the file or directory where they are granted. In order to change a file or directory's trustee assignments or Inherited Rights Filter, you must have rights to the file, specifically a right called the *Access Control right*. All of the possible rights to files and directories are discussed below.

We have been talking about how users are able to access files by having trustee assignments. Now we need to expand that idea, because any *object* in the Directory tree can be granted a trustee assignment to a file or directory. In previous versions of NetWare, only users and groups could be trustees. But in NetWare 4.0, a Profile object can be a trustee of a directory (for example), or an Organizational Unit object can be a trustee of a file. This makes it much easier to assign similar rights to a large group of people. We will see how in the next section.

As we talk about granting rights to users and other objects, a question may come to mind about whether there exists a special user account for a network administrator or supervisor who can always make the necessary trustee assignments. This type of account existed as the SUPERVISOR account in previous versions of NetWare, but this is no longer the case in NetWare 4.0. There is no

FIGURE 11.2

F I G U R E 11.2

How effective rights work

If User TOM needs access to a file:

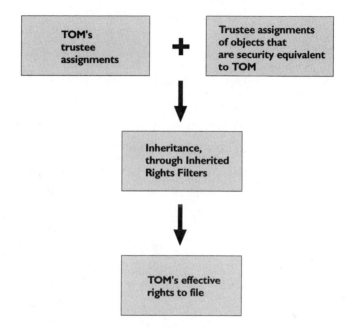

"superuser" who can log in and always make the necessary trustee assignments and rights changes. Instead, certain regular user objects in the Directory tree must be granted the rights to make changes. We will see much more about this when we talk about rights that objects have to change each other.

Directory Rights

The following lists the rights that a trustee can be granted to work on a directory in the file system. In many situations, you will see only the first character used by itself to indicate the right that has been granted.

RIGHT	DESCRIPTION
Supervisor	Grants all rights to the directory, its files, and subdirectories. The Supervisor right cannot be blocked by an Inherited Rights Filter. Users with this right can grant other users rights to the directory, its files, and subdirectories.
Read	Grants the right to open files in the directory and read their contents or run the programs.
Write	Grants the right to open and change the contents of files in the directory.
Create	Grants the right to create new files and subdirectories in the directory. If Create is the only right granted to a trustee for the directory, and no other rights are granted below the directory, a *drop-box directory* is created. In a drop-box directory, you can create a file and write to it. Once the file is closed, however, only a trustee with more rights than Create can see or update the file. You can copy files or subdirectories into the directory and assume ownership of them, but other users' rights are revoked.
Erase	Grants the right to delete the directory, its files, and subdirectories.
Modify	Grants the right to change the attributes or name of the directory and of its files and subdirectories, but does not grant the right to change their contents. (That requires the Write right.)
File Scan	Grants the right to see the directory and its files with the DIR or NDIR directory command.

RIGHT	DESCRIPTION
Access Control	Grants the right to change the trustee assignments and Inherited Rights Filter of the directory and of its files and subdirectories.

File Rights

The following lists the rights that a trustee can be granted to work on a file stored on any NetWare volume. In many situations, you will see only the first character used by itself to indicate the right that has been granted.

RIGHT	DESCRIPTION
Supervisor	Grants all rights to the file. The file Supervisor right cannot be blocked with an Inherited Rights Filter. Users who have this right can also grant other users any rights to the file, and can change the file's Inherited Rights Filter.
Read	Grants the right to open and read the file.
Create	Grants the right to salvage the file after it has been deleted.
Write	Grants the right to open and write to an existing file.
Erase	Grants the right to erase (delete) the file.
Modify	Grants the right to change the attributes and name of the file, but does not grant the right to change its contents. (That requires the Write right.)
File Scan	Grants the right to see the file with the DIR or NDIR directory command, including the directory structure from that file to the root directory.

RIGHT	DESCRIPTION
Access Control	Grants the right to change the trustee assignments and Inherited Rights Filter of the file.

Objects: A Simple Review

Let's do a quick review of objects in NetWare Directory Services. Objects are entries in a database that hold information about organizational structure, or about physical things on the network such as volumes, printers, and users. The objects in the database are organized in a tree structure, which makes some objects higher in the tree than others. We usually imagine the tree as having branches flowing down instead of growing up.

Objects that contain other objects underneath them in this analogy are container objects. These include Country, Organization, and Organizational Unit objects. Objects that cannot contain other objects are called leaf objects, and include things like Users, Printers, and Groups (a Group has a list of User objects, but it does not *contain* those User objects). A special case is the Volume object, which is both a leaf object in the Directory tree and the root directory of a physical volume. You must keep in mind the dual nature of this object, so that you can recognize where information that is presented in a volume comes from.

Think of an object as a box. Boxes can have other boxes beneath them in the Directory tree's hierarchical structure. The boxes are filled with information about the thing that the box represents. The pieces of information inside the box are the object's *properties*. One object can contain a great deal of information in its properties. A User object in particular holds a lot of information about a user and that user's account. This includes things like the user's password restrictions, login restrictions, station restrictions, group memberships, login script, etc.

Security in NetWare 4.0 allows us to control access to each object (box) individually, and also to each property (piece of information in the box) individually. We can grant access to the box without granting access to see inside the box, or we can grant access to see and change some information in the box, but not grant access to see other information in the same box.

This "granularity" of control allows great flexibility and power to the rights system. Unfortunately, it can make things enormously complex if good planning and a sound understanding do not precede our actions.

OBJECT AND PROPERTY RIGHTS

Access to the objects and properties of objects in Directory Services is controlled by two new sets of rights: object rights and property rights. This is a new concept in NetWare 4.0: instead of a user just having rights to the file system, a user can also have rights to another user, or more specifically, to see or change the information about that user stored in a User object. Object and property rights are different from the file and directory rights that are used in the file system, because different information must be protected.

First, we'll list the object and property rights that are used in NetWare 4.0 to access objects and the information that they contain. Then we can talk about how file-system concepts like trustees and inheritance apply to objects.

Object Rights

The following lists the rights that any trustee can be granted to work on any object in the NDS Directory tree. Except for the Supervisor object right, the object rights do not affect what a trustee can do with the object's properties. In many situations, you will see only the first character used by itself to indicate the right that has been granted.

RIGHT	DESCRIPTION
Browse	Grants the right to see the object in the Directory tree. The name of the object is returned when a search is made and matches the object.

RIGHT	DESCRIPTION
Create	Grants the right to create a new object below this object in the Directory tree. Rights are not defined for the new object. This right is available only on container objects, because non-container objects cannot have subordinates.
Delete	Grants the right to delete the object from the Directory tree. Objects that have subordinates cannot be deleted (the subordinates must be deleted first).
Rename	Grants the right to change the name of the object, in effect changing the naming property. This changes what the object is called in complete names.
Supervisor	Grants all access privileges. A trustee with the Supervisor object right also has unrestricted access to all properties. The Supervisor object right can be blocked by the Inherited Rights Filter below the object where the Supervisor right is granted.

Property Rights

The following lists the rights that any trustee can be granted to work on the properties of an object. These rights can be granted to a trustee for all of an object's properties, or for just one of an object's properties. In many situations, you will see only the first character used by itself to indicate the right that has been granted.

RIGHT	DESCRIPTION
Compare	Grants the right to compare any value to a value of the property. With the Compare right, an operation can return True or False, but you cannot see the value of the property. The Read right includes the Compare right.
Read	Grants the right to read the values of the property. Compare is a subset of Read. If the Read right is given, Compare operations are also allowed.
Write	Grants the right to add, change, or remove any values of the property. The Write right includes the Add or Delete Self right.
Add or Delete Self	Grants a trustee the right to add or remove itself as a value of the property. The trustee cannot affect any other values of the property. This right is only meaningful for properties that contain object names as values, such as group membership lists or mailing lists. The Write right includes the Add or Delete Self right.
Supervisor	Grants all rights to the property. The Supervisor property right can be blocked by an object's Inherited Rights Filter.

Rights are granted to objects and their properties in the same way that rights are granted to files and directories: through trustee assignments. As we described for the file system, however, any object can be a trustee of any other object. All of the rights in the tables above are used to grant one object access to another object and its properties.

Inheritance is still an important concept when granting object rights to trustees. If I grant a trustee assignment to a container object, the trustee has the same rights to all leaf objects in that container unless an Inherited Rights Filter blocks some or all of those rights. See Figure 11.3. (The figure shows object rights, but it could include property rights as well.) As in the file system, if a trustee has a trustee assignment on the container object, and a trustee assignment on a leaf object within that container, only the trustee assignment to the leaf object is valid; the rights that would have been inherited are not added to the explicit trustee assignment on the leaf object.

A trustee assignment to an *object* can include rights to the *properties* of that object as well. Such property rights can be assigned in two ways:

- I can grant a trustee the *All Properties right* to the properties of an object. If I grant the trustee the All Properties right, then those rights apply for that trustee to every property of the object for which specific property rights are not granted.
- Or I can grant a trustee *Specific Property rights* to one property of an object. If I grant a trustee Specific Property rights to one or several properties, then only access to those properties is defined, and that access overrides what would have been the default property rights from the All Properties right assignment.

Using the All Properties and Specific Property methods together to grant property rights to a trustee is useful when we want to control access to particularly

FIGURE 11.3

A user can have object rights to a container, but those rights can be blocked by an Inherited Rights Filter.

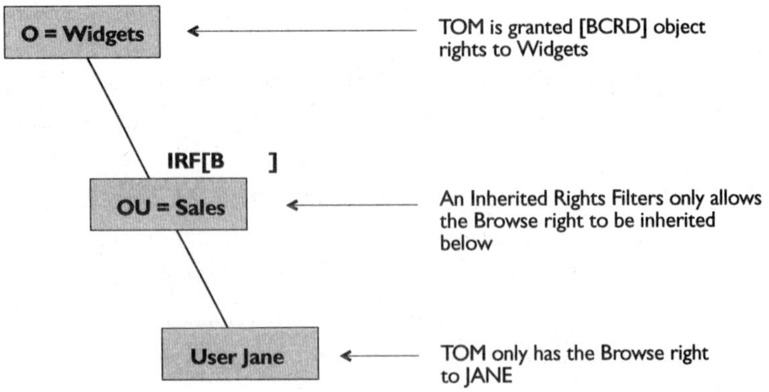

sensitive properties in an object. For example, we want a user to be able to read all of the properties of a Printer object, but not change any of them, so we grant Read All-Property rights. But if we want a user to be able to change all properties of a Profile object except the Login Script property, which the user should only be able to read, then we can grant both Write All-Property rights and Read Specific-Property rights to the Login Script property. The All Property assignment applies to every property of the profile except Login Script, which has a Specific Property assignment.

In NetWare Directory Services, it is important to know where trustee assignments to an object and an object's Inherited Rights Filter are stored. All are stored as entries in the Object Trustees–Access Control List (ACL) property of each object.

To change trustee rights or the Inherited Rights Filter of a file or directory, you must have the Access Control right to that file or directory. To change rights to an object or its properties, or an object's Inherited Rights Filter, you must have the Write Property right to the ACL property of that object. If you do, then you manage that object.

Inheritance with Object and Property Rights

Inheritance is even more important when working with objects than it is when working with files and directories. The reason is that objects must have both rights to other objects and rights to the file system in order for work to be done. A user must have rights to its own object, to the profile script that it uses, to printing objects that it uses, and to all areas of the file system that it will access in order to complete assigned tasks. If we did not have inheritance to assist in granting everyone rights to necessary areas, it might be impossible to keep up with the security needs of the users on a large network.

With inheritance, however, it is quite easy to make assignments to a large number of users with one trustee assignment.

Inheritance in NetWare 4.0 is just like the inheritance that one uses in the file system. If I grant User Jill a trustee assignment to a container object such as an Organization, then Jill has those same rights to every leaf object within that Organization. See Figure 11.4. (For simplicity, only object rights are shown in the figure.) If there are any Organizational Unit container objects in the Organization, then Jill's rights continue to flow down into that container. This continues to every object that is underneath the Organization where the original trustee assignment was made, unless an Inherited Rights Filter blocks the inheritance of the original trustee assignment at a lower level. If the Inherited Rights Filter is on a container object, then the rights are blocked for everything below that container, not just for that container object.

Suppose that all or several Directory Map objects pointing to all of your main application software packages are located under one of three organizational units in your Directory tree. User Megan needs to access all of these applications by having rights to each of the Directory Map objects that contains paths to applications that she uses. You could grant a trustee assignment to Megan for each of the Directory Map objects that she needs. That could take hours, and would be

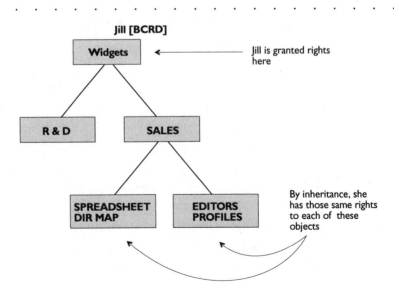

F I G U R E 11.4

Jill inherits object rights to lower objects in the Directory tree because she has a trustee assignment above.

Jill [BCRD]

Widgets ← ——————— Jill is granted rights here

R & D   SALES

SPREADSHEET DIR MAP   EDITORS PROFILES

By inheritance, she has those same rights to each of these objects difficult to update later when changes occurred. Now suppose instead that you grant Megan rights to the Organizational Unit APPLICATIONS that holds all of the Directory Map objects. By inheritance, Megan would have those same rights to each of the Directory Map objects within the APPLICATIONS Organizational Unit.

Remember this, however: only object rights and All Properties rights are inherited, or flow down the tree. Because specific property rights might grant rights to a property that does not exist on the object below, only the All Properties right is inherited and then applies to all properties of the object below. For example, if you grant a trustee rights to the Login Script property of an Organizational Unit, the trustee cannot inherit rights to the Login Script property of a Directory Map object in that Organizational Unit—because Directory Maps don't have login scripts. The trustee's All Properties assignment to the Organizational Unit would be inherited for the Directory Map.

In the previous example, we assume that no Inherited Rights Filters on the Directory Map objects are blocking Megan from inheriting the rights that are granted on the container APPLICATIONS. Objects also use Inherited Rights Filters to control the flow of inheritance, but the Inherited Rights Filter for objects must be more powerful than the one used for a file or directory in order to deal with the increased number of rights used with objects and properties.

We mentioned that only object and All Properties rights are inherited. The Inherited Rights Filter, however, can contain entries for each specific property of an object. Why is this so? First of all, the Inherited Rights Filter is not inherited itself, but is a part of each object, so the properties that it must apply to never change. Second, this allows the All Properties rights that are inherited from above to be selectively blocked for each property.

For example, suppose that you create an Inherited Rights Filter for a Group object named AUDITORS. You don't care if others read the identification information about this object, but you don't want anyone who does not have an explicit trustee assignment to that object to see who is a member of the auditing team. You create an Inherited Rights Filter for the object that includes:

▶ the Browse object right so that others can see the object;

▶ the Read All-Properties right, so that the identification information about this object can be seen but not changed by those with rights above this point;

▶ a Specific entry in the Inherited Rights Filter for the Members property that includes no rights, so that no one who is not granted rights explicitly to this property can read that membership list. Of course, if a trustee had the Supervisor object right, the trustee would also have access to all properties of the object, regardless of which property rights are inherited or blocked.

See Figure 11.5, which shows the details of this example, including both object and property rights.

Another important concept about the Inherited Rights Filter for an object is that it can block the Supervisor object or property right. Let me repeat that: The Inherited Rights Filter of an object can block the Supervisor object right or the Supervisor property right.

This can only be done under certain conditions: namely, that a trustee with the Supervisor object right already exists on the object where you want to block the Supervisor right from being inherited. The trustee with the Supervisor object right at that point is a manager of that branch of the tree. You cannot remove the Supervisor object right from that trustee's trustee assignment until the Supervisor right is added to the Inherited Rights Filter so it can be inherited again. This prevents cutting off supervisor-level access to a branch of the Directory tree.

At least it tries to. If you had a trustee who was the supervisor of a branch of the Directory tree, and some other supervisor deleted that User's object (not the trustee assignment, but the User object itself), then the trustee assignment would be invalid and there would be no supervisor of that area of the tree. If that part of the tree included a server and volumes, then Supervisor-level access to the file systems on those volumes might also be cut off.

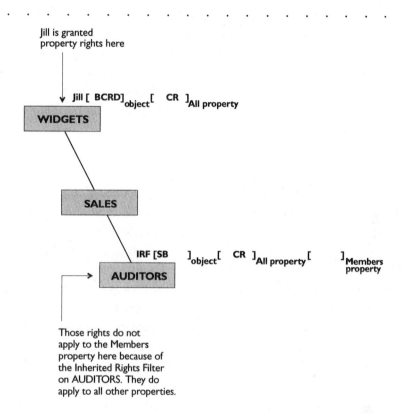

Jill cannot see the Members property of the AUDITORS group because an Inherited Rights Filter blocks Jill's rights.

Be careful when blocking the Supervisor object right. You must keep track of which users are branch supervisors and take care not to delete their User objects. NetWare utilities will not stop you from deleting a user even though the user is the only trustee with Supervisor rights to a part of the Directory tree.

Let's talk more about access to the file system through the Directory tree. Access to the file system is not automatic for any user. Access comes through the NetWare Server object representing the NetWare server to which a volume is physically attached. Any user that has Supervisor rights to a NetWare Server object will automatically have the Supervisor directory right to the root directory of every volume attached to that server.

Because the utilities have safeguards to prevent cutting off Supervisor-level access to part of the Directory tree, every object should always have a supervisor (or several supervisors), including every NetWare Server object. This attempts to ensure that every volume has a least one trustee with supervisor-level access at the root directory. A trustee with this access could then grant explicit trustee assignments to the root directory, granting someone rights that did not come through the server object. This might provide a safeguard if you are concerned about cutting off access. Of course, it is also less secure to have more supervisors.

Security Equivalence

The concept of security equivalence that we talked about for the file system is based on the idea that one object can be equivalent in rights to another object. That idea is used even more for rights to other objects in the NDS Directory tree. A User object can be security-equivalent to any other object. Each User object has a property that lists all of the objects that the user is security-equivalent to. The user has all of the rights granted to itself, plus all of the rights granted to each of the objects listed in its security equivalence property. Other objects do not have a security equivalence property.

Besides the objects listed in a User's security equivalence property, every object has three other security equivalences that are not shown anywhere and cannot be changed. These three extra security equivalences apply to every object, and not just to User objects:

1 • Every object is security-equivalent to the [Public] trustee, which is used mainly to grant rights to users who have not even logged in to Directory Services, such as the \LOGIN directory on a SYS volume. You probably won't use the [Public] trustee much anyway.

2 • Every object is security-equivalent to the [Root] object. This allows you to grant [Root] a trustee assignment to a file, a directory, or another object, and every object in the Directory tree will have those rights by security equivalence to [Root]. For example, you could make [Root] a trustee of your electronic mail directory so that everyone in the Directory tree would have rights to that directory.

3 · Every object is security-equivalent to all of the container objects that are part of its complete name. For example, in Figure 11.6, user TOM is security-equivalent to Organizational Unit SALES, Organizational Unit WEST, and Organization WIDGETS_INC. This security equivalence is not listed anywhere, but you can always see what an object is security-equivalent to by looking at its complete name. You also cannot change this security equivalence. Every object is always security-equivalent to the containers above it.

The third special security equivalence above provides one of NetWare Directory Service's most powerful security features. You can grant every user in a container rights to a file simply by granting the Organizational Unit a trustee assignment to the file. This operates like a group object, but with several

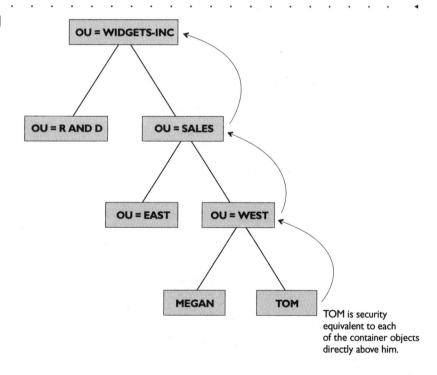

TOM is security-equivalent to all of the container objects above him in the Directory tree.

TOM is security equivalent to each of the container objects directly above him.

advantages. First, the membership of the group is automatic. You don't have to list member users, and when a user is no longer in the Organizational Unit, you don't have to change any trustee assignments—the user is automatically *not* security-equivalent to the Organizational Unit, and all of the rights granted to the Organizational Unit are *not* applied to that user.

Group objects should be used in place containers as trustees when the users that are part of the group are a subset of the users in a group, or a combination of a few users from each of several containers. See Figure 11.7.

You must remember three important points about security equivalence to use it effectively.

> ▶ **Security equivalence is not transitive.** That is, if Jill is security-equivalent to Tom, and Tom is security-equivalent to Maria, Jill is *not* security-equivalent to Maria through Tom. Only one level is resolved. This also applies to the security equivalence that each object has to every container above it. You cannot make TOM security-equivalent to

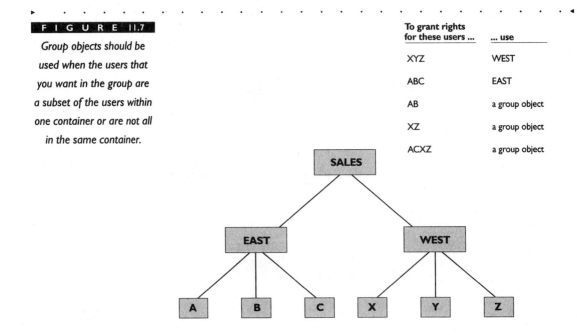

FIGURE 11.7

Group objects should be used when the users that you want in the group are a subset of the users within one container or are not all in the same container.

To grant rights for these users ...	... use
XYZ	WEST
ABC	EAST
AB	a group object
XZ	a group object
ACXZ	a group object

Organizational Unit SALES by making him security-equivalent to JANE, who *is* in SALES, because the only additional rights that TOM will have are those granted by explicit trustee assignment to JANE.

▸ **Security equivalence applies to the file system as well as objects.** That is, if Jill is granted a trustee assignment to a file, and Tom is security-equivalent to Jill, then Tom can access all the *files* that Jill has rights to, and not just all the *objects* that Jill has rights to.

▸ **Special rights are needed to make a user security-equivalent to another object.** The rights are special because they are different than the rights needed to perform any other action. In order to make BILL security-equivalent to MEGAN, you must list MEGAN in the security-equivalence property of BILL. But to do this, you do not need any rights to the security-equivalence property of BILL. Instead, you must manage User MEGAN, which means that you must have at least the Write property right to the ACL property of MEGAN. You do not need any rights at all to BILL.

This odd arrangement prevents you from adding to a security equivalence list people who have more rights than you do, and then using that security equivalence to gain Supervisor-level rights to a part of the Directory tree or file system.

What is security equivalence used for? We suggest three areas where it is useful. The first is when rights are granted to a Group or Organizational Role object. Any User listed as a member or occupant of the Group or Organizational Role is automatically listed as security-equivalent to that object, so that any rights granted to the Group are also granted to every user in the group.

Second, use security equivalence to temporarily grant one person all access to another persons' data while that person is away on vacation or business. Remember, however, that this also grants all rights to the user's home directory and personal data.

Third, use security equivalence to provide backup supervisors for areas of your Directory tree. For example, Jill is granted Supervisor right to an area of the tree and manages it from day to day. Tom is made security-equivalent to Jill so that if she is unavailable, Tom has the same rights to complete her tasks. By using security equivalence, Tom always has the same rights as Jill, even though Jill's rights change over time.

[Public] Trustee

A special case of granting rights is the [Public] trustee. [Public] is similar to the GUEST or EVERYONE account is NetWare 3.11, but operates a little differently. [Public] is used to grant rights to anyone who does not have other rights granted. Even users who are not logged in to the network have all rights that are granted to [Public]. Nevertheless, [Public] is not a real object of any kind, and no one can log in as [Public]. It simply says "if other rights are not granted to the person requesting access, grant these rights."

[Public] can always be entered as a trustee when creating a new trustee assignment, but should be used sparingly if at all because it grants rights to users who are not even logged in. It can be blocked by an Inherited Rights Filter, like any other trustee assignment. Do not confuse the [Public] trustee, used to grant rights, with the \PUBLIC directory on every SYS: volume, which holds utility programs that all users access.

Effective Rights

We have talked about many different ways that rights are assigned in Directory Services. Let's regroup by examining how effective rights to a file or to an object and its properties are determined.

Look at Figure 11.8 to see an example of how TOM's effective rights to a file are determined by NetWare each time TOM requests access to the file. Tom's effective file rights can come from any of the following:

1 · TOM's trustee assignments to the file, if there are any

2 · Inherited rights from Tom's trustee assignments to parent directories of the file, if nothing exists from 1

3 · Trustee assignments to objects that Tom is security-equivalent to, such as Group objects, or the containers above TOM.

If a user has a trustee assignment to a directory on a given level in the directory structure, and also one on a higher level, the current trustee assignment overrides the previous one. Trustee assignments to security-equivalent objects, such as Groups, however, are added to individual User trustee assignments.

Now that you know something about how rights work, let's see what rights are put in place automatically when we install NetWare 4.0 and create objects, and what additional rights you might need to grant to create a functioning Directory tree and network.

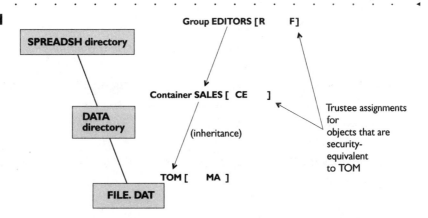

FIGURE 11.8

Tom's effective file rights are composed of several parts.

Group EDITORS [R   F]

SPREADSH directory

Container SALES [CE   ]

DATA directory

(inheritance)

Trustee assignments for objects that are security-equivalent to TOM

TOM [MA]

FILE. DAT

TOM's effective rights to FILE. DAT = [RCEMAF]

Rights Granted during Installation

Now that you know how rights work in 4.0, lets look at what rights are assigned during the installation process to get you started.

When you install your first NetWare 4.0 server, a Directory tree is created with several objects in place. An Organization object, an Organizational Unit object, a NetWare Server object, a Volume object for each volume attached to the server, and a User object named ADMIN are all created under the [Root] of the Directory tree.

During installation, User ADMIN is granted the Supervisor object right to the root object of the Directory tree. This allows ADMIN, the first user on the network, to perform any action on any object, because the trustee assignment on the [Root] object is inherited for all objects.

Similarly, the [Public] trustee is granted a trustee assignment to the [Root] object with the Browse object right. This allows all users on the network to see all objects in the Directory tree. You will probably want to remove this assignment if your network is large or your security demands are anything but simplistic. However, this provides a starting point so that everyone can work without the need to first create many trustee assignments. Some time may be needed before all of your users understand the idea of the Directory tree and of locating their User object in the tree to log in.

Another important trustee assignment is created when you create a SYS Volume object. This trustee assignment allows users to begin using the network and NetWare utilities without first creating many trustee assignments. The container of the SYS: volume is granted Read and File Scan Directory rights to the \PUBLIC directory of the SYS: volume. By security equivalence, this means that all users in the same container as the SYS: volume can access the utilities and information stored in the \PUBLIC directory.

When you create a new User in the Directory tree, you are prompted to create a home directory for the new user at the same time by simply specifying a path and directory name.

If you choose to create the home directory while creating the new user, the new user is granted all rights to the newly-created home directory. The new user can then log in to the network and have access to both the \PUBLIC directory for networking utilities and to a home directory on the network for personal work, all without special trustee assignments being made by the network administrator. If your user objects are created in the same container as the SYS: volume, and you create a home directory for each user when it is created, you will not have to create any additional trustee assignments for your users to be able to log in and work with the directory. The only catch is that a little additional work will be required to be able to access printing services.

Setting Rights with the NetWare Utilities

The default trustee assignments that are created when you install NetWare 4.0 allow users to begin working almost immediately. But how do you make other trustee assignments to serve other needs?

NetWare 4.0 provides two administrative utilities with which you can make trustee assignments. One is the text-menu utility NETADMIN. The other is the graphical utility NetWare Administrator, which can be run from Windows or OS/2.

If you are using the NETADMIN text utility, you can view or change the trustees and Inherited Rights Filters of a selected object by choosing "View or Edit the Trustee Assignments to this Object." You can also view or change the selected object's rights to files and directories on a volume by choosing "View or Edit this Object's Rights to Files and Directories."

The NETADMIN utility does not allow you to work directly with files and directories. You should use the FILER menu utility or the RIGHTS command-line utility to grant rights or change the Inherited Rights Filter of files and directories.

If you prefer to use the graphical NetWare Administrator, there are more options available. You can use the Object menu to view or change the trustees and Inherited Rights Filter of a selected object with "Trustees of this Object," or view or change the trustee assignments that the selected object has to other objects with "Rights to Other Objects."

The NetWare Administrator also includes the ability to work directly with files and directories. If you select a file or directory, you can choose "Details" from the Object menu and then view or change the trustees and Inherited Rights Filter of the selected file or directory with the "Trustees of this..." page. If you select an object and then open an object dialog with "Details," you can view or change the selected object's rights to files and directories on a volume with the "Rights to the File System" page.

In general, when using the NetWare Administrator, you use the Object menu to work with rights to files and directories, and the "Details" pages to work with rights to files and directories.

You need to be careful when working with volumes in the NetWare Administrator, however, because a Volume object displays both object properties and information about the root directory of the file system on that volume. Keep your eyes on which rights are listed in the dialog, and remember the rule in the preceding paragraph to keep track of which type of rights you are working on.

PART III

Creating the
User Environment

CHAPTER 12

Setting Up DOS and Windows Workstations

Fast Track

- ▶ Copies Windows-specific NetWare drivers, libraries, and files to the Windows program and SYSTEM directories
- ▶ Modifies Windows configuration files for using Windows with NetWare

Troubleshooting Windows workstations and troubleshooting DOS workstations 292

begin with the same procedures. Since Windows operates on a DOS platform, you should configure NetWare for DOS and Windows workstations to run on DOS first, and then you can pay attention to Windows-specific configuration parameters.

Workstations running MS-DOS 6.0 293

have advantages when troubleshooting CONFIG.SYS and AUTO-EXEC.BAT files. Use the F5 key at boot-up to bypass the CONFIG.SYS and AUTOEXEC.BAT files altogether, and the F8 key to confirm each line of code in the CONFIG.SYS file. This technique can uncover many DOS boot errors.

The NET.CFG file 294

must be in the same directory as your NetWare workstation ODI and NetWare DOS Requester files. If the NET.CFG file is not in the same directory, the parameters set in the NET.CFG file will not take effect.

NetWare 4.0 supports a wide range of workstation operating environments, including DOS, Windows, OS/2, Macintosh, and soon, UNIX. This chapter outlines the procedures for installing DOS and Windows workstations only.

For DOS and Windows workstations, the workstation environment is similar to that of previous versions of NetWare. In fact, you can use the workstation software from previous versions of NetWare to attach to a 4.0 file server, but your workstation will not support any of the NetWare Directory Services functions.

An Overview of the NetWare Workstation Drivers

This section provides an overview of the NetWare workstation drivers.

ANETX.COM

First we'll give you some background on the NetWare shells and how they have developed over time, to help you put the latest changes into perspective. Back in the days of NetWare 2.0a, one executable file acted as an interface between DOS and the workstation network board as well as between the network board and the rest of the network. This file was called ANETx.COM—the variable x represented the version of DOS being used by the workstation (for example, ANET2.COM for DOS 2.x and ANET3.COM for DOS 3.x). With NetWare 2.1, this shell file was divided into two separate files, IPX.COM and NETx.COM. (The x in NETx.COM also represented the DOS version.)

IPX.COM AND NETX.COM

With the division into IPX.COM and NETx.COM files, the network board-specific information was contained in the IPX.COM file. The network redirection functions were contained in the NETx.COM file.

A utility called SHGEN.EXE (SHell GENeration) was used to configure and compile the IPX.COM file. It combined a vendor-supplied network board driver and a standard set of code (IPX.OBJ) into a specific configuration for each network board. NETx.COM was compiled and shipped by Novell to work with the different versions of MS-DOS, but they were not configured in the SHGEN process.

Novell then replaced SHGEN.EXE with WSGEN.EXE (WorkStation GENeration) as an improved and updated shell generation utility. WSGEN was used to generate an IPX capable of being used transparently across NetWare 2.2 and 3.11. The generated IPX could also be used for most of the file-server-based menu utilities, such as ROUTEGEN.

OPEN DATALINK INTERFACE (ODI) DRIVERS

When NetWare 2.2 and 3.11 were released, a new technology was introduced, called Open Datalink Interface (ODI). ODI technology replaced IPX.COM by splitting its functions into three components: the Link Support Layer (LSL.COM), the Multiple Layer Interface Driver (MLID, or network board driver), and the Open Datalink Interface version of the Internet Packet Exchange (IPXODI.COM).

The MLID, or network board driver, is a generic term for the software components specific to the network board you are using. Some examples of popular network board drivers are NE1000.COM for the Novell NE1000 interface card and 3C503.COM for 3COM's 3C503 interface card.

For NetWare users, the significant advantage of the shift toward ODI technology was that users no longer needed to "generate" the IPX portion of the workstation shell. The manufacturer of the network board supplies a board driver in a compiled, executable form. All you have to do is choose the correct driver and load it in the proper sequence at the workstation. The proper sequence is as follows:

```
C:\>LSL.COM
C:\> network board driver
C:\>IPXODI.COM
```

Although eliminating the need for "generating" the IPX.COM file for each workstation was a good idea, it was in the generation procedure that the configuration parameters and type of driver were set. This procedure was crucial for the workstation shell to recognize the correct network board and driver settings.

Novell's engineers designed an ASCII (DOS text) configuration file called NET.CFG. This file lists the type of network board and settings used for such board parameters as hardware interrupt (INT), base input/output address (PORT), base memory address (MEM), and protocols. If you want to change a network board parameter, you simply need to edit the NET.CFG file to reflect the various board settings. The network board driver reads the correct board settings from this file. No longer do you have to regenerate a new IPX.COM from scratch.

Of course, there are other significant advantages to using the ODI versions of IPX, such as the ability to bind two different protocols to a single network interface card. If your network board is communicating with a standard NetWare LAN and a TCP/IP network at the same time, the ODI version of IPX will allow you to run both platforms through a single network board instead of dedicating a separate network board for each protocol. In some environments, this is not just a neat little trick but a central aspect of the connectivity needs of the enterprise.

Another advantage of the ODI version of IPX is that you can load and unload the individual drivers when necessary. It was necessary with the IPX.COM file to reboot the workstation each time you wanted to unload the IPX.COM file.

As people were becoming comfortable with Novell's ODI drivers, Microsoft and Digital Research were trying to outdo each other with their various DOS versions. Microsoft released its version 5.0, and Digital Research released its version 6.0. This presented a complex support issue for NetWare supervisors running the NETx.COM file, with workstations running every version from MS-DOS 3.3 through MS-DOS 5.0 and DR DOS 6.0.

Novell developed a replacement file called, simply, NETX.COM. This new file was not limited to any one version of DOS.

VIRTUAL LOADABLE MODULES (VLMs)

The NetWare workstation shell has developed from a monolithic, single-source shell file to a modular and more standardized approach to workstation connectivity. With NetWare 4.0, Novell has redesigned NETX.COM again by breaking it into individual components called Virtual Loadable Modules (VLMs). You do not load them individually, however, as you load the ODI drivers of IPX. VLMs are loaded by running the VLM.EXE program.

VLM.EXE searches its default directory and loads all modules that have the extension .VLM. If you want to avoid loading a particular module, all you have to do is rename it to another extension and it won't load. Some VLM modules are optional but most are required for your NetWare workstation to operate correctly.

You can adjust the VLMs with parameters in the NET.CFG file. One interesting parameter is the NETWORK PRINTERS= option. With a new maximum of nine printer connections, we think that many system administrators will be gratified by the enhanced flexibility.

The NAME CONTEXT= setting will be helpful for users running in NetWare Directory Services. Similar to the PREFERRED SERVER= setting for bindery-based networks, the NAME CONTEXT= setting is helpful because it directs the login utility to the exact location of your user information (User object) in the Directory tree. This eliminates the need to type your complete Directory Services context when logging in.

So if you're not using WSGEN anymore to generate the workstation shell files, and you have a large number of VLM files to copy to your boot disk, how do you know which files to copy? NetWare provides a workstation installation program that takes you through the steps for installing and configuring your NetWare workstation for DOS and Windows. We'll look closely at the DOS and Windows workstation installation routines in the following sections.

Installing NetWare 4.0 DOS and Windows Clients

Find the disks called WSDOS_1 (NetWare Workstation for DOS), WSWIN_1 (NetWare Workstation for Windows), WSDRV_1 (NetWare Workstation Drivers Disk 1), and WSDRV_2 (NetWare Workstation Drivers Disk 2). On the disk labeled WSDOS_1 there is a file called INSTALL.EXE. We'll start by loading the installation program by running INSTALL.EXE.

1 · Put the WSDOS_1 disk in drive A (you can use another drive, but for this walk-through we'll be using drive A).

2 · Change to drive A.

3 · Type **INSTALL** and press ↵. An example of the installation menu is illustrated in Figure 12.1.

Make the necessary modifications for your particular workstation setup, then highlight step 5 and press ↵ to continue with the workstation installation.

The first step asks you to define a directory on the local drive for the NetWare workstation files. This is where INSTALL will copy LSL.COM, your network board driver, IPXODI.COM, VLM.EXE, and the VLM files. The default directory is C:\NWCLIENT.

The second step confirms that the installation program should make any necessary changes to your current workstation's CONFIG.SYS and AUTO-EXEC.BAT files. The line "LASTDRIVE=Z" is added to the CONFIG.SYS file, and the line "Call STARTNET.BAT" is added to the AUTOEXEC.BAT file. This will load the shell files each time your workstation is booted.

The third step confirms that you want the Windows workstation software copied to the Windows program and SYSTEM directories. The default program directory is C:\WINDOWS. When you select *Install Windows pieces,* the installation program makes changes to your SYSTEM.INI, WIN.INI, and PROG-MAN.INI files.

▶ · ◀

FIGURE 12.1

The NetWare Workstation for DOS and Windows installation program opening screen

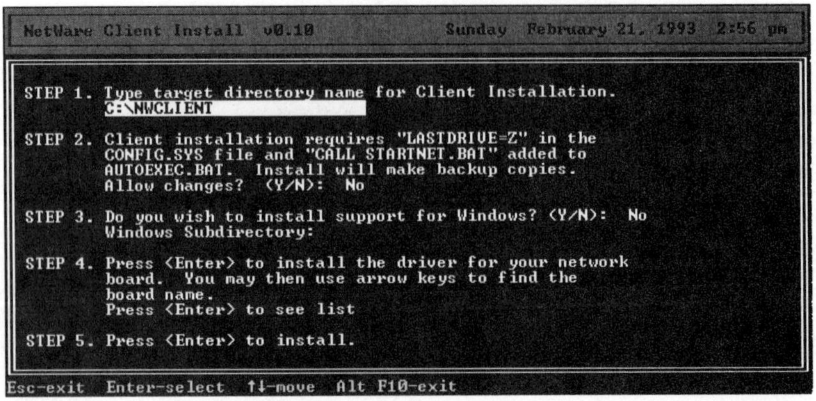

```
NetWare Client Install  v0.10              Sunday  February 21, 1993  2:56 pm

  STEP 1. Type target directory name for Client Installation.
          C:\NWCLIENT

  STEP 2. Client installation requires "LASTDRIVE=Z" in the
          CONFIG.SYS file and "CALL STARTNET.BAT" added to
          AUTOEXEC.BAT.  Install will make backup copies.
          Allow changes?  <Y/N>:  No

  STEP 3. Do you wish to install support for Windows? <Y/N>:  No
          Windows Subdirectory:

  STEP 4. Press <Enter> to install the driver for your network
          board.  You may then use arrow keys to find the
          board name.
          Press <Enter> to see list

  STEP 5. Press <Enter> to install.

Esc-exit  Enter-select  ↑↓-move  Alt F10-exit
```

If you are running Windows from the file server, there should be one shared program directory. We recommend that your Windows program directory (there is no SYSTEM directory on a network) be root-mapped as search drive W:\.

The fourth step is choosing the particular network board driver for your workstation. To choose a board driver, highlight step 4 and press ↵. A dialog box will appear, with a complete list of NetWare network board drivers (Figure 12.2):

Novell/Excelan EXOS 205T Ethernet, EXOS.COM, EXOS.INS, IE0

Novell/Excelan EXOS 215 Ethernet, EXOS.COM, EXOS.INS, 00M, 6205

ODI Module for the IBM LAN Support Program, LANSUP.COM, LANSUP.INS, IEM

Novell/Excelan LANZENET Ethernet, LANZENET.COM, LANZENET.INS, IE0

Novell/Eagle NE1000, NE1000.COM

Novell Ethernet NE1500T, NE1500T.COM

Ansel M1500, NE1500T.COM

Novell/Eagle NE/2, NE2.COM

Novell/Eagle NE2-32, NE2_32.COM

Novell/Eagle NE2000, NE2000.COM

Zenith Data Systems NE2000 Module, NE2000.COM

Novell Ethernet NE2100, NE2100.COM

Ansel M2100, NE2100.COM

Wearnes 2110T, NE2100.COM

Wearnes 2107C, NE2000.COM

EXOS 105, NE2100.COM

Novell Ethernet NE3200, NE3200.COM

INTEL EtherExpress32, NE3200.COM

EXOS 235T, NE3200.COM

Dedicated (Non-ODI) IPX, NULL.COM

Novell NTR2000 Token-Ring Adapter, NTR2000.COM

PCN II and PCN Baseband Driver, PCN2L.COM

PCN II/A and PCN Baseband/A Driver, PCN2.COM

IBM Token-Ring Network Adapter II & 16/4 Adapter, TOKEN.COM

IBM Token-Ring Network Adapter/A, TOKEN.COM

IBM Token-Ring Network 16/4 Adapter/A, TOKEN.COM

Novell RX-Net & RX-Net II, TRXNET.COM

Novell RX-Net/2, TRXNET.COM

Of course, some of the drivers listed are actually alternate names for the same network board driver. For example, Novell NE1000 Ethernet and Novell/Eagle NE1000 are identical.

When you select a network board driver, a box will appear with some parameters to set. Depending on the type and brand of network board that you are using, the parameters may be different. Figure 12.3 shows the parameters for a Novell NE1000 network board, including settings for hardware interrupt, base I/O, and Ethernet frame type.

F I G U R E 12.2

Selecting a network
interface driver

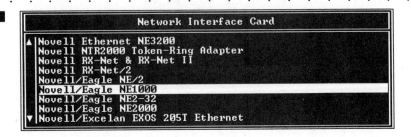

FIGURE 12.3

Sample parameters for an

NE1000 network board

driver

By choosing the different Frame Type options, you can save some workstation memory, but you will sacrifice some functionality. SPX functions are used by such utilities as RCONSOLE and PSERVER.EXE, so if you want to run either of these at a workstation, SPX must be loaded.

When the parameters for the network board are set, press Esc. Next, highlight step 5 and press ↵. The installation program will copy a set of files to the C:\NWCLIENT directory and then create the STARTNET.BAT file and NET.CFG text files.

When all of that is complete, a message similar to the one in Figure 12.4 will appear to signal that the client installation is complete.

Here is a sample STARTNET.BAT:

```
@ECHO OFF
C:
CD \NWCLIENT
SET NWLANGUAGE=ENGLISH
LSL
NE1000.COM
IPXODI
VLM
CD \
```

Here is a sample NET.CFG:

```
LINK DRIVER NE1000
   PORT 300
   INT 3
   FRAME Ethernet_802.2

NetWare DOS Requester
   FIRST NETWORK DRIVE = F
```

FIGURE 12.4

The DOS workstation

installation is complete.

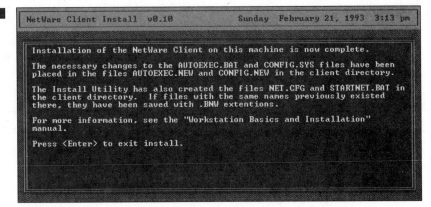

```
NetWare Client Install  v0.10                 Sunday  February 21, 1993  3:13 pm

  Installation of the NetWare Client on this machine is now complete.

  The necessary changes to the AUTOEXEC.BAT and CONFIG.SYS files have been
  placed in the files AUTOEXEC.NEW and CONFIG.NEW in the client directory.

  The Install Utility has also created the files NET.CFG and STARTNET.BAT in
  the client directory.  If files with the same names previously existed
  there, they have been saved with .BNW extentions.

  For more information, see the "Workstation Basics and Installation"
  manual.

  Press <Enter> to exit install.
```

USING ARCHETYPE CONFIGURATIONS FOR DOS WORKSTATIONS

If you have a number of DOS workstations that share configurations, you can avoid running INSTALL.EXE for each workstation. Once you have installed the first workstation, simply copy the AUTOEXEC.BAT and CONFIG.SYS files along with the contents of the C:\NWCLIENT workstation directory to any other DOS workstations that have identical configurations. Using this method, you will run INSTALL for each different configuration only once, and then simply copy the appropriate set of files to other machines as necessary.

Troubleshooting DOS and Windows Workstations

If you are having problems with a DOS or Windows workstation, start from the beginning: Does the workstation boot to DOS without errors? If there are errors, you should determine whether these errors are generated by commands in the CONFIG.SYS file, the AUTOEXEC.BAT file, or any other batch files that may be called from AUTOEXEC.BAT.

If you are running MS-DOS 6.0, this process is made significantly easier. Turn off the power to the workstation, wait about 15 seconds, and then power back on. Press the F5 key when the message "Loading MS-DOS..." appears. Pressing F5 bypasses the CONFIG.SYS and AUTOEXEC.BAT files entirely. Obviously, any device drivers that you normally load in the CONFIG.SYS file will be absent, but that's the point. If you see an error message after booting in this fashion, you can be certain that the error was generated by the power-on self test (POST) that a DOS computer runs every time it boots from a cold start.

If you don't see any errors, reboot once more, but instead of F5, press F8 when the message "Loading MS-DOS..." appears. This command tells DOS to step through each CONFIG.SYS command individually and to ask for confirmation for loading each one. Answer Y (for Yes) to each command, and watch closely for any error messages. If one appears, stop and look at the line that generated the error. If there's something wrong with it, fix it. If it looks all right, it may be a good idea to eliminate it until the workstation is working better.

The F8 boot also asks you to confirm execution of the AUTOEXEC.BAT file. If you want to step through AUTOEXEC.BAT, edit the file with a DOS text editor and insert a PAUSE command after each line in the file. That way, you can do almost the same thing as you did with the CONFIG.SYS file, checking each line for correct execution.

If you aren't running MS-DOS 6.0, you can come close to this level of troubleshooting by placing a PAUSE command at the beginning of the AUTO-EXEC.BAT file to halt execution after the CONFIG.SYS and before the AUTOEXEC.BAT commands are executed.

Nevertheless, most workstation problems occur after the workstation boots to DOS. There are a few tricks that we can suggest for debugging these. The first NetWare driver you load is LSL.COM. This one is usually easy to load.

The network board driver requires a NET.CFG file for nondefault board settings. Without the NET.CFG file, the board driver will recognize only default settings. The NET.CFG file is usually created by the DOS and Windows workstation installation program, but you can create or modify it with any ASCII text editor (such as EDLIN or EDIT, depending on your DOS version).

Keep in mind that the NET.CFG file must be located in the directory where the network board driver is actually executed. Failure to do this is probably the most common cause of problems encountered with the ODI drivers. If you load LSL.COM, NE1000.COM, and IPXODI.COM from the C:\NWCLIENT directory, you're in good shape.

However, if you decide to put the workstation files directory in your DOS path and then execute the commands from another directory, the network board driver will not recognize the board driver settings in the NET.CFG file unless you copy NET.CFG to the other directory as well. The safest way to avoid a problem is to change to the C:\NWCLIENT directory (the workstation files directory) and load your ODI drivers from the same directory.

The critical portion of the NET.CFG file as far as the network board driver is concerned is the Link Driver section. In this case the network board driver is NE1000.COM, which corresponds to the workstation's NE1000 network board. If the Link Driver option doesn't have the correct PORT setting (base I/O address) and the correct MEM setting (base memory address), the network board driver will not load correctly. If the INT setting (hardware interrupt, or IRQ) is incorrect, it will often load without an error message, but it will not find a file server when the NetWare DOS Requester (VLM) or NetWare shell (NETX.COM) is loaded.

If the network board driver is correct and the network board's settings match the NET.CFG file settings, the network board driver will probably load correctly. Then the protocol portion is loaded. This is usually IPXODI.COM. Loading the IPX doesn't usually generate a problem, so we'll move on to the NetWare DOS Requester or NetWare shell.

If you are using bindery services, you can choose to use the previous NetWare shell: NETX.COM. If that is your choice, type **NETX.COM** after loading the ODI drivers and you should be connected to a file server. If you aren't using bindery services, there might be a cable problem, or you may have a different INT setting (IRQ) in your NET.CFG file from what is actually configured on your network board. It is only at this stage that such a mistake will usually show up. This is because it is only on incoming traffic that the network board actually generates an interrupt. At that point the network board driver can't interpret the function because it's not configured to receive that hardware interrupt.

Connecting to a bindery-based network, NETX.COM sends out a "Get Nearest Server" packet and waits for a reply. Every network server that receives the packet replies with a "Give Nearest Server" packet, but only the nearest (or fastest, or least burdened) server gets its reply first to the workstation. When the first reply is received by the workstation, the rest are discarded.

You can use this understanding to help you troubleshoot your DOS or Windows workstation. If you type **Track On** at the file server console, you will bring up the router-tracking screen. Once you have the router-tracking screen at the network server, go to the workstation and load the NetWare shell or NetWare DOS Requester (NETX.COM or VLM.EXE). At the network server, you should see the workstation's "Get Nearest Server" request appear on the router-tracking screen and immediately after that the file server's "Give Nearest Server" reply.

If you don't see "Get Nearest Server," you know that communication between the workstation and the network server is not dependable—that is, there may be a cable break or a bad station cable. If you see "Get Nearest Server" and "Give Nearest Server" but the workstation returns a "File server not found" error message, you should suspect that the hardware interrupt is not correctly configured or that there is a problem with the ODI drivers themselves (check with the network board manufacturer to see if there is an update available).

If you are having problems with the NetWare DOS Requester (VLM.EXE) or its modules, try using NETX.COM instead and try to attach to a server that way. Using NETX.COM to log in to a NetWare 4.0 server requires that you have bindery emulation running at the NetWare 4.0 network server. To do that, set the bindery context at the colon prompt, or go into the "Miscellaneous" section of SERVMAN.NLM. The command at the console prompt is

```
SET BINDERY CONTEXT= <OU=Organizational Unit.OU=
Organizational Unit.O=Organizational>
```

The Organizational Units are the correct NetWare Directory Services Organizational Units, where Organizational represents your parent organization.

Once you can attach with NETX.COM, try again with VLM.EXE instead. Remember that the VLMs also need to be loaded from the same directory where the NET.CFG file resides.

Resources

There are a few publications available to help you with using Windows in a NetWare environment. Two of these are available directly from Novell, while others are full-length works.

- *Running Windows on NetWare,* by Stephen Saxon, M&T Books, San Mateo, Calif.

- *Integrating NetWare and Windows 3.1,* by Morgan B. Adair and Edward A. Liebing, Novell Research Publications, 122 East 1700 South E-23-1, Provo, Utah 84606-6194. U.S. orders: (800) 453-1267, ext. 5380. International orders (including Canada): (801) 429-5380.

- *Networking Windows, NetWare Edition,* by Howard Marks, Kristin Marks, and Rick Segal, SAMS, Carmel, Ind.

CHAPTER 13

Laying the Foundations for the User Environment

Fast Track

To view the directory structure,   *313*
use the NDIR command.

Loading programs and DOS files   *313*
on the file server is usually the responsibility of the NetWare network administrator. Some applications require a simple copy command for their
installation. However, it is more common for a network application to
come with a customized installation program or routine.

In evaluating a new application for use on your network, consider the   *317*
following questions:

- ▸ Is the software designed to be multiuser?

- ▸ Is the software tested and compatible with NetWare 4.0?

- ▸ Does the software have clear documentation for NetWare use?

- ▸ Are the software's rights requirements documented and
  reasonable?

- ▸ Are the software's file attributes requirements documented?

- ▸ Can the software's directory structure be configured?

This chapter reviews the basics of NetWare directory structures and the concept of drive mappings. With this foundation in mind, we show a way to develop a directory structure for a network that allows you to load and manage applications and multiple versions of DOS.

Using Directories and Subdirectories

As a personal computer user, you are probably familiar with directories and subdirectories. Directories are the "containers" of a file storage system. Whereas a file represents a collection of information (a letter, a spreadsheet, or a database, for example), a directory represents the logical location of the file. A multilevel file structure helps you manage large numbers of files by logically grouping them into subdirectories.

For example, your hard disk may contain programs such as Lotus 1-2-3 and WordPerfect as well as data files. Rather than mixing all the files together on the disk, you can group them into directories and subdirectories, as shown in Figure 13.1. In this figure, the full directory name for the file named COVER001.LTR in the LETTERS subdirectory would be

C:\DATA\LETTERS\COVER001.LTR

USING NETWARE DIRECTORIES
Like DOS, NetWare also lets you set up directory structures for managing files. However, since the network environment is more complex, the directory structure

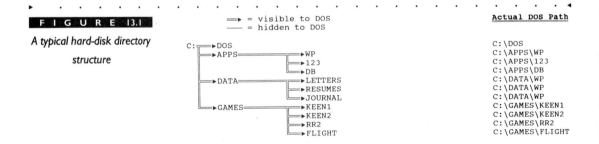

FIGURE 13.1

A typical hard-disk directory structure

hierarchy has an additional level. Figure 13.2 illustrates how the directory structure shown in Figure 13.1 might be modified for use on a file-server hard disk.

The file-server hard disk can be divided into volumes, then into directories, and finally into subdirectories. The directory structure shown in Figure 13.2 shows only two volumes (SYS: and VOL1:), residing on one file server (FS1). The full path for the file COVER001.LTR in the LETTERS subdirectory is now

FS1/VOL1:USERS\ME\LETTERS\COVER001.LTR

USING SYSTEM DIRECTORIES

When you installed the NetWare operating system, INSTALL.NLM automatically created a number of directories. The most important directories are the following:

SYS:SYSTEM

SYS:PUBLIC

SYS:LOGIN

SYS:MAIL

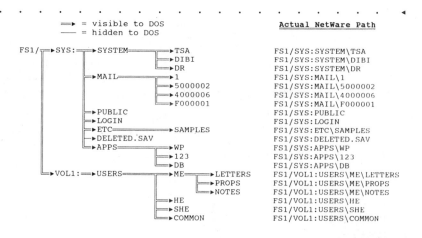

FIGURE 13.2

*A typical file-server
directory structure*

The SYSTEM directory contains various NetWare utilities that are usually restricted to use by the network administrator. The files stored in PUBLIC are mostly utility programs intended for general use. The LOGIN directory contains the programs required for logging in to the network.

The MAIL directory and its subdirectories are used by the operating system to store files that are specific to individual users. When each user is created, NetWare generates a number to identify the user internally. A mail subdirectory, named after the user's ID number, is then automatically created for that user. The directory contains the user's login script (which we'll explain in a later chapter) and the print-job configuration file, PRINCON.DAT (if the user has any personal print-job configurations).

To see this directory structure, log in to the network as **ADMIN**. Then type **CD** and press ↵ to return to the top level of the SYS: volume, type **DIR**, and press ↵. Your directory listing should be similar to Figure 13.3.

▶ · ◀

FIGURE 13.3	
A sample NetWare directory listing	

```
Volume in drive F is SYS
Volume Serial Number is 7A76-7CD9
Directory of F:\

LOGIN      <DIR>         10-16-93    1:07a
SYSTEM     <DIR>         10-16-93    1:07a
PUBLIC     <DIR>         10-16-93    1:07a
MAIL       <DIR>         10-16-93    1:07a
ETC        <DIR>         10-16-93    1:19a
VOL$LOG    ERR     25829 10-16-93    1:02p
TTS$LOG    ERR     32103 10-16-93    1:02p
```

CREATING DIRECTORIES WITH THE DOS MD COMMAND

You create new directories and subdirectories on a file-server hard disk the same way as on a disk drive in a standalone microcomputer. For example, to create a directory named APPS, simply enter the following command:

MD APPS

Now enter **DIR** to see the directory structure. The screen will look similar to Figure 13.4.

FIGURE 13.4

The directory listing after creating the APPS directory

```
Volume in drive F is SYS
Volume Serial Number is 7A76-7CD9
Directory of F:\

LOGIN       <DIR>       10-16-93    1:07p
SYSTEM      <DIR>       10-16-93    1:07p
PUBLIC      <DIR>       10-16-93    1:07p
MAIL        <DIR>       10-16-93    1:07p
ETC         <DIR>       10-16-93    1:19p
VOL$LOG     ERR   25829 10-16-93    1:02p
TTS$LOG     ERR   32103 10-16-93    1:02p
APPS        <DIR>       10-17-93    2:15p
```

CREATING NETWORK DIRECTORIES WITH THE FILER UTILITY

You can also create and modify directories using FILER, the NetWare file maintenance utility. To execute the FILER utility, enter **FILER** at the DOS prompt. A window will appear with a list of topics. Highlight Manage Files and Directories, then press ↵. A list of the current subdirectories and files will appear in a pop-up window. To add a new subdirectory named TOOLS, press the Insert key. Then simply type **TOOLS** in the box that appears, as shown in Figure 13.5.

FIGURE 13.5

The NetWare file-maintenance utility (FILER) screen

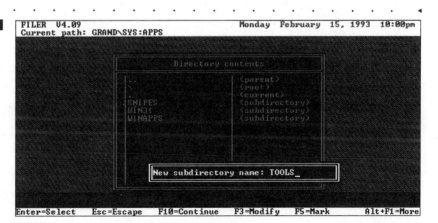

Using Drive Mappings

Drive mappings provide NetWare with a road map for finding files within the directory structure. Sometimes referred to as drive pointers, drive mappings specify particular network locations and permit easier navigation of the directory structure and access to executable files.

There are three types of drive mappings in a NetWare environment:

- ▶ Local drives

- ▶ Network drives

- ▶ Search drives

LOCAL DRIVES

Local drive mappings point to disk drives installed in a workstation. For example, drive A is usually a floppy-disk drive, and drive C is usually a local hard disk.

The disk operating system always reserves a certain number of drive letters for local storage devices. DOS versions after 3.1 reserve the first five letters (A to E) as local drive mappings.

NETWORK DRIVES

Network drive mappings are similar to local drive mappings except that they point to a directory on a file server's hard disk. In addition, network drive mappings can point to a specific subdirectory on the drive. For example, using the directory structure illustrated in Figure 13.2, you can map a drive to go directly to the LETTERS subdirectory. This map lets you change the current drive by simply entering the drive letter rather than typing the entire directory path. The syntax is as follows:

```
MAP J: = FS1_SYS:USERS\ME\LETTERS
J:
```

Of course, if you were only going to use that directory for a single operation, there's no reason to go to the extra effort. However, if you were planning to use your LETTERS subdirectory frequently, you would be better off with a drive mapping to it.

In previous versions of NetWare, the first network drive was always the first drive letter that was not reserved for local use. For example, the first network drive of a workstation running MS-DOS 3.1 through 5.0 was F by default.

One of the significant changes with NetWare 4.0 is that network drives are allocated from those available for DOS use instead of those that follow the DOS LASTDRIVE. For this reason, the DOS and Windows client installation routines add the following command to the CONFIG.SYS file:

LASTDRIVE=Z

In addition, you can use the NET.CFG file to specify the first network directory. For example, to set the first network directory to drive F, add the following command to NET.CFG:

FIRST NETWORK DRIVE = F

It is important to remember that network drive mappings are logical, not physical. That is, unlike local drives, a separate physical drive does not exist for the location of each network drive mapping.

In addition, network drive mappings can be different for individual users. For example, one user's drive G might be mapped to a different network directory than another user's drive G. Network drive mappings are normally set at the beginning of a session (in a login script), and they are lost when the user logs out of the network. (Chapter 15 covers login scripts.)

SEARCH DRIVES

Similar to normal network drive mappings, a search drive assigns a drive letter to a specific network directory, but the drive is added to (or inserted in) the DOS path, which allows the operating system to automatically search the mapped directory for an executable file.

When you execute a command at a DOS workstation, DOS looks first for an internal command (such as DIR, CD, or MD) that matches the one you issued. If your command isn't an internal DOS command, the operating system searches for an executable file by that name in the current directory. If the system cannot find an executable file, it searches any directories that are in the DOS path, including network search drives. Just as in a normal DOS environment, the order of directories or drives in the DOS path determines the order in which they are searched. Also, just like local directories on the path, search drives apply only to executable files: those with the extensions .COM, .EXE, and .BAT, in that order.

In most NetWare installations, the subdirectory that contains DOS is mapped as the second search drive. This mapping allows users to execute DOS commands from any place in the network without changing to the DOS subdirectory. The first search drive is, by default, mapped to SYS:PUBLIC, the directory that contains all the NetWare user utilities. With this order, any command conflicts are won by NetWare, the first search drive.

Generally, there are not many command conflicts. However, when Microsoft introduced the utility HELP.EXE in DOS 5.0, many NetWare users discovered the NetWare command HELP for the first time. They typed HELP at the command line and instead of MS-DOS's help information, up came the NetWare help interface. That was because DOS saw the executable Z:\PUBLIC\HELP.EXE before it tried searching for Y:\PUBLIC\IBM_PC\MSDOS\V5.00\HELP.EXE.

NETWARE'S DEFAULT DRIVE MAPPINGS

In a brand-new network, NetWare automatically assigns default drive maps. When you log in as the ADMIN user, NetWare's default drive mappings are as follows:

```
Drive A:  maps to a local disk.
Drive B:  maps to a local disk.
Drive C:  maps to a local disk.
Drive D: = FS1_SYS:SYSTEM
SEARCH1: = Z:. [FS1_SYS:PUBLIC]
SEARCH2: = Y:. [FS1_SYS:PUBLIC\%MACHINE\%OS\%OS\
%OS_VERSION]
```

This information indicates that drives A, B, and C are mapped as local drives. Drive D is a network drive that points to the SYSTEM subdirectory on the SYS: volume (the drive might be listed instead as F, depending on what drive letter you set for the FIRST NETWORK DRIVE= parameter in your NET.CFG file). The

SYSTEM directory contains the NetWare utilities commonly used only by network administrators.

Drive Z is a search drive that allows files in the PUBLIC directory to be executed from anywhere on the network.

Drive Y is a search drive mapped to a directory that contains DOS, if you've installed DOS on a network directory. When regular network users (not ADMIN) log in, their first network drive gets mapped to their home directory instead of to SYS:SYSTEM.

ADDING OR CHANGING DRIVE MAPPINGS

As you'll see in the next chapter, drive mappings are usually set in login scripts. (Login scripts contain a set of instructions that direct workstations to perform specific actions during the login process.) However, you can also modify drive mappings from the DOS prompt.

Suppose that you want to map drive G to a network directory you've created at the root of the SYS volume called APPS. The following command will do that:

```
MAP G: = SYS:APPS
```

Similarly, the following command adds a third search drive that points to a directory you might have created under APPS, called TOOLS:

```
MAP S3: = SYS:APPS\TOOLS
```

To make sure that mapping was successful, you can execute **MAP** at the DOS prompt with no parameters. The map information should reflect the changes, as follows:

```
Drive A:  maps to a local disk.
Drive B:  maps to a local disk.
Drive C:  maps to a local disk.
Drive D: = FS1_SYS: \SYSTEM
Drive G: = FS1_SYS: \APPS

-----
SEARCH1: = Z:. [FS1_SYS: \PUBLIC]
SEARCH2: = Y:. [FS1_SYS: \PUBLIC\IBM_PC\MSDOS\V5.00\
SEARCH3: = X:. [FS1_SYS: \APPS\TOOLS]
```

There are now three search drives, so the operating system will search for files first in the current directory and then in each of the search drives in order. If there are two executable files of the same name (as in the previous example, where HELP.EXE was in the PUBLIC and DOS directories), only the first one found will execute. If the second one is desired, it must be specified explicitly, as in the following command:

Y:HELP

or

Y:\PUBLIC\IBM_PC\MSDOS\V5.00\HELP

Developing a Directory Structure

Obviously, an unlimited number of directory structures could be employed on a NetWare volume. The task for our sample system is relatively simple, so we have only one file server and one volume. Nevertheless, we must plan the directory structure carefully.

When planning the directory layout, you should consider three important issues. The first issue to consider is the simplicity of the structure. You do not want the directory structure to be so complicated that users (and administrators) cannot find program and data files. The second issue to consider is security, because many of NetWare's security provisions relate to directories and subdirectories. The third issue to consider is logic. You should group files logically to enhance the efficiency of the network.

CREATING THE DIRECTORIES

In our sample network, we'll add the following directories to those created by NetWare:

APPS

APPS\TOOLS

PUBLIC\IBM_PC\MSDOS\V5.00 (though the previous example assumed that the DOS directory had already been created)

PUBLIC\IBM_PC\MSDOS\V3.30

USERS

USERS\COMMON

To create these directories, type **MD** (the Make Directory command in DOS), followed by the directory name, and press ↵. For example, to make the APPS directory, enter the following command:

```
MD \APPS
```

To create the rest of the directories, enter the following commands:

```
MD \APPS\TOOLS
MD \PUBLIC\IBM_PC
MD \PUBLIC\IBM_PC\MSDOS
MD \PUBLIC\IBM_PC\MSDOS\V5.00
MD \PUBLIC\IBM_PC\MSDOS\V3.30
MD \USERS
MD \USERS\COMMON
MD \GROUPS
```

You should add the V3.30 command line only if you plan to support MS-DOS 3.3 on your network.

Here are explanations of what the directories will contain:

▶ The **APPS** directory can contain various subdirectories that hold individual applications, such as Lotus 1-2-3 and WordPerfect. You use the APPS\TOOLS directory to provide a location for various utility programs, such as text editors, small shareware utilities, and so on.

▶ The **MSDOS** directory will contain subdirectories for each version of the disk operating system that your network will support. (The next section discusses DOS subdirectories in detail.)

▶ The **USERS** directory will be the parent directory for each user's home directory on the network. Home directories can be used by each user to store their personal files. Home directories are usually named with the user's own login name.

▶ The **USERS\COMMON** directory will provide a temporary storage location for files so they can be shared or passed from one user to another.

▶ The optional **GROUPS** directory might hold subdirectories that are shared by members of workgroups or those who are working on projects together.

Figure 13.6 illustrates a directory structure for a single-volume network hard disk. This approach meets the criteria established earlier for the directory layout. First, it is simple. The root of the SYS: volume contains only nine directories, and the names clearly reflect the directory contents. Of these nine, only three are not created by the system itself. It's hard to get much more efficient than that. Second, the directory structure facilitates effective security by allowing security rights to be assigned to individuals and groups. For example, you can assign access to the applications directories globally by allowing access to the SYS:APPS directory, or you can allow access to individual programs by assigning trustee rights to users or groups at the directories containing each individual application.

This kind of global or individual approach makes it easier to configure system security. Additionally, you can separate software applications from data files, because each user's data is generally kept in the user's home directory or its sub-directories.

After you create all these directories, executing the DOS DIR command at the root of the SYS volume should produce a directory listing similar to that shown in Figure 13.7.

FIGURE 13.6

A single-volume network
directory structure

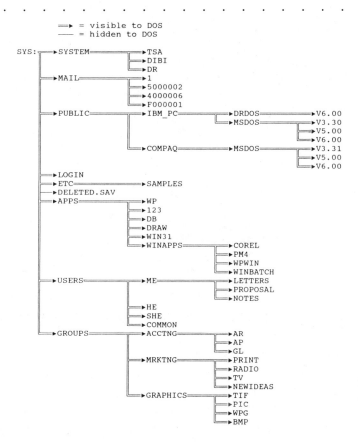

FIGURE 13.6

A single-volume network
directory structure

```
                        ===► = visible to DOS
                        ———  = hidden to DOS

SYS:──►SYSTEM═════════►TSA
        │              ►DIBI
        │              ►DR
        ├──►MAIL───────►1
        │              ►5000002
        │              ►4000006
        │              ►F000001
        ├──►PUBLIC─────►IBM_PC──────►DRDOS────────►V6.00
        │              │            ►MSDOS────────►V3.30
        │              │                           ►V5.00
        │              │                           ►V6.00
        │              │
        │              ►COMPAQ──────►MSDOS────────►V3.31
        │                                          ►V5.00
        │                                          ►V6.00
        ├──►LOGIN
        ├──►ETC────────►SAMPLES
        ├──►DELETED.SAV
        ├──►APPS───────►WP
        │              ►123
        │              ►DB
        │              ►DRAW
        │              ►WIN31
        │              ►WINAPPS──────►COREL
        │                            ►PM4
        │                            ►WPWIN
        │                            ►WINBATCH
        ├──►USERS──────►ME───────────►LETTERS
        │              │             ►PROPOSAL
        │              │             ►NOTES
        │              ►HE
        │              ►SHE
        │              ►COMMON
        └──►GROUPS─────►ACCTNG────────►AR
                       │              ►AP
                       │              ►GL
                       ►MRKTNG────────►PRINT
                       │              ►RADIO
                       │              ►TV
                       │              ►NEWIDEAS
                       ►GRAPHICS──────►TIF
                                      ►PIC
                                      ►WPG
                                      ►BMP
```

CREATING THE SUBDIRECTORIES

You also need to create the necessary subdirectories within each directory. The APPS directory should contain a subdirectory for each application that will be loaded on the network. In the MSDOS directory, you will need a subdirectory for each machine type (IBM_PC, COMPAQ, etc.). For more information on the LONG_MACHINE_TYPE login script identifier variable (which you can set in the NET.CFG file) and its uses in this context, see the chapter on login scripts and batch files (Chapter 15), and review the chapter on creating NetWare 4.0

FIGURE 13.7

The result of using the DIR command at the root of the SYS volume

```
Volume in drive F is SYS
Volume Serial Number is 7A76-7CD9
Directory of F:\

LOGIN        <DIR>        10-16-93    1:07p
SYSTEM       <DIR>        10-16-93    1:07p
PUBLIC       <DIR>        10-16-93    1:07p
MAIL         <DIR>        10-16-93    1:07p
ETC          <DIR>        10-16-93    1:19p
VOL$LOG  ERR      25829   10-16-93    1:02p
TTS$LOG  ERR      32103   10-16-93    1:02p
APPS         <DIR>        10-17-93    2:15p
USERS        <DIR>        10-17-93    2:45p
GROUPS       <DIR>        10-17-93    2:46p
```

clients (Chapter 12). If your network supports more than one version of DOS, you'll want another level of subdirectories for each version of the operating system that is in use.

The naming convention here is critical. To use the login script identifier variable %OS_VERSION, you must name the directories with the format V#.##, where V# represents the major DOS version and .## represents the minor DOS revision. In the example shown in Figure 13.6, Compaq DOS version 3.31 is placed in the directory V3.31, MS-DOS version 5.0 is placed in the directory V5.00, and so on. If you create a directory called V5.0 instead of V5.00, the value returned by %OS_VERSION will not match, and you will have difficulties.

The USERS directory can contain a subdirectory for each user. Naming these directories after the actual login names of the users is best. Such a convention makes a default mapping of each user to his or her home directory quite a simple matter in the system login script. Each user is commonly allowed to create a directory structure below his or her home directory to keep data organized. Limits can be set on total disk usage or even on the ability to create any new directories at all.

For the GROUPS directory, we can use an approach similar to the one we used in the USERS directory, but instead of subdirectories for each user, we will create a subdirectory for each workgroup or special project. In our example, we have created a subdirectory named ACCTNG for the accounting department, a subdirectory named MRKTNG for the marketing department, and a subdirectory named GRAPHICS to hold the various graphic-image formats in use on the network. Within each of these subdirectories, we have placed subdirectories that make sense for the various functions of the individual groups.

VIEWING THE DIRECTORY STRUCTURE

When you have finished creating the directories and subdirectories, you can use the NetWare utility NDIR to view the directory structure. From the root directory of the SYS: volume (drive F), enter the following command to list all the directories and subdirectories for the sample LAN:

```
NDIR /DO /SUB
```

The /DO parameter requests a listing of directories only. The /SUB parameter specifies that you want to view all levels of subdirectories.

If you are using DOS 5.0 or higher, you can use the DOS TREE command to look at your directory structure. At the root of the SYS: volume (F:\), type

```
TREE
```

The format of the resulting display should vaguely resemble the directory tree figures that are in this chapter.

Either format can be redirected to a text file and then imported into a word processing application or copied directly to a graphics printer (enter **TREE > TREE.TXT**). You can also redirect straight to the printer (enter **TREE > LPT1**). Periodically generating a graphic layout of the directory structure will help you manage your system more effectively.

Loading Files into Directories

Now that you've created the directories, you can begin to load files into them. In this section, you will load files into the DOS and APPS directories.

LOADING DOS FILES

Our sample network will have two types of DOS workstations attached to it: generic IBM-compatibles and Compaq workstations. Though we'll be showing you how to configure DOS directories for Compaq computers, you can use these techniques for any PC that uses a nonstandard brand of DOS.

Our definition of nonstandard is simply any copy of DOS that has a non-unique version or revision number but a COMMAND.COM file with a different date stamp or size. If your standard is Compaq DOS V5.00, any other DOS V5.00 would be nonstandard. However, since most networks have MS-DOS as the de facto standard, we'll use that condition in our scenario.

If you want to test the compatibility of two types of DOS, boot to one type, insert a bootable disk of the other type, and enter **COMMAND**. If you get a message like "Incorrect DOS version," the versions are not interchangeable and the following tricks will help you out. However, if you get a listing of the version and date of MS-DOS, the two versions are compatible and the following procedure is probably unnecessary for your system.

By default, all DOS PCs are assigned the value IBM_PC for the login script identifier variable LONG_MACHINE_TYPE (we'll explain identifier variables in Chapter 15 when we discuss login scripts). Because Compaq DOS is different from other brands of DOS, it can be helpful to identify Compaq PCs (or any other type that uses a brand of DOS that is not your network's primary standard) by using the workstation's NET.CFG file to set the LONG_MACHINE_TYPE variable to COMPAQ. That way we can branch the two types of computers to the directory holding the appropriate version of DOS when the system login script executes. We therefore created two DOS subdirectories, named IBM_PC and COMPAQ. (These directories are shown in Figure 13.6.)

To prepare the file server, you must copy the DOS files from the original DOS disks to the corresponding subdirectory. For example, to copy the Compaq DOS (version 5.00) files, place the first DOS disk in drive A and enter the following commands:

```
NCOPY A:\*.* SYS:\PUBLIC\COMPAQ\MSDOS\V5.00
FLAG SYS:\PUBLIC\COMPAQ\MSDOS\V5.00\*.* +SRO
```

NCOPY (similar to the DOS COPY and XCOPY commands, but optimized for NetWare) copies all the files from drive A to the network DOS subdirectory. The FLAG command makes all the files Shareable and Read-Only (SRO) so that multiple users can read them while at the same time prohibiting anyone from modifying or deleting them. Continue the copy process until all the DOS files have been copied to the file server.

Make sure that you are copying from the expanded (installed) DOS disks rather than from those that often come directly from the equipment or software manufacturer. If the files have extensions like .EX_ or .CO_, they were most likely compressed for distribution and will not execute. If the files have extensions like .EXE or .COM, you are probably fine.

LOADING APPLICATIONS AND DATA

The next step is to load the software applications and any data needed on the file server. In general, the installation procedure for network software is similar to that for applications on standalone computers. The principal difference is that the files are loaded on the file server's hard disk instead of on a local hard drive. For example, when you load WordPerfect, you might want the files to be copied to the SYS:APPS\WP directory.

Make sure, however, that you are installing a network version of the software. Not only is it often illegal to run single-user versions of application software on a multiuser network but such versions frequently will not perform as intended when multiple users attempt to access the same files, leading to possible data corruption or loss. After a lot of experience, we feel that it's just not worth it.

When loading network software, you will generally use the FLAG command to give the files the Shareable and Read Only (SRO) file attributes. Some software, however, needs to write to files during application execution. Thus, some files must be flagged Shareable Read/Write (SRW) or Nonshareable Read/Write. Since Nonshareable Read/Write is the default attribute for a file when it is created or copied into a NetWare volume, this set of attributes is labeled Normal (N).

To load applications properly, carefully follow the installation documentation; otherwise, problems may occur later. Diagnosing software anomalies that result from incorrect file attributes can be time-consuming and frustrating.

Most popular programs that are designed for network use have specific documentation for NetWare networks. The manuals usually have a special section for NetWare installation and/or special NetWare considerations. As well as giving a list of proper file attributes, the documentation should also give a listing of the necessary trustee assignments (rights) required by each user or group member in order to use the software. If there is no mention of rights, you may want to start out with Read and File Scan (RF) rights, as these are required to execute any program. If the application doesn't function properly, try adding Create (C), Write (W), Modify (M), and Erase (E).

Most well-designed programs do not require a normal user to possess the Erase trustee right to the application's main program directory, for the simple reason that such a user might erase a program file by accident. However, sometimes an administrator is forced to manage an application that violates this basic concept. In such cases, you should protect all critical files by flagging them as Shareable (if necessary) and Read-Only. Even a SUPERVISOR or SUPERVISOR-equivalent is not allowed to delete a Read-Only file (though if a user has the Modify right, he or she can change the Read-Only attribute to Read/Write; then anyone with the Erase right can delete the file).

Although the developers that are most responsive to the marketplace will likely have special instructions for NetWare 4.0 networks, many may not immediately revise their program design or documentation for NetWare 4.0. In such cases, consult the developer's sales or technical support representative to confirm that the software is compatible with NetWare 4.0, and check to see if there are any product updates that you will need. If the software is compatible, or if you can't get an authoritative answer (an all-too-common situation), try the software in a test environment—*not* on your production server—and follow the general instructions for installation on a 3.1 server.

Another source for product compatibility listings is the Network Support Encyclopedia (Professional Edition) from Novell. It has a current listing of those products that have undergone compatibility testing at the Novell labs, and it lists any caveats or limitations discovered with regard to the product's functionality on NetWare.

Multiuser software is usually licensed either by site or for a particular number of simultaneous users. With site-licensed software, an unlimited number of simultaneous users can usually run the application at the licensed site. Software licensed for a maximum number of simultaneous users may come with a counter or metering module that monitors the number of active users and blocks access when the maximum number is reached. Alternatively, the software manufacturer may rely on the honor system or a third-party metering utility to restrict the number of concurrent users.

With the application software installed, you can execute an application by changing to the program subdirectory and entering the appropriate command, or you can map a search drive to the application's directory and execute the application from your home or data directory.

Evaluating Network Applications

There are many factors that you should check into when evaluating a program for possible use on your NetWare network. While we don't want to be completely dogmatic about it, the following short list of factors should be of interest to NetWare 4.0 system administrators:

- Is the software designed to be multiuser?

- Has the software been tested with NetWare 4.0 and is the software compatible with it?

- Does the software have clear documentation for NetWare installation and use?

- Are the software's rights requirements documented and are they reasonable?

- Are the software's file attribute requirements documented?

- Can the software's directory structure be configured?

IS THE SOFTWARE DESIGNED TO BE MULTIUSER?

It is critical that any application on the network be designed for a multiuser environment. This includes the way the program treats open files, multiple accesses of data files, multiple accesses of program files, and so on. You cannot afford to find out about such issues by accident. The result of running single-user software in a network environment can be corrupted data or even corrupted application files. In short, if the software fails on this point alone, *don't use it!*

IS THE SOFTWARE COMPATIBLE WITH NETWARE 4.0?

As we mentioned before, the likelihood that the software has been tested with NetWare 4.0 and is compatible with it—at the time of NetWare 4.0's release—is probably minimal. However, as time goes on, the marketplace will adjust to the new standard, and developers will devote adequate resources to product testing and design modifications. Many applications that are compatible with previous versions of NetWare will be compatible with NetWare 4.0 with little or no change.

DOES THE SOFTWARE HAVE CLEAR DOCUMENTATION FOR NETWARE USE?

It is easy to check whether the software has clear documentation for NetWare use, though doing so before you buy it may be a challenge. Look for words like *NetWare, LAN,* and *Network Installation* in the index of the product installation or management manual. The answers to all the questions on the list above should be in the documentation. Of course, there can be quite a gap between "should be" and "are" in the real world.

ARE THE SOFTWARE'S RIGHTS REQUIREMENTS DOCUMENTED?

Look in the index of the application's manual for the terms *NetWare, Trustee Rights, Rights Assignments,* and so on. There may be different requirements for the application directory (often Read and File Scan) and the data directory (often Read, File Scan, Write, Create, Erase).

ARE THE SOFTWARE'S RIGHTS REQUIREMENTS REASONABLE?

If abnormal rights (All, Supervisory, and/or Access Control) are required for a normal user, suspect a poorly designed application and be careful with its use. If another application is available to perform the same function without the bad form of violating basic security sense, we recommend a close look at switching your application. Once again, you'll have to use some common sense about this, but keep it in mind.

ARE THE SOFTWARE'S FILE ATTRIBUTE REQUIREMENTS DOCUMENTED?

Like user trustee rights, the file attributes you need for your application can be fairly easily ferreted out even if they're not documented. If the requirements are not listed, however, pay attention to the possibility that the application's NetWare compatibility has not been tested fully.

CAN THE SOFTWARE'S DIRECTORY STRUCTURE BE CONFIGURED?

There are few things that are as irritating to a system administrator as software that will function properly only within a particular directory structure. The most common and most irritating example of this is a program that requires installation directly off the root of a drive. On a NetWare drive, that makes it the root of the volume.

With NetWare 4.0, you can still place the application files in a subdirectory, then map what is called a "fake root" to the subdirectory. The application will think it's at the root, even though it's in a subdirectory.

Whether or not you agree, sometimes bad program design is not, in and of itself, reason enough to ban a program from your system. In any case, don't keep your feelings to yourself. If you don't like the program, let the developer know by phone, fax, mail, or e-mail. We have been obliged to support applications that violated this point, but in most cases we have communicated our displeasure to the developers. It has even had some effect from time to time.

Creating
Users and Groups

Fast Track

It may be easier for you   **332**
to install your users from scratch than to modify them to fit in a global
naming scheme.

To create NetWare objects,   **333**
use the utility NETADMIN.

To create users with similar needs and configurations,   **337**
use user templates.

To make resources easy to use across the network's Directory,   **340**
use aliases.

One of the primary tasks of a system administrator is to maintain the users, groups, profiles, and other entities on the network. In this chapter you'll learn how.

What Are Objects?

NetWare uses the term *object* to denote network resources, such as users, groups, profiles, volumes, and so on. Some might need to rethink the concept they have of NetWare objects when they upgrade to version 4.0. A Printer object is the network's perception of a printer—not the printer itself. A User object is, from the point of view of the operating system, very similar to a Printer object, while you might not immediately think that to be the case. When making a catalog of network resources, the NetWare operating system considers users, printers, servers, etc., all to be objects.

OBJECTS IN PREVIOUS VERSIONS OF NETWARE

In previous versions of NetWare, objects existed on a file server. The bindery was a database of objects/users, their properties, and the values of those properties.

The key is that the bindery applied to only one file server. It couldn't handle objects that were associated with another file server. If you were a user on one file server, you were not necessarily known by any other file server on the same LAN segment, let alone on the same internetwork. Objects could be replicated across a network; a user could be on File Server 1 and File Server 2 with identical names and passwords. But, in fact, the user was two distinct objects, each residing on one of the file servers.

OBJECTS IN NETWARE 4.0

Objects in NetWare 4.0 exist on a network. Creating and maintaining the objects is the responsibility of the system administrator. As we've discussed earlier, the Directory is a database of every resource on the network. When you log in to the network, you can access objects according to your relationship to them in the Directory, rather than according to which file server they may be related to.

All the different types of objects fall into two categories: container objects and leaf objects. Figure 14.1 shows the relationship between the different container and leaf objects.

Container Objects

Container objects can contain other objects. Container objects are useful because they group other objects together. They are also useful because you can assign some characteristics to a container object that will then apply to all objects it contains. For example, if you assign trustee rights to the container object, all other objects in the container will automatically inherit the same trustee rights. The only available container objects are the following:

- ▸ Country objects

- ▸ Organization objects

- ▸ Organizational Unit objects

FIGURE 14.1

Container and leaf objects

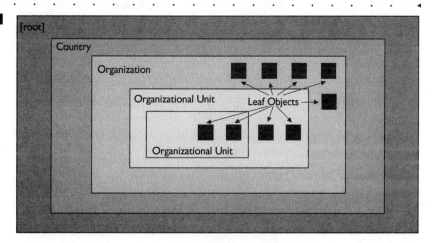

Technically, the Root object can be considered a container object. It is sometimes written in square brackets, [root]. The Root object, however, cannot contain any leaf objects or even any Organizational Unit objects; it can contain only Country or Organization objects.

In Chapter 8, you planned and installed the overall structure of your Directory tree, including the placement of these container objects.

Leaf Objects

Single-entity objects, such as users, printers, and servers, are referred to as *leaf objects*. Leaf objects cannot contain other objects. They are called leaf objects because they are the final element of the Directory tree; leaves cannot contain other branches or leaves. Table 14.1 shows the leaf objects you can have on your network in NetWare 4.0.

	OBJECT	DEFINITION
T A B L E 14.1 *Leaf Objects*	User	Each person that uses the network.
	Alias	Exists in one area of the Directory tree and points to an object located somewhere else in the tree.
	Organizational Role	Specifies a position that can be filled by a succession of people, such as team leader, network supervisor, party planner, etc.
	Group	A list of object names. The names represent individual users.
	Profile	A list grouping of users or groups or both. May have a login script that executes as each member-user logs in to the network.
	Computer	A computer that serves as an end-user workstation.
	Printer	A physical printing device on the network.
	Print Queue	A print queue on the network.
	Print Server	A network print server.

	OBJECT	DEFINITION
TABLE 14.1 *Leaf Objects (continued)*	AFP Server	An AppleTalk Filing Protocol server on the network. It provides a logical representation in the Directory database to view the actions and characteristics of the AFP server.
	NetWare Server	A NetWare Core Protocol (NCP) server.
	Bindery Object	An object that was upgraded from a bindery-based server but that cannot be identified.
	Bindery Queue	A print queue that was migrated from a previous version of NetWare but that could not be added to the Directory as an NDS print queue.
	Volume	A logical volume within a NetWare server. This is not the name of the volume; the name will be one of the properties of this Volume object. The Volume object might be MarketingSysVolume, even though the physical name of the volume is SYS.
	Directory Map	The logical name or alias of a file-system directory path on a volume. You can't look at the directory from the Directory Map object, but you can use the MAP command from login scripts or from the command line, specifying the Directory Map object to record the location of frequently used applications. If the application moves, only the path property of the Directory Map object must change; all login scripts calling that Directory Map object can remain the same.
	Unknown	Represents an NDS object that has been corrupted and cannot be identified as belonging to any of the other object classes.

Essential Elements of the Directory

Only two elements of the Directory tree are essential: The Directory must have the [root] and at least one Organization. Countries and Organizational Units are optional.

A typical Directory might look something like those shown in Figures 14.2 and 14.3. These two figures are graphical representations of the same directory. It is most common to see the Directory illustrated along the lines of Figure 14.2; the representation in Figure 14.3 better illustrates the concept of container and leaf objects.

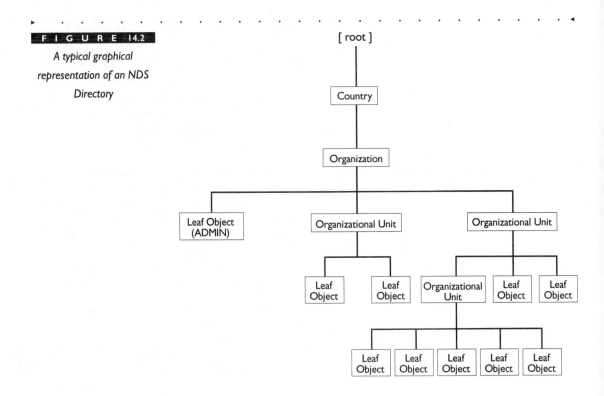

FIGURE 14.2

A typical graphical representation of an NDS Directory

Object Properties

Each object in NetWare Directory Services contains properties that describe it. You specify the information that goes into these properties. Properties vary for each type of object. For example, a User object can have properties such as telephone numbers, an electronic mail address, a postal address, and titles.

FIGURE 14.3

*A different style of
graphical representation of
the NDS Directory shown
in Figure 14.2*

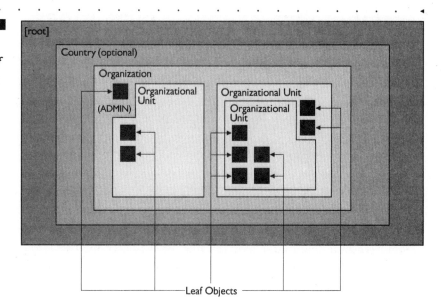

An important property of every object is the Access Control List (ACL) property. The ACL of an object is a list of all the other objects that have trustee rights to work with that object.

Properties add a whole new dimension to the Directory tree. Now, rather than just using the Directory tree to find a printer, you can also use it to look up a phone number for another user.

With properties, the reason behind the name "Directory Services" becomes clear. You can actually use the Directory tree like a telephone directory. You can use it like the white pages, searching for a particular name, such as "Marketing printer." You can also use the Directory tree like the yellow pages, searching for types of objects (printers) or even particular properties (for example, LaserJet printers that are located in Building 4, on the third floor).

Establishing Naming Conventions for Objects

Before you begin creating users, groups, printers, and other types of objects on your network, make sure you've established naming guidelines for the entire network. The Directory will be more useful and efficient if every network administrator who is responsible for creating new objects uses the same format for naming objects and describing object properties.

NAMING CONVENTIONS FOR USER OBJECTS

Etablishing global naming conventions for users may require some give and take if your system supports more than one security mechanism. For example, if you have a minicomputer, a mainframe, or even an e-mail system that requires each user to have a login name and password, it is helpful to make all of these systems conform to a unified set of naming and password conventions. The goal is to strike an appropriate balance between usability and security. If it's too open, there's insufficient security. If it's too secure, users may not be able to make efficient use of the system.

At any single context, there cannot be two objects with the same name. (An object's context is simply its location in the Directory Tree.) At another context, there can be an object with the same name, because the objects are in different container objects and therefore different contexts. Think of it as a family. You don't generally find two siblings with the same name (unless you look at George Foreman's family!), but you may encounter first cousins with the same name. Their nuclear families are different, and that is analogous to their NDS context.

A common naming convention is to use the first letter of the first name and the first seven letters of the last name. Alternatively, you can use the first letters of the first and middle names and the first six letters of the last name.

NETWORK DEVICES—OBJECTS THAT ARE NOT USERS

Keep names simple. If some users are logging in to the network away from their usual workstations, or if they must set up the environment manually at any time, they will have to type complete contexts for themselves and many of the devices or services that they need to use. Initials or cryptic names are generally a poor choice because people forget them. Naming a printer *p1* or *printer1* is less helpful than naming it *AcctOKI* if it is an Okidata printer in Accounting or *PSLaser* if it is a PostScript-compatible laser printer.

Catchy or clever names are good because they are easy to remember. Just don't use unusual spelling. If you have a large number of different devices that aren't manageable by descriptive names, use a convention that is completely non-descriptive, yet identifiable. We've mentioned the idea of alphabetical listings of different types of words or terms (for example, Amethyst, Beryl, Crystal, Diamond, Emerald, Ferrite, Garnet, and Hematite; or Alameda, Berkeley, Concord, Dublin, El Cerrito, Fremont, Gilroy, and Hayward). Users adapt to this kind of naming quite easily and often find it easier to remember than Printer1, Printer2, Printer3.

As with User objects, names within the same context or container object must be unique. Duplicate names are allowed only if they are not in the same container object. It is probably best to avoid duplicates in any case, since objects may be moved.

ALIASES

Aliases are extremely useful in making it easy for users to access network resources. Aliases enable you to specify a printer, a volume, or any other object type, from anywhere in the network. Aliases make for a kind of "speed dialing" of frequently used objects. An alias for the print queue might be placed in the context where you usually work. Then you could access the distant printer queue by capturing to the local alias.

For example, let's say that you have a color PostScript printer set to service a queue (COLOR) in the context of .OU=BOOKS.O=SDS, but you want to be able to send jobs to it from another context (say, .OU=MAGAZINES.O=SDS). By

configuring an alias (COLOR_PS) that relates to the object .CN=COLOR.OU=
BOOKS.O=SDS, you can capture to the alias, instead of specifying the complete
explicit context of the destination queue.

Migration vs. Installing Objects from Scratch

It may make sense for you to use the NetWare Migration Utility to bring your
NetWare 3.11 bindery objects into the NDS Directory, but that's not an entirely
sure bet. Give thought to how much work would be involved in migrating and
modifying those objects as opposed to redesigning them and installing them
from scratch in the new system.

MIGRATING BINDERY OBJECTS

Although we discussed migrating bindery objects in Chapter 9, it deserves
another look. If you are only going to have a single NetWare 4.0 server, or if your
naming conventions will be the same in your new network as they were in the
old one, using the Migration Utility is a very good choice. It automates
the process of reinstalling the same objects as NDS objects.

Migrating users from a bindery will also migrate their login scripts. While you
will probably need to update those login scripts with new drive mappings, it may
be easier to update them than to re-create them all from scratch.

INSTALLING NDS OBJECTS FROM SCRATCH

If you plan to overhaul your naming conventions or security structure, or if
you are not satisfied with the structure of your old network, think about starting
over. Rarely are there bindery servers that are easily convertible to an NDS environment. Usually there is quite a bit of fine tuning to do, and some users will
likely have new login names after all is said and done.

If it looks like you will be taking more time to fine-tune your migrated objects than you would to install them anew, don't be afraid to start over. With new objects and relationships, you can structure your network in an optimal way for the new NDS environment.

Creating Objects with NETADMIN

NETADMIN is the DOS-based network-administration menu utility. Use NETADMIN for creating, deleting, moving, viewing, and modifying objects in the Directory. It is located in the SYS:PUBLIC directory. (On a Windows or OS/2 workstation, you can use the NetWare Administrator graphical utility.)

When you create a new Organization or Organizational Unit object with the INSTALL utility, a new partition is automatically created for that object. This is *not* the case with NETADMIN. If you create an Organization or Organizational Unit object with NETADMIN, that object will be added to an existing partition. If you want to create a new partition for the object, you must use the PARTMGR utility after you create the object.

Log in to the network as User object ADMIN. You can also do this while logged in as any other user, as long as that user has object rights at the context where you intend to create new objects. Then type

    NETADMIN

You should see a screen similar to the one in Figure 14.4. Note that NETADMIN always shows your context at the top of the screen (in this case, O = SDS, which means Organization = Saxon Data Solutions).

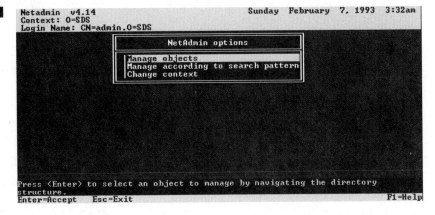

FIGURE 14.4

The opening screen of the NETADMIN menu utility

CREATING ORGANIZATIONS

If you are creating a new Organization, you must be at the context of [root] or Country, since they are the only objects capable of containing an Organization.

1 · Make sure that the context printed at the top of the screen is where you want to create your new Organization. If it is not [root], select *Change context* on the NETADMIN options menu and press ↵.

2 · When prompted with "Enter context," type [**root**] and press ↵.

3 · From the NETADMIN options menu, select *Manage objects* and press ↵. You will see a list of the objects that currently exist in your Directory at your present context. If you expect to see something on the list that isn't there, or if there are objects listed that you don't expect to see, you may be in the wrong context.

4 · If you are at the correct context and wish to create a new object, press the Insert key. A menu labeled *Select an object class* will list the possible object classes: Alias and Organization.

5 · Select Organization and press ↵. You should see a Create Organization screen similar to the one shown in Figure 14.5.

FIGURE 14.5

The Create Organization screen

```
                              Create Organization          •
Organization name:              New Org
Create user template in this Organization:      Yes
```

6 · Enter the organization name and press ↵. If this is the first time an Organization has been created, make a selection for *Create Template user in this Organization.*

7 · Press F10 to save the Organization object and continue.

CREATING ORGANIZATIONAL UNITS

Change context to your new Organization or to an Organizational Unit, since they are the only container objects that can contain Organizational Units. Be sure that the context printed at the top of the screen is correct. It should say O= or OU=, followed by the name of the Organization or Organizational Unit in which you want to create a new Organizational Unit.

1 · From the NETADMIN options menu, select *Manage objects* and press ↵. You should see a list of objects.

2 · Press the Insert key and you should see a menu labeled *Select an object class.*

3 · Select Organizational Unit and press ↵.

4 · Fill in the Organizational Unit name and press ↵. If this is the first time an Organization has been created, make a selection for *Create Template user in this Organization.*

5 · Press F10 to save your Organizational Unit and continue.

CREATING LEAF OBJECTS

Users, printers, NetWare servers, NetWare volumes, and so on are all considered leaf objects because they can't contain any other objects. The biggest adjustment that many will have to make in working with NetWare 4.0 is to stop thinking of a NetWare server as a container or an object of central importance. With NetWare 4.0, it's just another object. In the following example we'll be creating a user, but the procedure is substantially the same for any other leaf object.

1 · Change your context to an Organization or an Organizational Unit, since they are the only objects that can contain a user. Check to see that the proper context is listed at the top of the screen.

2 · From the NETADMIN options menu, highlight *Manage objects* and press ↵. You should see a list of objects, though if this is a new container object, the list may be virtually empty.

3 · Press Insert. The *Select an object class* menu appears (see Figure 14.6), displaying a list of object types that includes User.

4 · Use the cursor keys to highlight User (you can press U to move to it quickly), and press ↵.

5 · Type in the login name and other information on the New User Information screen.

6 · Press F10 to save.

▶

FIGURE 14.6

The menu for selecting an object class

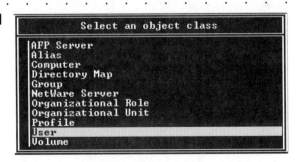

Creating Users with Similar Needs

There are three ways to automate the process of creating many users with similar needs. They involve user templates, groups, and profiles.

USER TEMPLATES

A user template is like a pattern, or a mold, for creating users. Technically, a user template is a leaf object in an Organization or Organizational Unit. It appears on the list of users as USER_TEMPLATE. You can use a user template only in the container where it was created. Once a user template exists, each time a user is created, you have the option of using the template. All future users created using the template will have the same properties, rights, and trustee assignments as the user template.

There are two ways to create a user template: The first way is to create it when its container object (Organization or Organizational Unit) is created. The second way is to create a user and name it USER_TEMPLATE.

When you have a user template at the current context or one above it in the Directory, the default is that each new user will have the same configuration with respect to the following properties:

Account Balance

Allow Unlimited Credit

Allow User to Change Password

Days Between Forced Password Changes

Default Server (if there is no Default Server for the user template or if there is no user template, the Default Server will be set to the name of the server where the master replica of the Directory partition that contains the user resides)

Department

Description

Email Address

Fax Telephone Number

Grace Logins Allowed

Home Directory Path (Volume and Path)

Language (if there is no Language specified for the user template or if there is no user template, the Language attribute will be set to the language of the workstation from which the new user is created)

Location

Login Script

Login Expiration Time

Login Time Restrictions

Maximum Connections

Minimum Account Balance

Minimum Password Length

Password Expiration Date

Require a Password

Require Unique Passwords

Postal Address

Street

Post Office Box

City

State or Province

Postal (Zip) Code

Mailing Label Information

Profile

Security Equals

See Also

Telephone Number

Title

Groups, Profiles and Organizational Roles

You can use a Group object to assign identical rights to several users. Using groups to assign rights to large numbers of users can simplify a network supervisor's job by eliminating the need to adjust each user's rights individually. Although a Group object appears to contain users, it really isn't a container object. Instead, it is merely a leaf object that has, as one of its properties, a list of all the User objects who are assigned to be members of the group.

When you grant trustee rights to a Group object, all the users who are listed as being members of that group also receive the same trustee rights. Assigning a user to a Group object is, relatively speaking, the same thing as granting the user a security equivalence to that Group object.

Group members can be located anywhere in the Directory tree; they do not have to be located in the same container object. For example, if users from two different Organizational Unit objects are working on the same project and need rights to use the same project directory, you can create a Group object called Project. Then, if you assign trustee rights for the necessary directory to the Project Group object, every user who is a member of the Project Group object will be able to access that directory.

A user can be a member of any number of groups.

A profile is an object specifically created to allow several users to have the same login script execute, even if those users are not located in the same container object. The users can be anywhere on the Directory tree. A user may be a member of only one profile. The profile login script executes after the system login script (which is a property of a container object) and before individual user login scripts.

An Organizational Role is a position or job in an organization. Like any other leaf object, it exists in a context and has properties such as location, occupant, and e-mail address.

The procedure for creating a Group, Profile, or an Organizational Role is virtually identical to that for creating a User object as described above. The difference is that instead of choosing User from the screen, you choose Group, Profile, or Organizational Role.

Creating Aliases

As we mentioned above, aliases make it easier to access distant resources. It saves time if you create aliases that point to resources you use frequently. For example, you can create an alias for a print queue. The alias is in your context, while the print queue may be on a distant branch of the Directory. If you give the alias the same name as the print queue, it will appear that the queue is local. Then you can access the queue by capturing the workstation print jobs to the alias.

Creating aliases is similar to creating users. The steps are the same, except that you must also specify the object that the alias points to. In addition, you can create an alias in any container object or context, including [root] and Country.

Editing Objects

Users, user templates, groups, profiles, organizational roles, and aliases are edited in a similar way. We will explain how to edit a user template because editing one template is faster than editing many users. Remember that editing the template will not change existing users; it will only affect users created after the template is edited.

Change the context to the container object that has a user object called USER_TEMPLATE. If there is none, you can create one by following the directions outlined earlier in the chapter for creating a User object.

Once you see it in the list of objects, highlight the object USER_TEMPLATE and press F10. You should see a screen similar to the one shown in Figure 14.7.

FIGURE 14.7

Using NETADMIN to

modify a user

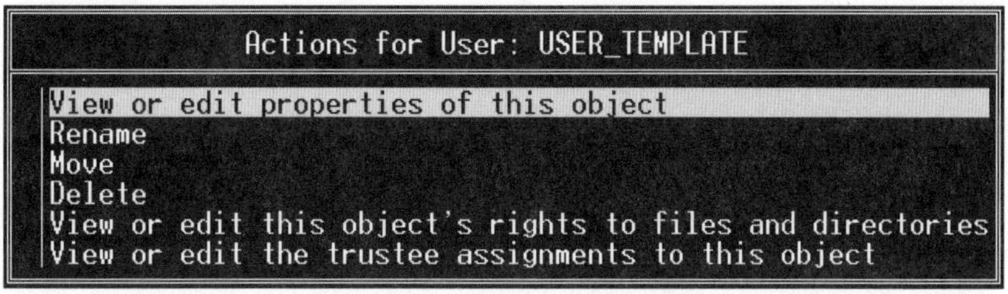

```
┌──────────────────────────────────────────────────────────────────┐
│                  Actions for User: USER_TEMPLATE                   │
├──────────────────────────────────────────────────────────────────┤
│ View or edit properties of this object                             │
│ Rename                                                             │
│ Move                                                               │
│ Delete                                                             │
│ View or edit this object's rights to files and directories         │
│ View or edit the trustee assignments to this object                │
└──────────────────────────────────────────────────────────────────┘
```

Highlight *View or edit properties of this object,* and press ↵. You will be able to edit the following properties of the user:

- ▶ Identification

- ▶ Environment

- ▶ Account Restrictions

- ▶ Login Script

- ▶ Memberships/Security Equals/Profile

- ▶ Change Password

- ▶ Postal Address

- ▶ See Also

See Also is a place for notes pertaining to the object. You could list the supervisor, printers, file servers, or any other object to which this user relates. You could also refer to some source of information that is not part of the network itself, such as personnel records and so on.

When you are finished editing the object, press Esc twice to get back to the list of objects in the same context. Press Esc again to get to the NETADMIN options menu.

EDITING LOGIN SCRIPTS

Login scripts execute when a user logs in to the network. They usually configure the user environment to set up a standard starting point for each user's session. They are analogous to the AUTOEXEC.BAT file in DOS.

Users, profiles, and container objects all may have login scripts. Since we will discuss login scripts in depth in Chapter 15, we will limit the discussion here to getting in and out of the login-script editing screen and leave syntax and function for later. The same steps can be used to edit the login script of a user, user template, profile, Organization, or Organizational Unit.

From the NETADMIN list of objects, highlight the profile, user, or container object whose login script you wish to edit and press ↵. Highlight *View or edit the properties of this object* and press ↵. Select *Login script* and press ↵. If NETADMIN responds with a message saying, "Script is empty. Copy script from another object?" you have two options. You can copy the login script from another user or profile, or you can start from scratch.

Copying the Script from Another Object

At the prompt "Script is empty. Copy script from another object?" select Yes and press ↵. At the "Object name" prompt, press Insert. Your context's list will be displayed. Select a user or profile and press F10. Now the Object Name screen has the name of the user or profile printed on it. Press ↵ to accept. You can now edit the copied login script. When you are finished, press F10 to save it.

Creating the Script from Scratch

At the prompt "Script is empty. Copy script from another object?" select No and press ↵. The screen will display a blank login script. Type in your login commands and press F10 to save the script.

Deleting, Renaming, and Moving Objects

You must have object rights to an object in order to delete, rename, or move it. Container objects may be renamed or deleted only if they are empty.

DELETING AN OBJECT

To delete an object, follow these steps:

1 · Change the context to the container where the object resides.

2 · Highlight the object and press F10.

3 · On the *Actions for [object_type]* screen, select Delete and press ↵.

4 · Choose Yes in response to the "Delete this object?" confirmation prompt and press ↵.

The context's updated list of objects should be displayed in about 60 seconds or less.

RENAMING AN OBJECT

To rename an object, follow these steps:

1 · Change the context to the container where the object resides.

2 · Highlight the object and press F10.

3 · On the *Actions for [object_type]* screen, select Rename and press ↵.

4 · Fill in the new name and answer whether you want to save the old name.

5 · Press F10 to save the name.

MOVING AN OBJECT

To move an object, follow these steps:

1 · Change the context to the container object where the target object resides.

2 · Highlight the object and press F10.

3 · At the *Actions for [object_type]* screen, select Move. You should see a screen similar to the one shown in Figure 14.8.

FIGURE 14.8

*The Move Object screen,
with a sample Old Context
filled in*

```
                                    Move Object
Old Context:     O=Oakland
New Context:
```

4 · You can move to the New Context field and manually type the new context for the object, or you can press Insert while the field is highlighted and be presented with Directory navigation options. Move around in the Directory until the proper destination context is listed and then press F10. The context you chose should now be displayed in the New Context field. (Figure 14.9 shows *San Francisco* as an example.)

FIGURE 14.9

*The Move Object screen,
with a sample New
Context filled in*

```
                                    Move Object
Old Context:     O=Oakland
New Context:     O=San Francisco.
```

5 · Press F10 to proceed.

When the Directory has finished updating, you should see a screen similar to Figure 14.10, confirming that the object was moved successfully.

FIGURE 14.10

*The Move Object
Successful screen*

```
            Move Object Successful

Object CN=GStein moved from context O=Oakland
to context O=San Francisco. successfully.
          Press <Enter> to continue.
```

Login Scripts and Batch Files

Fast Track

▸ **Workstation** variables: identify various aspects of the workstation from a physical and logical point of view.

▸ **DOS environment** variables: can be used within the login script or can be set in the login script and used later.

▸ **Miscellaneous**: allow you to test for other conditions that might exist at the time of login.

A batch file is   368
a file that contains a series of commands. When the file is executed, it runs all the commands in the file.

To automate environmental settings,   368
customize your AUTOEXEC.BAT file.

We've explained drive mappings and some of the other settings you can make to the user environment. So far, though, you have made all these settings using NetWare command-line utilities or the NetWare menu utilities (like NETUSER). The advantage of the menu utilities is that they are easier to maneuver through, because the range of options is displayed at each step along the way. The advantage of the command-line utilities (and the reason we have focused on them) is that they can be automated through batch files and the NetWare login scripts.

Let's say you have a series of commands that you have come up with to set up your user environment so that it's just the way you like it. It might involve five, ten, or more separate commands, and each time you log in they have to be executed again.

Types of Login Scripts

Wouldn't it be nice if you could set up the user environment once and then have it automatically return to that state whenever you logged in? You can do this with the NetWare login scripts, and you can enhance this capability even more through the creative use of DOS batch files.

The NetWare login scripts execute every time a user logs in to the network. There are four types of login scripts: system, profile, user, and default. Earlier versions of NetWare had only system, user, and default login scripts. The profile login script is new in version 4.0.

THE SYSTEM LOGIN SCRIPT

The system login script, if one is present, is the first script to execute when a user logs in. The system login script is a property of Organization and Organizational Unit objects. It executes the same set of commands for every user in that organization or organizational unit and generally contains settings and configuration information that apply to every user in that organization or organizational unit.

For example, you can include the following in the system login script: general drive mappings, service connections (such as printer redirections or CAPTURE statements), and settings that are relative to the physical workstation.

THE PROFILE LOGIN SCRIPT

The profile login script is an optional login script that will execute only for users who belong to a particular Profile object. It executes after the system login script. A Profile object is similar to a Group object, but its sole function is to provide a login script for its members.

A Profile object can include a subset of users within a single container object, or users from many different container objects. For example, if your tree is organized by departments, such as the Research, Development, and Sales Organizational Units, you may have created system login scripts for each of those three Organizational Unit objects.

Now suppose that a team has been formed to work on a particular project, and that team contains members from each of the three different Organizational Units. If all members of the project team need drive mappings to the same directories, you could create a Profile object called TEAM-A and put those drive mappings in that Profile object's login script. Then you could assign each of the users to the Profile object.

Then, when one of the project team members logs in, the system login script for that user's container object executes first. Next, the login script for the TEAM-A Profile object will execute, giving the user the drive mappings he or she needs to work on the special project. Other users in the container will not get these drive mappings unless they, too, have been assigned to the TEAM-A Profile object.

THE USER LOGIN SCRIPT

Each user can also have a personal user login script. If there are environment settings that are specific to the individual user, as opposed to the physical workstation or a workgroup or profile, the user login script might be useful. Another reason to use a user login script is if you allow the users to modify their own environments while operating on the network. By default, each user is allowed to modify his or her own user login script. The user login script can only be created or modified by the user or by someone who has the Write property right to that User object.

Many experienced NetWare system administrators avoid using the user login script because of maintenance considerations. To understand why, imagine a network in which every configuration parameter is set in the user login scripts. When a new user is installed, his or her script must be created (or copied) manually for the system defaults to apply to that user's environment.

Imagine further that the system administrator decides to change something in the system login procedure. To effect such a change, each user login script must be changed. That's not a fun way to spend your off-hours—take our word for it.

If systemwide defaults and environment settings are set at a more global level, for example at the Profile or Organizational Unit, you can make global changes by editing one script. By using the login-script identifier variables (discussed later in this chapter), including the one that represents the user's current login name (%LOGIN_NAME), you can effectively include even user-specific options in a global script without affecting other users.

THE DEFAULT LOGIN SCRIPT

The default login script is a built-in part of the LOGIN utility. The default login script contains a few basic drive mappings that are necessary to let users access the NetWare utilities they need to work on the network.

The default login script executes only for users who do not have individual user login scripts. The first time you log in as user ADMIN, this default login script will execute for you, because you haven't yet had an opportunity to create a user login script for ADMIN.

The default login script executes after the system and profile login scripts. If you don't want the default login script to execute and don't intend to create user login scripts, you can include the command NO_DEFAULT at the end of either the system or profile login script. This command will prevent the default login script from executing, even if there is no user login script.

Login Script Commands

Writing login scripts is a little bit like programming. Many of the rules of thumb for good programming apply to login scripts, such as documenting your routines within the script itself by using remarks (REMs), structuring the script in logical sections, and so on. The login script commands are the following (we'll examine each of them in the following sections):

ATTACH

BREAK [ON | OFF]

CLS

COMSPEC

CONTEXT

DISPLAY

DOS BREAK

DOS VERIFY

DRIVE

EXIT

FDISPLAY

FIRE PHASERS

GOTO

IF...THEN...ELSE

INCLUDE

LASTLOGINTIME

MACHINE

MAP

NO_DEFAULT

NOSWAP

PAUSE

PCCOMPATIBLE

REMARK

SET

SET_TIME [ON | OFF]

SHIFT

SWAP

WRITE

#

ATTACH

You can use this command to attach to a NetWare 4.0 server in bindery mode or to attach to bindery-based servers (NetWare 3.x or 2.x).

The syntax is

ATTACH *server/username*

BREAK [ON | OFF]

Using the BREAK ON command allows you to break out of the login script while it is executing by pressing Ctrl-Break. Using the BREAK OFF command disables your ability to halt the login script's execution by pressing Ctrl-Break.

CLS

This command functions precisely like the DOS CLS command, clearing the workstation screen of any previously displayed messages.

COMSPEC

If your users will be running DOS from a network directory instead of from a local disk, use the COMSPEC command to specify which network directory contains COMMAND.COM (the DOS command processor). This will allow the workstation to find the COMMAND.COM file on the network.

If users will run DOS from a local disk, do not put a COMSPEC command in their login scripts. Instead, those users can specify a path command in their AUTOEXEC.BAT files to indicate which local drive contains COMMAND.COM.

The syntax is

COMSPEC = *path* COMMAND.COM

CONTEXT

Use this command to change the current NDS context. It is somewhat analogous to the DOS CD command, except that CD changes a user's location in the DOS directory structure, and CONTEXT changes a user's location in the NDS directory structure.

The syntax is

CONTEXT *context*

DISPLAY

This command displays an ASCII text file on the screen. Use this command if you would like to compose a message in a word processor or text editor that can save files in pure ASCII text format. To display the file, include the file's name in the command, such as

DISPLAY MESSAGE.TXT

This command can be useful, for example, if you want to display "Message Of The Day." You can edit the text file instead of editing the login script every day.

The syntax is

DISPLAY *path/filename*

To display a file that contains word processing codes, see FDISPLAY.

DOS BREAK [ON | OFF]

Use the DOS BREAK ON command to enable DOS's Ctrl-Break keystroke, which lets users halt programs by pressing Ctrl-Break. The default setting is DOS BREAK OFF.

This command is different from the BREAK command, which lets users stop the login script from executing.

DOS VERIFY

This command verifies DOS data writes to a disk. This is especially useful for environments that disable NetWare's read-after-write verification process to enhance performance. It may be that some critical applications should have the extra security of verification even if it means a slight reduction in operating speed.

DRIVE

This command is equivalent to typing a drive letter followed by a colon and pressing ↵ at the DOS command line. Use it to change drives within the login script.

The syntax is

DRIVE *drive:*

EXIT

Use this command to halt the execution of all the login scripts for the user and to send the user directly into a program, such as an application, a batch file, or a menu. To specify the program that should be executed when the login script is shipped, include the name of the program's executable file in quotation marks after the word *EXIT.*

The syntax is

> EXIT "*filename*"

The following example would terminate the login process and execute the batch file TSRS.BAT:

> EXIT "TSRS.BAT"

If you want the login script to leave the user at the normal DOS prompt when the login process is completed, you do not need to use the EXIT command.

FDISPLAY

This command displays a word-processed file on the screen, filtering out any non-ASCII characters. Use this if you would like to compose a message in a word processor and don't want to go to the trouble of saving the message file as ASCII text or entering it into the login script.

The syntax is

> FDISPLAY *path/filename*

FIRE PHASERS

This command uses the workstation's speaker to blurt out an alarm that bears little or no resemblance to the sound effect used in the "Star Trek" television show (and that includes "Star Trek: The Next Generation" and even "Star Trek: Deep Space Nine"). Phasers are limited to nine blasts per command.

The syntax is

> FIRE PHASERS *n* TIMES

GOTO

What would any programming language, or pseudo–programming language, be without a GOTO command? It wouldn't allow you to use subroutines or bypass sections of code. Fortunately, the NetWare login scripts allow you to do both.

IF...THEN...ELSE

This command defines a segment of the script that executes only if a certain condition exists. The following example is a common use of IF...THEN:

```
If "%LOGIN_NAME"=="ADMIN" THEN
    WRITE "Please check the error logs while you're logged in."
    INCLUDE GRAND_SYS:SYSTEM\ADMINLOG.TXT
END
```

You can nest IF...THEN conditions up to ten levels in the login script, counting any sections executed because of INCLUDE statements.

INCLUDE

This command allows you to execute login script commands located in a separate text file or in another object's login script as a portion of your login script.

The syntax is

```
INCLUDE objectname or filename
```

LASTLOGINTIME

This command displays the last time the user logged in.

MACHINE

This command sets the DOS environment variable MACHINE to the default value of IBM_PC or any other value you specify.

The syntax is

```
MACHINE = name
```

MAP

Use the MAP command to map drives and search drives to network directories. For more information about mapping drives and search drives, see Chapter 13.

NO_DEFAULT

Use this command in either the system login script or the profile login script to prevent the default login script from executing.

NOSWAP

If you don't want LOGIN.EXE to leave the workstation's RAM to make room for any external programs, you can specify NOSWAP. If an external program tries to use more memory than LOGIN leaves available and you have NOSWAP set, the external program will fail to execute, but the login script will continue running.

PAUSE

Identical in effect to the DOS PAUSE command, this command pauses the execution of a login script until the user presses a key.

PCCOMPATIBLE

This command identifies the workstation as an IBM-compatible personal computer. You only need to use this command if you are also using the EXIT command.

REMARK

To add comments to your login scripts, use the REMARK command (or one of its variations: REM, *, or ;) at the beginning of the comment. The line will not be displayed on the workstation screen when the login script executes. Use remarks to document your login script commands.

For example, to include a note to yourself explaining why you included a drive mapping in the script, add the following line:

```
REM This drive mapping is for the payroll directory
```

SET

This command allows you to modify the DOS environment and set variables. The most useful advantage of this capability is that you can pass into the DOS environment any of the values that are returned from identifier variables and then use them outside the login scripts. We'll go into this in more detail when we talk about batch files later in this chapter.

The syntax is

SET *name* = *value*

SET TIME [ON | OFF]

By default, the workstation's time is set to that of the server to which it attaches when VLM.EXE executes (and a connection is made with a server) and then again each time the login script executes. If you want to avoid the second time adjustment, you can specify SET TIME OFF in the login script.

SHIFT

If you have used more than one command-line parameter (see the description of the identifier variable %*n* later in this chapter) when you execute the LOGIN utility, you can use SHIFT to discard the first parameter, and each one after it moves up in order. This ability is very useful if you have a routine that must run on each of the parameters in order. That way you can simply shift and then loop back to repeat the same section of code.

The syntax is

SHIFT *n*

SWAP

When you use # to invoke an external command, that command may require more memory than LOGIN.EXE leaves available. By default, LOGIN will first try to store itself in conventional memory. If that doesn't work, LOGIN.EXE will remove

itself to high memory or disk to make room for the external command. To force
LOGIN to be swapped to higher memory or to the disk without first checking to
see if it can be held in conventional memory, use the SWAP command.

WRITE

This command displays text on the workstation screen. Enclose all text to be
displayed in quotation marks ("text").
The syntax is

    WRITE "*message*"

#

The pound character, followed by a file name, indicates that the executable file
is not internal to the login script itself. This syntax is limited to COM and EXE
files for a DOS workstation. To execute an external batch file (.BAT), you must
execute the DOS command interpreter, COMMAND.COM, as in the following
example:

    #COMMAND /C RUN.BAT

Identifier Variables

One of the most powerful aspects of the NetWare login scripts is the
availability of the identifier variables. These are interpreted at the moment of the
login script's execution to reflect the current environment of the user's workstation or user status or both. Table 15.1 shows a listing of some of the identifier
variables and their general categories. In the following section, we will
demonstrate some ways of using them.

CATEGORY	IDENTIFIER VARIABLE
Date	DAY
	DAY_OF_WEEK
	MONTH
	MONTH_NAME
	NDAY_OF_WEEK
	SHORT_YEAR
	YEAR
Time	AM_PM
	GREETING_TIME
	HOUR
	HOUR24
	MINUTE
	SECOND
User	FULL_NAME
	LOGIN_NAME
	MEMBER OF "group"
	PASSWORD_EXPIRES
	USER_ID
Network	FILE_SERVER
	NETWORK_ADDRESS
Workstation	DOS_REQUESTER
	MACHINE
	NETWARE_REQUESTER
	OS
	OS_VERSION

	CATEGORY	IDENTIFIER VARIABLE
TABLE 15.1 *Login Script Identifier Variables (continued)*	**Workstation**	P_STATION
		SHELL_TYPE
		SMACHINE
		STATION
	DOS Environment	\<variable\>
	Miscellaneous	ACCESS_SERVER
		ERROR_LEVEL
		%n

The identifier variables are divided into seven general categories:

▶ Date

▶ Time

▶ User

▶ Network

▶ Workstation

▶ DOS Environment

▶ Miscellaneous

The first two categories indicate the current date and time in various formats at the instant that the login script executes. The User variables pertain to the User object whose account is being used for the login. The next two categories identify various aspects of the network and workstation from a physical and logical point of view. Variables from the DOS environment can be used within the login script, or they can be set in the login script and used later. Finally, the miscellaneous variables allow you to test for other conditions that might exist at the time of login.

You can use identifier variables with various syntaxes, depending upon whether they are being used within a WRITE statement. However, if you follow the rule of thumb that all of them should be preceded by a percent sign (%) and all of them should be capitalized, you will almost never use them incorrectly.

DATE VARIABLES

This section contains explanations of the Date identifier variables.

DAY   This variable returns the current day of the month as a two-digit number (01–31).

DAY_OF_WEEK   This variable returns the current day of the week as a word (Monday, Tuesday, etc.).

NDAY_OF_WEEK   This variable returns the current day of the week as a number (1–7, where 1 = Sunday, 2 = Monday, etc.).

MONTH   This variable returns the current month as a number (1–12, where 1 = January, 2 = February, etc.).

MONTH_NAME   This variable returns the current month name (January, February, etc.).

SHORT_YEAR   This variable returns the last two digits of the current year (93, 94, 95, etc.).

YEAR   This variable returns the current year in four-digit format (1993, 1994, 1995, etc.).

TIME VARIABLES

This section contains explanations of the Time identifier variables.

AM_PM   This variable returns whether the time is before or after 12:00 noon (AM or PM).

GREETING_TIME   This variable returns the time of day (morning, afternoon, or evening). It is most useful in constructing a generic greeting message. Using this variable lets the message adapt to the time of day.

HOUR   This variable returns the hour in 12-hour format (1–12).

HOUR24   This variable returns the hour in 24-hour format (00–23, where 00 = 12:00 midnight).

MINUTE   This variable returns the minute (00–59).

SECOND   This variable returns the second for those that need to be very precise (00–59).

USER VARIABLES

This section contains explanations of the User identifier variables.

FULL_NAME   This variable returns the complete name of the user, such as Mary.Sales.Lab_Products.HighTech.

LOGIN_NAME   This variable returns the first eight characters of the actual login name of the user.

MEMBER OF "group"   This variable returns tests for membership in a group. This variable is best used in an IF...THEN command, as in the following example:

IF MEMBER OF "ACCTG" THEN WRITE "Accounting Mtg. at 11:00 Today."

PASSWORD_EXPIRES   This variable returns the number of days that the user's password will remain valid. It can be used in a warning message, as in the following example:

IF "%PASSWORD_EXPIRES"<"15" THEN
WRITE "Please change your password. It is due to expire soon."
END

USER_ID   This variable returns the number that NetWare assigns each User object for mail directories and other internal functions. It is not often useful in login scripts, but you can find uses for it.

NETWORK VARIABLES

This section contains explanations of the Network identifier variables.

FILE_SERVER   This variable returns the NetWare server to which the user is connected.

MACHINE   This variable returns the type of machine being used as the workstation. DOS workstations by default will return IBM_PC_TYPE, but this value can be set differently in the NET.CFG file at the workstation (usually in the C:\NWCLIENT directory), by assigning a different value to the parameter LONG MACHINE TYPE=. This applies only to non-OS/2 workstations.

NETWORK_ADDRESS   This variable returns the address of the network. This is the same eight-digit hexadecimal number that is established in the server's AUTOEXEC.NCF file in the command that binds the protocol to the LAN driver.

NETWARE_REQUESTER   This variable returns the version of the Net-Ware Requester for OS/2 that is running on the workstation.

OS   This variable returns the type of DOS running at the workstation (either MSDOS or DRDOS).

OS_VERSION   This variable returns the version of DOS running at the workstation.

P_STATION   This variable returns the physical node address of the workstation. This value will be a 12-digit hexadecimal number. If the number doesn't contain 12 digits, the most significant digits will be packed with zeros. Therefore, an ARCnet workstation with a node address of 8F will return a value of 00000000008F.

SHELL_TYPE   This variable returns the version of the NetWare shell being used. It will display the version number for either the shell file in NetWare 2.*x* or 3.*x*, or the version of the NetWare DOS Requester in NetWare 4.0.

SMACHINE   This variable returns the short machine type of the workstation. The default value is IBM. This applies only to non-OS/2 workstations.

STATION   This variable returns the NetWare operating-system connection number allocated to the workstation while it is attached to the network. This value may be useful for keeping track of your use within the limits of your NetWare operating-system license, as in the example below:

```
IF "%STATION">"85" THEN BEGIN
   CLS
   WRITE "It's time to upgrade to 250 User NetWare..."
   FIRE PHASERS 5 TIMES
   PAUSE
   END
```

DOS ENVIRONMENT VARIABLE: <DOS_VARIABLE>

This syntax allows you to use an existing DOS environment variable in a login script command. For example, if you wanted to make sure that a workstation had a TEMP variable set for Windows, but you didn't want to change any existing definitions, you could use the following routine:

```
IF "<TEMP>"=="" THEN SET TEMP="C:\\"
```

As with some of the previous examples, you can use either one or two equal signs to indicate "equals." To indicate "not equals," use !=. We tend to use two because when we test for negative conditions, it keeps the script looking neat, as in the following example:

```
IF "DAY_OF_WEEK"=="FRIDAY" THEN WRITE "TGIF!"
IF "DAY_OF_WEEK"!="MONDAY" THEN WRITE "Did you back up
yesterday?"
```

The result of this example would be to display a message every Friday that says "TGIF!" Every day but Monday the user would be asked if he or she backed up the day before.

MISCELLANEOUS VARIABLES

This section contains explanations of the miscellaneous identifier variables.

ACCESS_SERVER   This variable returns either TRUE or FALSE for the condition "Is this session running on a NetWare Access Server?" The NetWare Access Server is a product that allows users to dial into the LAN and connect to a dedicated 386 (or better) computer that then runs up to 16 virtual 8086 sessions internally. You can use this variable to establish more stringent security or environment configurations, which might be needed, for example, when users are dialing in from remote sites.

ERROR_LEVEL   This variable returns a number between 0 and 255 (0 usually indicates no errors) after a command executes. It is a good way to make sure that certain commands execute normally, especially if they are running unattended.

%0   This variable returns the name of the NetWare server to which the workstation has connected. It returns the same value as the variable FILE_SERVER.

%1   This variable returns the user's login name. It returns the same value as the variable LOGIN_NAME.

%2, %3, etc.   These variables return any command-line parameters entered on the same line as LOGIN *username,* separated by spaces. For example, the command LOGIN ADMIN FIRST SECOND would be interpreted as follows:

```
%0 = Server Name
%1 = ADMIN
%2 = FIRST
%3 = SECOND
```

These variables are rarely used but can offer a safe back-door in case a login script is corrupted or written incorrectly. To use these variables, your first login script command must be the following:

```
IF "%2"= ="BREAK" THEN EXIT
```

To enable this line, you would log in as any valid user and then type BREAK after the login name (LOGIN ADMIN BREAK). The normal password prompt will appear, and the user will be validated on the system as they would at any other time. No one can get to this line of the script unless they have been validated as a user with a correct password.

Once they have been validated, all security parameters and rights are established, even though no drives have been mapped. As the first line of the login script, the EXIT command halts the environment configuration and dumps the user out to a DOS prompt with no mappings, menus, or anything else.

However, from that point, an administrator can map a few drives manually (or just change directories to SYS:PUBLIC, run NETADMIN, and fix the broken login script). This routine does not add any unauthorized access possibilities, yet it provides a fallback ability if a login script is fatally misconfigured.

Batch Files

A batch file is a file that contains a series of commands. When you execute the batch file, all the commands in the file execute. You can create a batch file to accomplish a variety of tasks.

Some basic formatting rules apply to batch files:

▶ They must have no control (formatting) characters besides tabs and spaces.

▶ They must be pure ASCII text.

▶ They must contain valid executable commands (whether they are internal DOS commands or external executable files does not matter).

▶ They must have the file-name extension .BAT.

CHANGING AUTOEXEC.BAT

On a standalone DOS computer, you can automate environmental settings by using AUTOEXEC.BAT. Every time the computer boots, it looks for a file, called AUTOEXEC.BAT, in the root directory of the boot drive (A: or C:). The name of the file describes its function; it is an AUTOmatically EXECuting BATch of commands.

As with any batch file, you can put anything in AUTOEXEC.BAT that would be a valid command at the DOS command line. However, whatever you put into your AUTOEXEC.BAT file will execute every time you boot the computer (turn it on).

Some people use a very simple AUTOEXEC.BAT to set a path and a prompt and that's about it. Others load special drivers or utility programs, a menu interface, or any of a wide range of options. You can also include commands to load NetWare files and LAN drivers and to log the user in to the network.

ADVANCED BATCH-FILE TECHNIQUES

As we already mentioned, a very powerful tool in administering a network is to pass login script variables into the DOS environment. To set a DOS environment variable, use the internal DOS command SET, or the login script command SET as follows:

> SET variable = value

where *variable* is the term you will assign in the DOS environment and *value* is the definition of that term. If this seems confusing, let's look at a DOS environment variable with which you are probably already familiar.

Changing the DOS Prompt

The DOS prompt is an environment variable. The most common DOS prompt is PG, which displays the current path followed by a greater-than sign (>). You can have other values for the prompt. One of our favorite tricks is to have the time (in military format) in the prompt, as in the following:

> SET PROMPT=$T PG

The effect would look something like this:

> 17:05:32:84 F:\USERS\STEPHEN>

Of course, this makes the prompt a little hard to read, with the seconds and hundredths of seconds displayed as they are. You can modify these with the following prompt:

> SET PROMPT=THHHHH$H PG

The $H is interpreted as a backspace, so with six of them, the prompt looks like this:

```
17:06 F:\USERS\STEPHEN>
```

Now if you want to see the current time, all you have to do is press ↵ and look at the prompt.

Passing Login Script Variables to the DOS Environment

Some useful identifier variable values to use in batch files are LOGIN_NAME, P_STATION, and OS_VERSION. If you add the following lines to your login script, you will be able to use these values in your batch files.

```
SET USER="%LOGIN_NAME"
SET NODE="%P_STATION"
SET DOS="%OS_VERSION"
```

To use these variables, you need to place them within percent signs (%USER%, %NODE%, %DOS%). Testing for the correct values in batch files is very similar to the IF…THEN syntax of the login scripts. To test for a particular version of DOS, use the following command:

```
IF "%DOS%"=="V5.00" echo You're using DOS 5.0
```

If you wanted to test to see if the workstation at which the tape backup software were being run had a tape drive, you could identify the node address of the computer that had a tape drive and then test for the existence of that value in the DOS environment variable NODE. If the tape drive were attached to a PC with the node address 8038CF49206D, you could set up a batch file routine like the following example:

```
IF "%NODE%"!="8038CF49206D" echo This PC has no tape drive."
```

Or, if you had to be logged in as SUPERVISOR to back up the system properly, you might want to put in a routine like this:

```
IF "%USER%"=="SUPERVISOR" THEN GOTO OK
ECHO You aren't logged in as SUPERVISOR. You can't run backups.
GOTO END
:OK
BACKUP.EXE
:END
```

This one is a little more complex. It tests to see if the user is SUPERVISOR. If the user is logged in as SUPERVISOR, the batch file skips the error message and goes on to the section labeled *OK* to perform the backup. If the user is not logged in as SUPERVISOR, he or she goes on to the error message and then skips to the final line, labeled :END. Since the last line is a commented line (because it is preceded by a colon), the file completes with no more actions. It's a little convoluted, but it works.

We could go on for chapters on the techniques of advanced batch files, but that's beyond the scope of this book. We will finish off this chapter with some sample login script segments and batch files for you to try out on your own system.

A Sample Login Script

Figure 15.1 shows the contents of a sample login script. Figure 15.2 shows the display produced by the script.

The first thing that you may notice is that there is documentation within the script itself. We strongly advise you to make all scripts and batch files self-documenting.

All the identifier variables were covered earlier in this chapter, so you should understand them pretty well at this point (as long as you have a photographic memory). There are several routines that bear explanation.

▶ · ◀

```
;;;;;;;;;;;;;;;;;;;;;;;;;;;;
;; SAMPLE LOGIN SCRIPT ::
;;;;;;;;;;;;;;;;;;;;;;;;;;;;
if "%2"=="OVERRIDE" then exit

map display off
map errors off
    ;;;;;;;;;;;;;;;;;;;;;;;;
    ;; Welcome message ;;
    ;;;;;;;;;;;;;;;;;;;;;;;;

write "************************************************************************ "
write "                            WELCOME!                                   "
write "************************************************************************ "
write "                    Good %GREETING_TIME, %LOGIN_NAME.  "
write "************************************************************************"
write "            Time:. . . . . . . . . %HOUR:%MINUTE %AM_PM"
write "            Day: . . . . . . . . . %DAY_OF_WEEK"
write "            Date:. . . . . . . . . %MONTH_NAME %DAY, %YEAR"
write "            Login Name:. . . . . . %LOGIN_NAME"
write "            Full Name: . . . . . . %FULL_NAME"
write "            User ID Number:. . . . %USER_ID"
write "            Network Address: . . . %NETWORK_ADDRESS"
write "            File Server Name:. . . %FILE_SERVER"
write "            Connection Number: . . %STATION"
write "            Node Address:. . . . . %P_STATION"
write "            Operating System:. . . %OS"
write "            OS Version:. . . . . . %OS_VERSION"
write "            Machine:. . . . . . . %MACHINE"
write "            NETX Shell:. . . . . . %SHELL_TYPE"
write "            DOS Requester:. . . . .%DOS_REQUESTER"
write "    "
write "                    LET'S GET BUSY!"
write "************************************************************************ "
map display off


    ;;;;;;;;;;;;;;;;;;;;;;;;
    ;; Global mappings ;;
    ;;;;;;;;;;;;;;;;;;;;;;;;
```

The sample login script

(continued)

```
map f:=sys:
if "%LOGIN_NAME"!="SUPERVISOR" then map root h:=sys:users\%LOGIN_NAME
if "%LOGIN_NAME"=="SUPERVISOR" then map root h:=sys:users\super

map ins        s1:=sys:public
map ins root   s2:=sys:public\%os\%os_version
map ins root   s3:=sys:apps\tools
map ins root   s4:=sys:apps\win31
map ins root   s5:=sys:apps\winapps
map ins        s6:=sys:apps\wp51


        ;;;;;;;;;;;;;;;;;;;;;;;;;;;;;;;
        ;; DOS environment settings ;;
        ;;;;;;;;;;;;;;;;;;;;;;;;;;;;;;;

comspec=s2:command.com
set WPC = "/nt-1/u-%LOGIN_NAME"
set USER = "%LOGIN_NAME"
set NODE = "%P_STATION"


        ;;;;;;;;;;;;;;;;;;;;
        ;; Special Cases ;;
        ;;;;;;;;;;;;;;;;;;;;

if "%LOGIN_NAME" = "SUPERVISOR" then begin
    dos set USER = "SUPER"
    dos set WPC  = "/nt-1/u-{WP"
    end
if member of "ADMIN_GROUP" then map s16:=sys:system


        ;;;;;;;;;;;;;;;;;;;;;;
        ;; Final Settings ;;
        ;;;;;;;;;;;;;;;;;;;;;;

drive h:
exit "TSRS.BAT"
```

▶ . . . . ◀

The display produced at
login

```
************************************************************
                          WELCOME!
                  Good morning, STEPHEN.
************************************************************
Time:................12:17 am
Day:.................Wednesday
Date:................February 10, 1993
Login Name:..........Stephen
Full Name:...........Stephen Saxon
User ID Number:......10000A6
Network Address:.....000CAB1E
File Server Name:....GRAND
Connection Number:...4
Node Address:........00AA00146163
Operating System:....MSDOS
OS Version:..........V5.00
Machine:.............IBM_PC
NETX Shell Type:.....V4.00A
DOS Requester:.......V1.00
LET'S GET BUSY!
************************************************************
H:\>
```

The first is the following:

```
if "%LOGIN_NAME"!="SUPERVISOR" then map root
h:=sys:users\%LOGIN_NAME
if "%LOGIN_NAME"=="SUPERVISOR" then map root
h:=sys:users\super
```

In the preceding lines, we account for the fact that SUPERVISOR has more than eight letters. For all other users on the network, the login name has eight characters or fewer, so we have established home directories that are keyed to those login names. For SUPERVISOR, that won't work, because the directory name turns out to be too long, so we name it SUPER instead.

There are two things wrong with this. The first problem is that there is not necessarily a user SUPERVISOR if you attach to the network through NDS. However, if you use NETX.COM, there is a user SUPERVISOR emulated on the system. The second problem isn't really a problem. Instead, it's a fix.

With the new login scripts, the variable %LOGIN_NAME is returned as the first eight characters of a login name. Thus, SUPERVISOR is returned as SUPERVIS, making a directory name quite doable. The identifier variable %FULL_NAME returns the whole name. You can see that this routine isn't really necessary, but it shows you how to use the comparison of two values in a login script.

By the way, when you compare a variable with a value, you must enclose the value in double quotation marks.

The second routine that needs some explanation is the following:

    if member of "ADMIN_GROUP" then map s16:=sys:system

This line tests for membership in the group ADMIN_GROUP. If the user is a member, a search drive is mapped to SYS:SYSTEM, the location of all supervisory utilities. Only system administrators should have access to SYS:SYSTEM. The group ADMIN_GROUP is one that we installed and configured manually. It is not a default object of NetWare 4.0.

The third routine that needs explanation is the following:

    exit "TSRS.BAT"

This line quits the login script (and all subsequent login scripts) and executes a batch file that may or may not load special drivers, TSR (memory-resident) programs, menus, etc. The advantage of loading them from a batch file is that they don't trap any of the memory used by LOGIN.EXE, because they don't load until LOGIN.EXE has already been removed from RAM.

A Sample Batch File: ADD2PATH.BAT

ADD2PATH.BAT (see Figure 15.3) adds a new directory to the existing path. It shows a lot of nice tricks that you can use in writing batch files.

► . . . . ◄

The sample batch file,

ADD2PATH.BAT

```
:::::::::::::::::::::::::::::::::::::::::::::::::
:: ADD2PATH.BAT                               ::
:: This file adds a directory specified at    ::
:: the command line to the existing DOS path. ::
:::::::::::::::::::::::::::::::::::::::::::::::::
@echo off
cls

if ~"%1"=="" goto SyntaxError

echo.
echo  The current path is:
echo.
echo        %PATH%
echo.
echo  If you want to add %1 to the existing path,
echo  please press a key to continue.
echo.
echo  If you do not wish to continue, hold down the [Ctrl] key
echo  while you press the [Break] key (the [Break] key might
echo  also be labeled [Pause]), and terminate this batch file.
echo.
pause
cls
echo  Thank you.
echo.
echo.
set OLDPATH=%PATH%
if "%OLDPATH%"=="%PATH%" goto EnvOk
goto EnvError

:EnvOk
SET PATH=%PATH%;%1

echo  The new DOS path is:
echo.
echo        %PATH%
echo.
echo.
goto End
```

▶ · ◀

FIGURE 15.3

The sample batch file,
ADD2PATH.BAT
(continued)

```
:SyntaxError
echo ^G
echo  You didn't supply a new directory for me to add to the path.
echo  Try it again, but this time specify a directory for me,
echo  for example:
echo.
echo        ADD2PATH C:\NEWDIR
echo.
echo  This example will place C:\NEWDIR at the tail end of the
echo  current DOS Path.
echo.
echo.
goto End

:EnvError
echo ^G
echo     You don't have enough space available in
echo     your DOS environment.  Try adding the following
echo     line to your CONFIG.SYS file:
echo.
echo            SHELL=COMMAND.COM /E:1024 /P
echo.
echo     Then reboot your workstation (if you are on a
echo     network, log out first), and try this batch file again.
echo.
goto End

:End
```

The whole purpose of this batch file is to change the value of the DOS variable, PATH. The idea is that a user can add a directory to the DOS path by typing **ADD2PATH Directory_Path**, where *Directory_Path* is the full path (including the drive) of the directory to be added.

There are also some error-checking mechanisms built in to account for some possible problems. It's when you start to think about how a batch file might be misused or mistaken that things start to get more complex.

The first error check is to make sure that the user supplies a directory for adding to the path. The first additional parameter (an argument entered at the same time as ADD2PATH and separated by a space) is identified within the batch file as %1. If you had more command-line parameters, they would be %2, %3, etc.

```
if "%1"=="" goto SyntaxError
```

When there is a directory specified, the equation will be interpreted as false. If there is no directory specified, the equation will be true and the conditional *goto* statement will execute, taking the user to an error message subroutine.

Later on there is a check to verify that there is enough environment space for the function of the batch file. It also passes onto a specific error message subroutine if there is a problem.

The first section of ECHO commands allows the user to confirm the action about to be taken. By explaining the process of breaking out of a batch file within the message itself, even users who aren't very comfortable with computers can be given some comfort and control over the situation.

Virtually all the lines in this batch file could be considered part of the "user interface." The only real command is right under the label *EnvOk,* which reads SET PATH=%PATH%;%1. That is the "engine" of the whole file. All the other commands support it in one way or another, either by checking for error conditions or by giving guidance to the user.

It's not uncommon for the number of supporting lines of code to be large when compared to the heart of the batch file's function. Don't be afraid to make a batch file "look pretty" when lots of people will be using it regularly. On the other hand, if it's not going to be viewed in public or affect many people, a quick-and-dirty batch file solution is sometimes appropriate.

CHAPTER 16

Creating
User Menus

Fast Track

382   *Using a menu system on your network has several advantages:*

- ▸ Menus provide a friendlier, more convenient interface for the user.

- ▸ Menus ensure that each user has a standardized operating environment while working on the network.

- ▸ Menus shield the user from the network, allowing you to prevent users from performing functions that are unrelated to their responsibilities on the network. This improves security.

384   *To create a menu script,*
make sure that it is pure ASCII text. No formatting codes (except for tabs and hard returns) are allowed.

384   *To compile the source file or menu script,*
use the MENUMAKE.EXE utility.

385   *The two structural identification terms in the menu script are the following:*

- ▸ MENU: identifies a discrete menu block.
- ▸ ITEM: identifies an individual menu option.

The essential menu commands are   385
EXEC, GETO, GETP, GETR, LOAD, and SHOW ##.

The essential menu parameters are   387
BATCH, CHDIR, PAUSE, AND SHOW.

To make your menus easier to maintain,   388
keep them centralized.

To keep the main menu files secure,   389
don't assign rights beyond Read and File Scan to any persons except
network administration staff.

To ease initial setup and long-term maintenance of a menu script,   389
use a batch file instead of individual commands in the script itself.

To convert old menu scripts to the new syntax in 4.0,   390
use MENUCNVT.EXE.

At the workstation, NetWare emulates the environment of the workstation. From a DOS workstation, operating on the network looks and feels like working in DOS. A Macintosh workstation sees the NetWare services as Macintosh items. An OS/2 workstation sees the NetWare resources as native to OS/2. This has advantages because any users who need to operate on a NetWare network can relate to the network in terms that they are already familiar with. They don't have to learn a whole new environment, as might be necessary when using some other systems.

That's great if the users happen to like the workstation's interface and they are fairly familiar with it to begin with. We don't know a whole lot of Macintosh users, for instance, who don't like the way the Macintosh works (besides possible performance complaints). Unfortunately, DOS is not the friendliest operating system around. Others are worse, but that's not the point.

Unlike using the graphical user interfaces available (Macintosh, OS/2, Windows, NeXT, X Windows, etc.), using DOS requires an understanding of a fairly lengthy command structure. NetWare respects that commands (eight characters or less, plus parameters) are the common currency of DOS. As such, all the NetWare functions are available as additional commands. So a DOS client on a NetWare LAN must actually "learn" NetWare to a greater extent than probably any other client that NetWare supports.

That can be a substantial amount of overhead when you consider the costs of training, lost productivity, and lost user comfort. In some environments, every new act for which the user is held responsible means a precise increase in the cost of doing business. This cost isn't just due to some amorphous fear of user responsibility. Some labor agreements are very explicit about the responsibilities of the workers, and a change in those definitions means a change in the cost of labor. Don't get us wrong; we are only saying that the change of an interface or a user's relationship to the network has far-reaching consequences. Adding NetWare commands is just such a change.

One answer is to shield the user from the actual command interface with a shell of some kind. There are many popular shells available, with lesser or greater implications for their use on a network. Some hold that Windows 3.*x* is little more than a DOS shell since it must run on top of DOS. For those who have managed Windows on a NetWare LAN, calling it a shell is to understate the administration requirements of such an endeavor.

Far more common is to provide menus of some sort to shield the user from the command line. Menus can provide a friendlier, or at least a more convenient, interface for the network user. They can assure that each user has a standardized operating environment while working on the network, avoiding a confusing combination of manuals, notes, cheat sheets, and so on that vary from user to user. Menus make these unnecessary for the normal network user.

You can also use a menu interface to shield the network from the user. You can prevent users from performing functions that are not related to their responsibilities on the network. Though security should be handled through a thoughtful and careful implementation of access rights and responsibilities, menus can help prevent users from finding holes in the security structure as it has been set up by the system administrator.

NetWare's Old Menu System

Previous versions of NetWare included a menu utility that could supply a manageable interface for network functions. To be honest, it had some serious shortcomings. First, it required access rights in the directories used by the menu utility that were somewhat more demanding than some system administrators wanted. Second, it consumed a fairly large chunk of workstation RAM during operation, varying from 34K to about 90K, depending on the version and revision used. Many workstations didn't have enough memory to run both the menu utility *and* the applications it called (such as a database or word processing application).

Part of the memory problem was solved with the release of a new version of MENU.EXE (available on NetWire). The new version took up only 32K of RAM, but many were still unhappy with the utility.

Saber Software's Menu Technology

Enter Saber Software. The engineers at Saber developed a very efficient and secure menu system. It can run with absolutely no memory overhead, or it can be configured to run a bit more quickly while still taking up less than half of what the smallest NetWare MENU.EXE file required in previous versions. It can be characterized as a batch file generator, though that is an oversimplification.

NetWare 4.0 ships with a limited version of the Saber menu utility, codeveloped by engineers from Novell and Saber. Whether or not you think that Saber is the best solution available, it is clearly one of the best utilities around. Now that it is included with NetWare, it is just about the most convenient, too.

While a simple press of the Escape key and then ↵ could get a user out of the NetWare menu utility to a NetWare DOS prompt, you can configure the Saber menu system to be significantly more secure.

An Overview of the New Menu System

The menu script that you create must be pure ASCII text. No formatting codes (except for tabs and hard returns) are allowed. This text file is called the source file, just as a programmer would call the ASCII text of an uncompiled program "source code."

The compiler in this case is the utility MENUMAKE.EXE. Once you have a complete source file and name it with an .SCR extension (for example, MENUFILE.SRC), you execute the MENUMAKE utility by entering

MENUMAKE MENUFILE

MENUMAKE compiles the source file, creates a noneditable menu script file, and renames the new file with a DAT (data file) extension (for example, MENUFILE.DAT).

The actual execution of the menu script file is quite similar to that of the old system. If you had a menu file called MENUFILE.DAT, the command to bring up the menu would be as follows:

NMENU menufile

NMENU.EXE is the menu file interpreter and is found with the other menu utility executables and support files in the SYS:PUBLIC directory.

MENU SCRIPT SYNTAX

There are two structural identification terms in the menu script: MENU and ITEM. MENU identifies a discrete menu block, such as a submenu or a list of options (for example, "Printing Utilities..."). ITEM identifies an individual menu choice (for example, "PCONSOLE: The Print Console" or "CAPTURE: The workstation print redirector").

The menu utility can support up to 99 separate MENU sections within a single source file. Additionally, you can use MENU sections from separate compiled source scripts as well, making the ability to call subroutines almost limitless. Each MENU screen is limited to 12 ITEMs.

THE MENU COMMANDS

The essential menu commands are as follows:

- ▸ EXEC
- ▸ GETO
- ▸ GETP
- ▸ GETR
- ▸ LOAD
- ▸ SHOW ##

EXEC

Of all the menu commands, EXEC is the most important and by far the most complex. There are three modifiers for EXEC, depending on the type of task or command to be executed. If the command is a DOS executable file (*.COM, *.BAT, or *.EXE), the syntax is simply

EXEC *filename*

EXEC EXIT is the only command that allows a user to leave the menu system entirely. If you don't have a selection on the menu that uses this command, the user cannot be dropped to a DOS prompt without rebooting the workstation.

EXEC DOS allows a user to "shell out" (go to the DOS command line). To return to the menu system, the user must type **EXIT**. As with any instance of shelling to DOS, you must take care if you try to change the DOS environment or environment variables.

EXEC LOGOUT performs a legal exit from the network. The user is returned to the LOGIN directory (displayed as F:\>), and the User object is logged out of the network.

GETO, GETP, GETR

Use GETO when the user response is to confirm or change a default value (such as *.* for a directory listing). Use GETR when the response is required; for example, when allowing the user to execute a single DOS command, you might want to require the user to respond with the executable command. Use GETP when you want user input to be used by other GET commands. The information is assigned to a variable.

SHOW

The SHOW ## command is just like a GOTO statement in a batch file or login script. It allows you to establish menu subroutines (submenus) within the same source file. The number (##) is the MENU number (1–99), not the menu title, within the source file.

LOAD

Similar to SHOW ##, the LOAD command allows you to call a menu sub-routine. The difference is that LOAD allows you to call a menu script from another source file, while EXEC SHOW ## is limited to the menus in the current source file.

MENU PARAMETERS

Each MENU or ITEM command can take a limited set of parameters. These are placed in braces ({}) after the ITEM description. The following parameters may be used in combination or separately. The syntax for using menu parameters is as follows:

ITEM Description {parameter1 parameter2...}

BATCH

The BATCH parameter removes the menu program from memory before it executes the item. It has nothing to do with running batch files from the menu. It refers to the operating mode of the menu utility itself. This parameter switches the menu utility into strict batch-file mode. This mode carries a bit of performance overhead because it generates batch files for each step of its execution. The advantage is that no workstation RAM is devoted to the menu system. This ability is critical for some networks that rely on large DOS applications and have to squeeze every little bit of RAM out of the user environment.

You may have a fixed set of applications that require BATCH mode while everything else can operate with the network in normal mode and take advantage of the enhanced speed of overall operation. That is the reason for the BATCH parameter.

You should not use BATCH with the DOS EXEC command.

CHDIR

The CHDIR parameter tells the menu to return after execution to the default directory that was in effect before the menu ITEM was executed. By default, any change in the default directory would remain after the ITEM completed.

PAUSE

As with a DOS batch file, the PAUSE parameter halts the execution of the menu item until a key is pressed. This is helpful when a message is displayed and you want to allow the user to read it at his or her own pace. Also, it can come in handy when you are debugging a menu script, or for commands that execute and terminate immediately, like MAP.EXE and DIR.

SHOW

Another debugging tool, the SHOW parameter (not to be confused with the command SHOW ##) tells the MENU utility to show each command as it executes. This is similar to the ECHO ON command in a DOS batch file.

Menu Examples, Tips, and Tricks

This section details some examples of menus you can create and some tips and tricks.

CENTRALIZE YOUR MENUS

As with login scripts, the more centralized you keep your menus, the easier they are to maintain. If you can get away from individualized menus, it will be much less time-consuming to make modifications later. If you must use personal menus, take advantage of the LOAD command and create a menu for each user.

You may want to map a drive to the menu area in the file system and key the LOAD statement to that variable, as in the following example. To set the variable, add one mapping to the system login script: MAP M:=SYS:USERS\COMMON\ MENUS.

Then, if you load M when the user selects Personal Menus, the menu will be called, corresponding to his or her login name.

```
ITEM Personal Menu
    LOAD M:%LOGIN_NAME.DAT
```

This way, all users can have their menu files in the M:\USERS\COM-MON\MENUS directory, but each one calls a different file when they choose Personal Menu from their network menu listings. This convention also allows you to store all personal menus centrally, making sure that they are backed up regularly and helping you to troubleshoot personal menu problems as warranted.

DON'T ASSIGN RIGHTS BEYOND RF TO NORMAL USERS

All users should have Read and File Scan (RF) rights to the SYS:PUBLIC directory, so the main menu files should stay there. Besides network administration staff, no one should have any more rights than RF in PUBLIC. If that is so, no one should be able to disturb the main menu files during normal network operations.

IF SECURITY ISN'T CRITICAL, USE BATCH FILES

If you use batch files instead of individual commands in the menu script itself, it can ease the initial setup and long-term maintenance tasks a bit. You can rewrite a batch file and test it fairly easily, just by editing the file with a text editor and running the file. If each command is in the menu script itself, you must compile the source file into a data file first, and then test it.

While this method makes the menu easier to take care of, it has a drawback. When all commands are within the menu, you have a more secure menu system. The commands are not visible to those who execute them as they are with a batch file. Most networks aren't too concerned with batch-file security (though they would probably benefit from an increased awareness of good security practices), so this drawback isn't too important to them.

Additionally, most network administrators are pretty comfortable with writing DOS batch files already and would prefer to carry those skills over into the new network operating system.

TAKE CARE IN ORGANIZING THE MENUS

Designing a logical flow to the menu structure is essential to a successful menu system. If you choose to define quick keys for some or all of the menu selections, make sure that they make sense. (A *quick key* is a single character or number that, when pressed, moves the highlight bar directly to a menu item.)

As a labeling convention, use ellipses (...) at the end of each menu selection that goes to a submenu. This helps the user to see how deep the choices go.

By default, the menus are organized with alphabetical quick keys. If you would prefer to override the arbitrary assignment of letters, you can precede ITEM labels with a caret (^) and the character you prefer for that item, as follows:

```
ITEM ^W WordPerfect
EXEC CALL WP.BAT
```

Converting Existing Menus

The syntax of the new menu scripts is different from the syntax for the old Net-Ware menu utility. As we mentioned previously, old menu scripts can be converted to the new syntax, using MENUCNVT.EXE. If you are extremely comfortable with the old syntax, you could continue to write scripts in that format and use the conversion utility rather than learn the new syntax right away.

To run the standard MAIN.MNU file that came with every box of NetWare since we can remember, go to the SYS:PUBLIC directory and use the following syntax:

```
MENUCNVT MAIN.MNU
MENUMAKE MAIN.SRC
NMENU MAIN
```

PART IV

Network Maintenance and Tuning

Disaster Planning and Recovery

Fast Track

Components of a fault-tolerant system include **404**
disk mirroring, disk channel duplexing, and even cable duplexing.

Regular maintenance tasks include **406**
regular backups, backup tape rotation, keeping and checking error logs,
running VREPAIR and DSREPAIR, and practicing disaster simulations.

Document your network **415**
to make it easier to troubleshoot and support.

Multiple levels of support **417**
can be available to you in order to help keep your network running
smoothly and with stability.

Every part of a computer network can be a source of trouble: hardware, software, and skinware (humans). The severity of the trouble depends on many things: what component has failed, what data is lost, and what day or time the problem happened and how quickly the problem was discovered, among other factors. Minor problems may be caused by a number of things: a file is deleted accidentally, electrical power goes out, someone knocks against a loose connection. Catastrophic losses can be caused by anything from a critical component failing (like a motherboard or a disk controller) to natural disasters like the 1989 San Francisco earthquake or Hurricane Andrew. In between is a range of causes, including fire, human error, sabotage, viruses, and hardware or software malfunctions.

The costs and implications of data loss are wide ranging. A company that loses its accounts-payable data could be in serious financial trouble. However, that's only money (and possibly jobs). Think about a hospital pharmacy, a doctor's office, or any other direct health-care provider; lost data there could conceivably result in a loss of life! The point is that for most businesses, the data is the business and the business is the data. The loss of one makes the other mean little.

Even if data is available in some other form, such as printouts or receipts, rebuilding a database is expensive and labor-intensive, and it delays accomplishing other essential tasks. Sales or payments due may be lost until the data is recovered, and customers may desert a company if it seems undependable or incompetent.

Most people wouldn't choose to live without car, fire, and health insurance. A disaster-prevention and recovery plan is like life insurance for the company. It is also professional (and mental) health insurance for MIS professionals.

What Is a Disaster Plan?

The two primary aims of a good disaster plan are the prevention of significant loss and recovery from whatever loss might be experienced.

Disaster prevention consists of designed redundancy (also called fault-tolerance), general maintenance measures to keep the equipment running smoothly, running antivirus programs, and so on. NetWare has built-in fault tolerant features such as Hot Fix redirection, disk mirroring, disk channel duplexing, and more.

Disaster recovery consists of secure storage and archival of system backups, on-site service contracts, and well-documented configuration information.

Virtually every piece of hardware in your network has a rating for MTBF (mean time between failures). What does that actually mean? It means that every component is bound to fail at some point in its lifetime. The objective in designing a disaster plan is not so much to ensure that key components never fail as to have procedures in place to manage the situation when they do.

Kinds of Failures

We will examine a number of problems that can occur on networks, starting with relatively minor ones. (Even the loss of individual files at the workstation or on the network can have serious effects.) We will then consider problems with more serious consequences and how to prepare for them.

FAULTY WORKSTATION COMPONENTS

There are many problems that can occur on individual workstations on the network, including disk-drive failures, interrupt conflicts, and so on. While there are many software utilities designed to troubleshoot workstation problems, there is no substitute for an experienced field engineer when the going gets rough. There is only so much information and experience that any part-time technician can keep current.

PHYSICAL FAILURES

Cables, connectors, network interface cards (NICs), and other network components can cause problems for the LAN, not limited to the actual workstation where the error is located. A missing terminator or broken cable in a coax Ethernet cabling system can bring down the whole network. We've seen this happen after nothing more drastic than a single user moving a PC from one position on the desk to another. By some estimates (mostly by cable-testing companies), up to 80 percent of LAN failures are the result of cable problems. While we think that this is a bit on the high side, it isn't completely out of line.

If your cabling system could have a break or disconnection that brings down the whole LAN, you may want to have some cable repair tools and components on-site and practice cable assembly every couple of months or so. The watchword is "Be Prepared!"

VIRUS INFECTIONS

Viruses are a significant danger for many networks. Your network is vulnerable to viruses if your workstations have floppy drives, or if you have a modem connected to both a telephone line and a workstation on the LAN. Many virus-protection programs are available. Since this particular niche market is so dynamic, it's a good idea to keep an eye out for current reviews and product evaluations. McAfee, Central Point, Intel, and Norton/Symantec virus control programs have rated well in the recent past.

You can help prevent virus infections by prohibiting users from loading public bulletin boards, demo disks, or beta products on the network. Also, scan the file server for viruses on a regular basis and control remote dial-in access to the server.

FILE SERVER CRASHES

File servers sometimes crash. The causes are as wide ranging as those for general PC failures, though often the file server will incorporate cutting-edge technology. That can have its drawbacks, as incompatibilities between parts and their software drivers sometimes don't appear right away. On occasion the server is disabled by the failure of an essential part, such as the power supply, the motherboard, a disk controller, or a RAM chip.

Backup tapes, external duplexed hard drives, and a spare computer can help you to recover from such a loss quickly. The spare should be configured as identically as possible to the original server.

Many offices have workstations that could be upgraded to the specifications of a file server simply by adding RAM. If you plan to have a workstation double as a "warm spare" file server, make sure that you upgrade the workstation in advance.

CATASTROPHIC LOSSES

Catastrophic loss of data can result from fire, earthquake, or other natural disasters; sabotage; viruses; or the malfunction of hardware or software. Preparing for this type of comprehensive loss requires the most planning.

A common method of recovery from the complete loss of an office is to recover lost data from recent backup tapes and a "warm spare" server off-site. You must move backup tapes off-site frequently for this option to work. Plans must include arrangements for the backup file server to be delivered and restored when the first one is lost. This plan, or plans like it, made recovery possible after the effects of the 1989 earthquake in Northern California and more recently Hurricane Andrew in Florida. In some cases, networks were reinstalled from backups and running with new machines in new buildings before anyone could enter the destroyed offices to make any attempt at salvaging anything.

Criteria for Planning Decisions

As a system manager, part of your responsibility is to identify the possible points of failure in your system and to design ways of overcoming failures at those points. Whether a failure is called a glitch, a bug, a malfunction, a problem, or a catastrophic loss is all a matter of degree. They should be planned for similarly. However, since businesses come in all sizes and shapes, it is useful to make your disaster-planning decisions based on the costs of downtime and lost data.

HOW DO YOU USE YOUR NETWORK?

One consideration is how many hours the network is used. Is your network up

- ► 8 hours a day, 5 days a week?

- ► 12 hours a day, 7 days a week?

- ► 24 hours a day, 365 days of the year?

Your support plan should be responsive to the actual needs of the network's operations. We had an accountant as a client, and he wanted a 30-minute maximum on-site response time guaranteed between 8:00 a.m. and 8:00 p.m. from January to April. He couldn't afford to be down for more than an hour during that quarter of the year. The rest of the year his business was quite calm and could adapt to system downtime. He ended up paying for a unique contract that addressed his needs, and it was well worth the investment.

HOW CRITICAL IS YOUR DATA?

Schedule your backups according to the amount of change that your data experiences. If your data is of little importance or if it is fairly static (unchanging), you may not need to back up frequently. If it changes constantly and is updated often, your backups will need to be much more frequent. A good place to start is with a full backup every evening of your workweek.

If you can lose one week's worth of data and not suffer too much trouble, perform a full backup once a week. If you can lose only one day's worth of data before your business suffers, you probably want to back up once every evening.

If your business cannot afford to lose more than an hour's worth of work, you should consider the more extensive of the fault tolerance options discussed below or even real-time archiving of your file system. There are a number of companies that offer such capabilities, though none are certified for NetWare 4.0 at this writing.

HOW MUCH PROTECTION CAN YOU AFFORD?

How much protection can you *not* afford? Again, this is like buying insurance. There is no way that we could tell you how much to invest in fault tolerance or a disaster plan. It is dependent upon the needs of each network's environment. Gauge the cost/benefit trade-off for your particular system.

Recovering a Deleted File

Let's start with what is probably the simplest problem you may face: inadvertent deletion of a file. Fortunately, MS-DOS 5.0 and DR DOS 6.0 have Undelete, a utility for recovering deleted files on DOS-formatted hard drives and floppy disks. You can recover files on systems with earlier versions of DOS by using Symantec's Norton Utilities, Central Point Software's PC Tools, or a similar utility.

If you delete a file from a NetWare drive, none of these utilities will work. They will work only on DOS disks. If you're familiar with previous versions of NetWare, you are probably thinking of the SALVAGE utility about now. In fact, SALVAGE is one of the utilities lost to restructuring in NetWare 4.0. The function is bundled into FILER and the NetWare Administrator graphical utility. Of course, when you think about it, FILER is a better place for it, since you're trying to recover a *file*, right? The following is a list of the steps necessary to undelete a file with the new functionality of FILER. (Note: You should make sure that the LAN administrator has enabled the option for saving deleted files.)

First, create or choose a file that you would like to use as the guinea pig for this demonstration. Our sample file is called TEST.DOC. Next, delete the file. The easiest way to do that is probably to type **DEL TEST.DOC** at the DOS command line. Now that you have a file that's ready to be undeleted, follow these steps:

1 • At the DOS command line, type **FILER** and then press ↵. You will see a screen similar to the one shown in Figure 17.1.

FIGURE 17.1

The FILER screen

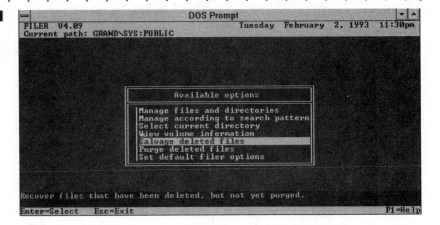

FIGURE 17.1

The FILER screen

2 · Highlight *Salvage deleted files* and press ↵. You will see the SALVAGE menu shown in Figure 17.2.

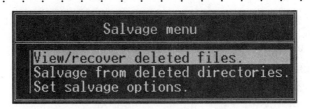

FIGURE 17.2

The SALVAGE menu

3 · Highlight the option *View/recover deleted files* and press ↵. You will be prompted to supply a file name or name pattern (with optional wildcards) to identify the file or files you want to recover. In a NetWare environment, the file specification *.* means only files that have extensions. The file specification * means all files.

4 · You will be presented with a list of files that matches your file name or pattern specification. Choose your target file from the list. Our sample file, TEST.DOC, is highlighted in Figure 17.3. At this time you can tag a series of files by pressing F5 as you highlight each file you want to mark.

FIGURE 17.3

The list of files, with
TEST.DOC highlighted

5 · When you have chosen your files, press ↵. You should be asked for confirmation with a message similar to that shown in Figure 17.4.

FIGURE 17.4

FILER requires confirmation
when you undelete a file.

The process of undeleting the file is actually quite fast. You will see that the file or files you chose for recovery are no longer listed on the screen as they are in Figure 17.3. The file in its undeleted state shows up in a directory listing, shown in Figure 17.5.

FIGURE 17.5

The file in its undeleted

state

```
TEST        DOC        18 02-02-93  11:38p
            1 file(s)              18 bytes
```

How the NetWare Transaction Tracking System (TTS) Protects Files

The NetWare Transaction Tracking System, or TTS, is a feature of NetWare that protects files, especially databases, against corruption if a transaction is interrupted or terminated before completion. TTS is enabled by default when NetWare 4.0 is installed. TTS protects the NDS Directory database and other critical system files, so it is necessary even if you do not use database applications.

If a file has the Transactional attribute set, TTS copies it to a backup area on disk whenever the file is opened. When the file is closed, NetWare deletes the backup copy. If, however, the file is not closed normally (as might happen if the power went out or the workstation rebooted while the file was open), TTS will roll back to the backup copy of the file, which represents the last version of the file that was not corrupt. TTS has been included in NetWare since version 2.15 SFT.

Most database applications and languages have the facility to perform TTS, or similar functions, at the record level. That's a lot better than at the file level, but it's not a bad idea to have a second line of retreat in times of trouble.

Designing a Fault-Tolerant System

The first aspect of a disaster plan is not really even a disaster plan. It is the design of the system itself.

A network can be designed so that many problems can be avoided entirely and so that recovery will be smooth if a critical component fails. *Fault tolerance* refers to measures that can be built into a network to prevent the crippling effects of the loss of critical components.

In the next section we'll look at some of the options available to those who want to design a fault-tolerant system.

SFT I: HOT FIX REDIRECTION

Over time, hard disks develop defects. NetWare uses a technique called Read after Write Verification to ensure the quality of disk writes. It reads back each byte of information after every write; if the data read back does not match the data written to the disk, the process is repeated. If the write fails three times, the area is marked as defective, and the block of data is written to another area of the disk, reserved for redirected blocks. This feature is called Hot Fix redirection (termed System Fault Tolerance, or SFT, level I).

When you create a NetWare 4.0 disk partition using the INSTALL utility, the Hot Fix redirection area defaults to 0.5 percent of the total volume space.

Note: Writes to the Hot Fix area should occur very rarely. If you see much activity in the Hot Fix area (check this statistic in MONITOR.NLM—see Chapter 18 and Part V for more information), it is an indication that the disk may be failing. The hard disk may need to be replaced.

SFT II: DISK MIRRORING AND DUPLEXING

With disk mirroring, all data written to a hard disk is also written to a second disk. If the server's disks are mirrored, the loss of a hard disk is a minor nuisance instead of a disaster. With disk duplexing, not only redundant disks but also redundant disk controllers and cables are installed. Then the system can bear the loss of any component in the disk channel itself. Disk mirroring and disk-channel duplexing are termed SFT level II.

Disk Mirroring

Mirrored disks are on the same channel, that is, they are attached to the same hard-disk controller. When you install a NetWare partition using INSTALL.NLM, you have the option of mirroring the disk.

The secondary drive must be at least as large as the primary drive. If the secondary drive is larger (in data capacity), NetWare will effectively shrink the secondary drive's size to match the primary drive's. Adding a DOS partition to each drive adds bootability in case of primary drive failure.

Disk Duplexing

Of course, hard disks are not the only components subject to failure. Disk controllers and cables can also malfunction. Disk duplexing is accomplished by installing redundant disks, disk controllers, and cables. All data written to the primary disk is also written to the secondary disk.

One advantage of duplexing when compared with mirroring is that performance is better with duplexed disk controllers. NetWare has the ability to seek information from the disk (and controller) that is closest to a block of information, improving response time for disk reads.

CABLE DUPLEXING

It is possible, though rare, to install redundant cabling for critical segments of a network. This option requires two NICs and twice the amount of cabling (a very expensive proposition!), but for some mission-critical environments the cost can be justified. (IPX workstations do not support dual cabling.)

Regular Maintenance Tasks

Part of making a network dependable involves performing regularly scheduled maintenance.

Backups and trial restorations of data are important. Tape drives are the most common devices for backing up hard disks. Optical disks, WORM (Write Once Read Many) devices, and others are valid options as well, but are not nearly as popular.

Whatever device you choose, there should be more than one person who has the skills to operate the device effectively. Operators should know both backup *and* restore functions. If, as the oft-misquoted saying goes, "The proof of the pudding is in the tasting," then the proof of the backup is in the restoring.

It is necessary to check the backup system regularly by restoring from tapes. In addition to testing the system, this helps keep personnel ready to deal with disasters before they occur. If your backup system has bugs, it is much better to find them before there is an emergency. We'll discuss some sample tape-rotation schemes shortly.

Some simple measures can prevent problems before they occur. Check (and keep) error logs. Unfortunately, it's not unheard-of for a mirrored hard disk to fail, and then it is only when the secondary drive begins to have problems that the network administrator looks into the situation. A notice is added to the file-server error log automatically, but if it's never checked it does no good at all.

Maintain wear-oriented devices. You should check the MTBF ratings of the components in your computers, especially the servers. Just as you don't wait for a tire to blow out on your car before buying a new one, you shouldn't wait for mechanical components to show their fatigue before replacing them.

You may want to run DSREPAIR.NLM (the Directory Services repair utility) to optimize and reindex the NDS Directory a couple of times a year—more if you are doing a lot of manipulation and making changes to the Directory often.

Since NetWare 4.0 automatically runs VREPAIR (the volume repair utility) if the operating system detects problems when the volume is mounted, it is not so crucial for an administrator to run it as a prophylactic measure.

TAPE ROTATION

When choosing a tape rotation schedule, you should have three things in mind: First, it should allow many different versions of the data to survive for as long as possible. Second, the tapes should be rotated out of use on a regular basis. Third, you should have a fairly current full backup somewhere off-site at all times. We'll discuss these points in more depth and suggest a couple of possible rotation schemes that meet all three requirements.

Why Allow Different Versions of Data to Survive?

There are quite a few examples of situations where it might be necessary to fall back to a previous version of a file. We feel that the most persuasive is when a virus strikes your system.

Imagine that you discover a virus that has infected your applications' directory structure. After determining the extent of the infection and eradicating all instances of the infection, you may be left with a large hole in your applications suite—that is, you may have to reinstall or restore some executables from backups. Imagine further that you check the condition of your last backup and find that some of the files there are also infected. Here is where it becomes crucial that you have multiple versions of your backups available. If you use the same tape to back up your system every time, you have only one iteration on which to depend. If it is corrupted, you're out of luck.

A well-thought-out rotation allows you a long list of versions or backup dates to choose from. The rotation schemes we will outline later offer daily, weekly, monthly, and even annual increments of backups for archival and restoration.

Why Rotate Tapes Out of Use?

We have worked in both academic and business settings. In both settings it is sometimes amazing to see how the big picture can be lost no matter what the education level of the users.

We had a client who backed up his system every day as soon as he was ready to quit working. Every day for three years he believed that he was safe from a system crash. Well, one day his system *did* crash, and we were called on to help him recover. After installing a new hard drive, we tried to restore his system from backups. For some reason the restore did not proceed normally. In fact, the tape drive wouldn't recognize the tape as valid media.

After some head scratching and general bewilderment, we examined the tape closely. It didn't look right; the tape seemed too clear. In fact, after over three years of daily use, the tape had virtually no magnetic media left on it. Every time our client had backed up his system, for who knows how long, he had been simply going through the motions because the tape had long since given up the ghost!

It isn't uncommon for a university help-desk technician to have a graduate student come in, frantic because he or she has "lost" a thesis or dissertation. "It's on this disk" begins the complaint, "but now I can't read it." "Where's your backup copy?" the technician usually asks. "It's on that same disk with another file name!" comes the sorrowful reply.

You may decide to rotate the tapes out of service as a set or individually, and we'll be doing both in our examples.

Why Have a Backup Off-Site?

We've covered this aspect pretty fully in our discussion of recovering from natural disasters. Just remember that unless and until you are prevented from entering a condemned building and recovering your vital possessions, you will never know the frustration of being only yards away but unable to reclaim them. Such situations are widespread after natural disasters and other calamities.

The only way to protect against losing all of your system data this way is to keep a copy of the backups at a different site. Often, system administrators take a copy home with them to accomplish this. Alternatively, there are archiving companies nationwide that offer off-site storage services.

Here's one more point about on-site storage: If you use a fire safe, make sure that it is a "dry" fire safe. Many fire safes protect their contents by releasing moisture to counteract the heat outside the chamber. Unfortunately, that can be almost as harmful to a backup tape as the fire itself. One of our clients had to wait for four or five days as their backup tapes sat in a dehumidifier drying out after a fire wiped out their office. The fire safe kept the tapes unharmed by the heat, but they were soaked through and unusable in that condition just the same.

The "Grandfather" Method of Tape Rotation

The "grandfather" method of tape rotation is a scheme that uses 20 (or 21) tapes over the course of a single year. This tape rotation method offers daily, weekly, and monthly archiving. The assumption here is that every day there will be a full system backup. This system can be adapted to alternating full and modified backups, but we strongly urge you to stick with full backups at all times if it's possible.

As illustrated by Figure 17.6, in this system there are daily tapes labeled Monday, Tuesday, Wednesday, and Thursday; weekly tapes labeled Friday-1, Friday-2, Friday-3, Friday-4 (and optionally, Friday-5); and monthly tapes labeled January, February, and so on. Every week you will back up over the previous tapes from Monday through Thursday. However, each Friday you will use a different tape, keeping all of the previous four (or five) Friday tapes available if they should be needed for a "previous history" restoration. At the end of each month, make an additional backup on the appropriate monthly tape and store that tape as an archive. Each Friday, the previous week's Friday tape should be taken off-site for storage.

You may notice that the daily tapes are used quite often, while the monthly tapes are used only once and then archived. This is one of the drawbacks of the grandfather method. In its favor, however, is the fact that it's pretty easy to understand and follow.

We generally recommend replacing the daily tapes every three to six months and the Friday tapes once a year. That works out to 13–26 uses for each of the

FIGURE 17.6

The "grandfather" method
of tape rotation

Monday	Tuesday	Wednesday	Thursday	Friday-1	
Monday	Tuesday	Wednesday	Thursday	Friday-2	
Monday	Tuesday	Wednesday	Thursday	Friday-3	
Monday	Tuesday	Wednesday	Thursday	Friday-4	January

Monday	Tuesday	Wednesday	Thursday	Friday-1	
Monday	Tuesday	Wednesday	Thursday	Friday-2	
Monday	Tuesday	Wednesday	Thursday	Friday-3	
Monday	Tuesday	Wednesday	Thursday	Friday-4	February

Monday	Tuesday	Wednesday	Thursday	Friday-1	
Monday	Tuesday	Wednesday	Thursday	Friday-2	
Monday	Tuesday	Wednesday	Thursday	Friday-3	
Monday	Tuesday	Wednesday	Thursday	Friday-4	Etc.

dailies and 12 uses for each of the Friday tapes, which we consider quite acceptable. You could decide to recycle the replaced daily and Friday tapes as the next year's monthly tapes.

Remember that the cost of tapes should not be so high as to seriously affect your decision on a rotation system. Compared with the other insurance costs that a business endures, backup tapes usually amount to a drop in the bucket.

The Saxon Method of Tape Rotation

The Saxon method is a bit less intuitive, but it is easier to determine the ordering of tapes for a recovery. It also uses about twenty tapes over the course of a year, but it allows each tape to be used equally over the course of a complete rotation. We say "about" twenty tapes because once the rotation is begun, the pool of tapes loses one and gains one each month. It may be easier to think of it as nine or ten tapes to start with and then one tape per month perpetually. Each tape will be used about twenty times or so.

As shown in Figure 17.7, this method doesn't depend so much on the calendar. It treats each week as a segment of a 52-week year and archives every 4 weeks instead of every calendar month. That means that after a year, there will be 13 archives instead of 12 monthly tapes.

Every four weeks, the last backup (the one with the smallest number) is taken out of rotation for archiving. The highest-number tape should be taken off-site at the beginning of the next week. If you look at Figure 17.7, you notice that in the first "month," on Friday of the first week, tape number 8 should be taken off-site. The next Friday it should be brought back, and tape number 7 should go off-site. On Friday of the first week of the second "month," tape 5 comes back from off-site in time to take its place back in the week's rotation, and the newly added tape 9 is taken off-site.

The numbering system allows for the archives to follow an easy pattern of 1, 2, 3, 4, and so on. The day after a tape leaves the rotation, a new tape is added to the pool, so at any one time you will have eight tapes in the pool.

F I G U R E 17.7

The Saxon method of tape

rotation

Day	Week 1	Week 2	Week 3	Week 4
Mon	8	7	6	5
Tue	7	6	5	4
Wed	6	5	4	3
Thu	5	4	3	2
Fri	4	3	2	1

This tape leaves the rotation

Day	Week 5	Week 6	Week 7	Week 8
Mon	9	8	7	6
Tue	8	7	6	5
Wed	7	6	5	4
Thu	6	5	4	3
Fri	5	4	3	2

This tape leaves the rotation

Day	Week 9	Week 10	Week 11	Week 12
Mon	10	9	8	7
Tue	9	8	7	6
Wed	8	7	6	5
Thu	7	6	5	4
Fri	6	5	4	3

This tape leaves the rotation

The restore order has a kind of elegance to it. If a failure should occur on a day when tape 2 would be used, the most recent backups will be tapes 3, 4, 5, 6, 7, 8, and 9, in descending order. When you exceed the numbered tapes within the current pool, you have the archived backups that were removed from rotation in the previous "months," or sets of four weeks.

This method may look a bit intimidating on the face of it, and it's not necessarily as easy to remember as the grandfather method, but it works very well for a long-term backup and archival system.

Other Rotation Schemes

There are other useful rotation schemes, including the "Tower of Hanoi" method used by Palindrome and others. Just make sure that they provide the three basic needs: allowing historic versions of the data to remain available, rotation of used tapes to archival (inactive) status, and a regular rotation of a fairly current backup to an off-site location.

By the way, there is one more critical component of a tape rotation system: It must be one that the person responsible for backups will actually follow! If it's too complex or intimidating, it's not worth a hill of beans, no matter how well thought out it is.

DATA COMPRESSION AND VERIFICATION

Your backup software should offer data compression and more important, data verification. Various types of files and compression algorithms have different compression ratios, but 50 percent is typical. Data compression effectively doubles the capacity of the tape. With verification, after data is written to the tape, it is read back and checked. We recommend data verification, even though it nearly doubles the time needed to back up a disk. Remember the guy with the three-year-old tape? If his backup system had featured data verification, he would have known that his tape had died before it was too late.

ERROR LOGS

You should check the file server and volume error logs at least once a week. Too often, error logs are ignored, and problems mount needlessly. Many problems are manageable if they are caught early enough. The system administrator or an assistant should check the log as a normal part of his or her weekly routine.

VREPAIR

Sometimes even minor damage prevents a volume from being mounted. Damage could result from a power failure, hardware problems, etc. An indication of damage is when the file server console displays a message about a mirroring error. You can use the VREPAIR utility to repair a damaged volume. VREPAIR is an NLM run at the console—just enter **LOAD VREPAIR**. You should run VREPAIR on each volume quarterly or semiannually for maintenance.

Two aspects of VREPAIR are worth noting. First, the Set VREPAIR Options screen is confusing to many people the first time they see it. Three "active" options are listed at the top of the screen. Three alternative options are listed at the bottom of the screen. The options are paired—the first at the top corresponds to the first on the bottom, etc. You can select the number-one option on the bottom, for example, to replace number one at the top. When the options listed at the top are what you need, continue to the next screen.

Second, if errors are detected, it may be necessary to run VREPAIR again. Running VREPAIR can fix errors on one pass that reveal other errors, requiring additional repair. Continue running the utility until no errors are found.

BINDFIX

BINDFIX is a utility for repairing the bindery. As such, BINDFIX is for versions of NetWare previous to 4.0. The bindery of a NetWare 3.*x* or 2.*x* server sometimes becomes corrupted. In essence, the bindery is a database. BINDFIX reindexes, or optimizes, the bindery database and fixes some problems.

DISASTER SIMULATION

Simulating disasters is a good weekend exercise. Of course, some may not think that anything to do with work is a good weekend exercise, but we won't argue that point. The idea is to simulate failures so that you are familiar with and have rehearsed the recovery process if it is required for real. It is far better to go through the exercise without the pressures of a crisis than to wait for a real disaster.

Start by fully restoring the operating system and the contents of the volumes. When you are comfortable with that procedure, move on to practicing replacing major components of the system. By the time you are comfortable with these examples, you'll surely be able to come up with more of your own.

Remember, experienced personnel should be on hand, and it is better to start with relatively minor difficulties and work up to simulated disasters. The idea is to train network personnel, not to break the system beyond recovery.

Documentation

Keep running documentation of your network; keeping everything in a three-ring binder is helpful. This information should include the physical layout (floor plans and the locations of servers, workstations, printers, cables, bridges, hubs, routers, etc.), the logical structure (login process, scripts, batch files, menus, etc.), and the network infrastructure (a graphical representation of the NDS Directory, the directory structure of each volume, etc.).

You should have a short introduction to the network for new or temporary employees, so they can come up to speed as fast as possible and more important, abide by the rules that you set for system access.

All procedures should be documented. This enables quicker recovery, and it helps tech-support people to give more efficient assistance, whether it's by phone or on-site.

Make a chart of the backup schedule and the location of backup tapes. What is the rotation of tapes that are kept off-site? The list should include names and phone numbers (and pager/mobile phone numbers) of responsible support staff.

UPDATING DOCUMENTATION

You should document every change to the system. In addition, you should document problems and service calls. If you don't keep the documentation current, there's no point in having it at all. It's difficult to be disciplined, but in the long run it is the only way to run any substantial network effectively.

DOCUMENTING SERVERS AND WORKSTATIONS

Make a list of the hardware and hardware configuration for each file server. The NetWare manuals have some lists and forms for keeping track of configurations. Copy them (it's legal!) and *use* them.

Print out the configuration files for each server. The following files are the most important:

- ▶ CONFIG.SYS

- ▶ AUTOEXEC.BAT

- ▶ STARTUP.NCF

- ▶ AUTOEXEC.NCF

List the contents (and DOS version) of the DOS partition for each NetWare server. List services provided (file, print, communication, database, routing, etc.).

DOCUMENTING WORKSTATIONS

Print out the configuration files for each workstation. Ideally, your workstations should be somewhat standardized in configuration. If not, this documentation is even more critical. The following files are the most important:

- ▶ CONFIG.SYS

- ▶ AUTOEXEC.BAT

- ▶ NET.CFG

List services provided (such as remote printing, communications, database, and routing), and make a chart of the standard workstation directory structure.

Support and Problem Escalation

There are normally three levels of support, ranging from the person who is on-site and can take care of minor problems to outside field engineers who can come on-site for high-level problem solving.

FIRST-LEVEL SUPPORT

Normally the person closest to the problem will try to handle it. If the problem is too difficult for that person, he or she will consult someone at the next level. First-level support may be a secretary or part-time network administrator who can add or modify users and do basic troubleshooting, perform backups, and so on.

SECOND-LEVEL SUPPORT

The second level of support is usually a higher-level (and more expensive) employee who oversees the more complex aspects of the network, such as writing login scripts and configuring menus, administering groups and profiles, and installing applications. This person may also be qualified to troubleshoot hardware problems at the workstation and possibly with the network cabling.

THIRD-LEVEL SUPPORT

This level of support may involve high-level network experts in your company or technical support from outside your corporation. This level of support will usually be provided by a full-time field engineer or consultant. Such a person should be a CNE (Certified NetWare Engineer) or ECNE (Enterprise CNE) with a good deal of practical experience.

In many cases, these engineers will make use of NetWire, a service sponsored by Novell on the CompuServe Information Service. Novell distributes patches and fixes to their software products primarily through NetWire.

A *patch* is software that replaces or enhances an existing program. Since the NetWare software in the retail box is not modified unless an official revision number is changed, you should keep up with the current fixes available on Net-Wire. Like any major product, NetWare 4.0 has its own area for downloads and updates. At the CompuServe "!" prompt, enter **GO NETWIRE** or **GO NOVELL** to move to the Novell forums.

USER GROUPS

NetWare Users International sponsors user groups all around the country. These are a good place to get advice about network problems. They often produce regional user conferences, where the emphasis is on technical information rather than sales pitches. They are often a very good place to come up to speed on the newest aspects of NetWare and LANs in general. We recommend that you join a local NetWare user group.

NOVELL TECHNICAL SUPPORT

Novell's technical support is an excellent source of expert advice. The phone number is 1-800-NETWARE (638-9273).

Additionally, Novell offers the Network Support Encyclopedia (NSE). The Standard edition of the NSE includes all the documentation for the NetWare operating-system products (all currently supported versions), technical specifications, and more. It is distributed on compressed floppy disks and is updated quarterly.

The Professional edition of the NSE comes on a CD-ROM and is updated monthly. It contains all the Standard edition's features but also includes all the current patches and fixes available on NetWire.

CHAPTER 18

Monitoring
and Troubleshooting

Fast Track

422   ***As you work on the network each day,***

▸ Get an idea of how long certain actions take to complete. This can clue you in to problems.

▸ Make sure you can do everything you expect to on the network. If a server or network service is unavailable, it could be an unreported problem.

423   ***Every week or so,***

▸ Check to see that all drives are mounted and running.

▸ Check the file-server error log.

▸ Check the file-server cache statistics.

▸ Check the space remaining on the network volumes.

425   ***Every month or so,***
go into NETADMIN and make sure there are no extra users or objects on the network that you can't account for.

426   ***Every six months or so,***

▸ Do a controlled trial of the UPS (uninterruptible power supply) to make sure it's operating correctly.

▸ Test the UPS's battery life.

▸ Test the server's floppy drives to make sure they're working correctly.

If you can't attach to the server,   **428**

- ▸ Check your network cabling.

- ▸ Check the hardware interrupt configuration in the NET.CFG file.

- ▸ Check frame types.

If you can't log in to the network,   **428**
check your context.

If you can't execute NETADMIN,   **429**
you may not be logged in as a user with sufficient rights, or you may be
logged in under bindery emulation instead of through Directory Services.

If you can't create, delete, or modify users and other objects,   **429**
you may not have sufficient rights to do so, or the Directory may be
corrupted.

Once your network is up and running, you need to think about how to keep it performing well over the long haul. The most important thing you can do is to monitor the network constantly, so that you can address any telltale signs of impending problems before they become disabling to the network. In this chapter we will list some of the statistics and tests that can help you stay in touch with your network.

While there could be a whole book devoted to troubleshooting NetWare 4.0, at the end of this chapter we'll discuss a few common errors and their possible solutions. We won't try to cover the art and craft of troubleshooting in this chapter, but we'll try to focus on a few problems that are new to NetWare 4.0.

Regular Monitoring

There are some aspects of your network that you should keep track of on a regular basis. They will help you anticipate problems before they become critical. We're going to look at some things you can do on a daily, weekly, monthly, quarterly, and semiannual schedule.

DAILY MONITORING

As you work on the network each day, take note of how the network is performing. You should get a good idea of how long certain actions take to complete. Maybe it takes you 10 seconds to log in, or it takes about 3 seconds to call your word processing application from a menu. Whatever it is, don't be so far removed from what you are doing that you don't notice how long normal activities take to complete. If there is a serious slump in performance, it could be an indication of problems on the network. This kind of problem is often your first clue to a network error that's affecting everyone on the LAN.

Also take the opportunity every day or so to make sure that you can do everything that you expect to on the network. If a server or network service is not available to you, it could be a problem that others are having but haven't reported yet. Stay on top of things so that the users feel like you're in control of the network.

WEEKLY MONITORING

Once a week or so you should check to see that all drives are mounted and running. If you have mirrored or duplexed drives, one might go bad and because the network doesn't fail, you don't know about it.

1 · At the file-server-console colon prompt (:), type **LOAD MONITOR.**

2 · Highlight DISK INFORMATION, and press ↵ to see a listing of all drives on the file server.

3 · Highlight each one and press ↵, making sure that the Drive Operating Status for each one of them is Active.

Once a week or so you should also check the file-server error log. This log lists all errors and notices that the operating system has generated since the last time it was cleared. To see the file-server error log, log in as ADMIN, move to SYS:PUBLIC, and type **NETADMIN.** You should see something similar to the screen shown in Figure 18.1.

Highlight Manage Objects and press ↵. Your list of objects will probably be quite different from the list shown in Figure 18.2, but it should have at least one

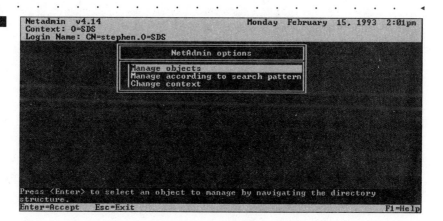

FIGURE 18.1

The opening screen of NETADMIN

object labeled (NetWare Server). Highlight it and press ↵. Highlight *View or edit properties of this object* and press ↵ to see a screen similar to the one shown in Figure 18.3.

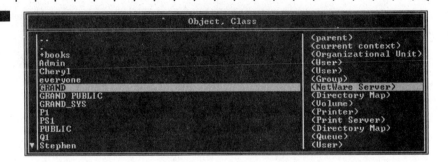

FIGURE 18.2

The list of objects in NETADMIN

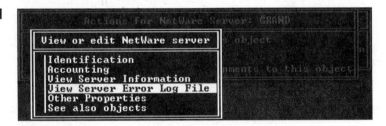

FIGURE 18.3

The View or Edit NetWare Server screen

Highlight the View Server Error Log File option and press ↵ to see a screen like the one shown in Figure 18.4.

The format of the error log is for each entry to be labeled by the date and time that the error or notice was generated, the module that generated it, the severity (0–5, with 0 being simple notifications and 5 being fatal errors of some kind), the locus and class of the error, and the actual error in English (or whatever you've chosen as the language). It's important to clear the error log periodically to keep it from using up too much disk space. You can use NETADMIN to clear it.

F I G U R E 18.4

The NetWare Server Error

Log screen

```
                        GRAND NetWare Server Error Log

2-01-93   3:28:00 pm:      DS-2.7-29
    Severity = 1  Locus = 17  Class = 19
    Bindery open requested by the SERVER

2-01-93   3:28:00 pm:      DS-2.7-27
    Severity = 1  Locus = 17  Class = 19
    Directory Service:  Local database is open

2-01-93   4:32:07 pm:      DS-2.7-31
    Severity = 0  Locus = 17  Class = 19
    Bindery close requested by the SERVER

2-01-93   4:32:07 pm:      DS-2.7-28
    Severity = 1  Locus = 17  Class = 19
    Directory Service:  Local database has been closed

This screen displays the errors logged since the last time the file was
cleared. Press <Esc> to exit.
Esc=Exit                                                        F1=Help
```

Another of the weekly monitoring tasks is to check the cache statistics of the file server. The file server cache should not go below 50 percent of the total cache of file server memory if you want to assure optimal performance. If the cache goes lower than that, plan on adding RAM to the server.

Finally, you should check the space remaining on the network volumes. The easiest way to do this is by using the command NDIR /VOL. The report you receive should be similar to the one shown in Figure 18.5, with a reading of the total volume space, space used, space remaining, etc. The key figure here is the figure for space remaining. Figure 18.5 shows that almost 500MB (just over 87 percent of the drive) is available. If that gets below about 10 percent or so, you should think about installing more disk storage, or at least getting off of your network some of the garbage files that no one is using.

MONTHLY MONITORING

Every month or so you should go into NETADMIN and make sure that there are no extra users or objects on the network that you can't account for. These could be security risks and should therefore be taken pretty seriously. The network administrator should know who each user is and what they need with respect to network access. If there are "strangers" on the network, you may have a security breach.

FIGURE 18.5

A report generated by the command NDIR /VOL

```
Statistics for fixed volume GRAND/SYS:
Space statistics are in KB (1024 bytes).

Total volume space:                        571,008    100.00%
Space used by 2,158 entries:                73,640     12.90%
Deleted space not yet purgeable:                 0      0.00%
                                           --------   -------
Space remaining on volume:                 497,368     87.10%
Space available to STEPHEN:                497,368     87.10%

Maximum directory entries:                   6,016
Available directory entries:                 2,263     37.62%

Space used if files were not compressed:    28,279
Space used by compressed files:             11,784
                                           --------
Space saved by compressing files:           16,495     58.33%

Uncompressed space used:                    85,400
```

QUARTERLY MONITORING

DSREPAIR is the Directory Services repair utility. It is an NLM that reindexes and optimizes the NDS Directory on a NetWare server. We generally advise running DSREPAIR about once per quarter. If your network is very static, this isn't too crucial. If your network has a lot of new objects added and old objects deleted, you might want to run DSREPAIR more often. To run DSREPAIR, go to the NetWare server colon prompt (:), type **LOAD DSREPAIR**, and follow the directions on screen.

About four times a year, we also recommend that you perform a trial restoration from your backup media. We covered disaster planning in detail in the previous chapter, but as a regularly scheduled maintenance task, you should make sure that your backups are providing the protection you count on. The only way to make sure of that is to perform a trial restoration periodically.

SEMIANNUAL MONITORING

About twice a year, you should perform some basic tests on the NetWare server to make sure that all the hardware is functioning properly. The first test is a controlled trial of the UPS (uninterruptible power supply). While the network is quiet (no users logged in), down the server and boot it to DOS. At this point the NetWare operating system is not at risk, and you can test the UPS by unplugging it from the wall. If the UPS is functioning correctly, the server should not have any problems at all. If the server powers down, you probably have faulty batteries in the UPS, and they should be replaced.

An additional test is to time the UPS's battery life. After a long time in service, the batteries may fade and no longer provide the length of service that you expect. You can create a test batch file for this purpose, as shown below:

```
@echo off
cls
echo.|time >> UPSTIMER.DAT
coldboot
```

This file should be the AUTOEXEC.BAT on a bootable floppy disk. The disk must have the normal system files of a bootable DOS disk, and you'll need any one of the many REBOOT utilities that are available as shareware or as part of various software "toolbox" packages. We use COLDBOOT from the *PC Magazine* DOS utilities.

This file will create a text file called UPSTIMER.DAT and then add to it each time the server reboots. The key to this function is *echo.|time,* which pipes a carriage return into the internal DOS command TIME. The >> UPSTIMER.DAT portion of the file appends the time to the text file. Let the server keep rebooting until the UPS finally gives out, and then figure the difference between the first time and the last time in the file UPSTIMER.DAT. That is how long the UPS batteries lasted.

The test above also accomplishes the last semiannual test—that of the floppy drive. You should boot the server to DOS and test the floppy drive to make sure that it is still functioning correctly. Read from a floppy disk, write to a floppy disk, and format a floppy disk. If there are no errors encountered, your floppy drive is probably fine.

. . . . ◄

Common Problems and Solutions

This section lists some common problems and tells you how to solve them.

CAN'T ATTACH TO SERVER

Network cabling is one of the first things to suspect when you can't attach to a NetWare server. Start with the back of the workstation, and make sure that it is plugged into the network cable correctly. Continue toward the server, making sure that each connection or device along the way is configured and attached correctly.

Another common cause is that the hardware interrupt configuration in the NET.CFG file doesn't match the actual hardware interrupt setting of the network interface card. If you've just switched the workstation from IPX.COM to ODI drivers, this might be your problem. To check the configuration of IPX.COM without actually loading it into memory, type **IPX I**. This parameter stands for "Information only." Check the IRQ/INT setting displayed and then edit the NET.CFG file to match it.

Still another possible cause in an Ethernet environment is that the frame types don't match. Previous versions of NetWare defaulted to a "raw" 802.3 Ethernet frame type. NetWare 4.0 defaults to the 802.2 frame type. Make sure that your workstations and servers are communicating with the same type of Ethernet packets.

CAN'T LOG IN

If you can't log in to your NetWare 4.0 server, check your context. If you are in a context that contains no users, or if you are trying to log in as a user who doesn't exist at the current context, you will be frustrated. Try logging in with the full context defined explicitly in the command line as follows:

LOGIN .CN=login_name.OU=organizational_unit.O=organization

where *login_name* is a valid user object, *organizational_unit* is a container object in which that login name exists, and *organization* is the parent organization of your particular Directory.

Another solution takes advantage of the fact that the utility CX.EXE is in the directory SYS:LOGIN so that you can change context even if you aren't currently logged in. Type CX to see your current context.

CAN'T EXECUTE NETADMIN

If you can't execute NETADMIN, you may not be logged in as a user with sufficient rights to accomplish anything with that utility. You also may be logged in under bindery emulation instead of through Directory Services. If you have loaded NETX.COM instead of VLM.EXE and the necessary Virtual Loadable Modules (VLMs), you are not logged in through Directory Services. You must install NetWare 4.0 workstation software on the workstation before you can use Directory Services. Then log in as ADMIN or another user with sufficient rights to use NETADMIN.

CAN'T CREATE, DELETE, OR MODIFY USERS AND OTHER OBJECTS

The first thing to suspect when you can't create, delete, or modify Directory objects is that you are logged in as a user without sufficient rights to perform these actions. If you have sufficient rights, the Directory may be corrupted. To fix the Directory, run DSREPAIR.NLM as mentioned in the section above, "Quarterly Monitoring."

If you can't see objects that should be there, you may be in the wrong context. Change the context to where the object should be and then look again.

If you are trying to delete a printer, print queue, or print server through NETADMIN, you will be unsuccessful. You can see or modify these objects, but to manage, add, or delete them, you must use PCONSOLE.

NetWare 4.0 Utilities

This part includes an explanation of the different types of utilities included in NetWare 4.0 and gives general information about each type. It also includes a summary of each utility's function. Where it is helpful or meaningful, the explanation is followed by examples of how to use the utility and some of its options. Following the utility summaries, you will find tables showing the utilities or loadable modules you can use to complete common NetWare tasks.

Overview

NetWare utilities fall into two general categories: workstation and server console.

Workstation Utilities

The first group of utilities, which is used to manage the network from a workstation, includes a graphical utility called the NetWare Administrator. You can use this utility on a workstation running either Windows 3.1 or OS/2 2.0 or later.

Also included are text utilities that you can use with a workstation running DOS 3.30 or later. Text utilities include both command-line and menu utilities.

Server Console Utilities

The second group of utilities is used to manage the network from the NetWare server console. These consist of command-line utilities, menu utilities, and NetWare Loadable Modules (NLMs).

The NetWare Administrator Utility

This workstation utility combines the functionality of the NETADMIN, PCONSOLE, FILER, PARTMGR, and RCONSOLE text utilities into a single graphical interface.

To get online help for the NetWare Administrator, use one of the following options:

- Highlight an item on the screen and press F1 to get specific help for the item.

- From a dialog box, choose the Help button to get instructions for that dialog.

- Choose the Help option on the menu bar. You can select from four choices, depending on the kind of help you need. The help options are explained in more detail in the section "The Help Menu."

THE OBJECT MENU

Use this menu to manage objects in the NDS tree and the NetWare file system. After selecting what you want to work with (object, volume, directory, file, etc.) from the Browser, choose an option from this menu to manage it.

You can do the following tasks with the Object menu:

- Create new objects.

- View or modify details about an object or file-system item.

- See who has rights to the object or item you selected.

- See what rights the object you selected has to other objects or file-system items on the network.

- Salvage deleted files and directories.

- Move leaf objects or files and directories.

- Copy files or directories to another location in the file system.

- Rename leaf objects or files and directories.

- Delete files or directories from the file system.

▸ View or modify a user template. (A *user template* is a set of defaults that are applied to users created in the container object it is associated with.) This option applies only when you have selected a container object from the Browser.

▸ Search for objects or files and directories according to a search pattern that you set.

▸ Exit the NetWare Administrator window.

THE VIEW MENU

This menu lets you set up the Browser window. You can set the following features for the window:

▸ Change the NetWare Administrator title bar to show hints for each menu item as it is scanned with the mouse.

▸ Set your context, or position, in the Directory tree. You can select the object you want to appear at the top of your Browser window. For example, you could set up the window to show your container object at the top so you would not need to move through objects above it in the tree to find your work area.

▸ Set the types, or classes, of objects that you want to see in your Browser window.

▸ Expand or collapse windows on your screen.

THE OPTIONS MENU

This menu allows you to specify some basic environment settings. You can do the following:

▸ Set the name-space type used by a file.

▸ Specify if you want a confirmation box to appear when you move or delete objects.

THE TOOLS MENU

Use this menu to access other workstation utilities. You can do the following:

► Open additional Browser windows.

► Start the Partition Manager utility to view, create, or merge NDS partitions. You can also add, delete, and modify replicas (copies of partitions).

► Start a remote console session with a server. This utility is available only if you have set up the necessary loadable modules on the servers you wish to access.

THE WINDOW MENU

Use this menu to arrange the open windows on the NetWare Administrator screen and to switch between Browser windows. You can do the following:

► Set open windows to cascade on the screen, so windows are not hidden behind other open windows.

► Set open windows to appear as "tiles" on the screen.

► Close all windows you have open.

► See the container in your current context.

THE HELP MENU

This menu allows you to access four types of help information. You can do the following:

► View lists of menu, keyboard, and mouse commands. This option includes an alphabetical listing of help topics under the "How to work with" heading. Main tasks are also listed by topic, so you can browse through the list for an overview of basic functions of the utility.

► See a glossary of NetWare terms. You can click on a term to see its definition.

► See error message explanations and suggestions for solving the problem.

► Get general information about the NetWare Administrator as well as system information.

Text Utilities

The text utilities are executed from a workstation's DOS command line. Two types of online help are available for these utilities:

► At the command line, enter a backslash and a question mark (\?) after the utility name to get syntax information and instructions for using the utility.

► From within the utility, highlight the item you want specific help for and press F1.

ATOTAL

If you have turned on the accounting function for a server, you can use this utility to see a total of all the accounting charges for the server.

You turn on accounting and set charge rates for services using the NetWare Administrator or the NETADMIN text utility. You decide which services to charge for, as well as the amount you want to charge for each service. You can charge for the following services:

► Each block of data read from the server

► Each block of data written to the server

► Each minute a user is logged in to the server

► Each request for a service provided by the server

If you have turned on the accounting function, you can see the total of all accounting charges on a server by entering the following at the command line:

ATOTAL

A screen is displayed showing totals for connection time (in minutes), service requests, blocks read and written, and disk storage per day (in blocks).

AUDITCON

This menu utility allows an auditor, who works independently of network supervisors and other users, to verify the security of your network. Auditing means examining records to make sure that network transactions are accurate and that confidential information is secure. Auditors can audit NetWare Directory Services (NDS) events as well as volume events (user and file-system activity). When auditing is enabled, a log file is created automatically. This file operates much like a system or error log file. When an audited event occurs, a record is entered in the log file.

The utility is designed to meet the Class F2 security criteria as specified by the Information Technology (IT) standards. The IT security standards and criteria are established and maintained by the German Information Security Agency (GISA). Class F2 specifies that a system must have tools for examining and maintaining audit records that meet the following criteria:

- A system must uniquely identify and authenticate auditors prior to all other interactions between the system and the auditor.

- All information gathered must be stored where only the auditor or other authorized users can access it.

- The auditor is not allowed to alter objects, directories, or files on the network; nor can the auditor mount or dismount volumes.

- The system must be allowed to log date, time, user ID, machine ID, operation performed, and completion status of items being audited.

When you enable auditing for a volume, an auditor can then take over and track the following types of events on that volume:

- ▸ File or directory events such as creations, deletions, and modifications. The auditor can also track when files or directories are salvaged, moved, or renamed.

- ▸ Server events such as bringing down a server and mounting or dismounting volumes. Changes to security rights can also be tracked. When you enable auditing for NetWare Directory Services (NDS), the auditor can then take over and track the following types of events in the Directory: when objects are added, deleted, moved, or renamed; when security equivalences are changed; and User object logins and logouts.

Although auditors can track activity on your network, they cannot open or modify network files (other than the audit files).

To start the auditing utility, simply enter the following command at the prompt:

AUDITCON

The main menu appears. You can use this menu to enable auditing and set up one or more users to audit the network.

CAPTURE

This command-line utility allows you to redirect print jobs so that you can print to a network printer from within network-unaware applications. You can also redirect screen displays to a network printer and redirect data to a network file. Additional options let you set up a print job to use a specific form (by name), specify the number of copies you want to print, etc. You do not need to use CAPTURE if you use a NetWare-aware application that can send print jobs to print queues or printers.

You have the option of sending print jobs to either a print queue or a printer, depending on the way you want to set up printing on your network.

For example, to send a print job to a printer named *Printer1*, you would use the following command:

CAPTURE P=Printer1

To send a print job to a print queue named *Sales* and use a form named *Charts*, you would use the following command:

CAPTURE Q=Sales J=Charts

To create a file and send data to it, use the Create option. For example, if you wanted to redirect data to a file in your current directory and name it *Myfile,* you would enter the following command at the prompt:

CAPTURE CR=MYFILE

If you wanted to create the file in another directory, you would enter the full path to the file instead of typing only the file name.

Other options are available that are not shown here. The CAPTURE utility has a total of 27 command-line options.

COLORPAL

You can use this menu utility to set the screen colors for NetWare menu utilities and menus you create for users (using the NMENU utility). When you change the default color settings, the changes apply to all utilities on your network. You can set colors for the following items:

▸ Active window border

▸ Active window text

▸ Alert window text and border

▸ Background and inactive windows

▸ Error window text and border

- ▸ Help window border
- ▸ Help window text
- ▸ Key description
- ▸ Key name
- ▸ Quick help area
- ▸ Screen header
- ▸ Selection bar

CX

This command-line utility allows you to see your context (where you are in the NDS tree). You can also change your location, or context, and view other objects in the tree.

Your context starts with the container object directly above you in the tree and follows the path up to the container at the top of the tree.

This utility lets you navigate the NDS tree, or change your context, much like the DOS CD command lets you move around in the file system. It also lets you view objects in an NDS container, similar to the way the DOS DIR command lets you view a list of subdirectories and files in a directory.

The following examples show you how to use the utility and its options from the command line.

To see your current context, enter

    CX

To move up one level, enter

    CX .

To move up additional levels, enter a period for each level you want to move up. To change your context to another location in the Directory tree, you must enter the complete name, or path, to the Root object. For example, to change your context to the Organizational Unit *Sales* in the Organization *USA,* you would enter

> CX .OU=SALES.O=USA

To see all objects at or below your current context, enter

> CX /A

Other options are available that are not shown here. The CX utility has a total of six command-line options.

DOSGEN

Use this command-line utility to set up workstations so they can boot from a server instead of from a boot disk or local drive. DOSGEN creates a boot file on the server and copies the workstation's boot files to this server file. The file, NET_DOS.SYS, is located in the server's SYS:LOGIN directory. You must run DOSGEN to create boot files for each workstation that will boot from the server. If you create multiple workstation boot files on the server, DOSGEN gives each set of boot files a unique name.

This utility has no command-line options.

FILER

Use this menu utility to manage the NetWare file system. Almost any task that is required for the file system can be done from FILER. This utility does not affect NDS objects (which are managed with NETADMIN or the NetWare Administrator graphical utility). Following is a list of the types of tasks you can do with FILER. For a detailed list of tasks, see the table at the end of this chapter.

- ▸ View information about files, directories, and volumes.
- ▸ Modify or view attributes of files and directories. (Attributes determine what operations can be done with a file or directory.)
- ▸ Modify or view rights and trustee assignments for files and directories.

▸ Search for files and directories according to a search pattern.

▸ Copy files and directories to another location in the file system.

▸ Purge deleted files and directories from the hard disk.

▸ Retrieve deleted files and directories (if they have not been purged).

To bring up the main menu, enter the following command:

FILER

FLAG

This command-line utility allows you to view or modify a file or directory's attributes. The attributes determine what operations can be done with a file or directory.

You can also use FLAG options to view detailed information about a file or directory or to change a file or directory's owner. When you use FLAG with an executable file, you can modify its search mode. A file's search mode determines where it looks for instructions for executing.

To run FLAG on a file or directory, either you must be at its location in the file system or you must include the complete path with the FLAG command. For example, if you are at the command line and you want to see the attributes of a file named *Accounts* in the SYS:PUBLIC directory, you enter

FLAG SYS:PUBLIC\ACCOUNTS

To add or remove attributes, use the plus (+) or minus (−) character. For example, to flag the directory in the previous example so its files will not be compressed or migrated to an online storage device, enter

FLAG SYS:PUBLIC\ACCOUNTS +DC +DM

If the Accounts directory's attribute is set to Read Only and you want to change it to Read Write, enter

FLAG SYS:PUBLIC\ACCOUNTS −RO +RW

Other attributes and options are available that are not shown here. The FLAG utility has a total of nine command-line options. File and directory attributes you can set include ten for directories and seventeen for files. There are seven search-mode options you can set for executable files.

LOGIN

This command-line utility allows you to log in to a NetWare server or an NDS tree. You can use LOGIN options to determine a login script to run or to specify that you do not want to run a login script. For example, to log in to Tree1 as User object *Fred* in the Organization object *International* without running any login scripts, enter

LOGIN TREE1/.CN=FRED.O=INTERNATIONAL /NS

Normally, your system, profile, and user login scripts are set up by a network supervisor, so using LOGIN options is unnecessary. Your workstation NET.CFG file will include a preferred tree or server setting and your current user context. When the workstation start-up files and login scripts are set up correctly, a user can log in by simply entering

LOGIN FRED

Other options are available that are not shown here. The LOGIN utility has a total of seven command-line options.

LOGOUT

Use this utility to log out of the network, or to log out of a specific server while remaining logged in to all other connections. For example, to end your network session and log out of all connections, enter

LOGOUT

If you are logged in to three servers and you want to log out of Server1 only, enter

LOGOUT SERVER1

You will remain logged in to all other servers except Server1.

The LOGOUT utility has two command-line options. The second option is /?, which gives you online help information.

MAP

This command-line utility allows you to view, create, or change network and search drive mappings. You can assign a total of 26 mappings, including network, search, and local drives.

A *local drive mapping* points to a hardware device, such as a hard drive in a workstation.

A *network drive mapping* points to a directory or file in the NetWare file system.

A *search drive mapping* also points to a directory or file. The difference is that the operating system automatically scans search drives for files when the files are not found in the current drive. This capability allows a user working in one directory to access application or data files located in a different directory. It is not necessary to move to the directory containing the needed file. For example, to see a list of all your drive mappings, enter

MAP

If you are not sure what drive letters you have assigned and you do not want to overwrite any of your existing mappings, you can assign the next available drive letter to a new mapping. To assign the next available drive letter to the Accounts directory (located in SYS:PUBLIC), enter

MAP N:=SYS:PUBLIC/ACCOUNTS

To assign the drive letter G to the same directory instead of assigning it to the next available drive letter, enter

MAP G:=SYS:PUBLIC/ACCOUNTS

To map your fourth search drive to the applications subdirectory in SYS:SYSTEM, enter

MAP S4:=SYS:SYSTEM/APPS

This map command assigns the search drive letter W to the applications directory.

Other options are available that are not shown here. The MAP utility has a total of eight command-line options.

NCOPY

This command-line utility allows you to copy files and directories from one location on the network to another and to specify how they are copied.

You can use NCOPY options to specify if you want extended attributes and name-space information retained, and whether to copy subdirectories of a directory. You can also specify if you want compressed files to stay compressed, archive bit settings to be changed, and other options.

For example, to copy the Accounts directory with its files and subdirectories from SYS:SYSTEM/ACCOUNTS to network drive G and maintain compressed files in their current state, enter

NCOPY SYS:SYSTEM/ACCOUNTS TO G: /R

Typing *TO* in an NCOPY command is optional.

To copy a file named *Sales* in the directory shown in the previous example to your local drive and rename the file *Sales2,* enter

NCOPY SYS:SYSTEM/ACCOUNTS/SALES TO C: SALES2

If you are in the Accounts subdirectory when you copy the Sales file, you do not need to enter the complete path name; you only need to enter the file name— for example,

NCOPY SALES TO C:

Other options are available that are not shown here. The NCOPY utility has a total of 11 command-line options.

NDIR

This command-line utility provides a powerful search function to help you find and sort information about files and directories in your file system. The following types of options are available:

Display Options

These options allow you to view specific volume information, including volume space limitations. You can also display only directories, only files, or only subdirectories. For example, to see a list of directories on drive G, enter

    NDIR *.* /DO

There are nine display options available for NDIR.

Format Options

These options allow you to view specific information about files and directories. You can display update, archive, access, create, and copy dates as well as name-space and rights information. You can also see compression and migration status. For example, to see a summary of the Inherited Rights Filter (IRF), effective rights, and attributes for all files in your current directory, enter

    NDIR *.* /R

If you are not in the directory you want information about, you will need to enter the complete path to the files.

There are six format options available for NDIR.

Sort Options

These options allow you to view files and directories according to criteria you specify, such as owner name, size, creation date, and file size. For example, to sort files in your current directory by date last accessed, from earliest to latest, enter

    NDIR *.* /SORT CR

There are eight sort options available for NDIR.

Attribute Options

These options allow you to sort file and directory information by attribute assignment. You can search for all files flagged Read Only or Read Write, or you can search for all files that have been compressed or migrated. For example, to search for all files in the directory SYS:PUBLIC/ACCOUNTS that are marked Execute Only, enter

NDIR SYS:PUBLIC/ACCOUNTS/*.* /X

There are 19 attribute options, including status flags.

Restriction Options

These options allow you to search for files within owner, size, or date restrictions that you set. You can also use NOT to view a list of all files except those within the specified limits. For example, if you want to view a list of all files except those created by user Ben in the current directory, enter

NDIR *.* /OW NOT EQ BEN

To view a list of all files created by Ben, you would enter the same command without NOT.

There are six restriction options available for NDIR.

NETADMIN

Use this menu utility to manage NetWare Directory Services objects. Almost any task that is required for objects in NDS can be done with NETADMIN. Following is a list of the types of tasks you can do with NETADMIN. For a detailed list of tasks, see the table at the end of this chapter.

- ▶ Browse the NDS tree
- ▶ Create, view, and modify container and leaf objects
- ▶ View and modify properties of an object
- ▶ Give an object rights to the file system

▸ Give objects rights to other objects

▸ Create a template of user defaults to simplify User object creation

To access the NETADMIN main menu, simply enter the following command at the workstation prompt:

NETADMIN

NETUSER

This utility was designed to simplify common user tasks by placing them in an easy-to-use menu format. Users do not need to learn NetWare and DOS commands to work in their network setting.

With this utility, users can do the following:

▸ Capture ports to printers or print queues

▸ Manage print jobs

▸ Send messages to other users on the network

▸ Disable and enable incoming messages from other users

▸ Map network drives

▸ Change the login script and password

▸ Attach to servers

To access the NETUSER main menu, users enter the following command from their workstations:

NETUSER

NLIST

This command-line utility provides a powerful search function to help you find and sort information about objects in your NetWare Directory Services database, much like the NDIR utility works in your file system. If you have servers on your network running previous versions of NetWare, you can also search them for information.

Because of the range of information available for you to search, each object class has a customized command syntax. You must use the appropriate syntax for each of the object classes shown below:

- ▸ NDS user
- ▸ Bindery user
- ▸ NDS server
- ▸ Bindery server
- ▸ NDS group
- ▸ Bindery group
- ▸ NDS Printer
- ▸ Bindery print queue
- ▸ NDS volume
- ▸ Bindery volume
- ▸ Other objects

The two types of options explained below can be used with any of the command syntaxes.

NDS Options

These options allow you to view all information in the database, or to limit your search to a context (or path) that you specify. You can also limit your search to object names, properties of an object, or all users who are currently logged in. For example, to see a list of all objects in your current context, enter

    NLIST USER /A /S

The A option specifies that you want to view all users logged in. The S option narrows the search to 4.0 users (those logged in to the database, or Directory tree).

There are nine NDS options available for NLIST.

Bindery Options

These options allow you to view information about 3.x servers on your network. For example, if you do not want to restrict your search of users in the previous example to those who are logged in to the 4.0 Directory tree, enter

NLIST USER /A

By not using the S option, you include all users who are logged in to the network, regardless of whether they are logged in to a server or the Directory tree.

There are seven bindery options available for NLIST.

NMENU

This command-line utility executes menus created for workstation users. You can bring up a menu automatically by using the EXIT command in a login script, or you can bring up the menu by entering **NMENU** and the menu's name at the command line. For example, to bring up a menu called *Wordprocessing,* a user would enter

NMENU WORDPROCESSING

If you want the Wordprocessing menu to appear on a user's screen whenever he or she logs in, put the following command at the end of the system or user login script:

EXIT "NMENU WORDPROCESSING"

NPRINT

You can use this command-line utility to print a file that has been formatted for a printer. You can also use the utility and its options to set up and print an

ASCII file. NPRINT options override default print queue and print job configuration settings.

If you have existing print-job configuration settings that you want to use with NPRINT, you can specify that you want to use them for the job you are sending. For example, to print a sales-report file and use a print job configuration named *Report,* enter

NPRINT SYS:SALES/SALES.RPT J=REPORT

Other options are available that are not shown here. The NPRINT utility has a total of 18 command-line options.

NVER

Use this command-line utility to see network, server, and OS/2 requester version information. To see version information for these items on your network, simply enter

NVER

This utility has only two options: Help and Continuous (which causes information on the screen to scroll without pausing).

NWEXTRACT

This command-line utility allows you to replace (reinstall) a NetWare system file if it is accidentally purged from the network. The utility locates and uncompresses the file you specify from the CD-ROM or the installation disks and copies it to the default location on the network. You can also copy the file to another location if you wish.

For example, if NETADMIN was deleted accidentally from your network, you could replace the utility in its default location on Server1 by entering

NWEXTRACT A:/NETADMIN.EXE /S=SERVER1

The utility looks in drive A for the master data file (FILES.DAT), where most of the files are located. If you want to search a different path, replace drive A in the example with the path you want to search.

Other options are available that are not shown here. The NWEXTRACT utility has a total of three command-line options.

PARTMGR

Use this menu utility to manage the partitions and replicas in your NetWare 4.0 network. Partitions are groups of objects. A replica is a copy of a partition. Following is a list of the types of tasks you can do with PARTMGR. For a detailed list of tasks, see the tables at the end of this chapter.

- ▸ Create and delete partitions

- ▸ Merge two partitions

- ▸ Add and delete replicas of a partition

- ▸ Change a replica's type

- ▸ See lists of replicas and partitions on your network

To bring up the main menu, enter the following command at the prompt:

    PARTMGR

PCONSOLE

Use this menu utility to set up and manage printers, print queues, and print servers on your network. Most printing setup and management tasks can be done from PCONSOLE. The following is a list of the types of tasks you can do with PCONSOLE. For a more detailed list of tasks, see the tables at the end of this chapter.

- ▸ Quickly create a default printer, print queue, and print server

- ▸ Create, monitor, and modify print queues, jobs, users, and operators

▶ Create, monitor, and modify printers and print queue assignments

▶ Create, monitor, and modify print servers, printers, and printer assignments

To bring up the main menu, enter the following command at the workstation prompt:

PCONSOLE

PRINTCON

Use this menu utility to manage print-job configurations on your network. You can create new configurations, and view or modify configurations that you have already set up. You can also specify default configurations to be used with print jobs sent using CAPTURE, NPRINT, or PCONSOLE.

To bring up the main menu, enter the following command at the workstation prompt:

PRINTCON

PRINTDEF

This menu utility allows you to create, view, or modify printer definitions. You can also use it to create and modify printer forms to use with CAPTURE, NPRINT, and PCONSOLE. If you have an existing printer definition that you want to use for another printer, you can import the definition to the new printer, saving you the time it would take to set up a definition for each printer.

To bring up the main menu, enter the following command at the workstation prompt:

PRINTDEF

PSC

Use this utility to control printers and print servers from the command line. You can also use it to view network printer information.

For example, to display the status of the printers on a print server named PSERV1, enter

    PSC PS=PSERV1 /STAT

To remove a printer named PRINT1 from a list of network printers, enter

    PSC P=PRINT1 /PRI

Other options are available that are not shown here. The PSC utility has a total of 13 command-line options.

PURGE

This command-line utility allows you to remove deleted files from your file system. Since deleted files are saved on a server's hard disk, you might want to purge the files to free disk space. PURGE removes deleted files from the path you specify. Using PURGE with the All option removes deleted files from subdirectories under a directory you specify.

For example, if you want to purge deleted files from the directory Accounts and all its subdirectories, move to the directory and enter

    PURGE *.* /A

This utility has two command-line options: All and Help. You can also use the FILER menu utility to purge files.

RCONSOLE

This command-line utility allows network supervisors to manage NetWare servers from a workstation or from a PC with a modem. RCONSOLE establishes a connection to the server you choose, turning the workstation or PC into a virtual server console. You can then manage the server as if you were at the console.

RCONSOLE will not work unless the NetWare Loadable Modules (NLMs) that enable remote sessions are loaded on the server. This utility has no command-line options.

RENDIR

This command-line utility allows you to rename a directory. Be careful when renaming directories, because it could affect your drive mappings. If you have mapped drives to a directory whose name is changed, you will need to change mappings to the new name.

To change a directory named *SALES* to *NY_SALES,* move to the directory and enter

> RENDIR :\ NY_SALES

The colon and backslash characters represent your current drive.

There are no command-line options, with the exception of help available for RENDIR.

RIGHTS

You can use this command-line utility to view or modify trustee rights to files, directories, and volumes.

For example, to see a list of trustee assignments for the directory Accounts, move to the directory and enter

> RIGHTS /TRUSTEE

If user Fred has only File Scan rights to the SYS:ACCOUNTS directory, and you want to add Read and Write rights for him, enter

> RIGHTS SYS:ACCOUNTS +R W /NAME=FRED

To add or remove rights, use the plus (+) or minus (−) sign with the rights. If you do not use one of these signs, the rights you list will replace the existing rights.

Other options are available that are not shown here. The RIGHTS utility has a total of eight command-line options.

SEND

This command-line utility allows you to send messages to other users on the network. You can also set the type of messages you want to receive at your workstation (all, none, or system only).

For example, if you do not want to get network messages on your workstation screen, enter

SEND /A=N

To send a message to members of the Sales group on your network, enter

SEND "Remember our meeting today at 2:00" TO SALES

All users in the group SALES will receive the message, unless some users have set the option to accept no messages at their workstations. To send a message to a user, substitute the user's name in place of SALES in the command.

Other options are available that are not shown here. The SEND utility has seven command-line options for workstations on an NDS network and four for workstations logged in to a bindery-based server.

SETPASS

This command-line utility allows you to change your password. For example, to change your password, enter

SETPASS

You will be prompted to enter your current password first, then you will be asked to enter the new password.

If you need to change another user's password, you must enter the user name. For example, to change user Fred's password, enter

SETPASS FRED

Of course, you must know Fred's current password before you will be allowed to change it.

If you are logged in to a bindery-based server, you must specify the server name. For example, to change your password on SERVER1, enter

SETPASS /B

The only other option available for SETPASS is Help.

SETTTS

Use this command-line utility to view and set the physical and logical record locks for the Transaction Tracking System (TTS), which protects database applications from corruption by backing out incomplete transactions in case of a hardware or software failure.

Valid TTS values are from 0 to 254. The number you set determines how many record locks will be ignored before a transaction is tracked. For example, if you set the value at 1, TTS tracks every transaction. The settings are reset to zero whenever you log out or turn off your workstation.

For example, if you want to see your current TTS settings, enter

SETTTS

Other options are available that are not shown here. The SETTTS utility has three command-line options.

SYSTIME

This command-line utility allows you to set your workstation's date and time to match the date and time of a server.

For example, if you want to set your workstation's date and time with those on your default server, enter

SYSTIME

To set your workstation's date and time with a server named SERVER1, enter

SYSTIME SERVER1

The only other option available for SYSTIME is Help.

UIMPORT

This command-line utility allows you to create User objects by importing data from an existing database to the NDS database. This utility saves time for network supervisors by automating the process of creating User objects.

Before you can use UIMPORT, you must save the existing database as an ASCII file (with a .DAT extension) and create an import control file (with a .CTL extension) to control where data is placed in the Directory tree.

For example, if you saved information from a database containing student records as STUDENT.DAT and created a control file named STUDENT.CTL, you would enter the following command to create User objects in your Directory tree:

UIMPORT STUDENT.CTL STUDENT.DAT

There are no command-line options for the UIMPORT utility.

WHOAMI

Use this utility to see connection information. You can see information such as groups you belong to, effective rights and security equivalences, etc.

For example, if you are logged in to a server named SERVER1, and you want to see a list of groups you belong to, enter

WHOAMI SERVER1 /G

To see all information available about your connection on this server, enter

WHOAMI SERVER1 /ALL

Other options are available that are not shown here. The WHOAMI utility has three command-line options for workstations on an NDS network and eight for workstations logged in to a bindery-based server.

WSUPDATE

This command-line utility allows you to search for and update workstation files in multiple directories or subdirectories. This utility is useful if you need to update files on several workstations.

For example, if you have a new NET3.COM file in your SYS:PUBLIC/WORK file, and you want to search all workstation local drives and copy the new file over existing ones, enter

WSUPDATE SYS:PUBLIC\WORK\NET3.COM /LOCAL /C

You cannot use wildcard characters in your source path statements.

Sometimes workstation and executable files are flagged Read Only to protect them from being deleted or overwritten. You can still update files with this attribute by using WSUPDATE.

For example, if the NET3.COM files in the previous example were marked Read Only, you would add another option to the command as shown below:

WSUPDATE SYS:PUBLIC\WORK\NET3.COM /LOCAL /C /O

To search all mapped drives instead of only local drives, you would use the All option instead of the Local option.

WSUPGRD

This utility makes it easy to upgrade workstations from IPX LAN drivers to ODI (Open Datalink Interface) drivers automatically. WSUPGRD can also modify workstation AUTOEXEC.BAT files so that the ODI driver is loaded instead of the IPX driver.

For example, if you want to update workstations to ODI drivers, and you want the AUTOEXEC.BAT files to load the new driver, enter

WUSUPGRD NE2000 /E1

The default is for the IPX drivers to be deleted before the new ODI driver is installed. If you want the IPX driver to remain, enter

WSUPGRD NE2000 /N

Other options are available that are not shown here. The WSUPGRD utility has a total of nine command-line options.

Server Utilities

You enter server utilities at the console prompt, or you can use them at a workstation if you have set up remote console software on your workstation and server.

When you start up a remote console session on your workstation, your keyboard and screen become the server console and monitor. You can do most server management tasks from a remote console, with the exception of file and directory coping. For security reasons, you can copy files to, but not from, a server.

Server utilities consist of console commands and NetWare Loadable Modules (NLMs).

Console Commands

Use the console commands to perform tasks such as controlling how server resources are used by workstations, changing how server memory is allocated, and monitoring server performance and resource use.

NetWare Loadable Modules

NetWare Loadable Modules (NLMs) link resources to the server operating system. For example, LAN and disk drivers are linked to the OS when they are loaded at the server console. You can also link in OS support for name spaces for Macintosh and OS/2 file systems. Some server management applications also link to the operating system as loadable modules.

Some NLMs are loaded automatically when you install and bring up a server. These modules are required for your network and servers to operate properly; do not unload them.

ABORT REMIRROR

If you have mirrored disks in your server, you must unmirror them if you make changes to a disk, such as changing the size of a disk partition. After making necessary changes, you can reset mirroring and synchronize the data on the changed partition by remirroring it with the secondary partition. If, for some reason, you decide to stop the remirroring process, you will use this command.

For example, if you are remirroring logical partition number three and you want to abort the process, enter

ABORT REMIRROR 3

ADD NAME SPACE

To store non-DOS files on a volume, the volume must be set up to support the name space required for the files. You do this by loading the name-space NLM on the server and then adding support for that name space to the volume where the files will be stored.

For example, if you want to store Macintosh files on volume SYS:, you load the MAC name space (using the LOAD command) on the server. After the name space is linked into the operating system, enter

ADD NAME SPACE MAC TO SYS

If you want to see a list of the name spaces you have loaded on a server, enter

ADD NAME SPACE

BIND

When you install a network board in a server, the board or its driver must be bound to the protocol being used to send packets across the network. When you install NetWare or add boards or drivers using INSTALL.NLM, the system defaults to binding the IPX protocol.

Most of the time you will not need to enter the commands to load drivers and bind a protocol to them, since INSTALL adds the applicable commands and options to the server's start-up file (AUTOEXEC.NCF) for you. However, you might want to use other protocols on the network. If so, you can edit the .NCF file and add the necessary commands so the drivers and protocol will be linked automatically whenever the server is booted.

For example, to bind a protocol at the command line and accept the server default settings (options), enter

BIND IPX TO NE2000

If you do not want to accept the default settings, you can specify options in the BIND command. There are six driver parameters and one protocol parameter. Additional parameters may be specified in the documentation that came with your network board.

BROADCAST

This command allows you to send a message from the server console to workstations on the network. You can send messages to all users (workstations) who are logged in, or you can send a message to a specific user, group, or workstation connection number.

For example, if you want to bring down the server and you need to notify all users so they can close their files and log out, enter

BROADCAST "Server going down in 5 minutes. Please log out."

If you want to send a message to a specific group, add the name of the group to the end of the command. For example, to notify the Sales group of a department meeting, enter

BROADCAST "Sales meeting in 20 mins." TO SALES

CDROM

This NLM allows you to use a CD-ROM disk as a read-only volume on your server. After this module is loaded, you can mount the volume represented by the CD-ROM disk and access the information stored there.

For example, to load volume INFO from the console, first make sure the CD-ROM module is loaded, and then enter

CD MOUNT INFO

For more information about how to load the module, see LOAD.

CLEAR STATION

If a workstation crashes while it is logged in to a server, you can use this utility at the console command line to clear the workstation's connection to the server. Clearing the connection closes all open files on the workstation and erases workstation information stored on the server's internal tables.

To use this command at the console prompt, you need to know the workstation's connection number. If you do not know the number, it is easier to clear the connection using MONITOR, which gives you a list of connections to choose from.

For example, if a workstation is attached to the server as connection number 18, you clear it by entering

CLEAR STATION 18

CLIB

This module is a C Interface Library. It provides other loadable modules with an interface to the operating system, so that each NLM does not need its own built-in library. CLIB is usually linked to the operating system at run time.

CLIB and STREAMS work together, so both must be linked to the operating system before dependent NLMs can be loaded.

Most NLMs that depend on CLIB and STREAMS will look for them at load time. If CLIB and STREAMS are not found, the module will autoload them before it loads itself.

Since STREAMS and CLIB are required for many other modules to run, they have probably already been loaded on your server. If they have not been loaded, and you want to be sure they are loaded each time the server is booted, consider adding them to an .NCF start-up file.

CLIB has no options or parameters available. To load it at the command line, enter

LOAD CLIB

If you need more information about loading modules, see LOAD.

CLS

Use this utility to clear information, messages, etc., from the server console screen. At the console prompt, enter

CLS

CONFIG

Use this utility at the console prompt to see configuration information about the server. You can see the following information:

- ▸ Server name

- ▸ Server internal network number

- ▸ LAN drivers loaded

- ▸ Network board information, such as node address, frame type, network number, and communication protocol

To see configuration information about the server, enter

CONFIG

DISABLE LOGIN

Use this utility if you want to prevent users from logging in to a server. If you must make changes or repairs to the server that affect its setup files (requiring you to reboot the server to use the new settings), or if you want to back up server information or load an application, you will probably want to disable user logins until you are finished.

If users are already logged in to the server when you disable logins, they are not affected. If you want all users to log out, you will need to send a BROADCAST message to all logged-in users and ask them to log out.

To disable logins to the server, simply enter the command at the console prompt:

DISABLE LOGIN

This utility has no options available.

When you want to allow users to log in again, you must enter ENABLE LOGIN at the console.

DISABLE TTS

Use this utility if you have used ENABLE TTS to enable transaction tracking on the server. In most cases, the server will disable TTS if it is necessary. For example, TTS will be disabled if the server runs out of memory or if the SYS: volume gets full (the SYS: volume is used as the back-out volume by TTS).

However, if you need to free up NetWare server memory that is being used by TTS, you can disable it yourself at the console prompt.

To disable TTS at the console, enter the command at the console prompt:

DISABLE TTS

This utility has no options available.

To enable TTS after you have disabled it, you will need to enter ENABLE TTS at the console prompt. TTS is also reenabled automatically if you reboot the server.

DISKSET

Use this utility when you install a disk subsystem or replace a hard disk on a server, before you bring up or reboot the server.

DISKSET adds identification and configuration information about the new hard disk or subsystem on the host bus adapter's EEPROM chip. It also formats external hard disks when you add them to your disk subsystem so they can communicate with the server through the adapter.

DISKSET

If you are not in the directory where DISKSET is stored, you will need to enter the complete path to the file instead of entering only the utility name.

DISMOUNT

This utility allows you to unload a volume from the server. When you dismount a volume, it is cleared from server memory.

You might want to dismount a volume if you need to repair it (using VREPAIR), or if you want to change or upgrade a disk driver without bringing down the entire server. You can also free up server memory if the server is running slow by dismounting volumes that are not used very often.

If you are using the INSTALL loadable module, you can select and unload the volume you want to dismount. If you are at the console prompt, you enter the command and the name of the volume you want to dismount.

For example, if you were having problems with volume SYS: and you wanted to run VREPAIR to see if it would find and solve your problem, you would send a message to anyone who might be logged in and using the volume and ask them to log out. Then you would enter

DISMOUNT SYS

When you want to reload the volume and make it available again, use the MOUNT command at the console prompt.

DISPLAY NETWORKS

Use this utility if you have a server set up as a router and you want to see all the networks available to the router. You can also see the network number of the cabling system for each available network.

To see the available networks for your router, enter this command at the router's console prompt:

DISPLAY NETWORKS

This utility has no options available.

DISPLAY SERVERS

Use this utility if you have a server set up as a router and you want to see all the servers available to the router. To see the available servers, enter this command at the router's console prompt:

DISPLAY SERVERS

This utility has no options available.

DOMAIN

This loadable module protects the server operating system from corruption by untested NLMs. If you want to run an NLM that you are not sure is safe, you can load it into a separate domain from the core NLMs. Then, if the NLM has problems, it will not affect your core operating system and crash or corrupt your server. After you test the NLM on your network and are certain that it is safe to run on your server, you can load it into ring 0 with the other NLMs.

For example, to run an NLM in the protected ring, load DOMAIN and then move to the protected area by entering

DOMAIN=OS_PROTECTED

Now you can load the NLM as you would any other, but it will be loaded into the OS_PROTECTED area (ring 3) instead of ring 0.

When you are certain that the NLM is safe to run with your operating system, unload it from the protected domain, load DOMAIN, and move to ring 0 area by entering

DOMAIN=OS

From this area, you can load the NLM into ring 0. The LOAD command is used to load all NLMs. If you need information about this command before using DOMAIN, see LOAD.

Options for this NLM are OS or OS_PROTECTED for domain names and 1, 2, or 3 for domain rings.

DOWN

This utility allows you to bring down the server in a way that protects data integrity. When you use this command, it ensures that all cache buffers are written to disk and files are closed before services are terminated.

Before you bring down a server, you might also want to use the BROADCAST command from the console to notify users who are logged in and allow them to save their work, close open files, and log out. Of course, if you just bring down the server, the files will be closed and the users logged out, so nothing will be corrupted, but it is better to let users know beforehand so they can finish whatever they are working on.

To bring down a server, at the server console, enter

DOWN

When you are ready to bring the server back up again, you must enter SERVER at the DOS prompt to execute the SERVER.EXE file.

DSREPAIR

This loadable module finds and corrects errors in the NDS database, similar to the way VREPAIR finds and corrects errors in volumes. DSREPAIR checks NDS partitions and replicas on the server where you run it. It also checks the file system for problems such as invalid trustee IDs, which occur when a user is deleted.

You can load and run this NLM if you suspect your NDS database is having problems. You will also have to run it if you get a message stating that the server could not open the local database. Running DSREPAIR can fix the problem so the database can be opened.

This module has two command-line options. If you want to run DSREPAIR, make changes to the database, and exit without being prompted before proceeding with each step, enter

DSREPAIR=U

If you do not use this option, you will be prompted after the database has been checked, before any corrections are made. You will also have to exit manually from the program.

Another command-line option allows you to specify a file for DSREPAIR to log all errors that are found. For example, if you want to log errors in a file called NDSERR.LOG, enter

DSREPAIR -l NDSERR.LOG

In addition to the command-line options, there are eight menu options you can use to specify the way the database is checked and errors are corrected. For more information about how to load the module, see LOAD.

EDIT

Use this NLM to create or edit text files on the server, such as the server .NCF files. You can edit files on either DOS or NetWare partitions. EDIT does have one limitation: You can only edit text files that are smaller than 8K. However, most server text files are smaller than this.

To use this module, you simply load it at the console prompt and then specify the name of the file you want to edit.

ENABLE LOGIN

Use this utility if you disabled logins for the server and you are ready to reenable them. You will only need to use this command if you are not rebooting the server after disabling logins, because logins are automatically enabled whenever the server is booted.

To enable logins, enter the following command at the console prompt:

ENABLE LOGIN

To find out about disabling server logins, see DISABLE LOGIN.

ENABLE TTS

Use this utility if you disabled TTS (transaction tracking) on the server using DISABLE TTS, or if it was disabled automatically by the operating system because of lack of memory or volume disk space.

You will only need to use this utility if you are not rebooting the server after TTS is disabled, because TTS is automatically enabled whenever the server is booted.

When you are ready to reenable TTS, enter the following command at the console prompt:

ENABLE TTS

To find out about disabling TTS on a server, see DISABLE TTS.

EXIT

This utility sends you back to DOS after you bring down a server. From there you can access DOS files if you want to. You also start NetWare on the server from this location, by entering SERVER.

If you removed DOS from the server earlier, to free up space, EXIT will not take you to the DOS level; it reboots the server.

For example, if you bring down a server and you need to access utilities on the DOS partition, enter the following command at the console prompt:

EXIT

This utility has no options available.

HELP

This utility gives you help information about the server utilities and NLMs. If you type HELP with no additional parameters, you will see a list of all the console commands. If you want help about a specific command, enter the name of the command after HELP.

For example, if you want to send a message to a group of users on your network and you need information about the BROADCAST command, enter

HELP BROADCAST

You will see a brief description of the command, an example showing you how it is used, and the command syntax.

INSTALL

This NLM is one of the most-often-used modules for managing, maintaining, and updating NetWare servers. The NLM is structured like a menu utility, which makes it easy to use.

You can do the following types of tasks with INSTALL:

▸ Create, delete, and manage disk partitions on the server, including DOS partitions

▸ Install NetWare (including the operating system and NetWare Directory Services)

▸ Update your license or registration disk

▸ Load and unload disk and LAN drivers

▸ Create, delete, and manage NetWare volumes on the server's hard disks

▸ Add, remove, mirror, unmirror, check, and repair hard disks

▸ Modify server start-up and configuration files (.NCF files)

▸ Install additional products (besides NetWare) on the server

Before you can use INSTALL to do any of these tasks, make sure it is loaded on the server. Sometimes NLMs are unloaded by network supervisors if the server's response time is slow and memory or disk space needs to be freed for other processes. If you need information about loading the module, see LOAD.

When INSTALL has been loaded on the server, enter the following command at the console prompt:

INSTALL

INSTALL has only one option. If you want to load INSTALL without the help screens (and save 16K of memory), enter

INSTALL NH

IPXS

This NLM must be loaded on your server before many other NLMs you might load. It supports the NetWare standard IPX protocol. Since other modules depend on this NLM, it should be loaded automatically whenever the server is booted.

To autoload the NLM, simply place the command to load it in a server start-up (.NCF) file. If you need more information about using the LOAD command for NLMs, see LOAD.

KEYB

This NLM allows you to use keyboard types on the server other than U.S. English. When you load KEYB, a list of valid keyboard types appears on the console screen. Five types are supported: English (U.S.), French, German, Italian, and Spanish.

For example, to load KEYB and use the German keyboard, enter

LOAD KEYB GERMAN

LANGUAGE

This utility allows you to set the language for the server operating system and NLMs. When the server's language is set, all messages from the operating system and NLMs will be in the specified language. The default language, unless you specify otherwise, is English.

NetWare 4.0 supports 16 languages for the operating system. Each supported language has an ID number, so you can specify the language you want by typing either the name or the ID number.

To see a list of the supported languages and their corresponding ID numbers, enter the following command at the console prompt:

LANGUAGE

From this list, select the language you want and write down either the name or the ID number, then exit the list.

If you wanted to set the messages to Japanese, you would enter either the word *Japanese* with the command or the following:

LANGUAGE 9

LIST DEVICES

This utility gives you a list of all devices, such as tape, disk, and optical disk or other storage device, attached to the server. From the console prompt, enter

LIST DEVICES

LOAD

This command is used with all loadable modules to link the modules to the NetWare operating system. To use a module, it must first be loaded. The following types of modules are loaded with this command:

- ▸ Disk drivers

- ▸ LAN drivers

- ▸ Name-space modules

- ▸ NetWare Loadable Modules (NLMs)

You can use LOAD to load commands at the console prompt, or you can put load commands in one of the server start-up (.NCF) files for modules that you want loaded automatically whenever the server is booted.

For example, to load a LAN driver, you would place the following command in an .NCF file (since you'll need the driver to load whenever the server is booted):

LOAD NE2000

If you use LOAD with only the module name, the operating system assumes the module is in the default directory (where it was copied during installation). If a module is moved to a different directory, you must enter the complete directory path to the module.

MAGAZINE

Use this utility at the console prompt after being prompted to insert or remove a magazine (a set of media) from the server. The server automatically prompts you to insert or remove a magazine when applicable, but you must enter an option to notify the server of your action. Four options are available:

- Removed
- Not removed
- Inserted
- Not inserted

Type one of these options after the MAGAZINE command at the console prompt. For example, if you were prompted to insert a magazine, you would insert it and then enter

MAGAZINE INSERTED

If you were prompted to insert a magazine and you decided not to insert it, you would enter

MAGAZINE NOT INSERTED

MATHLIB

If your server has a math coprocessor chip, you need to load this NLM to link it to the operating system. (If it does not, you must load MATHLIBC.)

This module cannot run without the CLIB and STREAMS modules. Most modules that depend on STREAMS and CLIB will autoload them if the modules are not linked to the operating system when the NLM tries to load.

Since STREAMS, CLIB, and either MATHLIB or MATHLIBC are required for many other modules to run, they have probably already been loaded on your server. If they have not been loaded, and you want to be sure they are loaded each time the server is booted, consider adding them to an .NCF start-up file.

To load MATHLIB, enter the following command at the server console:

LOAD MATHLIB

This module has no parameters or options available. If you need more information about loading modules, see LOAD.

MATHLIBC

If your server does not have a math coprocessor chip, you need to load this NLM. (If it does, you must load MATHLIB).

Like MATHLIB, this module relies on the CLIB and STREAMS modules. Most modules that depend on STREAMS and CLIB will autoload them if the modules are not linked to the operating system when the NLM tries to load.

Since STREAMS, CLIB, and either MATHLIB or MATHLIBC are required for many other modules to run, they have probably already been loaded on your server. If they have not been loaded, and you want to be sure they are loaded each time the server is booted, consider adding them to an .NCF start-up file.

To load MATHLIBC, enter the following command at the server console:

LOAD MATHLIBC

This module has no parameters or options available. If you need more information about loading modules, see LOAD.

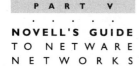
MEDIA

Use this utility at the console prompt after being prompted to insert or remove media from the server. The server automatically prompts you to insert or remove media when applicable, but you must enter a media option to notify the server of your action. Four options are available:

- ▶ Removed

- ▶ Not removed

- ▶ Inserted

- ▶ Not inserted

Type one of the options after the MEDIA command at the console prompt. For example, if you were prompted to insert media, you would insert it and then enter

MEDIA INSERTED

If you were prompted to insert media and you decided not to insert it, you would enter

MEDIA NOT INSERTED

MEMORY

Use this command to see how much of the server's installed memory the operating system can use. This command gives you information only. To see this information, enter the following command at the console prompt:

MEMORY

MIRROR STATUS

Use this command to see a list of all the server's partitions. You will also see information about the mirrored status of each partition. This command gives you information only. To see this information, enter the following command at the console prompt:

MIRROR STATUS

Mirrored partitions exist in one of five states:

▸ Not mirrored

▸ Fully synchronized (data is identical)

▸ Out of synchronization (data is not identical)

▸ Orphaned (integrity of data is not guaranteed)

▸ Being remirrored

MODULES

This utility allows you to see information about the loadable modules you have loaded on the server. You can see each module's short name and descriptive string (long name). Where applicable (such as for LAN and disk drivers), you will also see version numbers of the loaded modules.

This module is for information only. It has no options or parameters.

To see module information, enter the following command at the console prompt:

MODULES

MONITOR

This loadable module is the one you will use most often to get information about your server. Current statistics, updated as the server runs, let you assess how efficiently the server is running and how heavily it is being used. You can see information such as

▸ How long the server has been running since it was last booted

▸ The percentage of time the server's processor is busy

▶ The number of blocks available, and the number of blocks of data that are waiting to be written to disk

▶ Number of disk requests waiting to be serviced

▶ Buffer information, such as number available for station requests and directory caching

▶ Number of connections to the server

▶ Number of files being accessed

▶ Information about server disks, LAN drivers, volumes, and attached media devices

This information can help you configure your server in a way that will best use its resources, and it can help you track usage, see potential problems, and reallocate resources to solve them before they have an impact on the server.

Although you cannot change these statistics directly, you can make adjustments to your server and view additional information about its usage, because MONITOR provides a menu interface that allows you to perform maintenance tasks.

MONITOR also loads with a built-in screen saver, which protects your console and the MONITOR information from being accessed by unauthorized users. To access MONITOR, simply enter the command at the console prompt:

MONITOR

MOUNT

Use this command to load a volume onto the server. Mounting volumes makes the file-system data on the volume available to users.

You can mount volumes while the server is in use; there is no need to bring down the server to mount or dismount volumes. For example, if you are having problems with a server, you might want to dismount it, run VREPAIR to check and fix the volume, and then remount it.

MOUNT has two options available: You can mount a specific volume, or you can mount all volumes with a single command. For example, to mount a volume named VOL1, enter

>   MOUNT VOL1

If you want to mount all volumes, enter

>   MOUNT ALL

NAME

This utility lets you see the name of the server. This is the name that is assigned during the server installation. All you have to do is enter the command at the console prompt—for example,

>   NAME

The server name will appear.
   This utility has no parameters or options.

NMAGENT

This module is used with network hub and management programs. It passes network information from the server and LAN drivers to the management program. If you are using network management on your network, load this module on each server that you want to see on your program:

>   LOAD NMAGENT

This NLM has no parameters or options. If you need help loading the module, see LOAD.

NUT

This loadable module is the NLM utility user interface for NetWare 3.11 modules. It must be loaded on 3.11 servers in order for most utilities to function. (For 4.0 servers, use NWSNUT.)

You will probably not need to load the module at the command line, because the modules that depend on NUT will autoload it if they cannot find it when they try to load. You can see if NUT is loaded by using the MODULES utility at the console prompt to get a list of the modules currently loaded on your server.

If you must load this NLM at the console, enter the following command at the prompt:

```
LOAD NUT
```

NWSNUT

This loadable module is the NLM utility user interface for NetWare 4.0 modules. It must be loaded on 4.0 servers in order for most utilities to function. (For 3.11 servers, use NUT.)

You will probably not need to load the module at the command line, because the modules that depend on NUT will autoload it if they cannot find it when they try to load. You can see if NUT is loaded by using the MODULES utility at the console prompt to get a list of the modules currently loaded on your server.

If you must load this NLM at the console, enter the following command at the prompt:

```
LOAD NWSNUT
```

OFF

Use this utility to clear information, messages, etc., from the server console screen. At the console prompt, enter

```
OFF
```

This command does the same thing as the CLS command.

PROTOCOL

This utility allows you to see a list of the protocols and frame types registered on your server. You can also use it if you need to register additional protocols, although this is usually unnecessary because most protocols either register themselves or are automatically registered by the LAN driver they communicate with.

To see a list of protocols and frame types currently loaded on your server, enter this command at the console prompt:

    PROTOCOL

If you need to register a protocol (for a new, unusual media type, for example), enter this command, followed by the new protocol and its frame type:

    PROTOCOL REGISTER

You will have to get the protocol and frame-type information from the documentation that comes with the media or module you are adding to your server. To make sure the protocol is registered each time the server is booted, add the command to the server's AUTOEXEC.NCF file.

PSERVER

This loadable module links a print server to the server operating system. Loading this module is the final step in setting up printing for your network. Before you load it, you must use PCONSOLE to set up and configure the print server.

For example, after creating a print server named PSERV1, load this NLM by entering the following command at the console prompt:

    LOAD PSERVER PSERV1

This NLM has no parameters or options. If you need help loading PSERVER, see LOAD.

REGISTER MEMORY

If you add memory to your server, you will need to register the memory so the server knows where it starts and ends. This helps avoid memory address conflicts.

To register the memory, you need to specify the starting address of the memory and its length (in hexadecimal numbers). For example, if you added 8MB of memory to the server above its standard 16MB, you would enter the following command at the console prompt:

REGISTER MEMORY 1000000 800000

To make sure the memory is registered automatically whenever the server is booted, add the command to the server's AUTOEXEC.NCF file.

If you want to see how much memory the server is currently addressing, use the MEMORY command at the console prompt.

REMIRROR PARTITION

If your server stopped remirroring for some reason, or you aborted a remirroring procedure, use this command when you are ready to restart it.

You will not normally need to use this command, because the server automatically takes care of partition mirroring.

For example, if you had to abort a remirroring procedure for partition 3 and you wanted to restart the process, you would enter the following command at the console prompt:

REMIRROR PARTITION 3

REMOTE

This loadable module allows you to access the server console from a workstation or from a PC with a modem. The workstation utility RCONSOLE can establish a connection to any server running the REMOTE NLM and the RSPX NLM (the remote SPX protocol). When you have these modules linked to the server, you can manage the server as if you were at the console.

You can also set a password for REMOTE, so only users with the password can access the console. For example, to restrict access to the remote server console by adding the password *manage*, enter

LOAD REMOTE manage

Immediately after you load REMOTE, you must load RSPX. For more information, see LOAD and RSPX.

If you want the server to be available for remote access automatically each time it is booted, add these LOAD commands to the server's AUTOEXEC.NCF file. This NLM has no options or parameters.

REMOVE DOS

This command allows you to free the memory used by DOS on the server and return it to the NetWare operating system. You might want to remove DOS if your server's available memory is low and you want to alleviate the problem.

If you remove DOS, it is no longer resident on the server, so any modules loaded on the DOS drive are unavailable. When DOS is removed, the EXIT command, which normally takes you to the DOS level, will reboot the server.

To remove DOS from the server, enter the following command at the console prompt:

REMOVE DOS

This command has no parameters or options.

RESET ROUTER

If the router table in your server becomes corrupted or is inaccurate because servers are down, you can use this command to reset it. When a server is down, packets are still sent to that server until the other servers on the network update their router tables, which removes the inoperative server from the table. In the meantime, packets sent to that server for routing are lost.

Router tables are automatically updated every two minutes, so if you can wait that long, the router will be reset for you. If you do not want to wait, however, you can use the RESET ROUTER command on each server that is still running to update the router tables.

To reset a router table for a server, enter the following command at the console prompt:

RESET ROUTER

This command has no parameters or options.

ROUTE

This loadable module allows you to set up and control the routing of NetWare packets across an IBM bridge to a Token Ring network.

ROUTE has nine options available. However, in most cases where you have a simple configuration, loading ROUTE with the default settings (no parameters) will work fine. The only exception is the board number parameter, which will have to be specified if you do not have the Token Ring driver loaded first. For example, if you want to set up routing for a Token Ring network on your Net-Ware LAN, and you know that the driver for the Token Ring board will be the third one loaded by the system, enter

LOAD ROUTE BOARD=3

If you want routing to be enabled automatically whenever the server is booted, place this command in the AUTOEXEC.NCF file. If you need more information about loading modules, see LOAD.

RPL

The RPL (Remote Program Load) loadable module allows you to connect diskless workstations to your network by enabling them to boot from files on the server instead of requiring boot files on the workstation.

Before workstations can boot from a server, you must set up a directory on the server and copy boot files for each workstation to those files.

Once you have boot files set up, load this module on the server by entering the following command at the console prompt:

LOAD RPL

No parameters or options are available for this module. If you need help loading the module, see LOAD.

RS232

This loadable module sets up an asynchronous communications port on the server so workstations can access the server console through a modem. It works with the REMOTE module, so both modules must be loaded in order for a workstation to access the console through an asynchronous connection.

When you load RS232, you must specify the communications port number you will use and the baud rate of your modem. For example, after loading REMOTE (which must be loaded first), you can load RS232 and use communications port 2 with a 4800-baud modem by entering the following:

```
LOAD RS232 2 4800
```

If you don't specify the parameters with the LOAD command, you will be prompted for each parameter the system needs. If you want the communications port to be set up automatically whenever the server is booted, put the command immediately after the LOAD REMOTE command in the AUTOEXEC.NCF file.

RSPX

This loadable module loads the SPX driver on the server so that workstations cabled to the network can access the server console.

RSPX works with the REMOTE module, so both modules must be loaded in order for a workstation to access the console. For example, after loading REMOTE (which must be loaded first), you can load RSPX by entering

```
LOAD RSPX
```

No parameters or options are available for this module. If you need help loading modules, see LOAD.

RTDM

This loadable module allows the server to migrate data to an attached device, such as a CD-ROM disk changer.

Usually, you will not need to load RTDM from the console prompt, because devices that depend on it to communicate with the server will look for the NLM and autoload it if it is not already loaded.

You can see if it is loaded on the server by using the MODULES command. If you need to load RTDM, enter the following command at the prompt:

LOAD RTDM

No parameters or options are available for this module. If you need help loading the module, see LOAD.

SBACKUP

This loadable module allows you to back up data to and restore data from a storage device attached to a NetWare server. You can back up NetWare server data, such as Directory Services and the file system. You can also back up DOS, Windows, and OS/2 workstations to the storage device.

SBACKUP works with TSAs (Target Service Agents), which must be loaded on the machine whose data is being backed up. The TSA interprets the data and communicates information about its characteristics to SBACKUP, so that data types (such as name spaces) that are unfamiliar to the server can be backed up accurately.

To bring up the SBACKUP main menu, enter the following command at the console prompt:

SBACKUP

From the menu, you can choose F1 (Help) to get more information about running the program.

SCAN FOR NEW DEVICES

Use this utility to look for devices that have been added to the server since it was last booted. When a server is booted, it scans for all devices attached to it and gathers information about each device. However, if you add a device after the server is booted, the utility may not be aware of it.

To have the server scan for devices added since the last time it was booted, enter the following command at the console prompt:

SCAN FOR NEW DEVICES

This command has no parameters or options.

SCHDELAY

This loadable module allows you to specify how processes use the server's CPU by prioritizing them. You can delay the execution of some processes and give more CPU time to others.

You do this by assigning a number to a process. The number determines how many cycles will be skipped before the process will be allowed to run again. For example, the default setting of zero means that a process will run each time it is scheduled in the CPU cycle. If the process monopolizes the CPU and makes the other processes run too slowly, you might assign it the number 3. This means that it will only run every third time it is scheduled, freeing up the additional time for other processes to use.

If you want to see a list of current processes using the server CPU, enter

LOAD SCHDELAY

The list includes the current SCHDELAY setting of each process. You can change the setting by entering a process name and number after the command shown above. For example, if you are running SBACKUP and you don't want it to slow down your server, you might assign it a value of 2 so it will only run every other cycle. To do this, enter

LOAD SCHDELAY SBACKUP=2

If you want to retain schedule settings when the server is booted, put the command in the AUTOEXEC.NCF file. If you want to add a value to more than one process, you can place them one after another on the command line. In the example above, you would simply continue by entering a space and then the next process name and the number you want to assign it.

If you need help loading the module, see LOAD.

SEARCH

This command lets you set search paths that tell the server where start-up files and loadable modules are stored in the file system. It is similar to the MAP command used to map drives for workstations. The default search path for the server files is SYS:SYSTEM, so if you change the directory structure and move the loadable modules of the .NCF files, you will need to create new search paths so the server can find them.

This command allows you to add new server search paths, delete existing paths, and view the current paths. For example, to see a list of the search paths you already have, enter

    SEARCH

If you loaded new NLMs on your system at the root of the SYS: volume in a directory called NLMS, you would enter

    SEARCH ADD SYS:NLMS

SECURE CONSOLE

This utility allows you to use the console (if you are authorized), but it prevents security breaches. Although it does not lock the console (which can be done in MONITOR), it allows NLMs to load only from volume SYS:. This protects the server and the network from someone loading an NLM from a floppy disk or from DOS and then using it to break network security.

This utility also prevents anyone other than the console operator from changing the server date and time. Accounting and auditing features rely on date and time to determine exactly when certain procedures were done or when files or rights were changed.

If you use SECURE CONSOLE, you can only disable it by rebooting the server. To secure the console, enter the following command at the prompt:

SECURE CONSOLE

This command has no options or parameters available.

SEND

This command allows you to send a message from the server console to workstations on the network. You can send messages to specific users (workstations) who are logged in, or you can send a message to a workstation connection number.

For example, if you want to send a message to users, enter the message and the user names as follows:

SEND "Staff mtg. in 20 mins." TO Fred, Susan, Jeff

If you want to send a message to a group of users, or to all users who are logged in, use BROADCAST instead.

SERVER

This utility boots your server and starts NetWare. Whenever you bring down a server, you enter this command to start it up again.

When you run this utility, it executes the start-up files (STARTUP.NCF and AUTOEXEC.NCF) and mounts volume SYS:. SERVER has options that allow you to circumvent the start-up files and use replacements, and you can also change the block size of the cache buffer, but these changes are not recommended. Using the default files is the best way to bring up the server.

To bring up a server with NetWare, enter the following command at the DOS prompt:

```
SERVER
```

SERVMAN

This loadable module lets you manage your server and see information about the server, its volumes, and the network in a menu format. In addition to operating-system parameters, IPX/SPX settings, and device settings, you can see the following:

▶ How many processes are running

▶ How many NLMs are loaded

▶ How many volumes are mounted

▶ How many users are logged in

▶ How many name spaces are loaded

You can add or modify many SET parameters for the server by using SERVMAN, which provides an easier interface for users than the command-line SET parameters. To bring up the main menu, enter the following command at the console prompt:

```
LOAD SERVMAN
```

Online help is available by pressing F1. This module has no parameters or options available. If you need help loading the module, see LOAD.

SET

This utility allows you to set operating-system parameters from the command line. SET is an extensive utility with many parameters. You can add or modify many SET parameters by using SERVMAN, which provides an easier interface to SET than the command line.

To help you understand the types of parameters you can set for a server, they are divided into 12 categories.

Communications Parameters

These parameters let you set values for packet receive buffers (server memory set aside to hold data packets) and packet size. You can set watchdog functions, which automatically terminate workstation connections to the server if no activity is detected. You can also set (off or on) the *Get nearest server* option, which determines whether the server will respond to workstation requests to locate a server.

Memory Parameters

These parameters let you control the dynamic memory pool. You can set values for automatically registering memory above 16MB, set "garbage collection" intervals and memory usage limits, and turn on or off read/write emulation and notification of page fault errors.

File-Caching Parameters

These parameters let you manage file cache buffers in the server's memory. You can set Read Ahead on or off, set minimum file cache buffers, and manage disk cache settings.

Directory-Caching Parameters

These parameters let you manage how the Directory Entry Table (DET) is stored in memory by setting directory cache buffers and limits.

File-System Parameters

These parameters let you turn on and specify file compression settings, set warning thresholds for full volumes, set the maximum subdirectory depth for the file system, and manage how and when deleted files are purged from disk.

Locks Parameters

These parameters let you specify the number of open files that workstations can have and the number that the server can handle.

Transaction-Tracking Parameters

These parameters let you set TTS flags for backout and abort (off and on), and set TTS backout file truncation and unwritten cache wait times.

Disk Parameters

These parameters let you set remirroring requests and block size, and enable or disable Hot Fix functions, such as read and write verification.

Time Parameters

These parameters let you manage time synchronization of all servers on the network, which ensures that updates to the NDS database are correct. You can specify the time server type, add or remove a time source, and configure all servers to work in your time synchronization plan for the network.

NetWare Core Protocol Parameters

These parameters let you set the way the server handles NCP packets and boundary checking. You can also set the new NCP Server Packet Signature security level.

Miscellaneous Parameters

These parameters let you set alert messages and displays and specify whether passwords can be encrypted or unencrypted.

Error-Handling Parameters

These parameters let you set server and volume log file maximum size. You can also specify how the log files should be handled when they reach this size.

Most operating-system parameter defaults have been set so the server will perform efficiently and accurately. Make sure you do not change server settings unless you know how the change will affect your server.

If you want SET parameters to be implemented each time the server is booted, enter them in a server start-up (.NCF) file.

SET TIME

Use this utility to modify the server's internal date and time. This setting is only for date and time; it does not control the time synchronization settings used for validating network time across all servers (set with SERVMAN or SET).

The two parameters for the SETTIME command are *month/day/year* and *hour:minute:second*. Several formats are acceptable for each parameter. For example, to reset the server time to 2:30 p.m., April 18, 1993, enter

    SET TIME 4/18/93 2:30:00 PM

SET TIME ZONE

This utility sets a time reference in CLIB. The time information is used by other NLMs that depend on CLIB. It does not change the server time.

You can set parameters for the time zone, hours from Greenwich mean time, and daylight savings (if you live in an area where this applies). You can see the current setting by entering the command with no parameters.

For example, to change the time zone setting to central standard time, enter the code for that zone and its hours from Greenwich mean time by entering

    SET TIME ZONE CST6

SPEED

This utility allows you to see your processor's CPU speed setting. To get the most from your CPU, you should read the documentation that came with your computer to calculate and set the highest CPU setting allowed.

To see the CPU speed setting, enter

SPEED

This utility has no parameters or options available.

SPXCONFG

This loadable module allows you to set configuration parameters for SPX. You can change SPX parameters such as watchdog timeouts, retry counts, maximum concurrent SPX settings, and IPX socket table size.

A list of your current settings will appear if you enter the following command at the console prompt:

LOAD SPXCONFG

This module has a total of eight options available. You can also set SPX configuration parameters with SERVMAN, which provides an easier interface for the command and online help.

SPXS

Use this loadable module if you are using a STREAMS-based SPX protocol on your server. If you want this module loaded each time the server is booted, put the command to load it in a start-up (.NCF) file.

To load the SPXS module on the server, enter the following command at the console prompt or in a server .NCF file:

LOAD SPXS

If you need help loading the module, see LOAD.

STREAMS

This loadable module works with the CLIB module to provide C Interface Library and STREAMS protocol services to other NLMs. Since they work together, both modules should be loaded on the server before the NLMs that are dependent on them are loaded.

These NLMs are usually linked to the operating system at run time. Most NLMs that depend on CLIB and STREAMS will look for them at load time. If CLIB and STREAMS are not found, the module will autoload them before it loads itself.

Since STREAMS and CLIB are required for many other modules to run, they have probably already been loaded on your server. If they have not been loaded, and you want to be sure they are loaded each time the server is booted, consider adding them to a start-up .NCF file. STREAMS must be loaded before CLIB.

To load STREAMS, enter the following command at the console prompt or in the .NCF file:

LOAD STREAMS

This NLM has an option available for changing the maximum message file size, but the default is usually sufficient. If you need more information about loading modules, see LOAD.

TIME

This utility displays the server's date and time, the daylight savings time status, and information about the time synchronization setup on the server.

To get this information, enter the following command at the console prompt:

TIME

This utility has no parameters or options available.

TIMESYNC

This module controls time synchronization on the server, which is reported across the network to other servers. TIMESYNC loads automatically when the server is booted, so you should not need to load it at the console prompt.

If you need to change time synchronization settings or parameters, use the SERVMAN module.

TLI

This module provides the transport layer for network communications services. It is loaded with the modules it works with, such as STREAMS, CLIB, and
SPXS or IPXS.

You can see which modules are loaded on your server by using the MODULES
utility at the console. If this module is not loaded, you can load it at the console
prompt, or you can place the command to load it in an .NCF file so it is loaded
each time the server is booted.

To load TLI, enter the following command at the console prompt or in an
.NCF file (after the commands to load STREAMS and CLIB):

    LOAD TLI

No parameters or options are available for this module.

TRACK OFF

If you have the Router Tracking screen displayed, you can clear the console
screen and turn it off with this utility. Just enter the following command at the
console:

    TRACK OFF

TRACK ON

This utility displays the Router Tracking screen, which shows you incoming
information (network data received by the server), outgoing information (data
being broadcast to the network by the server), and responses by the server to "get
nearest server" requests.

This screen is for routing information only; you cannot set any router
parameters with this utility.

To display the screen, enter the following command at the console prompt:

    TRACK ON

No parameters or options are available for this utility. To turn off the Router
Tracking screen, see TRACK OFF.

UNBIND

If you want to remove a network board from your server or bind a different protocol to a board, you will first need to unbind the current protocol from the board's driver.

Specify the protocol and the name of the LAN driver you are unbinding so the operating system will know which protocol to unload. If you have several identical network boards, include enough information in the command to make it unique, such as its interrupt or port number.

For example, if you want to remove an NE2000 board from the server, unbind the protocol from its driver by entering the following command at the console prompt:

UNBIND IPX FROM NE2000

If you remove the network board permanently, you will need to remove the command to load and bind it from the AUTOEXEC.NCF file.

UNLOAD

This utility allows you to unload NLMs and other loadable modules from a server. Unloading the module removes its services from the server's operating system and returns the resources it was using.

If your server is running out of memory, you might want to use the MODULES command to see a list of the modules you are running and unload any that are not needed (such as old LAN and disk drivers, or a module you use occasionally, such as INSTALL).

For example, if you did not need the INSTALL module loaded all the time, you could unload it by entering the following command at the console prompt:

UNLOAD INSTALL

Anything that is loaded with the LOAD command can be unloaded using UNLOAD. Be careful about unloading modules such as CLIB, STREAMS, and drivers, since many other processes depend on them.

UPS

This loadable module allows you to link an uninterruptible power supply (UPS) system to your server. After installing the UPS hardware and connecting the power, load UPS.

You must specify several parameters when you load the module, to let the server operating system know what interface board and port number are being used. You can find this information in the documentation that comes with the UPS hardware. You can also specify how long the server will function on UPS power and how long the battery should recharge after it is used.

The easiest way to set up all this information is to enter the command to load the UPS and the driver, and then the system will prompt you for the additional information it needs. For example, enter

LOAD UPS TYPE=DCB

The system will prompt you for the information it needs to complete the linking process.

To have UPS loaded whenever the server is booted, place the LOAD command and parameters in a start-up (.NCF) file.

UPS STATUS

This utility allows you to view current information about your UPS system. You can also see the current network power status. This is helpful if the network is on battery power and you need to know how much power is left to keep the network running.

To see UPS information, enter the following command at the console prompt:

UPS STATUS

This utility has no parameters or options available.

UPS TIME

This utility allows you to change the discharge, recharge, and wait settings for the UPS. An older UPS will need the discharge and recharge settings adjusted, because it takes longer for it to recharge.

To change these settings for your power supply, enter all the settings at the command line, or simply enter UPS TIME and you will be prompted for the changes you want to make.

For example, to increase the recharge time to 175 minutes, enter the following command at the console prompt:

UPS TIME RECHARGE=175

You should also be aware that your current settings don't show on the screen at the time you make them. You have to use UPS STATUS to see the new settings.

VERSION

Use this utility to see the version of NetWare that is running on your server. At the console prompt, enter

VERSION

This utility has no parameters or options available.

VOLUMES

This utility allows you to list all the volumes currently mounted on the server. To see this list, enter the following command at the console prompt:

VOLUMES

This utility has no parameters or options available.

VREPAIR

This loadable module finds volume problems and corrects them so that the volume operates properly when it is remounted on the server. The server and its mounted volumes are not affected by VREPAIR; you do not need to bring down the server. All you have to do is dismount the volume before you run VREPAIR to fix it.

The following options are available for running VREPAIR:

- ▸ Specify if you want name-space support removed from the volume during the repair process. If you added a name space to a volume and then started having problems, you might want to remove it to see if the name space is the cause of the problem.

- ▸ Choose what directory and File Allocation Table (FAT) information is written to the disk. You can have the entire table rewritten or just the entries with errors.

- ▸ Choose whether to write changes to the disk immediately or to save them in memory and write them later. If you have enough memory available on the server, writing them later helps VREPAIR run faster.

- ▸ Choose whether to purge deleted files from the disk while it is being repaired.

For example, if you were having problems with VOL1 on your server, you would first use DISMOUNT to unload it from the server, and then you would enter

LOAD VREPAIR VOL1

If you need more information about loading modules, see LOAD.

Utilities and NLMs to Use for Common Network Tasks

The tables in this section will help you find a utility or loadable module that you can use for most network management tasks. The left column of each table lists common tasks that you might be required to do, and the right column lists the most common utilities or NetWare Loadable Modules (NLMs) that you can use to complete the tasks.

The "Utility or NLM" column does not contain a comprehensive list of every method available. For example, command-line utilities such as PURGE and RIGHTS are not listed in the table "Managing the NetWare File System" because they are harder to use (and less often used) than the FILER and NetWare Administrator utilities, which offer more helpful user interfaces to help you complete your tasks.

Tables V.1 to V.6 shows utilities and NLMs you can use for the following categories of tasks:

▸ Installing and upgrading NetWare

▸ Managing NetWare Directory Services (NDS)

▸ Managing the NetWare file system

▸ Managing NetWare servers

▸ Managing workstations

▸ Setting up and managing printing

	TASK	UTILITY OR NLM
T A B L E V.1 *Installing and Upgrading NetWare*	Install a new NetWare 4.0 server	INSTALL (.NLM)
	Install additional products on a server	
	Install Novell ElectroText (online documentation) on a server	
	Upgrade a server to NetWare 4.0	MIGRATE *or* 2XUPGRADE
	Install Novell ElectroText (online documentation) on a workstation	XCOPY
	Install networking software on a workstation	INSTALL (.EXE)

TABLE V.2

Managing NetWare

Directory Services

TASK	UTILITY OR NLM
Create a container object	INSTALL
	or NETADMIN
	or NetWare Administrator
Create a leaf object	NETADMIN
Create a user template	*or* NetWare Administrator
Delete an object	
Change an object's property values	
Create, modify, or copy a login script for an object	
Move an object	
Rename an object	
Set up accounting for user objects	
Add a trustee to an object	
Delete a trustee from an object	
Modify a trustee's rights to an object	
View or modify an Inherited Rights Filter (IRF)	
View a trustee's effective rights to an object	
Search for objects according to criteria you specify	NLIST
	or NetWare Administrator
Import users to the NetWare Directory from an existing database	UIMPORT

T A B L E   V.2

Managing NetWare
Directory Services
(continued)

TASK	UTILITY OR NLM
Create a new partition	PARTMGR
Merge or split partitions	*or* NetWare Administrator
Create or delete a replica	
Rebuild corrupted replicas	
View a list of partitions stored on a server	
View a list of replicas of a specific partition	
Change a replica's type	
View a list of partitions and replicas in a NetWare Directory tree	NetWare Administrator
Remove NDS from a server	INSTALL
Repair the NetWare Directory Services database	DSREPAIR
Manage time synchronization	EDIT
	or SERVMAN
Audit users and other NDS objects	AUDITCON
Back up or restore NDS data	SBACKUP

T A B L E   V.3

Managing the NetWare
File System

TASK	UTILITY OR NLM
Create a directory	FILER
Copy or move a file or directory	*or* NetWare Administrator
Add a trustee to a file or directory	
Delete a trustee from a file or directory	
Modify a trustee's rights to a file or directory	
View or modify an Inherited Rights Filter (IRF)	

TABLE V.3

Managing the NetWare
File System (continued)

TASK	UTILITY OR NLM
View a trustee's effective rights to a file or directory	
Salvage a file or directory	
Purge a file or directory	
View the name space that owns a file	
View a volume's owner	
View volume statistics (size, amount of space used, etc.)	
View volume features (type, name spaces supported, etc.)	
View information about a file or directory	FILER
View file size information	*or* NDIR
View creation, access, archive, and modification dates	*or* NetWare Administrator
View or change file and directory attributes	FILER
See if files have been compressed or migrated	*or* FLAG
View or change the owner of a file or directory	*or* NetWare Administrator
View or modify the search mode of an executable file	FLAG
Audit directory and file modifications	AUDITCON
Back up or restore the file system and data	SBACKUP

TABLE V.4

Managing Netware Servers

TASK	UTILITY OR NLM
Start up an existing server	SERVER
Bring down a server	DOWN
Load NetWare Loadable Modules (NLMs)	LOAD *or* DOMAIN
Create or edit a server batch (.NCF) file	INSTALL *or* EDIT

TASK	UTILITY OR NLM
Load LAN drivers	INSTALL
Enable data migration to save hard-disk space	
Check available disk space	
Create, delete, or rename volumes	
Modify the size of a volume	
Add a segment to an existing volume	
Enable file compression and memory suballocation for a volume	
Add or replace a hard disk	
Test a hard disk for bad blocks	
Mirror/unmirror a hard disk	
Duplex a hard disk	
Set up remote console access capability on a server	REMOTE *or* RSPX *or* AIO *or* RS232
Mount a volume	MOUNT
Dismount a volume	DISMOUNT
Use a CD-ROM disk as a volume	CDROM
Set up a volume to store non-DOS files	ADD NAME SPACE
Repair a volume	VREPAIR
Check available hard-disk space	NDIR
Create or view server search paths	SEARCH

TASK	UTILITY OR NLM
Set or view server time	SET TIME
Monitor server memory and processor utilization	MONITOR
View LAN driver statistics	
Check for disk errors	
View a server's error log	NETADMIN
View accounting totals on a server	ATOTAL
Manage workstation connections to the server	SERVMAN
Control file resource use	
Control file compression for a server	
Manage memory allocation	
Enable or disable transaction tracking (TTS)	
Set up an uninterruptible power supply	UPS
Back up or restore server data	SBACKUP

TASK	UTILITY OR NLM
Install workstation networking software	INSTALL (.EXE)
Copy NetWare programs to a workstation	XCOPY
Create user menus	NMENU
Set up remote console access capability on a workstation	RCONSOLE
Send messages to workstations from a server	BROADCAST or SEND

TABLE V.5

Managing Workstations
(continued)

TASK	UTILITY OR NLM
Send messages to workstations from a server or another workstation	SEND
	or NETUSER
Attach a workstation to a server	NETUSER
Capture printer or print queue ports	
Manage print jobs	
Clear workstation connections to the server	MONITOR
Back up or restore workstation files	SBACKUP
Update workstation files (such as applications) automatically	WSUPDATE
Upgrade workstations from IPX LAN drivers to ODI drivers	WSUPGRD

TABLE V.6

Setting Up and Managing
Printing

TASK	UTILITY OR NLM
Create print queue, print server, or printer objects	NetWare Administrator
Assign a printer to a print queue	*or* PCONSOLE
Assign a print server to a printer	
Modify printer configurations	
Modify print queue or print server assignments	
Set up printing with automatic defaults (Quick Setup)	PCONSOLE
Send a print job from an application not set up for network printing	CAPTURE
	or NPRINT

TABLE V.6

Setting Up and Managing

Printing (continued)

TASK	UTILITY OR NLM
Create, view, or modify printer forms	PRINTCON
Create, view, or modify a print job definition	
Set up default printer forms to use with CAPTURE or NPRINT	
Create, view, or modify printer forms	PRINTDEF
Create a print job definition	
View or modify printer forms	
Import an existing printer definition to another printer	
Control a printer or print server from the command line	PSC
View network printer information	

PART VI

Dictionary of Key Concepts

A

abend

(Abnormal end) A message issued by the operating system when it detects a serious problem, such as a hardware or software failure. The abend stops the NetWare server.

Access Control List (ACL)

A property of NetWare Directory Services objects that controls how other objects can access the object. An ACL contains trustee assignments that include object and property rights. The ACL also contains the Inherited Rights Filter. When you view an object's trustees or Inherited Rights Filter, you are seeing the values of that object's ACL.

Access Control right

A file-system right that grants the right to change the trustee assignments and Inherited Rights Filter of a directory or file.

accounting

The process of tracking resources used on a network. The network supervisor can charge for network services and resources by assigning account balances to users that they draw from as they use the services and resources.

The network supervisor can charge for blocks read, blocks written, connect time, disk storage, and service requests.

ACL

See *Access Control List*.

active hub

A device that amplifies transmission signals in network topologies. See *hub*.

Add or Delete Self right

A property right that grants a trustee the right to add or remove itself as a value of the property.

add-on board

A circuit board that modifies or enhances a personal computer's capabilities. Examples:

- *Memory board*—increases the amount of RAM within a personal computer.

- *Network board*—installed in each network station to allow stations to communicate with each other and with the NetWare server.

address

A number that identifies a location in memory or disk storage, or that identifies the location of a device on the network.

Address Resolution Protocol (ARP)

A process in Internet Protocol (IP) and AppleTalk networks that allows a host to find the physical address of a target host on the same physical network when it knows only the target's logical address. Under ARP, a network board contains a table that maps IP addresses to the hardware addresses of the objects on the network.

addressing, disk channel

The method of assigning numbers to identify hardware resources on disk channels. Each controller must have a unique address on the disk channel. You can find the physical address settings in the documentation shipped with the controller.

Depending on where you place the controller in your system, you may need to change the default setting (usually controller 0). Within one channel, the addresses can range from 0 to 7.

addressing space

The total amount of RAM available to the operating system in a NetWare 4.0 server. This amount can be divided for domains. Under NetWare, the maximum addressing space is 4GB, although practical hardware limits are much lower.

ADMIN object

A User object, created automatically during NetWare 4.0 installation, that has rights to create and manage objects. ADMIN doesn't have any special significance like SUPERVISOR did in earlier versions of NetWare. It is only the first User object created and therefore must have the ability to create other objects.

When you first create the Directory tree, ADMIN is given a trustee assignment to the Root object. This trustee assignment includes the Supervisor object right, which means that ADMIN has rights to create and manage all objects in the tree.

As you create other User objects in the Directory tree, you can give them the Supervisor object right to create and manage other container objects and all their leaf objects. Control of the network is as dispersed or centralized as you make it.

AFP

See *AppleTalk Filing Protocol*.

AFP Server object

A leaf object that represents an AppleTalk Filing Protocol-based server that is operating as a node on your NetWare network. (The AFP server is probably also acting as a NetWare router to, and the AppleTalk server for, several Apple Macintosh computers.)

alias object

A leaf object that points to the original location of an object in the Directory. Aliases can make NDS easier to use. Any Directory object located in one place in the Directory can also appear to be in another place in the Directory by using aliases.

For example, an administrator could create aliases pointing to all modems on the network. The aliases could all be created in one container. A user would then need to search only one area of the Directory tree to find out about all modems on the network.

AppleShare software

Networking software from Apple Computer, Inc., that enables a Macintosh computer to function as a file server in an AppleTalk network.

Also, AppleShare workstation software that allows a Macintosh computer to access an AppleShare server.

AppleTalk Filing Protocol (AFP)

A network file-system model from Apple Computer, Inc., that allows workstations to share files and programs on an AppleShare file server.

AppleTalk protocols

The underlying forms and rules that determine communication between nodes on an AppleTalk network. These protocols govern the AppleTalk network, from the network board to the application software.

The Link Access Protocol (LAP) works at the Data Link Layer (the bottom layer of the network), receiving packets of information and converting them into the proper signals for your network board. Examples of LAPs include LLAP (LocalTalk LAP), ELAP (Ethernet LAP), and DTLAP (Token Ring LAP).

Datagram Delivery Protocol (DDP)   The Datagram Delivery Protocol (DDP) works at the Network Layer and prepares packets of data to send on network cables. These packets, called Datagrams, include network address information and data formatting. They are delivered to one of the Link Access Protocols (LLAP, ELAP, or TLAP), according to the hardware in the computer.

Name Binding Protocol (NBP)   Each network process or device has a name that corresponds to network and node addresses. AppleTalk uses a Name Binding Protocol (NBP) to conceal those addresses from users.

Routing Table Maintenance Protocol (RTMP)   When many small networks are connected, a router connects them together in an internetwork. Information about other networks is stored in routing tables. Routers update routing tables by using the Routing Table Maintenance Protocol (RTMP) to communicate with each other.

Zone Information Protocol (ZIP)   In a large internetwork, all AppleTalk nodes are divided into groups, called zones, for ease of locating an object. The NBP uses a Zone Information Protocol (ZIP) to assist in finding the correct network and node addresses from a Zone List.

Printer Access Protocol (PAP)   When a network node prints to a network printer, the Printer Access Protocol (PAP) prepares a path to the requested printer using NBP.

application

A software program that makes calls to the operating system and manipulates data files, allowing a user to perform a specific job (such as accounting or word processing).

▸ *Stand-alone application.* An application that runs from the hard disk or floppy disk in a self-contained, independent computer. Only one user can access the application.

▸ *Network application.* An application that runs on networked computers and can be shared by users. Network applications use network resources such as printers. Advanced network applications (such as electronic mail) allow communication among network users.

archive

A transfer of files to long-term storage media, such as optical disks or magnetic tape.

Archive Needed attribute

A file attribute, set by NetWare, indicating that the file has been changed since the last time it was backed up.

ARP

See *Address Resolution Protocol.*

attach

To establish a connection between workstation and NetWare server. The server assigns each station a connection number and attaches each station to its LOGIN directory. When a user runs the NetWare DOS Requester or NetWare Requester for OS/2, the NetWare shell attaches the station to the server that responds first.

attributes

The characteristics of a directory or file that tell NetWare what to do with the directory or file; also called flags. NetWare reads the attributes you set (for example, to compress, back up, or restrict deletion of a file) and sets other attributes to tell you what has been done (for example, a file has been compressed, migrated, or indexed).

You can't override attributes. They can be changed, however, by a user who has been granted at least the Modify right.

DOS and OS/2 attributes work like attributes of the same name in DOS and OS/2, but apply to files and directories stored on NetWare volumes. NetWare attributes are unique to NetWare. They apply to files and directories stored on NetWare volumes.

auditing

The process of examining network transactions to ensure that network records are accurate and secure. NetWare auditing allows individuals, acting independently of network supervisors and other users, to audit network transactions.

Auditors can track events and activities on the network, but they don't have rights to open or modify network files (other than the Audit Data and Audit History files), unless they are granted rights by the network supervisor.

authentication

A means of verifying that an object sending messages or requests to NetWare Directory Services is authorized to do so. Authentication guarantees that only the purported sender could have sent a message or request, and that it originated from the workstation where the authentication data was created. Authentication works with login restrictions and access control rights to provide a secure network.

NetWare 4.0 authentication uses a Public Key Encryption system that is virtually unbreakable. It consists of a private key and a public key. The keys are strings of numbers used in complex mathematical functions.

The workstation uses a private key to encode messages sent to the NetWare server. The server then uses a public key to decode the messages. The server knows that the workstation sent it, because the workstation's private key is required to encode the message. Neither the two keys nor the user's password are ever sent across the network

AUTOEXEC.BAT

A batch file that executes automatically when DOS or OS/2 is booted on a computer.

A workstation's AUTOEXEC.BAT file, located on the bootable floppy or hard disk, can contain commands that load NetWare client files, load other files required by the hardware, set the DOS or OS/2 prompt, change the default drive to the first network drive, and log the user in.

A NetWare server's AUTOEXEC.BAT file, located on the hard disk's DOS or OS/2 partition, can contain the command that loads the NetWare operating system (SERVER.EXE).

AUTOEXEC.NCF

A NetWare server executable batch file, located on the NetWare partition of the server's hard disk, used to load modules and set the NetWare operating system configuration.

The AUTOEXEC.NCF file stores the server name and IPX internal network number, loads the LAN drivers and settings for the network boards, and binds the protocols to the installed drivers.

AUTOEXEC.NCF can also load NLMs, as well as make time-zone settings and bindery context settings. The network supervisor can also add executable server commands (such as LOAD INSTALL or LOAD MONITOR) to AUTOEXEC.NCF

automatic rollback

A feature of TTS (Transaction Tracking System) that returns a database to its original state. When a network running under TTS fails during a transaction, the database is "rolled back" to its most recent complete state, preventing corruption from an incomplete transaction.

B

backup

A duplicate of data (file, directory, volume), copied to a storage device (floppy diskette, cartridge tape, hard disk). A backup can be retrieved and restored if the original is corrupted or destroyed.

The type of backup you perform and the storage media rotation method you use are dictated by

- ▶ The number of backup sessions you are willing to restore in the event of data loss.

- ▶ The number of duplicate copies of data you want and are willing to store.

- ▶ The desired age of the oldest data copy.

Perform backups when the fewest files are likely to be open. (Files in use at the time of the backup aren't backed up.)

backup hosts and targets

A *backup host* is a NetWare server that has a storage device and a storage device controller attached.

A *target* is a server that contains data you back up or restore data to. Any server, workstation, or service (such as NetWare Directory Services) on the network can be a target, as long as it contains Target Service Agent (TSA) files.

baud rate

Under serial communication, the signal modulation rate, or the speed at which a signal changes.

bindery

A network database, in NetWare versions earlier than NetWare 4.0, that contains definitions for entities such as users, groups, and workgroups.

In NetWare 4.0, the bindery has been replaced by the NetWare Directory database, under NetWare Directory Services. The Bindery Emulator provides NetWare 4.0 networks with backward compatibility to NetWare versions that used the bindery.

bindery emulation

A feature of NetWare 4.0 that allows bindery-based utilities and clients to co-exist with NetWare Directory Services (NDS) on the network.

Objects in a bindery exist in a flat database instead of a hierarchical database like a Directory tree. Bindery emulation occurs when NDS emulates a flat structure for the objects within an Organization object or within an Organizational Unit object.

All objects within that container object can then be accessed both by NDS objects and by bindery-based clients and servers. Bindery emulation applies only to the leaf objects in that Organizational Unit.

Bindery object

A leaf object that represents an object placed in the Directory tree by an upgrade or migration utility, but that NetWare Directory Services can't identify. This object is for backward compatibility with bindery-oriented utilities.

Bindery Queue object

A leaf object that represents a queue placed in the Directory tree by an upgrade or migration utility, but that NetWare Directory Services can't identify. This object is for backward compatibility with bindery-oriented utilities.

binding and unbinding

The process of assigning a communication protocol to network boards and LAN drivers, or the process of removing it.

Each board must have at least one communication protocol bound to the LAN driver for that board. Without a communication protocol, the LAN driver can't process packets.

You can bind more than one protocol to the same LAN driver and board. You can also bind the same protocol stack to multiple LAN drivers on the server. You can also cable workstations with different protocols to the same cabling scheme.

BIOS

(Basic Input/Output System) A set of programs, usually in firmware, that enables each computer's central processing unit to communicate with printers, disks, keyboards, consoles, and other attached input and output devices.

block

The smallest amount of disk space that can be allocated at one time on a NetWare volume. In NetWare 4.0, to minimize RAM requirements, the block size depends on the size of the volume.

block suballocation

Allows the last part of several files to share one disk block, saving disk space. Block suballocation divides any partially used disk block into 512-byte suballocation blocks. These suballocation blocks are used to share the remainder on the block with "leftover" fragments of other files.

boot files

Files, like AUTOEXEC.BAT and CONFIG.SYS, that start the operating system and its drivers, set environment variables, and load NetWare.

BOOTCONF.SYS

A file used by a workstation using Remote Reset to determine which remote boot image file to use. See *Remote Reset*.

bridge

A device that retransmits packets from one segment of the network to another segment. A router, on the other hand, is a device that receives instructions for forwarding packets between topologies and determines the most efficient path.

Browse right

An object right that grants the right to see an object in the Directory tree.

Browsing

A way of finding objects in the Directory.

Objects in the Directory are in hierarchical order. Since the Directory can be very large, it can be difficult to remember an object's location. Rather than trying to remember an object's location, you can browse up or down the Directory tree and view different parts of the Directory to find the object you want.

Btrieve

A complete key-indexed record management system designed for high-performance data handling. Btrieve stores information in Btrieve data files. Numerous existing database programs recognize the Btrieve data file format, and you can use NetWare Btrieve with any of these database programs.

The Btrieve Record Manager can run on a NetWare server, called server-based Btrieve, or on a workstation, called client-based Btrieve.

buffer

An area in server or workstation memory set aside to temporarily hold data, such as packets received from the network.

C

cabling system

Part of a network's physical layout. See *topology*.

cache buffer

A block of NetWare server memory (RAM) in which files are temporarily stored. Cache buffers greatly increase NetWare server performance.

Cache buffers allow workstations to access data more quickly because reading from and writing to memory is much faster than reading from or writing to disk.

cache buffer pool

The amount of memory available for use by the operating system after the SERVER.EXE file has been loaded into memory.

The operating system uses cache buffers in a variety of ways:

- To cache a volume's File Allocation Table (FAT) and suballocation tables in memory.

- To cache parts of a volume's directory entry table.

- To cache parts of files for users to access.

- To build a hash table for directory names.

- To build Turbo FAT indexes for open files that are randomly accessed and have 64 or more regular FAT entries.

▶ To use with NLMs such as LAN drivers, disk drivers, INSTALL (used to create and modify NetWare partitions and volumes), VREPAIR (used to repair NetWare server tables), database servers, communications servers, and print servers.

cache memory

Available random access memory (RAM) that NetWare uses to improve NetWare server access time.

Cache memory allocates space for the hash table, the File Allocation Table (FAT), the Turbo File Allocation Table, suballocation tables, the directory cache, a temporary data storage area for files and NLMs, and an open space for other functions.

directory caching   A method of decreasing the time it takes to determine a file's location on a disk. The FAT and directory entry table are written into the server's memory. The area holding directory entries is called the directory cache. The server can find a file's address from the directory cache much faster than retrieving the information from disk.

file caching   A server can service requests from workstations up to 100 times faster when it reads from and writes to the server's cache memory, rather than executing direct reads from and writes to the server's hard disks.

Can't Compress attribute

A status flag indicating that, because of insignificant space savings, a file can't be compressed.

channel

The logical location of hard-disk controller hardware for the flow of data. For instance, a hard-disk controller in a PC is installed in a channel, or an HBA (Host Bus Adapter) and its disk subsystems make up a disk channel.

Available channels normally include 0 through 4. Channel 0 is normally used by internal controllers and hard disks.

character length

In serial communication, the number of bits used to form a character.

client

A workstation that uses NetWare software to gain access to the network. Under NetWare, client types include DOS, Macintosh, OS/2, UNIX, and Windows.

With the respective client software, users can perform networking tasks. These tasks include mapping drives, capturing printer ports, sending messages, and changing contexts.

CMOS RAM

(Complementary Metal-Oxide Semiconductor RAM) Random-access memory used for storing system configuration data (such as number of drives, types of drives, and amount of memory). CMOS RAM is battery powered to retain the date, time, and other information that requires power when the computer is turned off.

COM ports

Asynchronous serial ports on IBM PC compatible computers.

command format

Instructions that show how to type a command at the keyboard; also called syntax. In NetWare manuals, a command format may include constants, variables, and symbols.

communication

The process of transferring data from one device to another in a computer system.

communication protocols

Conventions or rules used by a program or operating system to communicate between two or more endpoints. Although many communication protocols are used, they all allow information to be packaged, sent from a source, and delivered to a destination system.

Workstation protocols   NetWare workstations may use protocols such as IPX (Internetwork Packet eXchange), SPX (Sequenced Packet eXchange), TCP/IP, NetBIOS, OSI, and AppleTalk (for Macintosh).

Server protocols   NetWare 4.0 has six layers of communication between an application and the hardware in the computer. These layers are based on the OSI model.

The six communication layers are

- ▶ Application Layer

- ▶ Service Protocol Layer

- ▶ Communication Protocol Layer

- ▶ Link Support Layer

- ▶ Driver Layer

- ▶ Hardware Layer

In the server, communication protocols allow the Service Protocol Layer to communicate with the Link Support Layer (LSL). IPX, part of the operating system, is the default communication protocol.

You can use more than one protocol on the same cabling scheme because the LSL, part of the Open Data-Link Interface (ODI), allows the LAN driver for a network board to service more than one protocol.

Compare right

A property right that grants the right to compare any other value to a value of that property.

Compressed attribute

A status flag indicating that a file is compressed.

Computer object

A leaf object that represents a computer on the network. In the Computer object's properties, you can store information such as the computer's serial number or the person the computer is assigned to.

configuration (hardware)

The equipment used on a network (such as servers, workstations, printers, cables, network boards, and routers) and the way the equipment is connected— the network's physical layout. Hardware configuration includes:

▸ The specific hardware installed in or attached to the computer, such as disk subsystems, network boards, memory boards, and printer boards.

▸ The set of parameters selected for a board. For many boards, these settings are made with jumper and switch settings; for other boards, settings are made using configuration software.

connection number

A number assigned to any workstation that attaches to a NetWare server; it may be a different number each time a station attaches. Connection numbers are also assigned to processes, print servers, and applications that use server connections.

The server's operating system uses connection numbers to control each station's communication with other stations.

connectivity

The ability to link different pieces of hardware and software (Macintoshes, PCs, minicomputers, and mainframes) into a network to share resources (applications, printers, etc.).

container object

An object that holds, or contains, other objects. Container objects are used as a way to logically organize all other objects in the Directory tree.

context

The position of an object within its container in the Directory tree. NetWare Directory Services allows you to refer to objects according to their positions within a tree.

When you add an object (such as a server or user) to the network, you place that object in a container object in the Directory tree.

When you move from one container object to another, you change contexts. Whenever you change contexts, indicate the complete name of the object you are changing the context to.

controller address

The number the operating system uses to locate the controller on a disk channel. The number is physically set (usually with jumpers) on a disk controller board.

controller board

A device that enables a computer to communicate with another device, such as a hard disk or tape drive. The controller board manages input/output and regulates the operation of its associated device.

Controller circuitry is incorporated in most new hard disks and tape drives; a separate controller board isn't used.

Copy Inhibit attribute

A file attribute (valid only on Macintosh workstations) that prevents users from copying the file.

Country object

A container object that designates the countries where your network resides and organizes other Directory objects with the country.

For example, you could use a Country object for the country where your organization headquarters resides or, if you have a multinational network, for each country that is a part of your network.

The Country object isn't part of the default NetWare 4.0 server installation. Using a Country object in NetWare Directory Services isn't a requirement for interoperability with other X.500-compliant directory services.

Create right

A file-system right that grants the right to create new files or subdirectories, or to salvage a file after it has been deleted.

Also, an object right that grants the right to create a new object in the Directory tree.

cylinder

A distinct, concentric storage area on a hard disk that roughly corresponds to a track on a floppy diskette. Generally, the more cylinders a hard disk has, the greater its storage capacity.

D

data fork

The part of a Macintosh file that contains information (data) specified by the user. See *Macintosh files*.

data migration

The transfer of inactive data from a NetWare volume to tape, optical disk, or other near-line or offline storage media.

Data migration lets you move data to a storage device, such as disk, tape, optical storage, etc., while NetWare still sees the data as residing on the volume. This frees valuable hard-disk space for often used files while still allowing slower access to infrequently used files.

data protection

A means of ensuring that data on the network is safe. NetWare protects data primarily by maintaining duplicate file directories and by redirecting data from bad blocks to reliable blocks on the NetWare server's hard disk.

Protecting data location information   A hard disk's Directory Entry Table (DET) and File Allocation Table (FAT) contain address information that tells the operating system where data can be stored or retrieved from. If the blocks containing these tables are damaged, some or all of the data may be irretrievable.

NetWare greatly reduces the possibility of losing this information by maintaining duplicate copies of the DET and FAT on separate areas of the hard disk. If one of the blocks in the original tables is damaged, the operating system switches to the duplicate tables to get the location data it needs. The faulty sector is then listed in the disk's bad block table, and the data it contained is stored elsewhere on the disk.

Protecting data against surface defects   NetWare hard disks store data in 4, 8, 16, 32, or 64K blocks. These blocks are specific data-storage locations on the disk's magnetic surface.

Due to the constant reading and writing of data to disk, some storage blocks lose their capacity to store data. NetWare prevents data from being written to unreliable blocks by employing two complementary features known as read-after-write verification and Hot Fix, as well as by storing duplicate copies of data on separate disks.

▶ *Read-after-write verification.* When data is written to disk, the data is immediately read back from the disk and compared to the original data still in memory. If the data on the disk matches the data in memory, the write operation is considered successful, the data in memory is released, and the next disk I/O operation takes place.

    If the data on the disk doesn't match the data in memory, the operating system determines (after making appropriate retries) that the disk storage block is defective. The Hot Fix feature redirects the original block of data (still in memory) to the Hot Fix redirection area, where the data can be stored correctly.

▶ *Hot Fix.* A small portion of the disk's storage space is set aside as the Hot Fix redirection area. This area holds data blocks that are redirected there from faulty blocks on the disk.

    Once the operating system records the address of the defective block in a section of the Hot Fix area reserved for that purpose, the server won't attempt to store data in the defective block.

▶ *Disk mirroring or duplexing.* You can also protect your data with disk mirroring or duplexing. Mirroring stores the same data on separate disks on the same controller channel; duplexing stores the same data on separate disks on separate controller channels.

data set

A group of data that can be manipulated by SBACKUP. Data sets can contain different items depending on which TSA they are related to.

DCB

See *disk coprocessor board.*

DDP

See *Datagram Delivery Protocol* under the entry *AppleTalk protocols.*

default drive

The drive a workstation is using. The drive prompt, such as A> or F>, identifies the current drive.

default server

The server you attach to when you log in. (The default server is specified in your NET.CFG file.)

Also, the server your current drive is mapped to.

Delete Inhibit attribute

A file-system attribute that prevents any user from erasing the directory or file.

Delete right

An object right that grants the right to delete an object from the Directory tree.

delimiter

A symbol or character that signals the beginning or end of a command or of a parameter within a command.

In the command NCOPY F:*.* G:, for example, the blank space between F:*.* and G: is a delimiter that marks two distinct parameters.

Other delimiters used in NetWare include the comma (,), the period (.), the slash (/), the backslash (\), the hyphen (-), and the colon (:).

destination server

The NetWare 4.0 server to which you migrate data files, bindery files, and other information from a previous NetWare version or another network operating system during upgrade.

device driver

An NLM that forms the interface between the NetWare operating system and devices such as hard disks or network boards. See *disk driver*; *LAN driver*.

device numbering

A method of identifying a device, such as a hard disk, to allow the device to work on the network. Devices are identified by three numbers:

> ► *Physical address.* Set with jumpers on the boards, controllers, and hard disks. The physical address is determined by the driver, based upon those jumper settings.

> ► *Device code.* Determined by the physical address of the board, controller, and hard disk. In the device code #00101, the first two digits (00) are reserved for the disk type. The third digit (1) is the board number; the fourth (0), the controller number; and the fifth (1), the disk number.

> ► *Logical number.* Determined by the order in which the disk drivers are loaded and by the physical address of the controller and hard disk.

After device numbers are assigned, NetWare also assigns physical and logical partition numbers to the partitions created on the hard disks. Hot Fix messages use the physical partition number when recording which hard disks have blocks of data that need to be redirected.

All physical partitions are assigned logical partition numbers. These numbers are assigned to both the mirrored disks and the DOS and nonNetWare partitions. Mirroring messages use the logical partition number to record which hard disks are being remirrored or unmirrored.

device sharing

The shared use of centrally located devices (such as printers, modems, and disk storage space) by users or software programs. By attaching a device to a network that several workstations are logged in to, you can use resources more efficiently.

An example of device sharing by software programs is that OS/2 and NetWare for OS/2 can reside on the same hard disk, although separate disk partitions are required.

Directory, directory

Directory   A common name for the NetWare Directory database, which organizes NetWare Directory Services objects in a hierarchical tree structure called the Directory tree. See *NetWare Directory Services*.

directory   A component in the NetWare file system, used to contain files and subdirectories. See *file system*.

directory and file rights

Rights that control what a trustee can do with a directory or file.

directory entry

Basic information for NetWare server directories and files, such as the file or directory name, the owner, the date and time of the last update (for files), and the location of the first block of data on the network hard disk.

Directory entries are located in a directory table on a network hard disk and contain information about all files on the volume. The server uses directory entries to track file location, changes made to the file, and other related file properties.

Directory management request

A request that controls the physical distribution of the NetWare Directory Services database. Through these requests, system administrators can install new Directory partitions and manage their replicas.

Directory Map object

A leaf object that refers to a directory on a volume.

You can't look at the file structure on the volume from the Directory Map object, but login scripts can use the MAP command with a Directory Map object to record the location of frequently used applications. If the application moves, you need to change only the directory map; all login scripts remain unchanged.

directory path

The full specification that includes server name, volume name, and name of each directory leading to the file-system directory you need to access.

directory rights

Rights that control what a trustee can do with a directory.

Directory services

A global, distributed, replicated database built into NetWare 4.0 that maintains information about every resource on the network. See *NetWare Directory Services*.

Directory services request

A request made to the Directory database by users or network supervisors. NetWare Directory Services requests can be divided into three types:

- ► *Directory-access requests.* These requests are submitted by users who are accessing or administrators who are managing the Directory database's contents. These requests support the Directory database's interface and allow objects to be created, modified, and retrieved.

- ► *Directory-access control requests.* These requests set access rights to Directory objects. In this respect, directory-access rights resemble file-access rights.

▶ *Directory-management requests.* These requests are submitted by administrators who manage the Directory database's physical distribution, such as through partitioning.

directory structure

The filing system of volumes, directories, and files that the NetWare server uses to organize data on its hard disks. See *file system.*

Also, a hierarchical structure that represents how partitions are related to each other in the Directory database. See *Directory tree.*

directory table

A table that contains basic information about files, directories, directory trustees, or other entities on the volume. The directory table occupies one or more directory blocks on the volume. Each block has 4K (4,096 bytes) of data. A directory entry is 32 bytes long, so each block can hold 128 directory entries.

Volume SYS: starts out with seven blocks for its directory table. When a volume needs to add another block to its directory table, the server allocates another block.

The maximum directory blocks per volume is 65,536. Since each block can accommodate 32 entries, the maximum directory table entries per volume is 2,097,152.

In NetWare 4.0, a volume can span multiple drives, so each drive can have more than one directory table.

Directory tree

A hierarchical structure of objects in the Directory database. The Directory tree includes container objects that are used to organize the network. The structure of the Directory tree can be based on a logical organization of objects, and not necessarily on their physical location.

disk

A magnetically encoded storage medium in the form of a plate (also called a platter). The following types of disks are used with personal computers:

- *Hard disks* use a metallic base and are usually installed within a computer or disk subsystem. (In some cases, they are removable.)

- *Floppy disks* (also called *diskettes*) use a polyester base and are removable.

- *CD-ROM* (Compact Disc Read Only Memory) is a small plastic optical disk that isn't erasable or writable.

- *Optical disks* are either erasable and writable or write-once, read-many (WORM).

disk controller

A hardware device that controls how data is written to and retrieved from the disk drive. The disk controller sends signals to the disk drive's logic board to regulate the movement of the head as it reads data from or writes data to the disk.

disk coprocessor board (DCB)

The Novell equivalent of a SCSI Host Bus Adapter. See *Host Bus Adapter (HBA)*.

disk driver

An NLM that forms the interface between the NetWare operating system and the hard disks. The disk driver talks to an adapter that is connected by an internal cable to the disk drives.

Basic disk drivers include

- *ISADISK.DSK* for Industry Standard Architecture hard disks.

- *IDE.DSK* for Imbedded Drive Electronics hard disks.

- *PS2ESDI.DSK* for hard disks connected to ESDI controllers in IBM Micro Channel Architecture PS/2 computers.

▶ *PS2SCSI.DSK* for hard disks connected to SCSI controllers in IBM Micro Channel Architecture PS/2 computers.

Other disk drivers are available from third-party vendors.

disk duplexing

A means of duplicating data to provide data protection. Disk duplexing consists of copying data onto two hard disks, each on a separate disk channel. This protects data against the failure of a hard disk or failure of the hard-disk channel between the disk and the NetWare server. (The hard-disk channel includes the disk controller and interface cable.)

If any component on one channel fails, the other disk can continue to operate without data loss or interruption, because it is on a different channel.

disk format

The way in which a hard disk is prepared or structured so that it can receive data from the computer's operating system. Disk formatting is a function of the operating system.

Hard-disk formats include FAT for DOS and NetWare, HPFS for OS/2, HFS for Macintosh, and FFS for UNIX.

disk interface board

An add-on board that acts as an interface between the host microprocessor and the disk controller.

disk mirroring

The duplication of data from the NetWare partition on one hard disk to the NetWare partition on another hard disk.

When you mirror disks, two or more hard disks on the same channel are paired. Blocks of data written to the original (primary) disk are also written to the duplicate (secondary) disk.

The disks operate in tandem, constantly storing and updating the same files. Should one of the disks fail, the other disk can continue to operate without data loss or interruption.

disk partition

A logical unit that NetWare server hard disks can be divided into. In NetWare 4.0, a NetWare partition is created on each hard disk. Volumes are created from the pool of NetWare partitions. A volume consists of one or more volume segments.

One of the server's internal hard disks can contain both an active, primary DOS partition and a NetWare partition. When the server boot files are copied to the DOS partition and included in the AUTOEXEC.BAT file, the NetWare operating system boots automatically.

You need only one DOS partition; the other hard disks need to contain only a NetWare partition. A NetWare partition consists of a Hot Fix redirection area plus a large data area. The logical sector 0 of a NetWare partition is the first sector of the data area.

disk subsystem

An external unit that attaches to the NetWare server and contains hard disk drives, a tape drive, optical drives, or any combination of these. The disk subsystem gives the server more storage capacity.

Don't Compress attribute

A file-system attribute that prevents files from being compressed.

Don't Migrate attribute

A file-system attribute that prevents files from being migrated to a secondary storage device (such as a tape drive or an optical disk).

DOS boot record

A record containing information that ROM-BIOS uses to determine which device to boot from. The boot record can be on either a floppy diskette, a local hard disk, or a remote boot chip.

ROM-BIOS then runs a short program from the boot record to determine disk format and location of system files and directories. Using this information, ROM-BIOS loads the system files (including two hidden files) and the command processor (COMMAND.COM).

DOS client

A workstation that boots with DOS and gains access to the network through either

 ▸ The NetWare DOS Requester and its VLMs (for NetWare 4.0).

 ▸ A NetWare shell (for NetWare versions earlier than NetWare 4.0).

With DOS client software, users can perform networking tasks. These tasks include mapping drives, capturing printer ports, sending messages, and changing contexts.

DOS device

A storage unit compatible with the DOS disk format—usually a disk drive or tape backup unit.

The UPGRADE and SBACKUP utilities both write to a DOS device. The DOS device should be a read/write device. Because the utilities read and write data, the media the DOS device uses must allow the data to be updated or changed.

DOS setup routine

The routine that sets up the system configuration of your DOS client or NetWare server. The setup routine records the system's built-in features (add-on boards, hard drives, disk drives, ports, math coprocessor) and available system memory. It also lets you set date and time, password, and keyboard speed.

The system configuration is accessed from the reference diskette (for IBM PS/2 systems) or from the setup or user diagnostics diskette (for most other systems).

DOS version

The version number and name of the kind of DOS you are using (DR DOS 6.0, MS DOS 3.3, etc.). Different machine types use different versions of DOS that are generally not compatible.

Since all DOS versions have identically-named utilities and command interpreters, you can't place the files of different DOS versions in the same directory. Create a DOS directory for each workstation type or DOS version you use and load the DOS files into it.

drive

Physical drive   A storage device that data is written to and read from, such as a disk drive or tape drive. A drive that is physically contained in or attached to a workstation is called a local drive.

Logical drive   An identification for a specific directory located on a disk drive. For example, network drives point to a directory on the network, rather than to a local disk.

drive mapping

A pointer to a location in the file system, represented as a letter assigned to a directory path on a volume.

To locate a file, you follow a path that includes the volume, directory, and any subdirectories leading to the file. You create drive mappings to follow these paths for you. You assign a letter to the path, and then use the letter in place of the complete path name.

NetWare recognizes four types of drive mappings: local drive mappings, network drive mappings, network search-drive mappings, and Directory Map objects.

Local drive mappings   Local drive mappings are paths to local media such as hard disk drives and floppy disk drives.

In DOS 3.0 and later, drives A: through E: are reserved for local mappings. To change this default, use the DOS LASTDRIVE command in your workstation CONFIG.SYS file.

Network drive mappings   Network drive mappings point to volumes and directories on the network. Drives F: through Z: can be used for network mappings. Each user can map drive letters to different directories.

Network search-drive mappings   Network search drive mappings are pointers to directories containing applications, DOS files, etc. Search-drive mappings let you execute a program even if it isn't located in the directory you're working in by enabling the system to search for the program.

When you request a file and the system can't find it in your current directory, the system looks in every directory a search drive is mapped to. The system searches, following the numerical order of the search drives, until either the program file is found or can't be located.

(Search-drive mappings aren't supported on OS/2 workstations. The search functionality is provided with the OS/2 PATH, LIBPATH, and DPATH commands.)

Directory Map objects   Directory Map objects can point to directories that contain frequently used files such as applications. If you create a Directory Map object to point to an application, users can access the application by clicking on the Directory Map icon from the Browser. If the application's location in the directory structure changes, you can update the object instead of having to change all users' drive mappings.

driver
An NLM that forms the interface between the NetWare operating system and devices such as hard disks or network boards.

dynamic configuration

A means of allowing the NetWare server to allocate resources according to need and availability. When the server boots, all free memory is assigned to file caching. As demand increases for other resources (directory cache buffers, for example), the number of available file cache buffers decreases.

The operating system doesn't immediately allocate new resources when a request is received. It waits a specified amount of time to see if existing resources become available to service the demand. If resources become available, no new resources are allocated. If they don't become available within the time limit, new resources are allocated.

The time limit ensures that sudden, infrequent peaks of server activity don't permanently allocate unneeded resources.

dynamic memory

The most common form of memory, used for RAM. Dynamic memory requires a continual rewriting of all stored information to preserve data.

If dynamic memory is too slow for a computer's microprocessor, overall performance will suffer while the CPU waits for requested information to arrive from memory.

A continuous electrical current is necessary to maintain dynamic memory. All data is lost from dynamic memory when the power is turned off.

E

effective rights

The rights that an object can actually exercise to see or modify a particular directory, file, or object. An object's effective rights to a directory, file, or object are calculated by NetWare each time that object attempts an action.

Effective rights to a file or directory are determined by

- An object's trustee assignments to the directory or file.

- Inherited rights from an object's trustee assignments to parent directories.

- Trustee assignments of Group objects that a User object belongs to.

- Trustee assignments of objects listed in a User object's security equivalences list.

Embedded SCSI

A hard disk that has a SCSI and a hard disk controller built into the hard disk unit.

Erase right

A file-system right that grants the right to delete directories, subdirectories, or files.

Ethernet configuration

The setup that allows communication using an Ethernet environment. In an Ethernet environment, stations communicate with each other by sending data in frames along an Ethernet cabling system.

Different Ethernet standards use different frame formats. NetWare 4.0 uses the IEEE 802.2 standard by default. In addition to 802.2, you can use one of the following frame types:

- *Ethernet 802.3.* The default frame type used in NetWare 3.11 and earlier. This frame type is also referred to as the raw frame.

- *Ethernet II.* The frame type used on networks that communicate with DEC minicomputers, and on computers that use TCP/IP or AppleTalk Phase I.

▸ *Ethernet SNAP.* The IEEE standard 802.2 frame type with an extension (SNAP) added to the header. Use this frame on networks that communicate with workstations that use protocols such as AppleTalk Phase II.

Using Novell's Open Datalink Interface (ODI) technology, NetWare 4.0 allows stations with different Ethernet frame types to coexist on the same Ethernet cabling system.

Because of ODI's Multiple Layer Interface Driver (MLID) and link support layer (LSL), a single workstation with one network board can communicate with other devices using different Ethernet frame types.

Execute Only attribute

A file-system attribute that prevents a file from being copied.

F

fake root

A subdirectory that functions as a root directory. NetWare allows you to map a drive to a fake root (a directory where rights can be assigned to users).

Some applications can't be run from subdirectories; they read files from and write files to the root directory. However, for security, don't assign users rights at the root or volume directory level. Instead, load the files in a subdirectory and designate it as a fake root directory in the login script.

Fake roots work with the NetWare DOS Requester, as well as with NetWare shells included with NetWare 2.2 and 3.x. Fake roots do not work for OS/2 clients. (Under OS/2, all mapped drives are roots, and search drives don't exist.)

FAT

See *File Allocation Table.*

fault tolerance

A means of protecting data by providing data duplication on multiple storage devices. See *System Fault Tolerance (SFT)*.

Also, distributing the NetWare Directory database among several servers to provide continued authentication and access to object information should a server go down. See *Replicas* under the entry *NetWare Directory Services*.

File Allocation Table (FAT)

An index table that points to the disk areas where a file is located. Because one file may be in any number of blocks spread over the disk, the FAT links the file together.

In NetWare, the FAT is accessed from the Directory Entry Table (DET). The FAT is cached in server memory, allowing the server to quickly access the data.

Each volume contains a FAT. NetWare divides each volume into disk allocation blocks that can be configured to 4, 8, 16, 32, or 64K. (All blocks on one volume are the same size.) NetWare stores files on the volume in these blocks. If a file consists of one or more blocks, the file may be stored in blocks that aren't adjacent.

When a file exceeds 64 blocks (and the corresponding number of FAT entries), NetWare creates a turbo FAT index to group together all FAT entries for that file. A turbo FAT index enables a large file to be accessed quickly.

The first entry in a turbo FAT index table consists of the first FAT number of the file. The second entry consists of the second FAT number, etc.

file compression

A means of allowing more data to be stored on server hard disks by compressing (packing) files that aren't being used. By enabling NetWare volumes for compression, you can effectively increase disk space up to 63 percent. For example, 600MB of files on a volume can be compressed to as little as 222MB.

File compression is managed internally by NetWare. Users can flag their files or directories so they are compressed after being used or flag them so they are never compressed.

After compression is enabled, files flagged "Immediate Compress" are compressed immediately; other files are automatically compressed when they haven't been accessed for a specific amount of time. Files are decompressed when accessed again by a user.

file indexing

The method of indexing FAT entries for faster access to large files. For example, to go to block 128 of a file, file indexing allows you to go right to the block instead of scanning through the 127 previous blocks.

NetWare 4.0 supports automatic file indexing above 64 blocks. The two levels of file indexing in NetWare 4.0 refer to the size of the table it uses to index the FAT. The first level indexes 64 to 1,023 blocks; the second level, 1,024 or more blocks.

file locking

The means of ensuring that a file is updated correctly before another user, application, or process can access the file. For example, without file locking, if two users attempt to update the same word-processing file simultaneously, one user could overwrite the file update of the other user.

file rights

Rights that control what a trustee can do with a file.

File Scan right

A file-system right that grants the right to see the directory and file with the DIR or NDIR directory command.

file server

A name used in previous NetWare versions for the computer that runs NetWare operating system software; now referred to as the NetWare server.

file sharing

A feature of networking that allows more than one user to access the same file at the same time.

file system

(Formerly *directory structure*) The system the NetWare server uses to organize data on its hard disks. Each file is given a file name and stored at a specific location in a hierarchical filing system so that files can be located quickly.

The NetWare server is divided into one or more volumes, which are divided into directories, which contain files or subdirectories.

Volume   The highest level in the NetWare file system, created from logical partitions using INSTALL. A volume can reside on one hard disk, or it can span multiple hard disks. To a user, a volume appears much like a hard disk in a stand-alone system.

You can store directories at the volume level. Storing files at this level is possible but, for security reasons, isn't recommended.

Directory   A place within a volume where you can store files or other directories. Directories within directories are called subdirectories. A directory can contain any number of files and subdirectories.

Files   Individual records that can be created in or copied to any level of the directory structure (except, in practice, the volume level).

Directory path   A file or directory is located by its path, which states where the directory or file is on a volume. Under DOS and OS/2, directory names and file names contain one to eight characters, followed with an optional file-name extension.

Basic NetWare server directories   When volume SYS: is created, it contains seven predefined directories:

▶ *SYS:DELETED.SAV* contains files that are deleted before they are purged.

▶ *SYS:ETC* contains sample files to assist the network supervisor in configuring the server.

▶ *SYS:LOGIN* contains programs necessary for users to log in. A subdirectory, SYS:LOGIN/OS2, contains OS/2 login programs.

▶ *SYS:MAIL* is used by mail programs compatible with NetWare. (NetWare creates a subdirectory in SYS:MAIL for user ADMIN.) If you upgrade from an earlier NetWare version, existing users still have subdirectories here, but their login script becomes a property of the User object. If you create new users after upgrading, the new users won't have directories in SYS:MAIL.

▶ *SYS:SYSTEM* contains NetWare operating system files as well as NLMs and NetWare utilities used for managing the network.

▶ *SYS:PUBLIC* allows general access to the network, and contains NetWare utilities and programs for network users. A subdirectory, SYS:PUBLIC/OS2, contains NetWare utilities and programs for OS/2.

▶ *SYS:DOC* contains electronic versions of the NetWare manuals.

Types of directories   You can create directories for both executable files and data files, depending on what types of directories best fit the needs of your network.

▶ *Operating system directories.* These store workstation operating system files. The number of DOS or other operating system directories you need depends on the number of different operating systems, versions, and workstation types on the network.

▸ *Application directories.* Although applications can be accessed from local drives, installing them on the network provides convenient access.

▸ *Data directories.* These are work directories for groups and users to keep work files in. You can also create a directory to transfer files between directories on the network.

▸ *Home or user-name directories.* To provide personal workspace for users, you can create home or user-name directories. You can create a parent directory in volume SYS: called HOME or USERS. Or, you can create a separate HOME or USERS volume, then you can create a subdirectory for each user. The name of each subdirectory should be the user name.

Although data can be created and stored in a home or user directory, when data is stored in a user's directory, no other user (except network supervisors or managers assigned file rights) can access it. So, to allow users to share data, you can create work directories and make trustee assignments for groups or users who need access to these directories.

file transfer protocol

A set of control procedures to prevent errors in information transmitted between network stations.

The data is sent from one station to another in packets. Each packet includes a discrete number that is derived from the data that makes up the packet, according to a mathematical algorithm. The algorithm is applied to each data packet a second time when it arrives on the receiving end.

If the number on the receiving end doesn't match the number included in the packet, the receiving station sends a signal to the transmitting station requesting that the packet be resent.

file-name extension

The extension used after the period in file names. Under the File Allocation Table (FAT) system used by DOS and OS/2, file-name extensions can be up to three characters. Under the High Performance File System (HPFS) used by OS/2, file-name extensions aren't restricted to three characters.

flag

See *Attributes* under the entry *security*.

frame

A packet data format for a given media.

Some media support multiple packet formats (frames), such as Ethernet 802.2, Ethernet 802.3, Ethernet II, Ethernet SNAP, Token Ring, or Token Ring SNAP. For NetWare 4.0, the default frame type is 802.2.

G

gateway

A link between two networks. A gateway allows communication between dissimilar protocols (for example, NetWare and nonNetWare networks) using industry-standard protocols such as TCP/IP, X.25, or SNA.

Group object

A leaf object listing several User objects, used to provide collective, rather than individual, network administration. A Group object isn't a container object like an Organization Unit object. A Group object has a list of User object names.

Whenever electronic mail is sent to a Group object, or whenever a trustee assignment names a Group object, each user in the list is part of that action.

You can create Group objects based on who uses the same applications, printers, or print queues; who performs similar tasks; or who has similar needs for information.

You can use Group objects to simplify trustee assignments and login scripts. For example, instead of repeating a trustee assignment for each user, you can create a Group object that lists the users and use just one trustee assignment.

H

handle
A pointer used by a computer to identify a resource or feature. For example, a directory handle identifies a volume and a directory, such as SYS:PUBLIC. Other types of handles used to access NetWare 4.0 include file handles, video handles, request handles, device handles, and volume handles.

handshaking
The initial exchange between two data communication systems prior to and during data transmission to ensure proper data transmission. A handshake method (such as XON/XOFF) is part of the complete transmission protocol.

A serial (asynchronous) transmission protocol might include the handshake method (XON/XOFF), baud rate, parity setting, number of data bits, and number of stop bits.

hard disk
A high-capacity magnetic storage device that allows a user to write and read data. Hard disks can be network or local workstation disks. Internal disks use channel 0 and external hard disks use channels 1 through 4.

hashing

A process that facilitates access to a file in a large volume by calculating the file's address both in cache memory and on the hard disk.

When a workstation wants to read a file from the NetWare server, the server performs a hash algorithm which predicts an address on a hash table. In NetWare 4.0, it is common to find the file on the first try 95 percent of the time. This method is much more efficient than searching for a file sequentially.

HBA

See *Host Bus Adapter.*

HCSS

See *high-capacity storage system.*

hexadecimal

A base-16 alphanumeric numbering system used to specify addresses in computer memory. In hexadecimal notation, the decimal numbers 0 through 15 are represented by the decimal digits 0 through 9 and the alphabetic digits A through F (A = decimal 10, B = decimal 11, etc.).

Hidden attribute

A DOS and OS/2 attribute that hides a directory or file from the DOS or OS/2 DIR command and prevents the directory or file from being deleted or copied.

high-capacity storage system (HCSS)

A data storage system that extends the storage capacity of a NetWare server by integrating an optical disk library, or jukebox, into the NetWare file system. HCSS moves files between faster low-capacity storage devices (the server's hard disk) and slower high-capacity storage devices (optical disks in a jukebox).

Users and programs can access files and directories on a jukebox using the same NetWare commands and function calls used to access them from the hard disk.

Migration and de-migration   HCSS uses free space on the server's hard disk to temporarily cache the jukebox's most active files. When space is needed on the hard disk to store additional files and the allocated space reaches a preconfigured capacity, the cache's least active files are moved to optical disks. This process is known as data migration.

Then, when a user requests a file stored on optical disk, HCSS copies the file from the jukebox onto the server's hard disk. This process, known as de-migration, allows users to access their most active files quickly.

The path name of a file remains the same whether the file resides on the hard disk or on an optical disk.

HCSS directory management   An HCSS directory is a file-system directory that logically groups one or more optical disks and their associated files. An HCSS directory resides on the NetWare volume that is associated with the directory's jukebox. The network supervisor can create one or more HCSS directories for each jukebox.

The network supervisor assigns unique labels to each side of the optical disks, and then assigns each optical disk to an HCSS directory. Once assigned, each label appears as a first-level subdirectory within the HCSS directory.

All optical disks in a jukebox can be assigned to one HCSS directory, or they can be grouped into several different HCSS directories.

An HCSS directory's contents can be viewed using any directory listing command (such as the DOS DIR or NetWare NDIR commands). Users can access and manipulate HCSS first-level subdirectories just like any other NetWare directory, except that users can't create or delete an HCSS first-level subdirectory.

home directory

A private network directory that the network supervisor can create for a user. The user's login script should contain a drive mapping to his or her home directory.

hop count

The number of network boards a message packet passes through on the way to its destination on an internetwork. The destination network can be no more than 16 hops (NetWare server or router interface boards) from the source.

host

A NetWare server you run SBACKUP from. A storage device and a storage device controller are attached to it.

Host Bus Adapter (HBA)

The HBA relieves the host microprocessor of data storage and retrieval tasks, usually improving the computer's performance time.

An HBA and its disk subsystems make up a disk channel. The NetWare operating system can handle up to 5 host adapter channels, with 4 controllers per channel and 8 drives per controller (up to a maximum of 32 drives).

The SCSI standard allows each host adapter a maximum of 8 SCSI controllers, with each controller supporting up to 2 disk drives.

External SCSI disk drive subsystems can be daisy-chained off the host adapter port. NetWare servers with ISA (AT bus) or EISA architecture can use HBAs.

Hot Fix

A method NetWare uses to ensure that data is stored safely. Data blocks are redirected from faulty blocks on the server's disk to a small portion of disk space set aside as the Hot Fix redirection area. Once the operating system records the address of the defective block in a section of the Hot Fix area reserved for that purpose, the server won't attempt to store data in defective blocks.

By default, 2 percent of a disk partition's space is set aside as the Hot Fix redirection area.

HSM

See *Hardware Specific Module* under the entry *Open Data-Link Interface.*

hub

A device that modifies transmission signals, allowing the network to be lengthened or expanded with additional workstations. There are two kinds of hubs:

- ▶ *Active hubs.* An active hub amplifies transmission signals in network topologies. Use an active hub to add workstations to a network or to extend the cable distance between stations and the server.

- ▶ *Passive hubs.* A device used in certain network topologies to split a transmission signal, allowing additional workstations to be added. A passive hub can't amplify the signal, so it must be cabled directly to a station or to an active hub.

I

identifier variables

Variables used in login scripts that allow you to enter a variable (such as LOGIN_NAME) in a login script command, rather than a specific name (such as RICHARD).

Immediate Compress attribute

A file-system attribute that causes files to be compressed as soon as the operating system can do so, without waiting for a specific event to occur (such as a time delay).

Indexed attribute

A status flag set when a file exceeds a set size, indicating that the file is indexed for fast access.

Inherited Rights Filter (IRF)

A list of rights that can be created for any file, directory, or object, which controls the rights that a trustee can inherit from parent directories and container objects. The Inherited Rights Filter (IRF) for any file, directory, or object is part of the access control information for that file, directory, or object.

To change the IRF of a file or directory, you must have the Access Control right to that file or directory. To change the IRF of an object, you must have at least the Write property right to the ACL property of that object.

The IRF can't grant rights, it can only revoke rights. The IRF's effect, for every object that doesn't have a trustee assignment to a file, directory, or object, is: "Whatever rights to this file, directory, or object you would have inherited, I am revoking all but these rights."

international use of NetWare 4.0

The adaptation of NetWare 4.0 for use with multiple languages. The NetWare 4.0 operating system, NLMs, and utilities use English as the default language, unless you set them otherwise.

These changes may be required for various network locations, since the formats for expressing dates, times, and numbers change not only across languages but also across locales within a given language area.

internetwork

Two or more networks connected by a router. Users on an internetwork can use the resources (files, printers, hard disks) of all connected networks, provided they have security clearance.

interoperability

The ability to use products from different vendors within the same system. For example, Novell's ODINSUP interface allows LAN Manager, LAN Server, or other NDIS protocols to co-exist with NetWare's ODI on a network.

Another example is Novell's network driver interface—the Open Data-Link Interface (ODI)—on which any protocol, including the native IPX protocol, can be used.

Communication protocols such as Internet Protocol (IP) or Appletalk Filing Protocol (AFP) can be used in ODI to process information from the network without the user having to know each protocol's required method of packet transmission.

Interoperability also means that an application running on different platforms (Macintosh, UNIX, etc.) can share files.

IPX

(Internetwork Packet eXchange) A Novell communication protocol that sends data packets to requested destinations (workstations, servers, etc.).

IPX addresses and routes outgoing data packets across a network. It reads the assigned addresses of returning data and directs the data to the proper area within the workstation's or NetWare server's operating system.

The NetWare DOS Requester prepares data packets in a form understandable to the intended destination before handing them to IPX. The IPXODI.COM file then uses the services of a LAN driver routine to control the station's network board for data delivery.

IPX external network number

A network number that uniquely identifies a network cable segment. An IPX external-network number is a hexadecimal number from one to eight digits in length (1 to FFFFFFFE). The number is arbitrary, and is assigned when the IPX protocol is bound to a network board in the server.

IPX internal network number

A logical network number that identifies an individual NetWare 4.0 server. Each server on a network must have a unique IPX internal-network number. The IPX internal-network number is a hexadecimal number from one to eight digits in length (1 to FFFFFFFE), and is assigned to the server during installation.

IPX internetwork address

A 12-byte number (represented by 24 hexadecimal characters) divided into three parts. The first part is the 4-byte (8-characters) IPX external-network number. The second part is the 6-byte (12-character) node number. The third part is the 2-byte (4-character) socket number.

IPXODI

(Internetwork Packet eXchange Open Data-Link Interface) A module that takes workstation requests that the DOS Requester has determined are for the network, packages them with transmission information (such as their destination), and hands them to the LSL.

IPXODI attaches a header to each data packet. The header specifies information that targets network delivery, announcing where the packet came from, where it's going, and what happens after delivery.

Because IPXODI transmits data packets as datagrams (self-contained packages that move independently from source to destination), it can only deliver the packets on a best-effort basis. Delivery is assured by SPX.

IRF

See *Inherited Rights Filter.*

J

jukebox

A high-capacity storage device, sometimes called an optical disk library, that uses an autochanger mechanism to mount and dismount optical disks as needed.

A jukebox typically contains one to four optical disk drives. A picker rotates, flips, and transports disks to and from the storage slots, drives, and the mail slot. The mail slot is the location in the jukebox used to insert and remove the optical disk cartridge.

jumper block

A group of jumper pins that can be connected (jumpered) or left unconnected to make hardware configuration settings on a circuit board.

L

LAN

See *local area network.*

LAN driver

An NLM that understands and controls the physical structure of a network board. A LAN driver serves as a link between a station's operating system and the physical network parts.

NetWare 4.0 is designed for LAN drivers written to the Open Data-Link Interface (ODI) specification. ODI drivers connect directly to the ODI model's Link Support Layer (LSL), which serves as an intermediary between the drivers and the communication protocols.

Large Internet Packet (LIP)

(Large Internet Packet) Functionality that allows the internetwork packet size limit to be increased from the default 576 bytes. By allowing the NetWare packet size to be increased, LIP enhances the throughput over bridges and routers.

leaf objects

Objects that don't contain any other objects, located at the end of a branch in the Directory tree.

Link Support Layer (LSL)

An implementation of the Open Data-Link Interface (ODI) specification that serves as an intermediary between the NetWare server's LAN drivers and communication protocols, such as IPX, AFP, or TCP/IP. The LSL allows one or more network boards to service one or more similar or dissimilar protocol stacks.

LIP

See *Large Internet Packet.*

loadable module

A program you can load and unload from NetWare server memory while the server is running. Two common types are NLMs (NetWare Loadable Modules) and VLMs (Virtual Loadable Modules).

loading and unloading

The process of linking and unlinking NLMs to the NetWare operating system. NLMs can be loaded and unloaded while NetWare is running.

local area network (LAN)

A network located within a small area or common environment, such as in a building or a building complex.

logical memory

Memory that may not have contiguous addresses, but which appears contiguous to NetWare 4.0 processes.

login

The procedure that provides access to the network by using the LOGIN command.

When a user initiates a login request, the operating system looks for security rights; the user is then asked for a password. All security information is placed into the NetWare server's connection list and the user is said to be logged in. At this point, LOGIN executes one or more login scripts (which initialize environment variables, maps network drives, etc.).

LOGIN directory

The SYS:LOGIN directory, created during network installation, that contains the LOGIN and NLIST utilities. Users can use these utilities to log in and view a list of available NetWare servers. For NetWare users running OS/2, the corresponding LOGIN directory is SYS:LOGIN/OS2.

login restrictions

Limitations on a user account that control access to the network, including requiring a password, setting account limits, limiting disk space, specifying the number of connections, and setting time restrictions.

When a user violates login restrictions, NetWare disables the account and no one can log in using that user name. This prevents unauthorized users from logging in.

login scripts

A file containing commands that set up your users' workstation environments whenever they log in. Login scripts are similar to configurable batch files and are executed by the LOGIN utility.

You can use login scripts to map drives and search drives to directories, display messages, set environment variables, and execute programs or menus.

Three types of login scripts   When a user logs in, the LOGIN utility executes the appropriate login scripts. Three types of login scripts can be used together to specify a custom environment for your users. All three types of login scripts are optional.

> ▸ *System* login scripts set general environments for all users in an Organization or Organizational Unit. These login scripts execute first.

> ▸ *Profile* login scripts set environments for multiple users. These login scripts execute after the system login script.

> ▸ *User* login scripts set environments specific to a single user, such as menu options or a user name for electronic mail. These login scripts execute after system and profile login scripts.

Login scripts are properties of objects.

logout

A procedure that breaks the network connection and deletes drives mapped to the network.

long machine type

A six-letter name representing a DOS workstation brand. (This doesn't apply to OS/2 workstations.) Use the long machine type in system login scripts (using the MACHINE identifier variable) to automatically map a drive to the correct version of DOS assigned to the station.

IBM computers use the long machine type IBM_PC. If the station is not an IBM computer, create a long machine type for the station in a NET.CFG file. Use the six-letter name for the long machine type as the subdirectory name when you use more than one brand of workstation. Example: COMPAQ.

LPT1

The primary parallel printer port of a personal computer.

LSL

See *Link Support Layer.* See also entry under *Open Data-Link Interface.*

M

Macintosh client

A Macintosh computer that attaches to the network. The Macintosh client can store and retrieve data from a NetWare server running NetWare for Macintosh support modules and can run executable Macintosh network files.

Macintosh clients can share files with other clients (DOS, Windows, OS/2, and UNIX) and can monitor queues.

Macintosh files

Files used on Macintosh computers. A Macintosh file contains two parts, the data fork and the resource fork:

- The *data fork* contains information (data) specified by the user.

- The *resource fork* contains file resources, including Macintosh-specific information such as the windows and icons used with the file.

When a Macintosh client accesses the file stored on the server, it accesses both the data and resource forks; both of these are required for the Macintosh to use the file. When a non-Macintosh client accesses the file stored on the server, only the data fork is used.

MAIL directory

The SYS:MAIL directory, created during network installation, used by mail programs that are compatible with NetWare.

In previous versions of NetWare, the MAIL directory held user login scripts. When you upgrade to NetWare 4.0, existing users still have subdirectories in the MAIL directory, but their login scripts become a property of the new User object. New users that you create under NetWare 4.0 won't have subdirectories in the MAIL directory.

major resource

A category of data defined by the Target Service Agent, and recognized by SBACKUP. A major resource contains data that can be backed up as a group—for example, server, volume, etc.

map

For DOS and OS/2 clients, to assign a drive letter to a directory path on a volume. Example: If you map drive F: to the directory SYS:ACCTS/RECEIVE, you access that directory every time you change to drive F:.

Media Manager

Routines within NetWare 4.0 that provide to applications a generic view of the different types of backup storage devices (disk, tape, autochanger, etc.). These routines enable applications to communicate with the different storage devices without having device-specific drivers.

memory

The internal dynamic storage of a computer that can be addressed by the computer's operating system; referred to frequently as RAM (random-access memory).

Memory accepts and holds binary data. To be effective, a computer must store the data that will be operated on as well as the program that directs the operations to be performed.

Memory stores information and rapidly accesses any part of the information upon request.

memory allocation

The process of reserving specific memory locations in RAM for processes, instructions, and data.

When a computer system is installed, the installer may allocate memory for items such as disk caches, RAM disks, extended memory, and expanded memory. Operating systems and application programs allocate memory to meet their requirements, but they can only use memory that is actually available to them.

NetWare 4.0 has only one memory allocation pool (compared to NetWare 3.11, which has at least five allocation pools).

memory board

An add-on board that increases the amount of RAM within a personal computer.

memory protection

The structuring of memory resources in NetWare 4.0 that guards NetWare server memory from corruption by NLMs.

Memory protection allows you to run NLMs in a separate memory domain called the OS_PROTECTED domain. Once you load an NLM in the OS_PROTECTED domain and find it safe, you can load it into the OS domain, where it can run most efficiently.

message packet

A unit of information used in network communication. See *packet*.

message system

A communications protocol that runs on top of IPX. It provides an engine that allows a node on the network to send messages to other nodes. A set of APIs (application program interfaces) gives programs access to the message system.

Migrated attribute

A status flag, set by NetWare, that indicates that a file is migrated.

migration

The conversion of servers from NetWare 2.x or 3.x, or from another network operating system, to NetWare 4.0.

minor resource

A category of data defined by the Target Service Agent and recognized by SBACKUP. A minor resource might be located in the directory structure below the selected major resource—for example, directories, subdirectories, or files.

MLID

See *multiple layer interface driver.* See also entry under *Open Data-Link Interface.*

Modify bit

A bit set by the operating system, when a file is changed, to indicate that data has been modified. When a backup is performed, SBACKUP can check to see whether Modify bits are set, and can back up only those files that have their Modify bit set.

Modify right

A directory or file right that grants the right to change the attributes or name of a directory or file.

MSM

See *Media Support Module.*

multiple-byte character

A single character made up of more than one byte.

One byte allows 256 different characters. Since the number of ASCII characters equals 256, a computer can handle any ASCII character with one byte. Asian character sets, however, include more than 256 characters; for this reason, a computer must use two bytes for each character in an Asian character set.

multiple layer interface driver (MLID)

A device driver written to the ODI specification that handles the sending and receiving of packets to and from a physical or logical LAN medium.

multiple name-space support

The method that allows various workstations running different operating systems to create their own familiar naming conventions. In other words, the file system can present multiple client views for any given file.

Each file stored on a given volume has a name that any workstation can recognize. This name is stored in a file entry in the volume's directory table.

Different operating systems (DOS, OS/2, Macintosh, Windows, and UNIX) have different conventions for naming files. These conventions include name length, allowable characters, case-sensitivity, data and resource forks, length of extensions, multiple extensions, etc.

multiserver network

A single network that has two or more NetWare servers operating. On a multiserver network, users can access files from any NetWare server they have access rights to.

A multiserver network isn't the same as an internetwork, where two or more networks are linked through a router.

► · ◄

N

name context

The position of an object in the Directory tree. See *context*.

name space

A special NLM that allows you to store non-DOS files on a NetWare 4.0 server. Files appear in native mode to users at different workstations.

Any non-DOS file types, such as Macintosh or OS/2, must have a name-space NLM linked with the operating system before the NetWare server can store such files. Name-space NLMs have a .NAM extension.

Once the name-space NLM is loaded, you must use the ADD NAME SPACE console command to configure the volumes so you can store other types of files. When name space support is added to a volume, another entry is created in the directory table for the directory and file naming conventions of that name space (file-system).

NBP

See *Name Binding Protocol* under the entry *AppleTalk protocols*.

NCP

See *NetWare Core Protocol*.

NCP Packet Signature

An enhanced security feature that protects servers and workstations using NCP (NetWare Core Protocol) by preventing packet forgery.

Without NCP Packet Signature installed, a workstation can pose as a more privileged workstation to send a forged NCP request to a NetWare server. By forging the proper NCP request packet, an intruder could gain SUPERVISOR rights and access to all network resources.

NCP Packet Signature prevents packet forgery by requiring the server and the workstation to "sign" each NCP packet. The packet signature changes with every packet. If NCP Packet Signature is installed on the server and all of its workstations, it is virtually impossible to forge a valid NCP packet.

NDIS

Network Driver Interface Specification. See *ODINSUP.*

NETBIOS.EXE

NetWare's NetBIOS emulator program that allows workstations to run applications written for peer-to-peer communication or distributed processing. The INT2F.COM file is used with NETBIOS.EXE.

NET.CFG

A workstation boot file, similar to DOS CONFIG.SYS, that contains configuration values that are read and interpreted when your workstation starts up. These configuration values adjust the operating parameters of the NetWare DOS Requester, IPX, and other workstation software.

Applications such as database, multitasking, or NetBIOS (involved in peer-to-peer communications or distributed processing) may require parameter values different from the default values to function properly on the network. Some network problems such as printing and file retrieval might also be solved by adjusting workstation parameters.

NetWare Core Protocol (NCP)

(NetWare Core Protocol) Procedures that a server's NetWare operating system follows to accept and respond to workstation requests. NetWare Core Protocols exist for every service a station might request from a server.

Common requests handled by NCP include creating or destroying a service connection, manipulating directories and files, opening semaphores, altering the Directory, and printing.

NetWare Directory database

The database (commonly referred to as the Directory) that organizes NetWare Directory Services objects in a hierarchical tree structure called the Directory tree.

NetWare Directory Services

A global, distributed, replicated database built into NetWare 4.0 that maintains information about, and provides access to, every resource on the network.

NetWare Directory Services treats all network resources (users, groups, printers, volumes, computers, etc.) as objects in a distributed database known as the NetWare Directory database (also referred to as the Directory). The NetWare Directory database organizes objects, independent of their physical location, in a hierarchical tree structure called the Directory tree.

Users and administrators can access any network service without having to know the physical location of the server that stores the service. NetWare Directory Services makes it possible to integrate a diverse network of resources into a single, easy-to-use environment.

The Directory replaces the bindery, which served as the system database for previous releases of NetWare. While the bindery supports the operation of a single NetWare server, NetWare Directory Services supports an entire network of servers. Compatibility with previous versions of NetWare is provided through bindery emulation.

Accessing NetWare Directory Services   Instead of logging in or attaching to individual servers, NetWare Directory Services users log in to the network. When a user accesses resources on the network, background authentication processes verify that the user has rights to use those resources. Authentication allows a user (who has logged in) to access any server, volume, printer, etc., that the user has rights to. User trustee rights restrict the user's access within the network.

Objects   A NetWare Directory Services object consists of categories of information, called properties, and the data in those properties. The information is stored in the NetWare Directory database.

Some objects represent physical entities. For example, a User object represents a user, a Printer object represents a printer, etc. Some objects represent logical entities, such as groups and print queues. Other objects, such as the Organizational Unit object, help you organize and manage objects.

Directory tree   NetWare Directory Services operates in a logical organization called the Directory tree. It is called a Directory tree because objects are stored in a hierarchical tree structure, starting with the Root object and branching out.

Two types of objects make up the Directory tree: container objects and leaf objects. A branch of the Directory tree consists of a container object and all the objects it holds, which can include other container objects. Leaf objects are at the ends of branches and don't contain any other objects.

Object names   The path from an object to the root of the Directory tree forms the object's complete name, which is a unique name.

Most leaf objects have a common name. For User objects, the common name is their login name, displayed in the Directory tree. Other leaf objects also have common names that are displayed in the Directory tree, such as a Printer object name or a Server object name. Container objects don't have common names. They are referred to by their Organizational Unit name, Organization name, or Country name.

An object's complete name consists of its common name (if it has one), followed by a period (.), then the name of the container object, also followed by a period, and on up through succeeding container object names to the root of the tree.

Object context   NetWare Directory Services allows you to refer to objects according to their positions within a tree. When you add an object (such as a server or user), you place that object in a container object in the Directory tree.

The position of the object within its container is its context. When you move from one container object to another, you change contexts. Whenever you change contexts, indicate the complete name of the object you are changing context to.

If you are referring to an object that is in the same container object as your User object, then you only need to refer to that object by its common name, instead of by its complete name.

User object ADMIN   The first time the network supervisor logs in, he or she logs in as User ADMIN, created automatically during NetWare 4.0 installation.

When ADMIN is created, it is given a default trustee assignment to the Root object. This assignment grants ADMIN all rights to all objects and all volumes (directories and files) in the entire Directory tree. This means that ADMIN has rights to create and manage all objects in the tree.

Partitions   To be more manageable, the NetWare Directory database is divided into smaller portions called partitions. Partitions are created by default when you install NetWare 4.0 on a server in a new context in the Directory tree.

Each partition consists of a container object, all objects contained in it, and data about those objects. Partitions don't include any information about the file system or the directories and files contained there. The Root object (at the top of the tree) is included in the first partition created.

To optimize access to different areas of the Directory, each partition can be replicated and stored at many locations. Partition replication improves access and provides the Directory with fault tolerance. Since a partition can be replicated at several locations, damage to one of the replicas doesn't need to interrupt access to the partition information.

Replicas   For NetWare Directory Services to be distributed across a network, the database must be stored on many servers. Rather than have a copy of the whole database on each server, replicas of each partition are stored on many servers throughout the network. A replica is a copy of a partition. You can create an unlimited number of replicas for each partition and store them on any server in the network.

Bindery compatibility   To provide compatibility with bindery-based versions of NetWare that may co-exist with NetWare Directory Services on the network, NetWare 4.0 features bindery emulation.

Objects in a bindery exist in a flat database instead of a hierarchical database like a Directory tree. Bindery emulation occurs when NetWare Directory Services emulates a flat structure for the objects within an Organization or Organizational Unit container object. All objects within that container object can then be accessed both by NetWare Directory Services objects and by bindery-based clients and servers.

Time synchronization   NetWare 4.0 allows servers to synchronize their time with each other. Time synchronization is critical to the operation of NetWare Directory Services because it establishes the order of events.

Whenever an event occurs in the Directory, such as when a password is changed, or an object is renamed, NetWare Directory Services requests a time stamp. A time stamp is a unique code that includes the time and identifies the event. The NetWare Directory Services event is assigned a time stamp so that the order in which replicas are updated is correct.

NetWare DOS Requester
The DOS client software portion of NetWare 4.0. The NetWare DOS Requester replaces the NetWare shell under 4.0, while maintaining backward compatibility with previous NetWare shell versions.

The NetWare DOS Requester includes a redirector that, in contrast to the NetWare shell, is called by DOS. Under the redirector, DOS makes specific requests for services from the redirector (such as for file and print services from the server) that DOS can't provide. (These functions were previously performed by the NETX shell, without involving DOS.)

The NetWare DOS Requester also continues to provide network services for file and print redirection, as well as for connection maintenance and other NetWare-specific support.

NetWare Express

Novell's private electronic information service that provides access to Novell's Network Support Encyclopedia. NetWare Express uses the GE Information Services network and software and requires a connection through an asynchronous modem.

NetWare Loadable Module (NLM)

A program you can load and unload from server memory while the server is running. (Some NLMs that are depended on by other NLMs are loaded automatically.) NLMs link disk drivers, LAN drivers, name spaces, and other NetWare server management and enhancement utilities to the operating system.

The NetWare server allocates a portion of memory to the NLM when the NLM is loaded. The NLM uses the memory to perform a task, and then returns control of the memory to the operating system when the NLM is unloaded.

NetWare 4.0 has four types of NLMs:

▶ *Disk drivers* (.DSK extension) control communication between the operating system and hard disks.

▶ *LAN drivers* (.LAN extension) control communication between the operating system and the network boards.

▶ *Management utilities and server applications modules* (.NLM extension) allow you to monitor and change configuration options.

▶ *Name-space NLMs* (.NAM extension) allow non-DOS naming conventions to be stored in the directory and file naming system.

Some NLMs, such as utilities, can be loaded, used, and then unloaded. Other NLMs, such as LAN driver and disk driver NLMs, must be loaded every time the server is booted.

NetWare-managed node

A NetWare 4.0 server that has the NetWare management agents enabled, making more information available to management console software than is available with IPX/SPX function calls.

NetWare Management Agents

A group of NLMs that bring together manageable software, hardware, and data components of a NetWare server and an external network management software package.

When NetWare Management Agents are loaded, they create a hierarchical representation of all managed objects and their attributes, including a server's hardware, software, or data components.

NetWare operating system

The network operating system developed by Novell, Inc. NetWare runs on the server and provides several functions to the network and the applications running on it, including file and record locking, security, print spooling, and interprocess communications.

The NetWare operating system also determines performance, multivendor support, and reliability of the network.

NetWare partition

A partition created on each network hard disk, from which volumes are created. See *disk partition*.

NetWare Requester for OS/2

Software that connects OS/2 workstations to NetWare networks allowing OS/2 users to share network resources. The NetWare Requester performs the following functions:

▶ Directs network requests from the workstation to the network.

▶ Allows application servers (such as SQL Server) and their workstations to communicate on the network without using a NetWare
server. Users can run advanced distributed applications or back-end
server engines on their OS/2 workstations. DOS and OS/2 users can
access data on those application servers without using a NetWare
server.

A stand-alone computer running OS/2 is converted into an OS/2 client by
adding a network board and installing the NetWare Requester for OS/2 software.

NetWare Runtime

A single-user version of the NetWare 4.0 operating system that provides Net-
Ware services to clients of NetWare Loadable Module (NLM) applications.

NetWare Runtime is a network server platform supporting front-end or back-
end applications as well as basic NLM services such as communication services,
database servers, electronic mail, and other third-party applications. NLM application developers have the flexibility to determine which client services will
be available in their product.

NLMs, loaded on a NetWare Runtime server, provide client connection services (using IPX, SPX, AppleTalk, or TCP/IP).

NetWare server

A computer that runs NetWare operating system software. A NetWare server
regulates communications among personal computers attached to it and
manages shared resources, such as printers.

A NetWare 4.0 server must have at least one hard disk, either internal or external, and a recommended minimum 8MB of RAM. The server must also contain
at least one network board.

Some NetWare servers are dedicated (used as a server only) or nondedicated
(used as a server and a workstation). NetWare servers running NetWare 4.0 can
be used only as dedicated servers, except NetWare 4.0 for OS/2 servers, which
are nondedicated only.

NetWare server console operator

A user or a member of a group in NetWare 3.11 to whom SUPERVISOR delegates certain rights in managing the NetWare server with FCONSOLE.EXE.

In NetWare 4.0, a user needs RCONSOLE to perform tasks on the server console from a DOS workstation. A user can perform the same tasks as if using the NetWare server's keyboard. For example, a user could load MONITOR.NLM, unload a print server (PSERVER.NLM), or down the server.

NetWare Server object

A leaf object that represents a server running NetWare on your network. The network address property identifies its location on the network. The NetWare Server object is referred to in several other objects to specify where to find items such as volumes.

NetWare Tools

Utilities that enable users to perform a variety of network tasks such as accessing network resources, mapping drives, setting up printing, and sending messages. NetWare Tools, new under NetWare 4.0, come with their own installations, separate from the server installation program.

NetWire

Novell's online information service, which provides access to Novell product information, Novell services information, and time-sensitive technical information for NetWare users.

NetWire is accessed through the CompuServe Information Service. It requires a PC or compatible workstation, a modem, and a communications program.

network

A group of computers that can communicate with each other, share peripherals (such as hard disks and printers), and access remote hosts or other networks.

A NetWare network consists of workstations, peripherals, and one or more NetWare servers. NetWare network users can share the same files (both data and program files), send messages directly between workstations, and protect files with an extensive security system.

network backbone

A cabling system that NetWare servers and routers are attached to. If your network has three or more NetWare servers, this may be an efficient way to improve network performance. The central cable handles all network traffic, decreasing packet transmission time and traffic on the network.

network board

A circuit board installed in each workstation to allow stations to communicate with each other and with the NetWare server. Some printers contain their own network board to allow them to attach directly to the network cabling.

network communication

Data transmission between workstations. Requests for services and data pass from one workstation to another through a communication medium such as cabling.

Network Driver Interface Specification (NDIS)

See *ODINSUP.*

Network interface card (NIC)

A circuit board installed in each workstation to allow stations to communicate with each other and with the NetWare server. NetWare documentation uses the term "Network board" instead of "Network Interface Card."

network node

A personal computer or other device connected to a network by a network board and a communication medium. A network node can be a server, workstation, router, printer, or fax machine.

network numbering

The system of numbers that identifies servers, network boards, and cable segments. These network numbers include the following:

- *IPX external network number.* A number that uniquely identifies a network cable segment.

- *IPX internal network number.* A number that identifies an individual NetWare 4.0 server.

- *Node number.* A number that identifies a network board (in a server, workstation, or router).

network printer

A printer shared in a network environment.

network supervisor

A generic term in NetWare 4.0 for the person responsible for configuring the NetWare server, workstations, user access (security), printing, etc.

Network Support Encyclopedia (NSE)

Novell's electronic information database containing comprehensive information about network technology.

The NSE includes downloadable NetWare patches, fixes, drivers, and utilities as well as Novell technical bulletins and manuals. NSE contains NetWare Application Notes (with graphics), the NetWare Buyer's Guide, Novell press releases, and additional product information. The NSE also includes Novell Labs' hardware- and software-compatibility test results.

NETX

A VLM (NETX.VLM) under the NetWare DOS Requester that provides backward compatibility with NETX and other older versions of the shell.

NIC

See *Network interface card.*

NLM

See *NetWare Loadable Module.*

node number

A number that uniquely identifies a network board. Every node must have at least one network board, by which the node is connected to the network. Each network board must have a unique node number to distinguish it from all other network boards on that network.

Node numbers are assigned in several ways, depending on the network board type:

> ▸ Ethernet boards are factory set. (No two Ethernet boards have the same number.)

> ▸ ARCnet and Token Ring board numbers are set with jumpers or switches.

node schematic

A graphical representation of a node (NetWare server) and its managed objects.

A node schematic is the main graphical display available in the NetWare Management System software. The node schematic is the focal point of the node with other graphical displays being launched from it.

The node schematic can display network boards, server disks, volumes, queues, users, memory, NLMs, and event and alert messages.

Normal attribute

A file-system attribute that indicates that no NetWare attributes are set.

NSE

See *Network Support Encyclopedia.*

O

object

A NetWare Directory Services structure that stores information about a network resource (a user, group, printer, volume, and so on). An object consists of categories of information, called *properties*, and the data in those properties. The information is stored in the NetWare Directory database.

Some objects represent physical entities. For example, a User object represents a user and a Printer object represents a printer. Some objects represent logical entities, such as groups and print queues. Other objects, such as the Organizational Unit object, help you organize and manage objects.

Objects and the Directory tree   Two types of objects make up the Directory tree: container objects and leaf objects. A branch of the Directory tree consists of a container object and all the objects it holds, which can include other container objects. Leaf objects are at the ends of branches and don't contain other objects.

Object names   The path from an object to the root of the Directory tree forms the object's complete name, which is a unique name. Most leaf objects have a common name. For User objects, the common name is their login name, displayed in the Directory tree. Other leaf objects also have common names displayed in the Directory tree, such as a Printer object name or a Server object name.

Container objects don't have common names. They are referred to by their Organizational Unit name, their Organization name, or their Country name.

An object's complete name consists of its common name (if it has one), followed by a period (.), then the name of the container object, also followed by a period, and on up through succeeding container object names through the root of the tree.

Object contexts   NetWare Directory Services allows you to refer to objects according to their positions within a tree. When you add an object (such as a server or user) to the network, you place that object in a container object in the Directory tree.

The position of the object within its container is its context. When you move from one container object to another, you change contexts. Whenever you change contexts, indicate the complete name of the object you are changing contexts to.

Object properties   Each type of object has certain properties that hold information about the object. For example, some User object properties include the login name, password restrictions, and group memberships. Some Profile object properties are the profile name, login script, and volume.

object rights

Qualities assigned to an object to control what the object can do with directories, files, or other objects.

ODI

See *Open Data-Link Interface*.

ODINSUP

(Open Data-Link Interface / Network Driver Interface Specification SUPport) An interface that allows the co-existence of two network driver interfaces: the Network Driver Interface Specification (NDIS) and the Open Data-Link Interface (ODI) specification.

ODINSUP allows you to connect to dissimilar networks from your workstation and use them as if they were one network.

ODINSUP also allows NDIS protocol stacks to communicate through the ODI's LSL and MLID. This way, NDIS and ODI protocol stacks can coexist in the same system, making use of a single ODI MLID.

Open Data-Link Interface (ODI)

An architecture that allows multiple LAN drivers and protocols to coexist on network systems. The ODI specification describes the set of interface and software modules used to decouple device drivers from protocol stacks and to enable multiple protocol stacks to share the network hardware and media transparently.

The major components of the ODI architecture are described in the following sections.

Multiple Layer Interface Driver (MLID)

The MLID is a device driver written to the ODI specification that handles the sending and receiving of packets to and from a physical or logical LAN medium. Each driver is unique due to the adapter hardware and media, but the ODI eliminates the need to write separate drivers for each protocol stack. ODI allows LAN drivers to function with protocol stacks independent of the media frame type and protocol stack details.

MLIDs interface with a network board and handle the appending and stripping of media frame headers. They also help de-multiplex the incoming packets by determining their frame format.

Link Support Layer (LSL)

The LSL is a software module that implements the interface between drivers and protocol stacks. It essentially acts like a switchboard, directing packets between the drivers and protocol stacks.

Any ODI LAN driver can communicate with any ODI protocol stack through the LSL. The LSL handles the communication between protocol stacks and MLIDs.

Media Support Module (MSM)   The MSM standardizes and manages primary details of interfacing ODI MLIDs to the LSL and operating system. The MSM handles generic initialization and run-time issues common to all drivers.

Topology-Specific Module (TSM)   The TSM manages operations unique to a specific media type, such as Ethernet or Token Ring. Multiple frame support is implemented in the TSM so that all frame types for a given media type are supported.

Hardware-Specific Module (HSM)   The HSM is created for a specific network board. The HSM handles all hardware interactions. Its primary functions include adapter initialization, reset, shutdown, and removal. It also handles packet reception and transmission. Additional procedures may also provide support for timeout detection, multicast addressing, and promiscuous mode reception.

optical disk
A form of removable media used to store data. An optical disk can be one- or two-sided. Some optical disks are read-only; others can be read from and written to. Rewritable optical disks are used as the media type for HCSS.

optical disk library
A high-capacity storage device, sometimes called a jukebox, that uses an autochanger mechanism to mount and dismount optical disks as needed.

Organization object

A container object that helps you organize other objects in the Directory and allows you to set template information for users created in this container. For example, you could use an Organization object to represent a company, or a university with various departments, or a department with several project teams.

The Organization object is a level below the Country object (if used), and a level above the Organizational Unit object (if used).

Organizational Role object

A leaf object that defines a position or role within an organization. Use the Organizational Role object to specify a position that can be filled by different people, such as Team Leader or Vice President.

Organizational Unit object

A container object, a level below the Organization object, that helps you to further organize other objects in the Directory and also allows you to set template information for users created in this container. For example, you could use an Organizational Unit object to designate a division, a business unit, a project team, or a college or department within a university.

OS/2 client

An OS/2 computer that connects to the network using NetWare Workstation for OS/2 software. The OS/2 client can store and retrieve data from the network and can run executable network files.

OS/2 client workstations support IPX/SPX, NetBIOS, and Named Pipes to allow users access to OS/2-based applications such as the SQL Server.

P

packet

A unit of information used in network communication. Messages sent between network devices (workstations, NetWare servers, etc.) are formed into packets at the source device. The packets are reassembled, if necessary, into complete messages when they reach their destination.

A packet might contain a request for service, information on how to handle the request, and the data that will be serviced.

Packet Burst Protocol

A protocol built on top of IPX that speeds the transfer of multiple-packet NCP (NetWare Core Protocol) file reads and writes. The Packet Burst Protocol speeds the transfer of NCP data between a workstation and a NetWare server by eliminating the need to sequence and acknowledge each packet.

Packet Burst Protocol is more efficient than the one-request/one-response protocol in earlier NetWare versions. With Packet Burst Protocol, the server or workstation can send a whole set (burst) of packets before it requires an acknowledgment. By allowing multiple packets to be acknowledged, Packet Burst Protocol reduces network traffic.

packet receive buffer

An area in the NetWare server's memory set aside to temporarily hold data packets arriving from the various workstations. The packets remain in this buffer until the server is ready to process them and send them to their destination. This ensures the smooth flow of data into the server, even during times of particularly heavy input/output operations.

Paging

A feature of the Intel 80386/80486 architecture that NetWare 4.0 uses to create memory domains. A memory page is a contiguous 4K block of RAM.

Rather than assign memory to processes in large blocks of contiguously-addressed pages, NetWare 4.0 assigns memory in a noncontiguous range. Page tables map the noncontiguous pages into contiguous logical address spaces. A group of page tables is a domain.

PAP

See *Printer Access Protocol* under the entry *AppleTalk protocols*.

Parallel port

A printer interface that allows data to be transmitted a byte at a time, all eight bits moving in parallel.

Parent directory

The directory immediately above any subdirectory. For example, the parent directory of the subdirectory SYS:ACCTS/RECEIVE would be SYS:ACCTS.

Parent objects

Container objects that contain other objects.

Parity

A method of checking for errors in transmitted data.

Partition

A logical division of the Directory's global database. A partition forms a distinct unit of data in the Directory tree that you use to store and replicate Directory information.

Each partition consists of a container object, all objects contained in it, and data about those objects. Partitions don't include any information about the file system or the directories and files contained there.

To optimize access to different areas of the Directory, each partition can be replicated and stored at many locations. Partition replication improves access and provides the Directory with fault tolerance. Since a partition can be replicated at several locations, damage to one of the replicas doesn't need to interrupt access to the partition information.

Partition replicas are stored on NetWare servers. Multiple partitions can be stored on the same NetWare server; none of the partitions need to be contiguous to another.

Partition management

The method of managing NetWare Directory database partitions and replicas. Partition management divides the directory into partitions and makes and manages various replicas of these partitions.

Partition management allows you to

► Create, delete, rebuild, and synchronize partitions

► Display partitions and partition details

► Add, delete, and display replicas

Partition management won't allow you to modify the structure of existing partitions; partitions can't be split, combined, or moved.

passive hub

A device used in some network topologies to split a transmission signal, allowing additional workstations to be added. See *hub*.

password

The characters a user must type to log in with. NetWare allows the supervisor to specify whether passwords are required and, if so, to assign a login password to each user on the network.

In NetWare 4.0, login passwords are encrypted at the workstation and put into a format that only the NetWare server can decode. This format helps prevent intruders from accessing network files.

path
The location of a file or directory in the file system. For example, the path for file REPORT.FIL in subdirectory ACCTG in directory CORP on vol SYS: of server ADMIN is

ADMIN\SYS:CORP\ACCTG\REPORT.FIL

physical memory
The RAM installed in a computer. NetWare servers use paging to address physical memory in 4K blocks, or pages.

port

Hardware port   A connecting component that allows a microprocessor to communicate with a compatible peripheral.

Software port   A memory address that identifies the physical circuit used to transfer information between a microprocessor and a peripheral.

power conditioning
Methods of protecting sensitive network hardware components against power disturbances. Power disturbances can be categorized in several ways:

- *A transient* (sometimes called a spike or surge)—a very short, but extreme, burst of voltage.

- *Noise or static*—a smaller change in voltage.

- *Blackouts and brownouts*—the temporary drop in or loss of electrical power.

Three types of protection are available:

▶ *Suppression.* Protects against transients. The most common suppression devices are surge protectors that usually include circuitry to prevent excess voltage.

▶ *Isolation.* Protects against noise, using ferro-resonant isolation transformers to control voltage irregularities.

▶ *Regulation.* Protects against brownouts and blackouts. The uninterruptible power supply (UPS) is the most commonly used form of regulation.

Primary time server

A server that synchronizes the time with at least one other Primary or Reference time server, and provides the time to Secondary time servers and to workstations. See *time synchronization.*

print device

A printer, plotter, or other peripheral that prints from the network. Print devices require print jobs to be formatted with the correct control sequences that set and reset the printer, produce bolding, underlining, etc.

Most applications provide you with a printer definition to correctly format print jobs. Each printer definition has a .PDF extension and must be imported into NetWare print services using the NetWare Administrator or PRINTDEF.

print device mode

A sequence of print functions (also called printer commands, control sequences, or escape sequences) that determines the appearance of the printed file. A print device mode can define the style, size, boldness, and orientation of the typeface.

Print device modes are designated using the NetWare Administrator or PRINTDEF.

print job

A file stored in a print queue directory waiting to be printed. As soon as a print server sends a print job to the printer, the print job is deleted from the queue directory.

print job configuration

A group of characteristics that determine how a job is printed. The characteristics may include the following:

- ▸ The printer the print job will be printed on

- ▸ The print queue the print job is sent through

- ▸ The number of copies to print

- ▸ The use of a banner page

- ▸ The printer form number

- ▸ The print-device mode

print queue

A network directory that stores print jobs. When the printer assigned to a print queue is ready, the print server takes the print job out of the print queue and sends it to the printer. The print queue can hold as many print jobs as disk space allows.

When you create a print queue in NetWare Administrator or PCONSOLE, a corresponding directory is created. In NetWare Directory Services mode, the print queue directory resides in the QUEUES directory on the volume specified. In bindery mode, the print queue directory resides in the SYSTEM directory on volume SYS: of the current server.

print-queue operator

A user who can edit other users' print jobs, delete print jobs from the print queue, or modify the print queue status by changing the operator flags. Print-queue operators can also change the order in which print jobs are serviced. They can also change the service mode.

User ADMIN can assign users to be print-queue operators as necessary.

print-queue polling time

The time interval the print server waits between checking the print queues for jobs ready and waiting to be printed. Users can specify the time period.

print server

A server that takes print jobs out of a print queue and sends them to a network printer. NetWare print servers run as PSERVER.NLM on a NetWare server and can service up to 255 printers (and any number of print queues assigned to the printers).

Print Server object

A leaf object that represents a network print server.

Print Server operator

A user or member of a group delegated rights by ADMIN to manage the print server. A Print Server operator has rights to control notify lists, printers, and queue assignments.

printer

Computer equipment used to produce printed material. Network printers can be attached directly to the network, to the printer port of a NetWare server, or to the printer port of a PC workstation.

In NetWare 4.0, users can specify printer names as the destination of their print jobs. In previous versions, users had to specify the print queue. (Users can still specify print queues.)

In bindery-based NetWare, printers are a subset of the print server. For that reason, a print server must exist before you can define printers.

In NetWare Directory Services, printers are objects used in conjunction with Print Server and Print Queue objects. They can be added, modified, or removed independently.

printer definition

A set of printer control characters used to interpret commands to bold, italicize, and center text. Printer definitions are specific to a printer brand and model.

Over 50 printer definitions ship with NetWare 4.0. If your printer, plotter, etc. doesn't function with one of the available print-device definitions, you can create your own set of control characters and specify what forms your print device accepts.

printer form

A print option designed to prevent print jobs from being printed on the wrong paper. NetWare print services allow you to send print jobs that will not print until you make sure that the correct paper is in the printer.

For each type of paper (such as regular, letterhead, and bond paper), you can create a printer form. Each form has a unique name and number (between 0 and 255). If you specify this form in a print-job configuration or in NPRINT or CAPTURE with the form option, the print job won't print unless the mounted form matches the number required by the print job.

Printer object

A leaf object that represents a physical printing device on the network.

printing

The ability to transfer data from computer files to paper. NetWare 4.0 allows users to share printing hardware, where previously each personal computer had to have a printer attached to one of its printer ports.

NetWare 4.0 uses a print queue and print server to allow workstations to print to a printer. The print server takes print jobs from the print queue and sends them to the printer.

privilege level

(Also called *protection rings*.) The rank assigned to server memory segments in NetWare 4.0. By running an NLM at a different privilege level than the operating system (OS), you can protect OS memory from the NLM.

Privilege levels are made possible by the Intel microprocessor architecture. Four privilege levels are available: 0, 1, 2, and 3. NetWare uses levels 0 and 3.

NetWare assigns memory segments to one or two memory domains, depending on how you configure the server. One is the OS domain at privilege level 0, and the other is the OS_PROTECTED domain at privilege level 3.

By loading an NLM into level 3, you can protect the OS from writes the NLM may errantly make to memory it doesn't "own." This keeps a "poorly-behaved" NLM from bringing down the server. NLMs you load into the OS_PROTECTED domain must be specially coded to run at level 3.

profile login script

A type of login script that sets environments for a group of users. Use profile login scripts if there are groups of users with identical login script needs.

Profile login scripts are optional; if used, they execute after the system login script and before the user login script.

Profile object

A leaf object that represents a login script used by a group of users who need to share common login script commands. The group of users may not necessarily be located under the same container in the Directory tree, or they may be a subset of users in the same container.

prompt

A character or message that appears on the display screen and requires a response (such as a command or a utility name) from the user.

Standard types of prompts include:

- ▸ *The DOS prompt,* which, by default, displays the current drive letter followed by a > symbol: **F>**

- ▸ *The OS/2 prompt,* which, by default, displays the current drive mapping in brackets: [C:\]

- ▸ *The NetWare server console prompt,* which displays : (a colon)

property

A characteristic of a NetWare Directory Services object. Each type of object (such as a User object, Organization object, or Profile object) has certain properties that hold information about the object.

For example, a User object's properties include login name, E-mail address, password restrictions, group memberships, etc. As another example, a Profile object's properties include profile name, login script, volume, etc.

The only properties required for objects are those you enter when you create a new object. You must enter a value in each field. Properties you must enter when you create an object can be properties that name the object, or properties required to create the object but that don't name it.

property rights

Rights that apply to the properties of a NetWare Directory Services object.

protected mode

The mode that 80286, 80386, and 80486 processors run in by default. When running in protected mode, these processors aren't subject to the same memory constraints as 8086 processors.

The 80286 processor uses a 24-bit address bus, and can address up to 16MB of memory. The 80386 and 80486 processors use a 32-bit address bus, and can address up to 4GB of memory.

Protected-mode operating provides the capability of multitasking (running more than one application or process at a time). Protected mode allocates memory to various processes running concurrently so that memory used by one process doesn't overlap memory used by another process.

By contrast, 8086 processors can address only 1MB of memory, and can run only one application or process at a time. 80286, 80386, and 80486 processors can be set to run in *real mode*, in which case they emulate an 8086 processor (and are subject to its memory constraints).

protection ring

See *privilege level*.

PUBLIC directory

The SYS:PUBLIC directory, created during network installation, that allows general access to the network and contains NetWare utilities and programs for network users.

NetWare users running DOS have a search drive mapped to SYS:PUBLIC through the system login script and are assigned Read rights and File Scan rights to this directory.

NetWare users running OS/2 access NetWare utilities from the SYS:PUBLIC/OS2 directory.

public files

Files that must be accessed by all NetWare users, including NetWare utilities, help files, and some message and data files. By convention, the files are located in SYS:PUBLIC for DOS users, and in SYS:PUBLIC/OS2 for OS/2 users.

All NetWare users have Read rights and File Scan rights to the files.

Public trustee

A special trustee that can be added to any object, directory, or file. [Public] is only used in trustee assignments and must always be entered within square brackets. [Public] can be added or deleted like any other trustee. An Inherited Rights Filter will block inherited rights for [Public].

Whatever rights are granted to [Public] are effective for any object in NetWare Directory Services that doesn't have any other effective rights. This is similar to granting trustee rights to user GUEST or group EVERYONE in previous NetWare versions.

Make [Public] a trustee of areas that every object should have access to. (A user doesn't have to log in to access areas where [Public] is granted rights.)

In most cases, it is better to make a container object a trustee, rather than making [Public] a trustee. This grants rights only to the objects within the container, improving security control.

Purge attribute

A file-system attribute that causes NetWare to purge the directory or file when it is deleted.

R

RAM

(Random Access Memory) The internal dynamic storage of a computer that can be addressed by the computer's operating system.

Read-after-Write verification

A means of assuring that data written to the hard disk matches the original data still in memory.

If the data from the disk matches the data in memory, the data in memory is released. If the data doesn't match, the block location is recognized as "bad," and Hot Fix redirects the data to a good block location within the Hot Fix redirection area.

Read-Only attribute

A file-system attribute that indicates that no one can write to the file.

Read right

A file-system right that grants the right to open and read files.

Also, a property right that grants the right to read the values of the property.

real mode

The mode that allows 80286, 80386, and 80486 processors to emulate an 8086 processor and run as though they actually were an 8086 processor.

The 8086 processor uses a 20-bit address bus, and can address up to 1MB of memory. The 8086 processor is also limited to running only one application or process at a time.

When running in protected mode, the 80286, 80386, and 80486 processors are capable of multitasking and addressing much more than 1MB of memory.

When running in real mode, these processors are subject to the same 1MB memory constraint as the 8086 processor, and they can run only one application or process at a time. However, the 80286, 80386, and 80486 processors running in real mode perform more efficiently than the 8086 processor, because they operate at a faster clock rate.

record locking

A feature of NetWare that prevents different users from gaining simultaneous access to the same record in a shared file, preventing overlapping disk writes and ensuring data integrity.

recursive copying

The process of copying a specified source directory to a destination directory until all files and subdirectories in and below the specified source directory are copied.

Recursive copying copies all directories and files of a logical drive to the destination, keeping them exactly as they were in the source directory. Whether a trustee's rights are copied with the files and directories depends on what rights are assigned in the destination directory.

The DOS and OS/2 XCOPY and BACKUP utilities use recursive copying, as does the NetWare NCOPY command.

Reference time server

A server that specifies the time for all other time servers and workstations to synchronize to. See *time synchronization*.

registered resources

Network resources that report information to the NetWare Management Agent.

Registration is the process by which key software, hardware, and data components identify themselves, along with the objects they control and all associated attributes to the NetWare Management Agent. A registered resource then becomes monitorable and manageable by a management software program designed to work with the NetWare Management Agent.

For example, a server could have its disk drive and certain drive attributes registered as a manageable object. A management software program would then be able to monitor and manage the server's disk drive.

remote boot

A method that allows a user to boot a workstation from remote boot image files on a NetWare server rather than from a boot diskette in the workstation's local drive.

When a workstation is booted, the Remote Reset PROM (installed on the workstation's network board) directs the nearest (default) NetWare server to run the remote boot image file commands contained in the default server's LOGIN directory.

remote connection

A connection between a LAN on one end and a workstation or network on the other, often using telephone lines and modems. A remote connection allows data to be sent and received across greater distances than those allowed by normal cabling.

Remote Console

Software that allows network supervisors to manage servers from a DOS workstation or from a PC using a modem. Remote Console gives you greater server security since you can lock servers in a safe place and remove the keyboards and monitors.

From a remote console, supervisors can

- Use console commands as if they were at the server console.

- Scan directories and edit text files in both NetWare and DOS partitions on a server.

- Transfer files to (but not from) a server.

- Bring down or reboot a server.

- Install or upgrade NetWare on a remote server.

Remote Reset

Software that allows you to boot a DOS workstation (including a diskless workstation) from a remote boot image file on a NetWare server, rather than from a boot diskette in the workstation's local drive.

To use Remote Reset to boot a workstation, install a Remote Reset PROM on the station's network board and run the DOSGEN utility. DOSGEN uploads the station's boot files into a remote boot image file, NET$DOS.SYS, in the server's LOGIN directory.

The remote boot image file includes the station's AUTOEXEC.BAT file, used by the station as if the file were present on a local boot diskette. Copy the workstation's AUTOEXEC.BAT file to the remote boot image file, to the LOGIN directory, and to any default directory named in the workstation's login script.

Using Remote Reset with multiple servers   If you have multiple NetWare servers on your network, copy the remote boot image files onto each server that may come up as the remote boot workstation's default server. Then, if the first default server isn't available, the station can boot from the next available server.

Using multiple remote boot image files   For more than one workstation to use Remote Reset, upload multiple remote boot image files for each station into SYS:LOGIN.

Instead of the single NET$DOS.SYS file, upload a separate remote boot image file for each workstation. Name the image files for each user (FRED.SYS for user FRED, JANE.SYS for user JANE, etc.). Then, in the LOGIN directory, create a BOOTCONF.SYS file, which is a DOS text file that, for each station's network board, identifies the

- IPX external network number
- node number
- remote boot image filename (FRED.SYS, JANE.SYS, etc.)

Remote workstation   A terminal or personal computer connected to the LAN by a router or through a remote asynchronous connection. A remote workstation can be either a stand-alone computer or a workstation on another network.

Rename Inhibit attribute

A file-system attribute that prevents any user from renaming the directory or file.

Rename right

An object right that grants the right to change the name of an object, in effect changing the naming property.

replica

A copy of a Directory partition.

For a NetWare Directory Services database to be distributed across a network, the database must be stored on many servers. Rather than have a copy of the whole database on each server, replicas of each partition are stored on many servers throughout the network. You can create an unlimited number of replicas for each partition and store them on any server.

Purpose   Replicas serve two purposes:

1 • *To eliminate any single point of failure.* For example, if a disk crashes or a server goes down, a replica on another server can still authenticate users to use the network and can provide information on objects in that partition.

   With the same information distributed on several servers, you aren't dependent on any single server to authenticate who can use the network.

2 • *To provide faster access to information for users across a WAN link.* For example, if a WAN link is used to access information, you can decrease access time and network traffic by placing a replica containing the needed information on a server that users can access locally.

   Distributing replicas among servers lets you access information more quickly and reliably because the information comes from the nearest available server.

Types of replicas   There are three types of replicas:

▸ *Master replica*. Although many replicas can exist in the Directory, only one is the Master replica. Use it to create a new partition in the Directory database, or to read and update Directory information, such as adding or deleting objects.

▸ *Read-Write replica*. Use to read or update Directory information (such as adding or deleting objects).

▸ *Read-Only replica*. Use to view, but not to modify, Directory information.

Synchronization   To maintain their fault tolerance, a partition's replicas must be periodically updated, or synchronized. When changes are made in one replica, synchronization ensures that those changes are made in all other replicas of that partition, so that each partition's replica contains the same data as the other replicas.

resource fork

The part of a Macintosh file that contains file resources, including Macintosh-specific information such as the windows and icons used with the file. See *Macintosh files*.

resource tags

Operating system tags that keep track of NetWare server resources such as screens and allocated memory.

NLMs request a resource from the NetWare server for each kind of resource they use and give it a resource tag name. NLMs return resources when they no longer need them. When the NLM is unloaded, the resources are returned to the NetWare server.

Resource tags ensure that allocated resources are properly returned to the operating system upon termination of an NLM.

resources

The manageable components of a network, including:

▸ Networking components—cabling, hubs, concentrators, adapters, and network boards.

▸ Hardware components—servers, workstations, hard disks, printers, etc.

▸ Major software components—the NetWare operating system and resulting network services such as file, mail, queue, communication, etc.

▸ Minor software components that are controlled by the operating system of its subsystems—protocols, gateways, LAN and disk drivers, etc.

▸ Data structures and other network resources that don't easily fit into one of the above categories, or are created by a combination of network components—volumes, queues, users, processes, security, etc.

restore

A retrieval of data previously copied and backed up to a storage media. Perform a restore if data has been lost or corrupted since the backup.

ribbon cable

A cable in which the wires are placed side by side in the insulation material instead of being bunched or twisted together in a circle inside the insulation material. Typically, ribbon cables are used for connecting internal disk or tape drives.

rights

Qualities assigned to an object that controls what the object can do with directories, files, or other objects. Creating, reading, and other operations can be done only if an object has rights to perform them.

Rights are granted to a specific directory, file, or object by trustee assignments. An object with a trustee assignment to a file, directory, or another object is a trustee of that file, directory, or object.

Within each object is a list of who has rights to the object. This list is the ACL property of the object. (Files and directories contain similar information, but not an ACL.)

Directory, file, object, and property rights   Directory rights apply to the directory in the NetWare file system that they are assigned to, as well as to all files and subdirectories in that directory (unless redefined at the file or subdirectory level).

Directory rights are a part of the file system. They aren't assigned to NetWare Directory Services objects. But a User object can be granted Directory rights to a directory on a volume.

> *File rights* apply only to the file they are assigned to. A trustee can also inherit rights to a file from the directory above the file.

> *Object rights* apply to NetWare Directory Services objects. Object rights don't affect the properties of an object (see property rights below). A trustee can inherit rights to an object from the object above it.

> *Property rights* apply to the properties of a NetWare Directory Services object. They can be assigned to each property, and a default set can apply to properties that do not have specific rights set.

To grant directory or file rights to other objects, a trustee must have the Access Control right to a directory or file.

To grant object or property rights to other objects, a trustee must have the Write, Add or Delete, Self, or Supervisor right to the ACL property of the object.

RIP

See *Router Information Protocol.*

root directory

The highest directory level in a hierarchical directory structure. With NetWare, the root directory is the volume; all other directories are subdirectories of the volume.

Root object

An object in the Directory tree whose purpose is to provide a highest point to access different Country and Organization objects, and to allow trustee assignments granting rights to the entire Directory tree. The Root object is a place holder; it contains no information.

router

A workstation or NetWare server running software that manages the exchange of information (in the form of data packets) between network cabling systems.

A NetWare router runs as part of a NetWare server. It connects separate network cabling topologies or separate networks by way of the server's NetWare operating system.

NetWare router vs. traditional bridge   A NetWare router, unlike a traditional bridge, does more than just transfer data packets between networks that use the same communications protocol. A NetWare router is intelligent. It not only passes packets of data between different cabling systems, but also routes the packets through the most efficient path.

A NetWare router can also connect cabling systems that use different kinds of transmission media and different addressing systems. For example, a NetWare router can connect a network using the Ethernet addressing structure and RG/58 coaxial cable to another network using the ARCnet addressing structure and RG/62 coaxial cable.

Local vs. remote   When a router is used within the cable length limitations for its LAN drivers, it is a local router. If the router is connected beyond its driver limitations or through a modem, it is a remote router.

Router Information Protocol (RIP)

A protocol that provides a way for routers to exchange routing information on a NetWare internetwork. RIP allows NetWare routers to create and maintain a database (or router table) of current internetwork routing information. Workstations can query the nearest router to find the fastest route to a distant network by broadcasting a RIP request packet.

Routers send periodic RIP broadcast packets containing current routing information to keep all routers on the internetwork synchronized. Routers also send RIP update broadcasts whenever they detect a change in the internetwork configuration.

RTMP

See *Routing Table Maintenance Protocol* under the entry *AppleTalk protocols*.

S

salvageable files

Files saved by NetWare, after being deleted by users, that can be salvaged (recovered). Salvageable files are usually stored in the directory they were deleted from. If the user deletes that directory, the file is saved in a DELETED.SAV directory located in the volume's root directory.

The user can view a list of deleted files in a directory and recover files by using the FILER utility. Recovered files contain information about who deleted the files and when they were deleted.

Deleted files are saved until the user deliberately purges them or until the NetWare server runs out of disk allocation blocks on the volume. When the NetWare server runs out of blocks, it purges deleted files on a first-deleted, first-purged basis.

SAP

See *Service Advertising Protocol.*

SCSI

(small computer system interface) Commonly pronounced "scuzzy." An industry standard that sets guidelines for connecting peripheral devices and their controllers to a microprocessor. The SCSI interface defines both hardware and software standards for communication between a host computer and a peripheral.

Computers and peripheral devices designed to meet SCSI specifications have a large degree of compatibility.

SCSI bus

An interface that connects additional HBAs to controllers and hard disks. (If you are using a SCSI bus, make sure connected peripherals are properly terminated and addressed.)

SCSI disconnect

A feature in NetWare 4.0 that allows the SCSI driver to inform a disk that the disk should prepare for I/O.

While that disk is preparing for I/O, the SCSI driver can either send messages to other hard disks or actually perform I/O to other hard disks. When the disk is ready to receive or send data, the disk sends a message back to the SCSI driver, informing the driver that the disk is ready for I/O. The SCSI driver then performs the I/O.

SDI

See *Storage Device Interface.*

search drive

A drive that is searched by the operating system when a requested file isn't found in the current directory. Search drives are supported only from DOS workstations.

A search drive allows a user working in one directory to access an application or data file located in another directory.

search modes

Methods of operation that specify how a program will use search drives when looking for a data file.

When an .EXE or .COM file requires an auxiliary file, it makes an open request through the operating system. The request may or may not specify the path to that file.

If a path is specified, the operating system searches that path. Otherwise, it only searches the default directory. If the file isn't found, the NetWare shell uses the search mode of the executable file to determine if it should continue looking for the file in the search drives.

Secondary time server

A server that obtains the time from a Single Reference, Primary, or Reference time server and provides the time to workstations. See *time synchronization*.

security

Elements that control access to the network or to specific information on the network. Six categories of security features are: login security, trustees, rights, inheritance, attributes, and effective rights.

Login security The LOGIN command controls who can access the network by determining if a valid user is attempting to log in. A person must know the User object's name and the correct password (if required) to log in.

The network supervisor establishes this login security by creating a User object in NetWare Directory Services and by then assigning values to the properties of that user. Those values determine how the user can access the network.

A User object's properties affect when a user can log in, which workstations can be used, when the user's account is disabled, and information about the user's password, among other things.

Passwords are encrypted and are never displayed on the monitor or transmitted across the network. The password authenticates every action of a user.

Trustee A trustee is a User or Group object that has been granted access to a directory, file, or object. Access is granted through a *trustee assignment*. A trustee assignment says, in effect, "This user can access this directory, file, or object in these ways."

- *Trustee List*. Each directory, file, and object has a list of trustee assignments, called a trustee list, that specifies who can access that directory, file, or object. An object's trustee list is stored in the object's ACL property.

- *Trustees of groups*. For several users to access a directory, file, or object, a trustee assignment is required for each user. Rather than make trustee assignments for each user, create a Group object, include the users in the group, and then grant access for the group with one trustee assignment.

- *[Public] trustee*. [Public] is a special trustee. You can always specify [Public] as the trustee of a file, directory, or object. Anyone who tries to access a directory, file, or object without any other rights at least has the rights granted to the [Public] trustee.

Rights Rights determine the type of access a trustee has to a directory, file, or object. For example, if a trustee assignment grants the Create right to a directory, a trustee can create files in the directory.

A trustee assignment grants to one object the rights to another object. Rights are granted within the object a trustee has rights to, not within the trustee object. For example, to grant JILL the right to delete a Printer object, make JILL a trustee of the Printer object with the Delete right—don't make the Printer object a trustee of JILL. There are four kinds of rights in NetWare 4.0:

▸ *Directory rights* control what a trustee can do with a directory.

▸ *File rights* control what a trustee can do with a file.

▸ *Object rights* control what a trustee can do with an object.

▸ *Property rights* control a trustee's access to information stored within the object—that is, the information stored in the object's properties.

Inheritance   Creating a trustee assignment for every user and for every directory, file, and object would be a huge job. Inheritance simplifies the task. By inheritance, rights granted by a trustee assignment apply to everything below the point where the assignment is made, unless another trustee assignment is made or unless the rights are blocked by an Inherited Rights Filter (IRF).

Inheritance applies both to objects in the Directory tree and to directories and files on a volume.

Inherited Rights Filter   If you were to create a file, but didn't want everyone who has rights in the directory to have rights to your file, you could create a filter that stops those rights from being inherited.

An Inherited Rights Filter has the same set of possible rights as a trustee assignment, but instead of granting rights, it revokes rights. Its effect is this: "Whatever rights to this file, directory, or object you would have inherited, I am revoking all *but* these rights."

Every directory, file, and object has an Inherited Rights Filter. With this filter, you can grant access more freely at the top of the object tree or volume; then filter out rights in sensitive areas.

Attributes   Attributes (also called *flags*) describe the characteristics of a directory or file and tell NetWare what actions are allowed (and in a few cases, what actions have been performed). They aren't used for objects.

NetWare reads the attributes you set (for example, to compress, back up, or not allow deletion of a file) and sets other attributes to tell you what has been done (for example, a file has been compressed, migrated, or indexed).

Effective rights   Effective rights are the rights that a user actually has to a directory, file, or object. NetWare calculates your effective rights to a directory, file, or object whenever you take an action.

Effective rights to a file or directory are determined by

1 · An object's trustee assignments to the directory or file.

2 · Inherited rights from an object's trustee assignments to parent directories.

3 · Trustee assignments of Group objects that a User object belongs to.

4 · Trustee assignments of objects listed in a User object's security equivalences list.

security equivalence

A property of every User object that lists other objects. The user is granted all rights that any object (User, Group, Printer, etc.) in that list is granted, both to objects and to files and directories. Use security equivalence to give a user temporary access to the same information or rights another user has access to.

When a user is added to the membership list of a Group object or the occupant list of an Organizational Role object, the Group or Organizational Role is listed in that user's security equivalence. By using a security equivalence, you avoid having to review the whole directory structure and determine which rights need to be assigned to which directories, files, and objects.

semaphore

A flag that coordinates activities of both programs and processes to prevent data corruption in multiprocess environments.

Semaphores with byte value 0 allow a file to be shared. Byte value 1 locks the file while in use, thereby preventing another user from accessing or altering the shared file.

Semaphores can lock resources so that only one user or process has access to the resource. Semaphores can also allow a limited number of users access to a resource, such as to network applications with limited-user licenses. When the specified number is reached, the semaphore denies access to additional users.

Sequenced Packet Exchange (SPX)

A NetWare DOS Requester module that enhances the IPX protocol by supervising data sent out across the network.

SPX verifies and acknowledges successful packet delivery to any network destination by requesting a verification from the destination that the data was received. The SPX verification must include a value that matches the value calculated from the data before transmission. By comparing these values, SPX ensures not only that the data packet made it to the destination, but that it arrived intact.

SPX can track data transmissions consisting of a series of separate packets. If an acknowledgment request brings no response within a specified time, SPX retransmits it. After a reasonable number of retransmissions fail to return a positive acknowledgment, SPX assumes the connection has failed and warns the operator of the failure.

serial communication

The transmission of data between devices over a single line, one bit at a time.

NetWare uses the RS-232 serial communication standard to send information to serial printers, remote workstations, remote routers, and asynchronous communication servers. The RS-232 standard, developed by the Electronic Industries Association (EIA), enhances the delivery of information from one system to another.

A system can be any device or group of devices that can handle and process the data received. For example, a printer can be thought of as a system that transforms the binary data it receives from the computer into printed text.

Parameters   The RS-232 standard uses several parameters that must match on both systems for valid information to be transferred:

▶ *Baud rate.* The signal modulation rate, or the speed with which a signal changes.

▶ *Character length.* The number of data bits used to form a character.

▶ *Parity.* A method of checking for errors in transmitted data. You can set parity to even or odd, or not use parity at all.

▶ *Stop bit.* A special signal that indicates the end of that character. Today's modems are fast enough that the stop bit is always set to 1. Slower modems formerly required two stop bits.

▶ *XON/XOFF.* One of many methods that prevents the sending system from transmitting data faster than the receiving system can accept it.

serial port

A port that allows data to be transmitted asynchronously, one bit at a time. Typically, serial ports are used for modems or serial printers.

On IBM PC compatible computers, COM1 and COM2 are asynchronous serial ports.

serialization

The process of serializing software to prevent unlawful software duplication.

Each NetWare operating system has a unique serial number. If two NetWare operating systems with the same serial number exist on the same internetwork, each NetWare server displays a copyright violation warning at the server console and at each logged-in workstation.

server

NetWare server   A computer running the NetWare operating system software. See *NetWare server.*

Print server   A computer that takes print jobs out of a print queue and sends them to a network printer. See *print server.*

server console

The monitor and keyboard where you view and control NetWare server activity. You can view network traffic, send messages, set configuration parameters, shut down the server, and load and unload NLMs.

Many server console tasks are done in MONITOR and PSERVER. MONITOR allows you to view server and memory use, connections, and many disk and network statistics. PSERVER allows you to control active printers on the network.

server protocol

Procedures that a NetWare server follows to accept and respond to workstation requests. See *NetWare Core Protocol (NCP)*.

Service Advertising Protocol (SAP)

A protocol that provides a way for servers to advertise their services on a NetWare internetwork.

Servers advertise their services with SAP, allowing routers to create and maintain a database of current internetwork server information.

Routers send periodic SAP broadcasts to keep all routers on the internetwork synchronized. Routers also send SAP update broadcasts whenever they detect a change in the internetwork configuration.

Workstations can query the network to find a server by broadcasting SAP request packets. When a workstation logs in to a network, it broadcasts a "Get Nearest Server" SAP request and attaches to the first server that replies.

SFT

See *System Fault Tolerance.*

Shareable attribute

A file-system attribute that allows a file to be accessed by more than one user at a time.

short machine type

A four-letter (or less) name representing a DOS workstation brand. The short machine type is similar to the long machine type, except the short machine type is used specifically with overlay files.

Files using the short machine type include the IBM$RUN.OVL file for windowing utilities and the CMPQ$RUN.OVL file that uses a default black-and-white color palette for NetWare menus.

The short machine type is set in the NET.CFG file, using the SHORT MACHINE TYPE parameter. The default is IBM.

Single Reference time server

A server that provides time to Secondary time servers and to workstations. The Single Reference time server is the sole source of time on the network. See *time synchronization.*

SMS

See *Storage Management Services.*

socket

The part of an IPX internetwork address, within a network node, that represents the destination of an IPX packet.

Some sockets are reserved by Novell for specific applications. For example, IPX delivers all NCP request packets to socket 451h. Third-party developers can also reserve socket numbers for specific purposes by registering those numbers with Novell.

source routing

IBM's method of routing data across source-routing bridges. NetWare source routing programs allow an IBM Token Ring network bridge to forward NetWare packets (or frames).

IBM bridges can be configured as either single-route broadcast or all-routes broadcast. The default is single-route broadcast.

▶ *Single-route broadcasting.* Only designated single-route bridges pass the packet and only one copy of the packet arrives on each ring in the network. Single-route bridges can transmit single-route, all-routes, and specifically routed packets.

▶ *All-routes broadcasting.* Sends the packet across every possible route in the network, resulting in as many copies of the frame at the destination as there are bridges in the network. All-routes bridges pass both all-routes broadcasts and specifically routed packets.

source server

The server from which you migrate data files, bindery files, and other information to a NetWare 4.0 destination server during upgrade.

sparse file

A file with at least one empty block. (NetWare won't write any block that is completely empty.)

Databases often create sparse files. For example, suppose the disk allocation block size for volume VOL1: is 4K. Also suppose that a database opens a new file, seeks out the 1,048,576th byte, writes five bytes, and closes the file.

An inefficient operating system would save the entire file to disk. The file would be comprised of 256 zero-filled disk allocation blocks (the first 1MB) and one more disk allocation block with five bytes of data and 4,091 zeros. This method would waste 1MB of disk space.

However, NetWare writes only the last block to disk, saving time and disk space.

The NetWare NCOPY command doesn't write to sparse files automatically. NCOPY has a /f option that forces the operating system to write to sparse files.

SPX
See *Sequenced Packet Exchange*.

STARTUP.NCF
A NetWare server boot file that loads the NetWare server's disk driver and name spaces and some SET parameters.

station
Usually a shortened form for *workstation*, but can also be a server, router, printer, fax machine, or any computer device connected to a network by a network board and a communication medium.

Stop bit
A signal that indicates the end of a character.

Storage Device Interface (SDI)
A set of routines that allows SBACKUP to access various storage devices and media.

If more than one storage device is attached to the host, Storage Device Interface sends SBACKUP a list of storage devices and media, each labeled Available or Unavailable. SBACKUP displays this list so you can select an available device to store backup data on.

If a storage device is unavailable, it is being used by another application. Such a device remains unavailable until the application gives it up, or until the application is exited.

Storage Management Services (SMS)

Services that allow data to be stored and retrieved. SMS is independent of backup/restore hardware and file systems (such as DOS, OS/2, Macintosh, Windows, or UNIX).

SMS architecture   SMS provides NLMs and other software modules that run on NetWare servers. Modules used in SMS are

- *SBACKUP.* Provides backup and restore capabilities.

- *SMDR (Storage Management Data Requester).* Passes commands and information between SBACKUP and Target Service Agents (TSAs).

- *Storage Device Interface.* Passes commands and information between SBACKUP and the storage devices and media.

- *Device drivers.* Acting on commands passed through the Storage Device Interface from SBACKUP, device drivers control the mechanical operation of storage devices and media.

- *NetWare-server TSAs (Target Service Agents).* Pass requests for data (generated within SBACKUP) to the NetWare server where the data resides, then return requested data through the SMDR to SBACKUP.

- *Database TSAs.* Pass commands and data between the host server (where SBACKUP resides) and the database where the data to be backed up resides, then return the requested data through the SMDR to SBACKUP.

- *Workstation TSAs.* Pass commands and data between the host server (where SBACKUP resides) and the station where the data to be backed up resides, then return the requested data through the SMDR to SBACKUP.

▶ *Workstation Manager.* Receives "I am here" messages from stations available to be backed up. It keeps the names of these stations in an internal list.

STREAMS

An NLM that provides a common interface between NetWare and transport protocols such as IPX/SPX, TCP/IP, SNA, and OSI that need to deliver data and requests to NetWare for processing. By making the transport protocol transparent to the network operating system, STREAMS allows services to be provided across the network, regardless of the transport protocols used.

If the applications support multiple protocols, Network managers can install the protocols of their choice or change the protocols used without affecting the level of services delivered to the user.

NetWare 4.0 STREAMS and related NLMs are as follows:

▶ *STREAMS.NLM* includes the STREAMS application interface routines, the utility routines for STREAMS modules, the log device, and a driver for the Open Data-Link Interface (ODI).

▶ *SPXS.NLM* provides access to the SPX protocol from STREAMS.

▶ *IPXS.NLM* provides access to the IPX protocol from STREAMS.

▶ *TCPIP.NLM* provides access to the TCP and UDP protocols from STREAMS.

▶ *CLIB.NLM* is a library of functions that some NLMs use.

▶ *TLI.NLM* is an application programming interface that sits between STREAMS and applications, allowing interface with transport-level protocols such as IPX/SPX or TCP/IP.

subdirectory

A directory below another in the file-system structure. For example, in SYS:ACCTS\RECEIVE, RECEIVE is a subdirectory of SYS:ACCTS.

Supervisor right

A file-system right that grants all rights to the respective directory and files. Also, an object right that grants all access privileges to all objects. Also, a property right that grants all rights to the property.

surface test

A test in the NetWare INSTALL program that lets you test the NetWare partition on a hard disk for bad blocks. The surface test can run in the background on one or more dismounted hard disks so that you (or other users) can work on mounted volumes on other hard disks.

You can choose either a destructive or a nondestructive surface test:

▶ *Destructive test.* Acts like a disk format—it destroys data as it makes several passes over the disk surface, reading and writing test patterns.

▶ *Nondestructive test.* Prereads and saves existing data while it reads and writes test patterns to the hard disk. Then the program writes the data back to the disk.

switch block

A set of switches mounted to form a single component.

In some NetWare servers, a switch block is used to control system configuration data, such as type of monitor, amount of memory, and number of drives. Network boards often use switch blocks to set system addresses (such as station, base I/O, and base memory addresses).

synchronization

Replica synchronization   A means of ensuring that replicas of a Directory partition contain the same information as other replicas of that partition. See *Replicas* under *NetWare Directory Services*.

Time synchronization   A method of ensuring that all servers in a Directory tree report the same time. See *time synchronization*.

syntax
See *command format*.

System attribute
A file-system attribute that marks directories or files for use only by the operating system.

SYSTEM directory
The SYS:SYSTEM directory, created during network installation, that contains NetWare operating-system files as well as NLMs and NetWare utilities for managing the network.

System Fault Tolerance (SFT)
A means of protecting data by providing data duplication on multiple storage devices; if one storage device fails, the data is available from another device.

There are several levels of hardware and software system fault tolerance; each level of redundancy (duplication) decreases the possibility of data loss.

system login script
A type of login script that sets general environments for all users in an Organization or Organizational Unit. System login scripts are optional; if used, they execute first, before profile and user login scripts.

T

tape backup unit
Typically, an external tape drive that backs up data from hard disks.

target
A server from which you back up data or to which you restore data. Any Net-Ware server, workstation, or service on the network can be a target, as long as the Target Service Agent (TSA) files are loaded.

A target can be either a different server than the host or the same server as the host. If you are backing up and restoring on the same server, the target and the host are the same.

Target Service Agent (TSA)
A program that processes data moving between a specific target and SBACKUP. SBACKUP, running on the host, sends requests to the TSA, which

1 • Receives the commands from SBACKUP and processes them so that the target operating system can handle the request for data.

2 • Passes the data request from SBACKUP to the target.

3 • Receives the requested data from the target and returns it to SBACKUP in standard SMS format.

Servers and workstations running different software releases, or having different operating systems, require NetWare-compatible TSAs to communicate with SBACKUP.

TCP/IP
(Transmission Control Protocol/Internet Protocol) An industry-standard suite of networking protocols, enabling dissimilar nodes in a heterogenous environment to communicate with one another.

TCP/IP is built upon four layers that roughly correspond to the seven-layer OSI model. The TCP/IP layers are:

- ▸ Process/application

- ▸ Host-to-host

- ▸ Internet

- ▸ Network access

NetWare TCP/IP   A collection of NLMs that support applications requiring TCP/IP connectivity. Its routing capabilities forward IP traffic from one network to another.

NetWare TCP/IP uses Routing Information Protocol (RIP) to communicate the Internet's configuration with other routers. It also provides communication between NetWare (IPX) networks across an IP internetwork that doesn't directly support IPX. This is known as IPX/IP tunneling.

NetWare TCP/IP also provides a transport interface for higher-level network services. This interface is used by the Network File System (NFS) and third-party applications written for either the 4.3 BSD UNIX socket interface or the AT&T Streams Transport Layer Interface (TLI).

termination

Placing a terminating resistor at the end of a bus, line, chain, or cable to prevent signals from being reflected or echoed.

Data signals travel along a cable or bus that is in many ways analogous to a pipe. You must terminate the end components to ensure that the signal doesn't echo back along the cable or bus and cause corruption.

time synchronization

A method of ensuring that all servers in a Directory tree report the same time. Clocks in computers can deviate slightly, resulting in different times on different servers. Time synchronization corrects these deviations so that all servers in a Directory tree report the same time and provide a timestamp to order NetWare Directory Services events.

Whenever an event occurs in the Directory, such as when a password is changed, or an object is renamed, NetWare Directory Services requests a *time stamp*.

time stamp   A time stamp is a unique code that includes the time and identifies this event. The NetWare Directory Services event is assigned a time stamp so that the order in which replicas are updated is correct.

NetWare Directory Services uses time stamps to:

▸ Establish the order of events (such as object creation and partition replication)

▸ Record "real world" time values

▸ Set expiration dates

Time stamps are especially important when NetWare Directory Services partitions are replicated and need to be concurrent with one another.

time servers   When you install NetWare 4.0 on a server, you are prompted to designate it as a Single Reference, Primary, Reference, or Secondary time server. Each designation performs a particular time-synchronization function:

▸ *Single Reference time server.* Provides time to Secondary time servers and to workstations. This server determines the time for the entire network and is the only source of time on the network. The network supervisor sets the time on the Single Reference time server.

▸ *Primary time server.* Synchronizes the time with at least one other Primary or Reference time server, and provides the time to Secondary time servers and to workstations. Primary time servers also "vote" with other Primary or Reference time servers to determine what the common network time should be.

▶ *Reference time server.* Provides a time to which all other time servers and workstations synchronize. Reference time servers may be synchronized with an external time source, such as a radio clock.

Reference time servers "vote" with other Primary or Reference time servers to determine what the common network time should be. However, Reference time servers don't adjust their internal clocks; instead, the Primary servers' internal clocks are adjusted to synchronize with the Reference time server.

Therefore, a Reference time server acts as a central point to set network time. Eventually, all Primary time servers will adjust their clocks to agree with a Reference time server.

▶ *Secondary time server.* Secondary time servers obtain the time from a Single Reference, Primary, or Reference time server. They adjust their internal clocks to synchronize with the network time, and they provide the time to workstations.

A Secondary time server doesn't participate in determining the correct network time.

SAP and custom configuration   Time source servers use one of two methods to find each other: SAP and custom configuration.

▶ *SAP (Service Advertising Protocol).* By default, Primary, Reference, and Single Reference servers use SAP to announce their presence on the network. Primary and Reference time servers use SAP information to determine the other servers to poll in order to determine the network time. Secondary time servers use SAP information to pick a time server to follow.

An advantage of SAP is that it allows quick installation without regard to the network layout. It also allows automatic reconfiguration if operating modes are changed or if new servers are added to the network.

A disadvantage of the SAP method is that a small amount of additional network traffic is generated.

▶ *Custom configuration.* You can list the specific time servers that a particular server should contact. You can also specify that a server shouldn't listen for SAP information from other time sources, and that it isn't to advertise its presence using SAP.

An advantage of custom configuration is that the network supervisor maintains complete control of the time-synchronization environment. Also, custom configuration helps eliminate nonessential network SAP traffic, as well as errors associated with accidental reconfiguration.

A disadvantage of custom configuration is the increased time required for planning and installation.

topology

The physical layout of network components (cables, stations, gateways, hubs, and so on). There are three basic topologies:

▶ *Star network.* Workstations are connected directly to a NetWare server but not to each other.

▶ *Ring network.* The NetWare server and workstations are cabled in a ring; a workstation's messages may have to pass through several other workstations before reaching the NetWare server.

▶ *Bus network.* All workstations and the NetWare server are connected to a central cable (called a trunk or bus).

Transaction Tracking System (TTS)

A system that protects database applications from corruption by "backing out" incomplete transactions that result from a failure in a network component. When a transaction is backed out, data and index information in the database are returned to the state they were in before the transaction began.

TTS is a standard feature on NetWare 4.0 servers. This function can be turned on and off.

Transactional attribute

A file-system attribute that indicates the file is protected by TTS.

trustee

A user or group granted rights to work with a directory, file, or object; the object is called a trustee of that directory, file, or object.

Rights are granted to objects (making them trustees) by *trustee assignments*. Trustee assignments are part of the directory, file, or object to which they grant access. Trustee assignments are stored in a trustee list. An object's trustee list is stored in the object's ACL property.

For example, to make group WRITERS a trustee of directory PROJECTS, go to PROJECTS and make a trustee assignment with the name of group WRITERS.

[Public] is a special trustee. You can always specify [Public] as the trustee of a file, directory, or object. Anyone who tries to access a file, directory, or object without any other rights is allowed the rights granted to the [Public] trustee.

When you make a trustee assignment to a directory, file, or object, the trustee has access to the directory, its files, and its subdirectories (unless rights are redefined at the file or subdirectory level) or to the subordinate objects. This is called *inheritance*.

Through inheritance, rights granted to a trustee flow down through the structure unless one of the following is true:

- ▶ Other trustee assignments are granted for the same object at a lower level of the directory structure, or

- ▶ The Inherited Rights Filter of a subdirectory or file or subordinate object revokes rights granted in a trustee assignment above that point.

A *trustee through inheritance* is an object that has a trustee assignment to a directory, file, or object higher in the structure and inherits rights for the current directory, file, or object.

TSA

See *Target Service Agent*.

TSA resources

Categories of data, referred to as *major resources* and *minor resources*, created by each TSA (Target Service Agent). Because these resources vary with each TSA, SBACKUP processes these resources in different ways.

TSM

See *Topology Specific Module* under the entry *Open Data-Link Interface.*

TTS

See *Transaction Tracking System.*

TTS protection

TTS protects data from failure in certain situations (see below) by making a copy of the original data before it is overwritten by new data. If a failure occurs during the transaction, TTS can "back out" the transaction and restore the original data.

A transaction on a network can be saved improperly in any of the following situations:

- ▸ Power to a server or a station is interrupted during a transaction.

- ▸ Server or station hardware fails during a transaction (for example, a parity error or a network board failure).

- ▸ A server or a station "hangs" (a software failure) during a transaction.

- ▸ A network transmission component (such as a hub, a repeater, or a cable) fails during a transaction.

How TTS operates   TTS guarantees that all changes to a file are either wholly completed or aren't made at all. To track transactions on a given file with TTS, flag the file as Transactional.

When a workstation begins a transaction in a database file, TTS follows four basic steps to maintain the integrity of the file:

1 · TTS makes a copy of the original data so that the original data can be restored if the transaction fails. The copy is placed in a file external to the database file. This external file contains all transaction backout information; only the operating system uses it.

2 · TTS writes the changed data to the database file after the copy of the original has been written to the backout file.

3 · TTS repeats Steps 1 and 2 for additional transactions. (A single transaction can consist of a sequence of changes.)

4 · When all changed data has been written to disk, TTS writes a record to the backout file, indicating that the transaction is complete. Completed transactions won't be backed out if the NetWare server, workstation, or network transmission components fail.

Turbo FAT index table

A special FAT (File Allocation Table) index table used when a file exceeds 64 blocks (and the corresponding number of FAT entries). NetWare creates a turbo FAT index to group together all FAT entries for that file. The turbo FAT index enables a large file to be accessed quickly.

See also *File Allocation Table (FAT)*.

U

unbinding

The process of removing a communication protocol from network boards and LAN drivers. See *binding and unbinding*.

uninterruptible power supply (UPS)

A backup power unit that supplies uninterrupted power if a commercial power outage occurs.

Types of UPS are online and offline:

▸ *Online UPS.* Actively modifies the power as it moves through the unit. If a power outage occurs, the unit is already active and continues to provide power. An online UPS is usually more expensive than an offline UPS, but provides a nearly constant source of energy during power outages.

▸ *Offline UPS.* Monitors the power line. When power drops, the UPS is activated. The drawback to this method is the slight lag before the offline UPS becomes active. However, most offline UPS systems are fast enough to offset this lag.

Attaching a UPS to a server enables the server to properly close files and rewrite the system directory to disk.

Unknown object

A leaf object that represents a NetWare Directory Services object that has been corrupted and can't be identified as belonging to any of the other object classes.

Unicode

A 16-bit character representation, defined by the Unicode Consortium, that supports up to 65,536 unique characters. Unicode allows you to represent the characters for multiple languages using a single Unicode representation.

All objects and their attributes in the NetWare Directory database are stored in their Unicode representation. However, clients (including DOS and OS/2) use 256-character code pages (using 8-bit characters).

Not every character created using a given code page will display correctly on a workstation using a different code page. When you change code pages, you need a different set of Unicode translation tables in order to run NetWare utilities and manage the NetWare Directory database.

For example, to use code page 850 (Europe) with country information for France (for which the international telephone country code is 33), you need the following Unicode files:

- ▸ *850_UNI.033*—translates code page 850 to Unicode
- ▸ *UNI_850.033*—translates Unicode to code page 850
- ▸ *UNI_MON.033*—handles monocasing (the proper alphabetization of upper and lowercase letters)
- ▸ *UNI_COL.033*—collation, sorted lists

For different code pages and locales, you need Unicode tables with corresponding code-page numbers and country codes.

UNIX client

A UNIX computer connected to the network. The UNIX client stores and retrieves data from the NetWare server and runs executable network files. The UNIX client provides multiple NetWare-client multitasking on a single station.

UNIX clients include IPX/SPX and NCP/IPX communication protocols to allow other NetWare clients access to UNIX applications.

unloading

The process of unlinking NLMs from the NetWare operating system. See *loading and unloading*.

upgrade

The process of converting your network from any earlier version of NetWare or from another operating system platform to NetWare 4.0.

Migration   Migration converts servers from NetWare 2.x or 3.x, or from another network operating system, to NetWare 4.0 using either of two methods:

▸ *Across-the-wire,* where you transfer network information from a Net-Ware 2.x or 3.x server or a LAN Server to an existing NetWare 4.0 server on the same network.

▸ *Same-server,* where you change your NetWare 2.x or 3.x server to a NetWare 4.0 server.

In-Place Upgrade   In-Place Upgrade allows you to upgrade a 2.1x or 2.2 server to NetWare 3.11 using SERVER.EXE. You can then continue the upgrade to NetWare 4.0.

The In-Place Upgrade includes three parts:

1 · The file system is upgraded.

2 · The new operating system is installed. At this point, you have a NetWare 3.11 file system. The new operating system and utilities have not been installed in the SYSTEM and PUBLIC directories on volume SYS: yet.

3 · You must now install 4.0 to complete the upgrade to NetWare 4.0.

UPS

See *uninterruptible power supply.*

UPS monitoring

The process a NetWare server uses to ensure that an attached UPS (uninterruptible power supply) is functioning properly.

A Novell-certified UPS is attached to a server to provide backup power. (You can also attach a UPS to workstations without installing UPS monitoring hardware on the stations.) When a power failure occurs, NetWare notifies users. After a timeout specified in SERVER.CFG, the server logs out remaining users, closes open files, and shuts itself down.

user login script

A type of login script that sets environments specific to a user. Use user login scripts to contain items that can't be included in system or profile login scripts. User login scripts are optional; if used, they execute after system and profile login scripts.

User object

A leaf object in NetWare Directory Services that represents a person with access to the network. The following items are important to managing User objects:

- *Login name.* The login name is the name the user logs in with. A login name is mandatory when creating a User object.

- *Group membership.* You can assign a user to Group objects. When added to a group, a user inherits the rights assigned to that group.

- *Home directories.* A home directory serves as a user's personal workspace. If you create home directories, plan a parent directory (such as SYS:HOME or SYS:USERS) for them. Or, for a large system, set aside a separate volume for users' home directories.

- *Trustee rights.* If users need to access specific directories and files (other than those assigned by the system), you must grant users trustee rights to these directories.

- *Security equivalences.* Security equivalences allow users to exercise rights equivalent to those of another user. Assigning security equivalences is convenient when you need to give a user access to the same information that another user already has access to.

- *User login scripts.* These configurable batch files customize the network environment for users by initializing environment variables, mapping drives, and executing other commands.

- *Print-job configurations.* Each user can use printing defaults, or you can create print-job configurations for a container or User object.

▶ *Account management.* Any user who has the Supervisor object right to another User object manages that User object and can modify information about that user. Users who don't have the Supervisor object right can be granted rights to other User objects to fulfill specific responsibilities. For example, the network supervisor may want only the phone-book manager to be granted rights to each user's phone-number property.

▶ *User account restrictions.* Every user account can be restricted to prevent unauthorized users from accessing the network. Some restrictions can even disable the account so that no one can log in as that user.

User template

A file containing default information you can apply to new User objects to give them default property values. This helps if you are creating many users who need the same property values. You create user templates in Organization or Organizational Unit objects.

When you create a User object, you can specify that you want to use a user template. In this case, the property values entered in the user template for that container (or the container above, if no user template exists in the current container) are copied into the new User object as it is created.

The user template saves you from re-entering information—a fax number, login time restrictions, addresses, password restrictions, language, etc.—that is common to every User object in a container.

When you create a user template in a container, you can copy information from the parent container's user template.

utilities

Programs that add functionality to the NetWare operating system. NetWare 4.0 utilities support Windows, OS/2, and DOS environments. (Refer to the *Utilities Reference* for more information.)

Server utilities and NLMs   NetWare server utilities and NLMs run at the server console of a NetWare 4.0 server or a NetWare for OS/2 server. Use the server utility commands at the server console prompt to change memory allocations, monitor how the server is being used, and control workstations' use of the resources on the server.

The server NLMs link disk drivers, LAN drivers, name-space modules, management applications, etc., with the server's operating system.

Workstation utilities   NetWare workstation utilities can be run from a DOS, Windows, or OS/2 workstation.

Graphical utilities, new under NetWare 4.0, allow network supervisors to manage the network through Microsoft Windows 3.0 and 3.1 or OS/2 Presentation Manager 2.0.

Text utilities for DOS and OS/2 support both bindery and NetWare Directory Services.

► . . . . ◄

V

Value-Added Process (VAP)

A process that ties enhanced operating system features to a NetWare 2.x operating system without interfering with the network's normal operation. VAPs run on top of the operating system in much the same way a word processing or spreadsheet application runs on top of DOS.

NLMs provide this type of enhancement for NetWare 3.x and 4.0. (See *Net-Ware Loadable Module (NLM)*.

value-added server

A separate, specialized, dedicated computer (such as a print server or a database server) that fulfills a specific function for network users.

VAP

See *Value-Added Process.*

Virtual Loadable Module (VLM)

A modular executable program that runs at each DOS workstation and enables communication with the NetWare server. A VLM file has a .VLM file-name extension. For example, the IPX VLM file is IPXNCP.VLM.

The NetWare DOS Requester is composed of several VLMs. These VLMs replace, and provide backward compatibility with, NetWare shells used in previous NetWare versions.

There are two types of VLMs: *child VLMs* and *multiplexor VLMs.*

Child VLMs   Child VLMs handle a particular implementation of a logical grouping of functionality. For example, each NetWare server type has its own child VLM:

▸ *NDS.VLM,* for NetWare Directory Services–based (NetWare 4.0) servers.

▸ *BIND.VLM,* for bindery-based servers (prior to NetWare 4.0).

▸ *PNW.VLM,* for NetWare desktop-based servers.

Multiplexor VLMs   A multiplexor is a VLM that routes calls to the proper child VLM. Requester multiplexors can be considered parent VLMs, ensuring that requests to child VLMs reach the appropriate VLM module.

VLM

See *Virtual Loadable Module.*

volume

A physical amount of hard-disk storage space, fixed in size. A NetWare volume is the highest level in the NetWare directory structure (on the same level as a DOS root directory).

In NetWare Directory Services, each volume is also a Volume object in the Directory. When you create a volume with the INSTALL utility, INSTALL puts a Volume object in the same context as the NetWare server within the Directory tree. By default, INSTALL names the Volume object *servername_volumeobject*.

You can create a new volume on any hard disk that has a NetWare 4.0 partition. A NetWare 4.0 server supports up to 64 volumes. NetWare volumes are subdivided in two ways:

▸ *Logically,* volumes are divided into directories by network supervisors and users having the appropriate rights.

▸ *Physically,* volumes are divided into volume segments; different segments of a volume can be stored on one or more hard disks. A single hard disk can contain up to 8 volume segments belonging to one or more volumes, and each volume can consist of up to 32 volume segments.

The first network volume is named SYS:. Additional volumes can be defined with INSTALL, and are assigned volume names between 2 and 15 characters in length.

When you boot the NetWare server, each volume is "mounted," meaning that

▸ The volume becomes visible to the operating system.

▸ The volume's File Allocation Table (FAT) is loaded into memory. Each file block of data takes up one entry in the FAT. Because of this, volumes with a smaller block size require more server memory to mount and manage. However, if most of your files are small, a large block size wastes disk space.

▸ The volume's Directory Entry table is loaded into memory.

volume definition table

A table that keeps track of volume segment information such as volume name, volume size, and where volume segments are located on various network hard disks. Each NetWare volume contains a volume definition table in its NetWare partition.

Volume object

A leaf object that represents a physical volume on the network.

In the Volume object's properties, you can store information about which NetWare server the physical volume is located on and the volume name recorded when the volume was initialized at the server (for example, SYS:). You can also store information such as the volume's owner, space use restrictions for users, or a description of its use.

volume segments

A physical division of a volume. A volume can have up to 32 volume segments. The maximum number of volume segments on a NetWare disk partition is 8.

A volume can have multiple physical segments spanning multiple hard disks, allowing you to create large volumes. NetWare maintains a volume definition table that maps the segments on the hard disk to the volume.

W

wait state

A period of time when the processor does nothing; it simply waits. A wait state is used to synchronize circuitry or devices operating at different speeds. For example, wait states used in memory access slow down the CPU so all components seem to be running at the same speed.

wait time

In a NetWare UPS system, the number of seconds the UPS will wait before signaling to the NetWare server that the normal power supply is off. The NetWare server then alerts attached workstations to log out.

WAN

See *wide area network.*

watchdog

Packets used to make sure workstations are still connected to the NetWare server.

If the server hasn't received a packet from a station in a certain time, a watchdog packet is sent to the station. If the station doesn't respond within a certain time, another watchdog packet is sent. If the station still doesn't respond to a certain number of watchdog packets, the server assumes that the station is no longer connected and clears the station's connection.

wide area network (WAN)

A network that communicates over a long distance, such as across a city or around the world.

A local area network becomes a part of a wide area network when a link is established (using modems, remote routers, phone lines, satellites, or a microwave connection) to a mainframe system, a public data network, or another local area network.

Windows client

A workstation that boots with DOS and gains access to the network through either

▶ The NetWare DOS Requester and its VLMs (for NetWare 4.0)

▶ A NetWare shell (for NetWare versions earlier than NetWare 4.0)

The computer also runs Windows and, with the client software, is able to perform networking tasks in the Windows environment. These tasks include mapping drives, capturing printer ports, sending messages, and changing contexts.

workstation

A personal computer connected to a NetWare network and used to perform tasks through application programs or utilities. Also referred to as a *client* or, simply, a *station*.

Write right

A file-system right that grants the right to open and write to files.

Also, a property right that grants the right to add, change, or remove any values of the property.

X

XON/XOFF

A handshake protocol that prevents a sending system from transmitting data faster than a receiving system can accept it.

Z

ZIP

See *Zone Information Protocol* under the entry *AppleTalk Protocols*.

zones

Arbitrary groups of nodes on an AppleTalk internetwork. Zones provide divisions in a large internetwork. Each node belongs to only one zone at a time. The zone that a node belongs to is determined automatically when that node connects to the network.

Zones are referred to by names, which can be up to 32 characters each. The zone names are converted to addresses on the internetwork by the Name Binding Protocol and the Zone Information Protocol. (In a network without routers, only one zone exists, and the zone name is invisible to users.)

Zone names and addresses are maintained in a Zone Information Table within each router. A NetWare server can act as a router for AppleTalk nodes connected to it.

*I*ndex

G

H

X

Y

Z

SYBEX

FREE BROCHURE!

Complete this form today, and we'll send you a full-color brochure of Sybex bestsellers.

Please supply the name of the Sybex book purchased.

_____

How would you rate it?

_____ Excellent   _____ Very Good   _____ Average   _____ Poor

Why did you select this particular book?

_____ Recommended to me by a friend

_____ Recommended to me by store personnel

_____ Saw an advertisement in _____

_____ Author's reputation

_____ Saw in Sybex catalog

_____ Required textbook

_____ Sybex reputation

_____ Read book review in _____

_____ In-store display

_____ Other _____

Where did you buy it?

_____ Bookstore

_____ Computer Store or Software Store

_____ Catalog (name: _____)

_____ Direct from Sybex

_____ Other: _____

Did you buy this book with your personal funds?

_____ Yes   _____ No

About how many computer books do you buy each year?

_____ 1-3   _____ 3-5   _____ 5-7   _____ 7-9   _____ 10+

About how many Sybex books do you own?

_____ 1-3   _____ 3-5   _____ 5-7   _____ 7-9   _____ 10+

Please indicate your level of experience with the software covered in this book:

_____ Beginner   _____ Intermediate   _____ Advanced

Which types of software packages do you use regularly?

_____ Accounting	_____ Databases	_____ Networks
_____ Amiga	_____ Desktop Publishing	_____ Operating Systems
_____ Apple/Mac	_____ File Utilities	_____ Spreadsheets
_____ CAD	_____ Money Management	_____ Word Processing
_____ Communications	_____ Languages	_____ Other _____

(please specify)

Which of the following best describes your job title?

_____ Administrative/Secretarial _____ President/CEO

_____ Director _____ Manager/Supervisor

_____ Engineer/Technician _____ Other _____
(please specify)

Comments on the weaknesses/strengths of this book: _____

_____

_____

_____

_____

Name _____

Street _____

City/State/Zip _____

Phone _____

PLEASE FOLD, SEAL, AND MAIL TO SYBEX

-- -- -- -- -- -- -- -- -- -- -- -- -- -- -- -- -- -- -- --

SYBEX INC.
Department M
2021 CHALLENGER DR.
ALAMEDA, CALIFORNIA USA
94501

SYBEX

SEAL